Lecture Notes in Computer Science　13558

More information about this series at https://link.springer.com/bookseries/558

Robert Thomson · Christopher Dancy ·
Aryn Pyke (Eds.)

Social, Cultural, and Behavioral Modeling

15th International Conference, SBP-BRiMS 2022
Pittsburgh, PA, USA, September 20–23, 2022
Proceedings

 Springer

Editors
Robert Thomson 🆔
Army Cyber Institute
West Point, NY, USA

Christopher Dancy 🆔
Pennsylvania State University
Pennsylvania, PA, USA

Aryn Pyke 🆔
United States Military Academy
West Point, NY, USA

ISSN 0302-9743   ISSN 1611-3349 (electronic)
Lecture Notes in Computer Science
ISBN 978-3-031-17113-0   ISBN 978-3-031-17114-7 (eBook)
https://doi.org/10.1007/978-3-031-17114-7

This Springer imprint is published by the registered company Springer Nature Switzerland AG
The registered company address is: Gewerbestrasse 11, 6330 Cham, Switzerland

Preface

In this 15th year of the International Conference on Social Computing, Behavioral-Cultural Modeling and Prediction and Behavior Representation in Modeling and Simulation conference, SBP-BRiMS 2022, we highlight the many advances in the computational social sciences. Improving the human condition requires understanding, forecasting, and impacting socio-cultural behavior both in the digital and non-digital world. Increasing amounts of digital data, embedded sensors that collect human information, rapidly changing communication media, changes in legislation concerning digital rights and privacy, spread of 4G technology to developing countries, and others changes are creating a new cyber-mediated world, in which the very precepts of why, when, and how people interact and make decisions is called into question. For example, Uber understood human behaviors regarding commuting. It then developed software to support this behavior, which ended up saving time (and so capital) and reducing stress, which indirectly created the opportunity for people to evolve new behaviors. Scientific and industrial pioneers in this area are relying on both social science and computer science to help make sense of and impact this new frontier. To be successful pioneers, a true merger of social science and computer science is needed. Solutions that rely only on the social sciences or computer science are doomed to failure. For example, Anonymous developed an approach for identifying members of terror groups, such as ISIS, on the Twitter social media platform using state-of-the-art computational techniques. These accounts were then suspended. This was a purely technical solution. The consequence was that those individuals with suspended Twitter accounts just moved to new platforms and resurfaced on Twitter under new IDs. In this case, failure to understand basic social behavior resulted in an ineffective solution.

The goal of this conference is to build this community of social cyber scholars by bringing together and fostering interaction between members of the scientific, corporate, government and military communities, who are interested in understanding, forecasting, and impacting human socio-cultural behavior. It is the mission of this community to build a new field, its theories, methods and its scientific culture in a way that does not give priority to either social science or computer science, and to embrace change as the cornerstone of the community. Despite decades of work in this area, this scientific field is still in its infancy. To meet this charge, to move this science to the next level, this community must meet the following three challenges: deep understanding, socio-cognitive reasoning, and reusable computational technology. Fortunately, as the papers in this volume illustrate, this community is poised to answer these challenges. But what does meeting these challenges entail?

Deep understanding refers to the ability to make operational decisions and theoretical arguments based on an empirically-based deep and broad understanding of the complex socio-cultural phenomena of interest. Today, although more data is available digitally than ever before, we are still plagued by anecdotally-based arguments. For example, in social media, despite the wealth of information available, most analysts focus on small samples, which are typically biased and cover only a small time period, to explain all events and make future predictions. The analyst finds a magic tweet or an unusual tweeter and uses that to prove their point. Tools that can provide more data or less biased data are not widely used, are often more complex or time-consuming than what the average analyst would refer to use for generating results. Not only are more scalable technologies needed, but also a better understanding of the biases in the data and ways to overcome them, as well as a cultural change to not accept anecdotes as evidence.

Socio-cognitive reasoning refers to the ability of individuals to make sense of the world and to interact with it in terms of groups and not just individuals. Currently, most social-behavioral models either focus on (1) strong cognitive models of individuals engaged in tasks -and thereby produces a model showing a small number of agents with high levels of cognitive accuracy, but with little if any social context, or (2) light cognitive models and strong interaction models, which results in model depicting massive numbers of agents with high levels of social realisms and little cognitive realism. In both cases, as realism is increased in the other dimension, the scalability of the models fail, while their predictive accuracy on one of the two dimensions remains low. In contrast, as agent models are built where the agents are not just cognitive by socially cognitive, we find that the scalability increases and the predictive accuracy increases. Not only are agent models with socio-cognitive reasoning capabilities needed, but so too is a better understanding of how individuals form and use these social-cognitions.

More software solutions that support behavioral representation, modeling, data collection, bias identification, analysis and visualization are available to support human socio-cultural behavioral modeling and prediction than ever before. However, this software is generally just piling up in giant black holes on the web. Part of the problem is the fallacy of open source, that is, the idea that if you just make code open-source, others will use it. In contrast, most of the tools and methods available in Git or R are only used by the developer, if at all. Reasons for its unpopularity with analysts include: the lack of documentation, interfaces, interoperability with other tools, difficulty of linking to data, and increased demands on the analyst's time due to a lack of tool-chain and workflow optimization. A part of the problem is the "not-invented here" syndrome. For social scientists and computer scientists alike, it is just more fun to build a quick and dirty tool for your own use than to study and learn tools built by others. Another issue is the insensitivity of people from one scientific or corporate culture to the reward and demand structures of the other cultures that impact what information can or should be shared and when. A related problem is double standards in sharing: universities are expected to share and companies are not, but increasingly universities are relying on that intellectual property as a source of funding just like other companies. While common standards and representations would help, a cultural shift from a focus on sharing to a focus on re-use is as or more critical for moving this area to the next scientific level.

In this volume, and in all the work presented at the SBP-BRiMS 2022 conference, you will see suggestions of how to address the challenges just described. The SBP-BRiMS 2022 carries on the scholarly tradition of the past conferences out of which it has emerged like a phoenix: the Social Computing, Behavioral-Cultural Modeling, and Prediction (SBP) Conference and the Behavioral Representation in Modeling and Simulation (BRiMS) Society's conference.

A total of 50 papers were submitted as regular track submissions. Of these, 24 were accepted to these proceedings, resulting in an acceptance rate of 48%. All papers were single-blind reviewed by 2 to 3 non-chair reviewers, and any papers from conference committee members were independently reviewed by 2–3 non-committee members. Additionally, committee member's students were excluded from reviewing their papers. Overall, the accepted papers come from an international group with papers submitted with authors from many countries, showing the broad reach of the computational social sciences community.

The conference has a strong multi-disciplinary heritage. As the papers in this volume show, people, theories, methods, and data from a wide number of disciplines are represented including computer science, psychology, sociology, communication science, public health, bioinformatics, political science, and organizational science. Numerous types of computational methods are used include, but not limited to, machine learning, language technology, social network analysis and visualization, agent-based simulation, and statistics.

This exciting program could not have been put together without the hard work of several dedicated and forward-thinking researchers serving as the organizing committee, listed on the following pages. Members of the Program Committee, the scholarship committee, publication, advertising, and local arrangements chairs worked tirelessly to put together this event. They were supported by the government sponsors, the area chairs, and the reviewers. We thank them for their efforts on behalf of the community. In addition, we gratefully acknowledge the support of our sponsors – the Army Research Office (W911NF-21-1-0102) and the National Science Foundation (IIS-1926691). We hope that you enjoy the conference and welcome to the community.

September 2022

Robert Thomson
Aryn A. Pyke
Christopher L. Dancy II

Organization

Conference Co-chairs

Kathleen M. Carley   Carnegie Mellon University, USA
Nitin Agarwal   University of Arkansas at Little Rock, USA

Program Co-chairs

Christopher L. Dancy II   Pennsylvania State University, USA
Aryn A. Pyke   United States Military Academy, USA
Robert Thomson   United States Military Academy, USA

Advisory Committee

Fahmida N. Chowdhury   National Science Foundation, USA
Rebecca Goolsby   Office of Naval Research, USA
Paul Tandy   Defense Threat Reduction Agency, USA
Edward T. Palazzolo   Army Research Office, USA

Advisory Committee Emeritus

Patricia Mabry   Indiana University, USA
John Lavery   Army Research Office, USA
Tisha Wiley   National Institutes of Health, USA

Scholarship and Sponsorship Committee

Nitin Agarwal   University of Arkansas at Little Rock, USA
Christopher L. Dancy II   Bucknell University, USA

Publicity Chair

Donald Adjeroh   West Virginia University, USA

Proceedings Chair

Robert Thomson   United States Military Academy, USA

Agenda Co-chairs

Robert Thomson   United States Military Academy, USA
Kathleen M. Carley   Carnegie Mellon University, USA

Journal Special Issue Chair

Kathleen M. Carley   Carnegie Mellon University, USA

Tutorial Chair

Kathleen M. Carley   Carnegie Mellon University, USA

Graduate Program Chairs

Fred Morstatter   University of Southern California, USA
Kenny Joseph   University at Buffalo, USA

Challenge Problem Committee

Kathleen M. Carley   Carnegie Mellon University, USA
Nitin Agarwal   University of Arkansas – Little Rock, USA

Technical Program Committee

Billy Spann   University of Arkansas at Little Rock, USA
Geoffrey Dobson   Carnegie Mellon University, USA
Jonathan Morgan   Duke University, USA
Samer Al-Khateeb   Creighton University, USA
James Kennedy   USITC, USA
Vito D'Orazio   West Virginia University, USA
Palvi Aggarwal   Carnegie Mellon University, USA
Mainuddin Shaik   University of Arkansas at Little Rock, USA
Andrew Crooks   University of Buffalo, USA
Joshua Uyheng   Carnegie Mellon University, USA
Hamdi Kavak   George Mason University, USA
Kiran Kumar Bandeli   University of Arkansas at Little Rock, USA
Nathan Bos   John's Hopkins Applied Physics Laboratory, USA
Prakruthi Karuna   Perspecta Labs, USA
Alina Vereshchaka   University of Buffalo, USA
Lu Cheng   Arizona State University, USA
Martin Smyth   Stony Brook University, USA
Farnaz Tehranchi   Pennsylvania State University, USA

Jose Padilla	Virginia Modeling, Analysis & Sim Center, USA
Akshay Aravamudan	Florida Institute of Technology, USA
Chitaranjan Mahapatra	Indian Institute of Technology Bombay, India
Juliette Shedd	George Mason University, USA
Khalid Kattan	Wayne State University, USA
Md. Saddam Mukta	United International University, Bangladesh
Wen Dong	SUNY Buffalo, USA
Yuzi He	Meta Platforms, Inc., USA
Salem Othman	Wentworth Institute of Technology, UK
Aruna Jammalamadaka	HRL Laboratories, LLC., USA
Murali Mani	University of Michigan Flint, USA
Keith Burghardt	University of Southern California, USA
Emanuel Ben-David	US Census Bureau, USA
Huan Liu	Arizona State University, USA
Peng Fang	Huazhong University, China
Rey Rodrigueza	Sorsogon State University, Philippines
A. S. M. Ahsan-Ul Haque	University of Virginia, USA
Juan Fernandez-Gracia	Harvard University, USA
Patrick Rice	Rice University, USA
Friederike Wall	Alpen-Adria-Universitäet Klagenfurt, Austria
Gayane Grigoryan	Old Dominion University, USA
Stephan Leitner	University of Klagenfurt, Austria
Edward Cranford	Carnegie Mellon University, USA
Antonio Luca Alfeo	University of Pisa, Italy
Laurie Fenstermacher	Air Force Research Labs, USA
Nasrin Akhter	University of Buffalo, USA
Shuyuan Mary Ho	Florida State University, USA
Jordan Richard Schoenherr	Concordia University, Canada
Kai Shu	Arizona State University, USA
Christian Lebiere	Carnegie Mellon University, USA
Jessica Dawson	United States Military Academy, USA
Sahiti Myneni	University of Texas, USA
Xupin Zhang	University of Rochester, USA
Talha Oz	George Mason University, USA
Sterling Somers	Carnegie Mellon University, USA

Contents

Modeling and Simulation

Theory and Methods

Social Cybersecurity

Chasing the Wrong Cloud: Mapping the 2019 Vaping Epidemic Using Data from Social Media

Parush Gera[1]([✉]) and Giovanni Luca Ciampaglia[1,2]

[1] University of South Florida, Tampa, FL, USA
parush@usf.edu
[2] University of Maryland, College Park, MD, USA

Abstract. The digital trails of activity on social media are valuable for public health due to their potential to reveal risky health behavior, but there are still considerable methodological issues associated to using data from social media. One particular source of bias is the presence of automated accounts, or social bots, whose activity may compromise predictive tasks based on social media data. In this work, we collected a corpus of public tweets about electronic vaping and combine them with data from the CDC to predict the incidence of lung injuries by state. We show that only when likely bot accounts are removed the relative volume of tweets about vaping predicts injuries, but this correlation disappears otherwise. We compare the predictive power of these data against survey-based predictions, and show that our models achieve the lowest generalization error. These results highlight the importance of bot detection as a data cleaning step and the potential value of social media data in the context of public health.

Keywords: Vaping · E-cigarettes · Lung injuries · EVALI · Twitter · Social bots

1 Introduction

Social media platforms have become a hub for entertainment, commerce, news, and civic engagement. The "digital trails" of metadata associated to activities such as online purchases, interpersonal communication, content consumption, etc. have made available enormous data which has been used extensively by researchers for many predictive tasks. Examples of these include: product sales [15], stock market [6], elections [16], and disease outbreaks [1,18]. In addition to these digital traces of activity, previous research shows that social media data comprises of unstructured data about opinions, stance, sentiments and many other attributes that reflect human behavior and preferences, such as ideology [7] or even health-related states like depression [11]. These trends have been especially consequential in domain of public health, as highlighted by the recent

The original version of this chapter was revised: An error in figure 2 has been corrected. The correction to this chapter is available at
https://doi.org/10.1007/978-3-031-17114-7_26

© The Author(s), under exclusive license to Springer Nature Switzerland AG 2022, corrected publication 2022
R. Thomson et al. (Eds.): SBP-BRiMS 2022, LNCS 13558, pp. 3–12, 2022.
https://doi.org/10.1007/978-3-031-17114-7_1

COVID-19 pandemic, with social media platforms facilitating both access to accurate health-related information worldwide [9], as well as misinformation [14].

Despite their enormous success, there are still considerable challenges associated to the application of social media data in the study of human behavior at scale [20]. Biases associated to the way social media data are produced, sampled, or created could result in biased estimates and flawed predictions, something especially worrisome in the domain of public health [18]. In this study, we highlight one such challenge, namely the widespread presence of automated accounts, or social bots [12], as a factor that can potentially bias or even hide valuable signals about public health issues [2,3,8].

Even though the use of social media has increased exponentially in the past decade, and the population of its users has become more and diverse and representative, the usage of social media bots has also grown. Although social bots are sometimes used for harmless purposes, they have also been shown to amplify content from low-credibility sources [21]. Therefore, it becomes important to assess how automated amplifiers bias predictions drawn from social media data for the purpose of studying and understanding health related behavior at scale.

To illustrate a concrete example, here we focus on the recent public health crisis associated to vaping and e-cigarette products that took place in the United States right before the COVID-19 pandemic in 2019. During this crisis, the usage of e-cigarette and vape products caused several lung injuries and deaths across United States [13]. Later this incident was classified as epidemic by the healthcare authorities. The source of these injuries in the composition of liquid chemical in vape products was unknown at that time, and later was found to be the presence of vitamin E acetate in many commercial vaping products. The Centers for Disease Control and Prevention (CDC), asked providers to report all e-cigarette related injuries or deaths cases to their state health department. By the end of the year of 2019, there were more than 2,500 confirmed cases of lung injuries and 55 deaths across the United States.

For the purpose of this study, we used the social media platform Twitter as the source of our data. Twitter is widely used as micro-blogging platform, centered around news sharing and public conversation; it has thus been compared to a public square. To date, there are 206 million active users on Twitter, producing approximately 500 million tweets every day. Social media skew younger [5], and the fact that the typical person who uses vape products also tends to be young motivated us to select Twitter as a rich source of information about vaping and an ideal forum for vape-related conversations. Our main hypothesis is thus that the chatter on Twitter about vaping and e-cigarettes may be a signal that could let us predict in which locations vaping-related injuries occurred, and perhaps extract meaningful insights that could help in understanding the outbreak in various parts of the United States.

To test this hypothesis we compiled a list of representative keywords associated to vaping and e-cigarettes (see Table 1), and used this list to collect a corpus of vaping-related public tweets in English. Using simple pattern matching methods, we geolocated the authors to these tweets to any of the 50 U.S.

states. Because larger states may have both more tweets and more injuries by virtue of their larger populations, we normalized tweet counts by the number of tweets we would see from that state by chance alone and injuries by the total population in the state. This normalized volume of tweets gives us a rough sense of the vaping-related chatter in each of state, and thus could be used as a predictive feature to determine the number of per capita *E-cigarette or Vaping Use-Associated Lung Injury* (EVALI) in that state.

This data was used to predict number of EVALI reported by the CDC. In particular, we sought to answer the following research questions:

– Are data from Twitter able to provide a signal about the presence of injuries due to vaping in different states?
– What is the impact of social bots on this signal?
– Given a set of potential keywords for collecting tweets, can we find specific keywords which can be used for lung injury predictions?
– What is the predictive power of these data compared to survey-based estimates of vaping activity?

To evaluate our method, we used data from the Behavioral Risk Factor Surveillance System (BRFSS) as a baseline for predicting EVALI. The BRFSS (www.cdc.gov/brfss/) is the premiere health telephonic survey system in the nation. It collects information from residents about various chronic diseases. The information is collected by asking the residents various questions about different chronic diseases, like diabetes and includes specific questions about vaping.

To preview our findings, we show that Twitter data do provide a useful signal in predicting lung injuries if one accounts for the presence of social bots: if unaccounted, our study shows that bots can completely mask the signal. Thus, researchers in public health should take into account their presence and clean the data from bots. In addition to these findings, we also show that using linear models with regularization we are able to identify the keywords and hashtags which are more predictive of injuries.

2   Methods

Twitter Data. As part of a class project, we collected 72,023 vaping-related tweets from November 28, 2019 to November 30, 2019 using the 'filter' endpoint of the Twitter streaming API, which returns 100% of all tweets with the specified keywords (i.e., not a random sample). To select the keywords and hashtags that were representative of vaping, we relied on Google Trends. Table 1 shows the 25 keywords used. Simultaneously to this collection, for the same time period we collected 11,776,299 tweets from the 'sample' endpoint of the Twitter API (also known as the 'Spritzer' API), which provides access to a 1% pseudo-random sample of all tweets posted on Twitter during the same time period. Even though the 'sample' endpoint is known for producing potentially biased samples due to the nature of the tweet selection procedure employed by Twitter, which uses a millisecond sampling window [17], and can be thus tampered with by automated

Table 1. Keywords used to collect tweets from the 'filter' endpoint of the Twitter API.

#antivaping	#fighttheflavor	thc vaping	vapecommunity	vaper
ecigarettes	iambigvape	truthaboutvaping	vape death	vaping
ecigs	in2020imgoingtoquit	vape	vapefam	vaping illness
e pen	noecigs4kids	vape	vape juice	vapingindustry
e vaping	quitlying	vape ban	vape porn	vapingsa

accounts [19], it should be noted that we relied on this API for the sole purpose of establishing baseline tweeting volumes for each U.S. state. Assuming that the choice of disclosing one's location is not associated to the act of tampering with the Twitter API, this sample should give an accurate picture of the baseline volume of activity in each U.S. state. Furthermore, as we show below, we do apply bot detection techniques to these data (see below), which are likely to reduce the over-representation of automated accounts that post systematically within the millisecond sampling window used by Twitter.

All tweets were collected using Tweepy. There were 46,678 unique users in the vape-related tweets and 5,741,318 unique users in the random sample tweets. The tweets from both datasets were filtered so that only tweets that met the following two requirements were used in subsequent analysis: (i) they were written in English, as detected by the language attribute present among the tweet metadata, and (ii) they were posted by someone located in one of the 50 states of the United States, where the location was determined by applying a simple pattern matching expression to the self-reported user profile information of the author. The regular expression we used recognized place names followed by either a state name (e.g. `Tampa, Florida`) or its 2-letter code (e.g. `Tampa, FL`).

Having collected and filtered both samples of tweets, we counted the number of tweets in each state and then normalized them to obtain the per capita tweeting activity about vaping of a state as the number of 'vape' tweet (i.e. those collected the 'filter' endpoint) divided by the estimated number of tweets in the state, which is number of 'random' tweets (i.e. from the 'sample' endpoint) of that state multiplied by 100. We refer to this variable as the *relative vaping tweets*, or *relative tweets* in a state.

Finally, similar to way we calculated relative vaping tweets for each state, we also calculated relative vaping tweets of each of the 25 keywords and hashtags used in the data collection from the 'filter' API (see Table 1). This was done by calculating relative vaping tweets corresponding to each keyword and hashtag which was used to collect vape related tweets.

EVALI Data. To collect data on per capita EVALI in each U.S. state, we scraped the number of lung injury cases and of death cases caused by vaping illness from the website of the Centers for Disease Control and Prevention (CDC) until Nov 30, 2019, along with data the population of each state from the U.S. Census. In the following, because the total number of deaths reported was very low, we focus on lung injuries only for all subsequent analyses.

Survey Data. To provide a baseline against which to compare the predictive power of our models trained on social media data, we used data from The Behavioral Risk Factor Surveillance System (BRFSS). Friedman [13] used 2017 and 2018 BRFSS data to estimate e-cigarettes use in states. The 2017 data represents the current vaping rates of a state as a weighted mean of binary indicator for options 'every day' or 'some days' for responses to: *'Do you now use e-cigarettes or other electronic "vaping" products every day, some days, or not at all?'*, fielded in all US states. Unfortunately, not all states included this question in both years of the survey. Similar to prior work [13], for these states, missing 2018 vaping rates were estimated by multiplying the reported 2017 rate by the average 2018-to-2017 ratio in states in the same census region.

Social Bot Detection. We used the BotometerLite API (botometer.osome.iu.edu/ botometerlite) to obtain the bot scores of all the unique twitter user accounts from both sample and vape tweet datasets. BotometerLite is based on a supervised machine learning algorithm which is trained on thousands of features which were extracted from publicly available data and metadata about Twitter accounts [22]. It evaluates the extent to which an account exhibits properties similar to a social bot and discriminates between accounts operated by humans and bots. Given a tweet, BotometerLite returns the probability that the user who posted that tweet is a bot. We used this probability value as a threshold for categorizing all tweets.

Regression Models. To predict per capita EVALI by state, we used linear regression models. We consider three groups of predictive features: 1) the overall relative vaping tweets, 2) the relative vaping tweets for each of the 25 keywords/hashtags from Google Trends (see Table 1), and the current vaping rates estimated from BRFSS data. Since counts for different keyword/hashtags are likely correlated with each other, we applied regularization using the ElasticNet method [23], with hyperparameters selected via 10-fold cross-validation. Unlike LASSO, ElasticNet can select groups of features together, which is more useful in our case since different hashtags/keywords may co-occur in some of the tweets. To evaluate the models, we report the root mean squared error. All regression scripts were implemented using scikit-learn.

3   Results

Effect of Social Bots. We begin by checking whether social bots are present in our data. The left panel of Fig. 1 shows the bot score distribution for all Twitter users in the vape and sample corpora (see Sect. 2). Although most users display very little signs of automation, we observe a fraction of users that are likely automated, suggesting further investigation about their impact. Furthermore, despite having used two different APIs to collect the two corpora, the two samples are not statistically different (two-sided Kolmogorov-Smirnov test, $D = 0.073, p < 10^{-4}, N_1 = 46,678, N_2 = 5,741,312$).

The above results apply to the filtered tweets, which were filtered of non-English tweets and users that could not be geolocated to any of the 50 U.S. states (see Sect. 2). We repeated the analysis on the full dataset (Fig. 1, center left), obtaining similar results (two-sided K-S test, $D = 0.03999, p < 10^{-4}, N_1 = 31,951, N_2 = 1,797,525$). This suggests that our filtering decision should not be affecting our results.

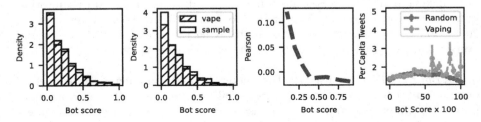

Fig. 1. Left: the distribution of bot scores (lower values indicate less chances of automation) of users in the vape and sample corpora, after filtering out non-English tweets and tweets by users that could not be geolocated (see Sect. 2). Center left: the same distribution but for all tweets (i.e., before filtering). Center right: The Pearson correlation between EVALIs and relative vaping tweet volume as a function of the maximum bot score in the data. Right: the per capita number of tweets posted by users as a function of their bot score for users in the vaping tweets corpus (orange) and in the random tweets corpus (blue). Error bars represent the standard error of the mean. (Color figure online)

Having confirmed that our social media data do include instances of automated accounts, we consider the impact of these social bots on the tweeting activity and the signal about EVALIs across states. To do so, we applied an increasing threshold on the bot score and removed from the corpora all tweets posted by accounts whose bot score exceeded the threshold. Since the bot score returned by BotometerLite is a probability of automation, by varying the thresholds we can observe how the association between Twitter activity and EVALIs changes as we change the likelihood that our social media data have been produced by automated accounts. When we set our acceptance threshold high (>0.4), this is equivalent to considering all tweets in our corpora and thus including tweets by likely bots together with those by likely humans. In that case, Fig. 1 (center right) shows that there is almost no correlation between tweeting activity and EVALIs in a state. However, when we consider only tweets by likely humans, we observe a positive correlation, suggesting that the signal about EVALIs is masked by automated tweeting activity.

To better understand the impact of bots on the public conversation about vaping and e-cigarettes, we focus on the tweeting rate of an individual account as a rough proxy for its impact on the conversation. In Fig. 1 (right) we compare the number of tweets per capita for accounts in the vape and sample corpora as a function of their bot score. We observe that in the random sample of tweets the per-capita tweeting rate *decreases* as the likelihood of automation increases. When we consider the vape tweets, however, we observe that more automated accounts also tend to tweet more. This suggests one way social bots may be responsible for the obfuscation of the signal about EVALIs, and may also point to the simpler nature of social bots deployed in this context, which may be programmed to produce large quantities of spam about vaping and e-cigarettes.

These results strongly suggest that social bots can bias statistics that are based on social media data. Thus, it is important to filter them out in any social media analysis for analyzing human behaviour. We now turn to quantifying the usefulness of social media data that have been cleaned of social bots.

EVALI Prediction. Figure 2 (top left) shows the average out- of-sample RMSE over 10^3 iterations of 10-fold cross-validation. We used different features and combinations of features to predict EVALIs in a state. As a baseline to compare our method, we used the current vaping rate estimated from BRFSS. The lowest error is achieved by models trained on the relative vaping tweets stratified by keyword/hashtag (see Table 1), suggesting that not all keywords obtained from Google Trends were equally predictive of EVALIs. The error reduction relative to the BRFSS baseline is significant for all alternative model (see Table 2).

Table 2. Mann-Whitney U test, two-sided test, $N = 10^3$.

Comparison	U_1	p-value
BRFSS vs Tweets (all)	388, 721	$< 10^{-4}$
BRFSS vs BRFSS + Tweets (all)	429, 669	$< 10^{-4}$
BRFSS vs Tweets (by HT)	13, 054	$< 10^{-4}$
BRFSS vs BRFSS + Tweets (by HT)	16, 244	$< 10^{-4}$
BRFSS vs Tweets (all + by HT)	14, 209	$< 10^{-4}$

Content and Geographic Analysis. As a diagnostic check to our results, we also analysed the content of tweets to make sure that they are bona fide examples of social media conversations on the topic of vaping and e-cigarettes. Our content analysis consists of two parts. First, to better understand the impact of keyword choice on our results, we calculated the signal-to-noise ratio (SNR) of the relative vaping tweets across states for all 25 keywords/hashtags used to collect the vape-related tweets (see Table 1). A value of SNR > 1 usually indicates that a feature contains enough signal for prediction purposes. From Fig. 2 (top right) we can observe that only two of the 25 keywords/hashtags from Google Trends meet this threshold (**vape** and **vaping**), further confirming the importance of applying regularization to the ML model.

Second, using the above two keywords, we selected all vape-related tweets that contained those two keywords and had been posted by accounts with a

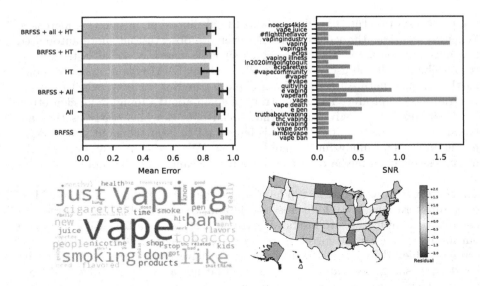

Fig. 2. Top left: Average root mean squared error from 10^3 iterations of 10-fold cross-validation for models trained on different groups of features. Here, 'Tweets (all)' refers to the relative vaping tweets by state, and 'Tweets (by HT)' refers to the relative vaping tweets stratified by the 25 keywords/hashtags from Google Trends (see Table 1). The error bar represent the standard error of the mean. Top right: Signal-to-noise ratio of all the keywords and hashtags used to collect the data (see Table 1). Bottom left: Terms with highest TF-IDF score from vape-related tweets. Only tweets with the keywords **vape** and **vaping** and that were posted by a likely human user (bot score ≤ 0.1 were included in the visualization. Word size proportional to TF-IDF score. Bottom right: Map of the residuals of EVALI prediction with the best-performing model.

bot score ≤ 0.1. We computed TF-IDF scores for all words in those tweets and inspected them. Figure 2 (bottom left) shows a word cloud made with the words with the highest TF-IDF score and gives a rough idea of the content of our data, confirming the bona fide nature of the tweets collected. Few interesting observations are words like 'ban', 'kids', 'health', 'lungs', 'stop', which suggest Twitter users were engaged on conversation about the health implications of vaping and a possible stop due to the reports of EVALIs in the media.

Finally, to get a better sense of the predictions of our model, we conducted an additional visualization exercise. We computed, using leave-one-out, the residuals of the predictions of our best-performing model (see Fig. 2 (bottom left)) and visualized them in a map of the United States. States with large positive residuals indicate areas of concern that should be prioritized by public health officials. Figure 2 (right) shows a geographic cluster of midwestern states (Minnesota, Illinois, Indiana, and North Dakota) of special concern.

4   Related Work

Other studies looked at vaping and associated health risks. Friedman studied the same 2019 EVALI outbreak studied here and the relationship between the mass-marketed e-cigarettes and an additive in regionally available black market vape products [13]. Adolescents or young adults are especially prone to vaping [4], and Colditz et al. [10] expresses the need of collecting vape relevant data for better understanding the vaping culture, as an opportunity to understand health benefits, policies, and the attitudes associated to vaping [10]. While all these studies used social media to observe the signals of vape smoking behavior on social media, our approach uses these data to predict lung injuries due to vaping.

5   Conclusions

In this work we used data from Twitter to predict e-cigarettes and vaping lung injuries during the 2019 US vaping epidemic. Our work shows that the usefulness of data from social media for public health can be severely hampered by the presence of automated amplifiers, whose activity can mask the bona fide signal due to human activity. Thus, care should be taken to detect and remove content produced by social bots when attempting to use data from social media for studies of human behavior. Even though our analysis was based on a limited dataset collected for a brief period, we show that nonetheless regression models trained on this data outperform those trained on data about current vaping usage from gold-standard probability surveys, suggesting the potential of this type of data. Future work should investigate the possibility of using data from social media to build digital surveillance tools for health risks associated to electronic cigarettes, despite the challenges posed by the presence of automated accounts.

Acknowledgement. The authors would like to thank Filippo Menczer and Kai-Cheng Yang for providing access to the BotometerLite API, and to Hunter Morera for help with data collection and coding during the initial part of this project.

References

1. Achrekar, H., Gandhe, A., Lazarus, R., Yu, S.H., Liu, B.: Predicting flu trends using twitter data. In: 2011 IEEE Conference on Computer Communications Workshops (INFOCOM WKSHPS), pp. 702–707 (2011)
2. Allem, J.P., Ferrara, E.: Could social bots pose a threat to public health? Am. J. Publ. Health **108**(8), 1005–1006 (2018)
3. Allem, J.P., Ferrara, E., Uppu, S.P., Cruz, T.B., Unger, J.B.: E-cigarette surveillance with social media data: Social bots, emerging topics, and trends. JMIR Publ. Health Surveillance **3**(4), e98 (2017)
4. Arrazola, R.A., et al.: Tobacco use among middle and high school students-united states, 2011–2014. Morb. Mortal. Wkly Rep. **64**(14), 381 (2015)
5. Auxier, B., Anderson, M.: Social media use in 2021. Technical report, Pew Research Center, April 2021

6. Bollen, J., Mao, H., Zeng, X.: Twitter mood predicts the stock market. J. Comput. Sci. **2**(1), 1–8 (2011)
7. Bond, R., Messing, S.: Quantifying social media's political space: estimating ideology from publicly revealed preferences on Facebook. Am. Polit. Sci. Rev. **109**(1), 62–78 (2015)
8. Broniatowski, D.A., et al.: Weaponized health communication: Twitter bots and Russian trolls amplify the vaccine debate. Am. J. Publ. Health **108**(10), 1378–1384 (2018)
9. Chan, A.K.M., Nickson, C.P., Rudolph, J.W., Lee, A., Joynt, G.M.: Social media for rapid knowledge dissemination: early experience from the COVID-19 pandemic. Anaesthesia **75**(12), 1579–1582 (2020)
10. Colditz, J.B., Welling, J., Smith, N.A., James, A.E., Primack, B.A.: World vaping day: contextualizing vaping culture in online social media using a mixed methods approach. J. Mixed Methods Res. **13**(2), 196–215 (2019)
11. De Choudhury, M., Gamon, M., Counts, S., Horvitz, E.: Predicting depression via social media. In: Proceedings of the International AAAI Conference on Web and Social Media, vol. 7, no. 1, pp. 128–137 (2021)
12. Ferrara, E., Varol, O., Davis, C., Menczer, F., Flammini, A.: The rise of social bots. Commun. ACM **59**(7), 96–104 (2016)
13. Friedman, A.S.: Association of vaping-related lung injuries with rates of e-cigarette and cannabis use across us states. Addiction **116**(3), 651–657 (2021)
14. Gallotti, R., Valle, F., Castaldo, N., Sacco, P., Domenico, M.D.: Assessing the risks of 'infodemics' in response to COVID-19 epidemics. Nat. Hum. Behav. **4**(12), 1285–1293 (2020)
15. Gruhl, D., Guha, R., Kumar, R., Novak, J., Tomkins, A.: The predictive power of online chatter. In: Proceedings of the Eleventh ACM SIGKDD International Conference on Knowledge Discovery in Data Mining. KDD 2005, pp. 78–87. Association for Computing Machinery, New York, August 2005
16. Kennedy, R., Wojcik, S., Lazer, D.: Improving election prediction internationally. Science **355**(6324), 515–520 (2017)
17. Kergl, D., Roedler, R., Seeber, S.: On the endogenesis of Twitter's spritzer and gardenhose sample streams. In: 2014 IEEE/ACM International Conference on Advances in Social Networks Analysis and Mining (ASONAM 2014), pp. 357–364 (2014)
18. Lazer, D., Kennedy, R., King, G., Vespignani, A.: The parable of google flu: traps in big data analysis. Science **343**(6176), 1203–1205 (2014)
19. Pfeffer, J., Mayer, K., Morstatter, F.: Tampering with Twitter's sample API. EPJ Data Sci. **7**(1) (2018)
20. Ruths, D., Pfeffer, J.: Social media for large studies of behavior. Science **346**(6213), 1063–1064 (2014)
21. Shao, C., Ciampaglia, G.L., Varol, O., Yang, K.C., Flammini, A., Menczer, F.: The spread of low-credibility content by social bots. Nat. Commun. **9**(1), 1–9 (2018)
22. Varol, O., Ferrara, E., Davis, C., Menczer, F., Flammini, A.: Online human-bot interactions: Detection, estimation, and characterization. In: Proceedings of the International AAAI Conference on Web and Social Media, vol. 11, pp. 280–289, May 2017
23. Zou, H., Hastie, T.: Regularization and variable selection via the elastic net. J. Roy. Statis. Soc. Ser. B (Statis. Methodol.) **67**(2), 301–320 (2005)

Mitigation of Optimized Pharmaceutical Supply Chain Disruptions by Criminal Agents

Abhisekh Rana[1]([✉]), Hamdi Kavak[1], Andrew Crooks[2], Sean Luke[1], Carlotta Domeniconi[1], and Jim Jones[1]

[1] George Mason University, Fairfax, VA 22030, USA
{arana6,sean,cdomenic,jjonesu}@gmu.edu
[2] University at Buffalo, Buffalo, NY 14261, USA
atcrooks@buffalo.edu

Abstract. Disruption to supply chains can significantly influence the operation of the world economy and this has been shown to permeate and affect a large majority of countries and their citizens. We present initial results from a model that explores the disruptions to supply chains by a criminal agent and possible mitigation strategies. We construct a model of a typical pharmaceutical manufacturing supply chain, which is implemented via discrete event simulation. The criminal agent optimizes its resource allocation to maximize disruption to the supply chain. Our findings show criminal agents can cause cascading damage and exploit vulnerabilities, which inherently exist within the supply chain itself. We also demonstrate how basic mitigation strategies can efficaciously alleviate this potential damage.

Keywords: Pharmaceutical supply chains · Criminal agents · Evolutionary computation · Mitigation

1 Introduction and Background

Supply chains are a critical part of modern society and the operation of the world economy. Recently, the COVID-19 pandemic has brought supply chains and disruptions to them front and center. These disruptions have not only led to massive shortages in critical goods such as semi-conductors, personal protective equipment and medical supplies, but also impacted the roll out of vaccinations [3,12].Though the effects of disruptions to supply chains by natural disasters have been well studied (e.g., [6]), potential disruptions to their operations by nefarious criminal agents remains an area of limited research [9].

In this paper, we discuss our initial study of the effects of disruptions by a criminal agent to pharmaceutical supply chains and ways to mitigate their impact. We have developed a discrete event simulation model of a supply chain for drug production drawn from real systems in the pharmaceutical industry

R. Thomson et al. (Eds.): SBP-BRiMS 2022, LNCS 13558, pp. 13–23, 2022.
https://doi.org/10.1007/978-3-031-17114-7_2

(e.g., [7,13,14]). Our ultimate goal is to build an agent-based model of a criminal organization and use it to disrupt the supply chain, then develop mitigation or protection strategies against this attack. As an initial step, we are using an optimizer to search for ways to maximize damage to the supply chain and analyze its recovery. This paper discusses results from this initial approach.

Given the importance of supply chains, it should not be surprising that efficient supply chain management has received a lot of attention, from mitigating the negative impacts of natural disasters, such as the current COVID-19 pandemic, and attacks by criminal or terrorist organisations (e.g., [3,6,9,17]). In order to explore the effect of these different scenarios, supply chains have long been modelled and studied via simulation (e.g., [5]). Much of this work has focused on the supply chain itself, including the identification of potential bottlenecks, which represent the most vulnerable points in the chain [10]. Supply chain optimization is also another major research area. For example, in the pharmaceutical industry efforts have been made to balance capacity and future demand [14]. There is also a growing interest in disruptions to supply chains from external factors such as criminal organisations (e.g., [2,9]). These disruptions include adulteration to key materials, physical attacks or theft of key ingredients and cyber-attacks on the software used in the logistics of the supply chain [7,13,14,17].

To the reader it might seem obvious that there exists a significant risk stemming from supply chain disruptions to the operation of the global economy and individual companies. However, it has been argued that up to 75% of Fortune 500 companies, which include the major pharmaceutical companies, remain unprepared to handle disruptions to their supply chains [18]. Having basic mitigation strategies such as access to third party manufacturers and secondary materials suppliers, in case of disruptions to delivery from your main provider, have been shown to protect supply chains from disruptions [15,18]. In the remainder of this paper we first present our supply chain simulation model in Sect. 2, we then discuss the results (Sect. 3), which include mitigation strategies. We then conclude with a summary and discussion of areas for further work (Sect. 4).

2   Methodology

This paper proposes to analyze supply chains and their bottlenecks using various computational modeling tools and technologies. We utilize discrete event simulation to model a simplified pharmaceutical supply chain [7,14] as our case study (Sect. 2.1). We then simulate attacks (Sect. 2.2) on this supply chain by a criminal agent (Sect. 2.3) whose aim is to maximize damage to its operations. The supply chain is provided with mitigation strategies to protect itself from such attacks. Details of our methodology are outlined in the following subsections.

2.1   Supply Chain Model

Our example pharmaceutical supply chain is illustrated in Fig. 1. This model represents a generic pharmaceutical company that purchases the materials required

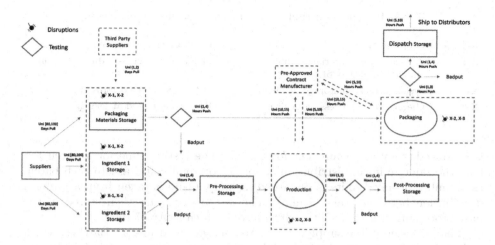

Fig. 1. A simplified version of a typical pharmaceutical supply chain.

to produce drugs from a supplier pool (e.g., [7]). The resources available to the supplier pool to meet these purchase orders are assumed to be infinite. Thus, a request for a purchase order for any material from the pharmaceutical company is always honored. There are three different types of materials the pharmaceutical company requires to produce its drugs and deliver them to its distributors: two separate ingredients that are combined to produce the actual drug and packaging materials used to package the drugs once production is completed. Once purchased, these materials are stored in separate storage facilities, all of which have a maximum capacity of 1000 units. If the number of units of the materials in any of the storage facilities falls below the critical threshold of 350 units, a restocking request is sent to the supplier pool for 800 additional units. The time to fulfill this restocking request is modeled using a uniform distribution between 80 and 100 h. It should be noted these numbers and several of the values chosen below were arbitrarily chosen but mimic the basic principles and dynamics seen within supply chains. In future work, these values could be parameterized from real-world data.

Once the materials arrive at their respective storage facilities, they are separated into batches of 20 units and sent for testing, which is the norm in such supply chains [14]. The testing time for each batch is modeled using a uniform distribution between 1 to 4 h. For each batch, a certain number of units fail at testing and are discarded as badput. The number of failed units in each batch is also modeled using a uniform distribution between 1 and 6 units. After testing, the two different ingredients are transferred to a pre-processing storage facility which has a capacity of 1000 units. Two batches, each containing 10 units of the two ingredients, are then combined during the production phase to produce 10 units of the actual drug. The time to produce these 10 units of the drug is modeled using a uniform distribution between 1 to 3 h. Once a batch of drugs

Table 1. Type of disruption and its effect on the supply chain.

X-Code	Disruption type	Effect on supply chain
X-1	Adulteration of materials secured from the supplier pool	Failure rate increases during testing
X-2	Physical attack on storage facilities	Stored inventory destroyed at facility
X-3	Cyberattack in processing facilities	Processing halted at facility

is produced, they are again sent for testing. The testing time for a batch follows the same uniform distribution as for the original materials. In each batch, the number of failed units is discarded as badput and is taken from a uniform distribution between 1 and 3 units. The tested drugs are then stored in the post-processing storage facility, which also has a capacity of 1000.

The next step in the supply chain is to package the drugs [7]. Batches, which include 10 units of packaging material and 10 units of the completed drugs, are packaged together and sent to the dispatch storage facility. The time for the packaging of each batch is modeled using a uniform distribution between 1 to 3 h. Similar to the production phase, batches of 10 units of the packed drug are tested; units that fail testing are discarded from the batch as badput. The units that pass testing are moved to the dispatch storage facility for collection by the distributors. The dispatch storage facility has a capacity of 1000 units. Once the inventory of packaged drugs at the dispatch storage facility exceeds 50 units, a request is sent to the distributors to collect the drugs to be passed on to the end customer. The time for this pickup request to be fulfilled is modeled using a uniform distribution between 5 to 10 h. For our simulation, once a drug has been picked up by the distributors, the drug is considered sold and leaves the system.

2.2 Disruptions

As noted before, supply chains can be disrupted in a number of ways. In this paper, we model the effects of three different types of disruptions, which can be executed by the criminal agent [7,17]. There are five separate points in the supply chain, marked by a bomb symbol in Fig. 1, where these disruptions can occur. These disruptions are represented using X-Codes (i.e., X1), and the type of disruption (X-Code) and its effect on the supply chain are detailed in Table 1. The effect and duration of each of these disruptions at different points in the supply chain are directly related to the resources allocated to the criminal agent, which is detailed in the next section.

2.3 The Criminal Agent

In this paper, we model a generic and lone criminal agent who can directly affect the supply chain via the disruptions outlined above. The design of the criminal agent is detailed in Fig. 2. The criminal agent is allocated a fixed amount

Fig. 2. Design of the criminal agent.

of resources, represented by a resource allocation vector (akin to money). The total amount of resources available to the agent is set to 1500. These resources can be allocated to disrupt the five points in the supply chain detailed in Fig. 1. The allocation of these resources is represented by a vector of length five (corresponding to the five potential disruption points). The first element in this vector represents the number of resources allocated to disrupt the ingredient one storage facility. Similarly, the other elements in the vector represent the resources allocated to disrupt the other four disruption points.

This resource allocation vector is then multiplied by a set of weights, represented by the weight vector, which equals one. These weights are used to quantify the effect on the supply chain from the resource allocation for each disruption at the corresponding five disruption points. Additionally, a lower weight results in a lower magnitude of disruption at each point. Thus, these weights can be changed to make certain points in the supply chain more difficult to disrupt (i.e., a point with heavy physical security). Once the resource allocation vector is multiplied by the weight vector, we obtain a vector that represents the magnitude of each disruption at the five different disruption points. The first three elements of this vector represent a disruption to the storage facilities. They measure the number of drugs destroyed or adulterated by a physical attack. The last two elements represent a cyber or physical attack on the production and packaging facilities. They disable the operation of the facilities and their effect is represented by the number of hours either facility is unable to produce or package any drugs. Using this design the criminal agent is able to directly interact and disrupt the operation of the supply chain. This is executed by optimizing the resource allocation vector while the elements of the weight vector remains fixed at 0.2.

2.4   Simulation and Optimization

The supply chain model was implemented using Python's SimPy [11] library and the optimization is carried out using the Optuna [1] library. Each simulation in this study is run for 6 months, representing a total of 3600 h hours of simulation time. We measure the efficacy of the disruptions caused by the criminal agent using the total number of drugs sold by the supply chain during the simulation.

We use an optimization algorithm to find how the criminal agent might apply fixed resources, via the resource allocation vector, to attack the supply chain so as to minimize the number of drugs sold during the simulation period. Because the parameter space involved has no known derivative, we rely on the *CMA-ES* algorithm to accomplish this task [4]. CMA-ES is part of a family of sample-based optimization techniques collectively known as *evolutionary algorithms* [8]. Broadly speaking, CMA-ES starts with a sample of random candidate solutions to optimize. It then iteratively assesses the quality of each candidate solution, then performs resampling based on their quality to produce a new sample of candidates. In CMA-ES, the resampling is done by fitting a multidimensional Gaussian distribution over the samples warped according to their respective quality. The new samples are then randomly sampled under the distribution. By combining our supply chain model with our criminal agent, and by leveraging CMA-ES, in what follows we attempt to identify the main bottlenecks and the most vulnerable points in the pharmaceutical supply chain.

We also investigate the effects of adding mitigation strategies to the supply chain. There are two types of standard mitigation strategies made available to the supply chain, both based on using third-party suppliers or contractors [16]. For disruptions to the inventory storage facilities, when an attack destroys units stored, the supply chain has access to a third party supplier to quickly re-stock its goods. The restocking request is fulfilled at a faster rate than if secured from its regular supplier. This restocking request is triggered if the inventory at a point in the supply is depleted by amount 3X or greater than the average hourly depletion rate. A depletion in inventory of this size is used by the supply chain to determine an attack has occurred and a mitigation should be implemented. The second set of mitigations involve the production and packaging facilities. These mitigations are triggered when these facilities lie idle for more than 80 h. This value is chosen since it is 4X greater than the max average idle time across 500 simulations. Thus, if the facility lies idle for longer than this time the supply chain assumes an attack has occurred. The mitigation involves outsourcing production or packaging to a third party. An additional, time delay is also added in order to model the extra time taken to transport the goods from the pharmaceutical companies' facilities to the third-part facility and return the produced or packaged goods.

3   Results

In our first set of simulations, we explore the effect on the supply chain from a disruption by the criminal agent where all its resources are focused on a single disruption point. These simulations model a single disruption that occurs halfway through the 6-month simulation period. These simulations allows us to ascertain the weakest points in the supply chain. Figure 3 details representative sample simulations for the baseline model, which is a simulation without any disruption, and results for an attack at the five disruption points in the supply chain. It charts the total weekly drug sales during the entire simulation period. The dotted red line indicates the time the disruption took place. Correspondingly, Table 2 outlines the key statistics derived from running the simulations 500 times.

The first result of interest is the lag between the time the disruption occurs and its effect on the weekly drug sales between the packaging materials facility

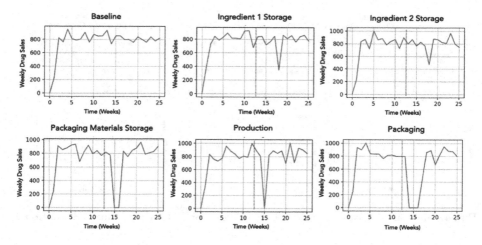

Fig. 3. Sample simulations for the baseline model, without any disruption, and attacks at the five main disruption points in the supply chain.

and the ingredient facilities. This lag is the due to the location of the facilities in the supply chain. The ingredient facilities are located at the beginning of the chain, thus the result of a disruption at these locations takes time to permeate through the network. In contrast, a disruption to the packaging materials facility, which is directly linked to the end of the supply chain, creates a more immediate and more damaging effect. The magnitude of this effect is larger since the packaging material facility also represents a bottleneck. Without access to packaging materials no drugs can be packaged and sold.

Table 2. Key statistics for the baseline model, without any disruption, and attacks at the five main disruption points in the supply chain.

Disruption point	Mean drugs sold	Std. dev.	99% confidence interval
Baseline	20947	211	[20971–20923]
Ingredient 1 storage	20667	352	[20708–20626]
Ingredient 2 storage	20635	392	[20680–20590]
Packaging materials storage	19358	276	[19390–19326]
Production facility	19641	183	[19662–19620]
Packaging facility	18283	158	[18301–18265]

It is also important to note that none of the 99% confidence intervals for the average drugs sold for the disruptions overlap with the baseline. Thus, all the disruptions implemented significantly affect the operation of the supply chain. Furthermore, the most vulnerable point in the supply chain was identified as the

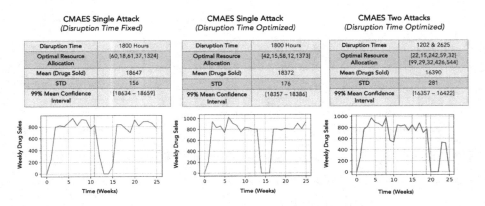

Fig. 4. Summary statistics and sample simulations for CMA-ES optimized disruptions.

packaging facility. This is because it represents a bottleneck in the supply chain and is located at the end point.

Next, we utilize CMA-ES to optimize the resource allocation vector of the criminal agent (as discussed in Sect. 2.4). This allows us to not only analyze the best way for the criminal agent to attack the supply chain, but also determine whether causing multiple disruptions at the same time creates additional vulnerabilities and therefore does more damage. For consistency with the previous results, we carry out this optimization at the same time as the attacks in the previous simulations and then pass the timing of the attack as a further parameter to the CMA-ES. This enables us to analyze whether there is an optimal time in the simulation to mount an attack.

We also study the effect of multiple attacks on the supply chain at different times using the same number of resources utilized for a single attack (i.e., 1500 as discussed in Sect. 2.3). Specifically, we focus on two attacks with the aim being to establish whether the first attack significantly weakens the supply chain so that a second attack creates a cascading effect and thus causes more damage. The results for 500 simulations is outlined in Fig. 4. From the results (Fig. 4) one can observe that the optimal resource allocation derived from using the CMA-ES optimizer allocates the majority of its resources to disrupting the packaging facility. This again illustrates the point that there exist bottlenecks in supply chains and bottlenecks further down the chain are the most vulnerable points. The mean 99% confidence intervals for the drugs sold during the simulation when the timing of the attack is fixed and optimized also do not overlap. Thus, we demonstrate that optimizing the timing of disruptions does greater damage. It is also clear from these results that distributing the resources of the criminal agent over two separate attacks does result in generating additional vulnerabilities to the supply chain and that there exists a cascading effect.

In our final set of experiments, we study the efficacy of mitigation strategies, outlined in Sect. 2.4, our rationale being that many companies are not geared

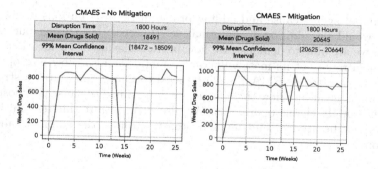

Fig. 5. Summary statistics and sample simulations for CMA-ES optimized disruptions with and without mitigation in place.

towards supply chain disruptions [18]. However, our methodology could help alleviate this. Specifically, we use the single attack model optimized via CMA-ES with and without mitigation in place. The results for 500 simulations are detailed in Fig. 5. From these results, one can observe that having adequate mitigation strategies in place protects the supply chain from disruptions. The mean 99% confidence intervals also do not overlap; thus, this result is significant.

4 Summary and Outlook

In this paper we analyze the operations of a pharmaceutical supply chain and the effects on it from disruptions by a single criminal agent. We demonstrate how a supply chain can be effectively simulated via a discrete event simulation. We then construct a single simple criminal agent with fixed resources whose goal is to disrupt the supply chain. The design of the criminal agent allows it to interact with the supply chain and attack and damage key points within it. By studying the operation of the supply chain and using CMA-ES to optimize the criminal agent's resource allocation, we are able probe and identity the main bottlenecks and weak points in the supply chain. This also allows us to discover the optimal approach for a criminal agent to disrupt the supply chain and to optimize the timing of its attacks. We also demonstrate how mounting multiple attacks on the supply chain creates additional vulnerabilities and creates a cascading effect of damage to its operations. Finally, we study the effects of utilizing basic mitigation strategies to protect the supply chain from attacks. We find that these basic strategies are effective in ameliorating the damage caused by attacks from the criminal agent.

The effects and possible damage to supply chains from disruptions caused by nefarious criminal agents remains an understudied area [15]. One of the limitations in our approach is that we utilize a simplified version of a typical pharmaceutical supply chain. Thus, implementing a more complex model would further improve the analysis of the key aspects of our results. The complexity and structure of the criminal agent can also be improved. Studying the typical disruptions these criminal agents cause and adding probabilistic distributions to these disruptions would be additionally informative. However, even using our current approach we are able to demonstrate how bottlenecks and their locations in the supply chain represent its most vulnerable points. We also show how optimization approaches such as CMA-ES can be used to find optimal attack strategies for a criminal agent and how these attacks can be timed to cause the most damage to the supply chains operations. We also demonstrate different mitigation strategies can be studied and implemented to protect the supply chain from disruptions.

References

1. Akiba, T., Sano, S., Yanase, T., Ohta, T., Koyama, M.: Optuna: a next-generation hyperparameter optimization framework. In: ACM SIGKDD International Conference on Knowledge Discovery and Data Mining, pp. 2623–2631 (2019)
2. Basu, G.: The role of transnational smuggling operations in illicit supply chains. J. Transp. Secur. **6**(4), 315–328 (2013)
3. Chowdhury, P., Paul, S.K., Kaisar, S., Moktadir, M.A.: COVID-19 pandemic related supply chain studies: a systematic review. Transp. Res. Part E Logist. Transp. Rev. **148**, 102271 (2021)
4. Hansen, N., Ostermeier, A.: Adapting arbitrary normal mutation distributions in evolution strategies: the covariance matrix adaptation. In: IEEE International Conference on Evolutionary Computation (CEC), pp. 312–317. IEEE (1996)
5. Kleijnen, J.P.: Supply chain simulation tools and techniques: a survey. Int. J. Simul. Process Model. **1**(1–2), 82–89 (2005)
6. Kleindorfer, P.R., Saad, G.H.: Managing disruption risks in supply chains. Prod. Oper. Manag. **14**(1), 53–68 (2005)
7. Koh, R., Schuster, E.W., Chackrabarti, I., Bellman, A.: Securing the pharmaceutical supply chain. Techncial report, Auto-ID Labs, Massachusetts Institute of Technology, 400 Technology Sq., Building NE46, 6th Floor, ambridge, MA 02139 (2003)
8. Luke, S.: Essentials of Metaheuristics, 2nd edn. Lulu (2013). http://cs.gmu.edu/~sean/book/metaheuristics/
9. Männistö, T., Hintsa, J., Urciuoli, L.: Supply chain crime-taxonomy development and empirical validation. Int. J. Shipp. Transp. Logist. **6**(3), 238–256 (2014)
10. Mizgier, K.J., Jüttner, M.P., Wagner, S.M.: Bottleneck identification in supply chain networks. Int. J. Prod. Res. **51**(5), 1477–1490 (2013)
11. Muller, K., Vignaux, T.: SimPy. https://gitlab.com/team-simpy/simpy/
12. Rizou, M., Galanakis, I.M., Aldawoud, T.M., Galanakis, C.M.: Safety of foods, food supply chain and environment within the COVID-19 pandemic. Trends Food Sci. Technol. **102**, 293–299 (2020)
13. Settanni, E., Harrington, T.S., Srai, J.S.: Pharmaceutical supply chain models: a synthesis from a systems view of operations research. Oper. Res. Perspect. **4**, 74–95 (2017)
14. Shah, N.: Pharmaceutical supply chains: key issues and strategies for optimisation. Comput. Chem. Eng. **28**(6–7), 929–941 (2004)
15. Shekarian, M., Nooraie, S.V.R., Parast, M.M.: An examination of the impact of flexibility and agility on mitigating supply chain disruptions. Int. J. Prod. Econ. **220**, 107438 (2020)

16. Tang, C.S.: Robust strategies for mitigating supply chain disruptions. Int. J. Logist. Res. Appl. **9**(1), 33–45 (2006)
17. Urciuoli, L., Männistö, T., Hintsa, J., Khan, T.: Supply chain cyber security–potential threats. Inf. Secur. Int. J. **29**(1) (2013)
18. Wu, T., Blackhurst, J., O'Grady, P.: Methodology for supply chain disruption analysis. Int. J. Prod. Res. **45**(7), 1665–1682 (2007)

Evolution of Intent and Social Influence Networks and Their Significance in Detecting COVID-19 Disinformation Actors on Social Media

Chathika Gunaratne[1]([⊠]), Debraj De[1], Gautam Thakur[1],
Chathurani Senevirathna[2], William Rand[3], Martin Smyth[4],
and Monica Lipscomb[4]

[1] Oak Ridge National Laboratory, Oak Ridge, TN 37831, USA
{gunaratnecs,ded1,thakurg}@ornl.gov
[2] University of Central Florida, Orlando, USA
[3] North Carolina State University, Raleigh, USA
[4] U.S. National Geospatial-Intelligence Agency, Fairfax, USA

Abstract. Online disinformation actors are those individuals or bots who disseminate false or misleading information over social media, with the intent to sway public opinion in the information domain towards harmful social outcomes. Quantification of the degree to which users post or respond intentionally versus under social influence, remains a challenge, as individuals or organizations operating the profile are foreshadowed by their online persona. However, social influence has been shown to be measurable in the paradigm of information theory. In this paper, we introduce an information theoretic measure to quantify social media user intent, and then investigate the corroboration of intent with evolution of the social network and detection of disinformation actors related to COVID-19 discussions on Twitter. Our measurement of user intent utilizes an existing time series analysis technique for estimation of social influence using transfer entropy among the considered users. We have analyzed 4.7 million tweets originating from several countries of interest, during a 5 month period when the arrival of the first dose of COVID vaccinations were announced. Our key findings include evidence that: (i) a significant correspondence between intent and social influence; (ii) ranking over users by intent and social influence is unstable over time with evidence of shifts in the hierarchical structure; and (iii)

Supported by the U.S. National Geospatial-Intelligence Agency (NGA).
Thanks to Cody Buntain of University of Maryland for supplying the Twitter dataset.
This manuscript has been authored by UT-Battelle, LLC, under contract DE-AC05-00OR22725 with the US Department of Energy (DOE). The US government retains and the publisher, by accepting the article for publication, acknowledges that the US government retains a nonexclusive, paid-up, irrevocable, worldwide license to publish or reproduce the published form of this manuscript, or allow others to do so, for US government purposes. DOE will provide public access to these results of federally sponsored research in accordance with the DOE Public Access Plan (https://energy.gov/downloads/doe-public-access-plan).

R. Thomson et al. (Eds.): SBP-BRiMS 2022, LNCS 13558, pp. 24–34, 2022.
https://doi.org/10.1007/978-3-031-17114-7_3

both user intent and social influence are important when distinguishing disinformation actors from non-disinformation actors.

Keywords: Disinformation · Misinformation · COVID-19 · Intent · Social influence · Twitter · Transfer entropy · Information theory

1 Introduction

Quantitative study into the role of user *intent* in online social dynamics is not yet well documented in the scientific literature. Nevertheless, intent is an important feature to consider when distinguishing regular users and misinformation actors from disinformation actors. Disinformation has been defined as the intentional dissemination of false or misleading information by malicious actors with the intent of swaying public opinion towards socially dangerous outcomes [6,24,25]. Therefore, by definition, without the measurement of intent, it is impossible to distinguish those instances of disinformation from misinformation. In this paper, we present a novel, information theoretic approach for estimating user intent on social networks. We applied this technique to analyze user intent and social influence expressed in COVID-19 discussions on Twitter, during the period 1st January 2021 to 21st May 2021. We chose this time period as it was when the first doses of COVID-19 vaccinations started to be discussed online [20,22]. In particular, we investigated whether there was a correspondence between user intent and social influence, and whether the ranking of users by intent and social influence remained stable over time. Users with high intent are likely to express their own agendas, acting as gate-keepers of new information and ideas into a social network, and users with high social influence have a stronger impact in swaying the opinions and behaviors of the other users in the network. Therefore, users with both high intent and high social influence were identified as those, who pose the highest risk of disinformation propagation, if their motivations were to be malicious or manipulative. Establishing whether the agendas of the users are malicious or manipulative is beyond the scope of this paper.

2 Background

During the COVID-19 pandemic, both misinformation and disinformation have played a major role in spreading confusion, fear, insecurity, and anti-public health narratives among targeted populations [5,19]. Certain properties of disinformation help distinguished it from misinformation. While misinformation constitutes a claim that contradicts or distorts common understandings of verifiable facts [6], disinformation refers to such falsehoods that are *intentionally* propagated to actively undermine integrity in the information domain [6,21]. In other words, disinformation may be distinguished by the intentional purpose to deceive, while misinformation may simply be a result of inadvertent or unintentional action [6]. Thus, *intent or intentionality is the major discriminator between misinformation and disinformation* [24]. Proving intent in users or accounts can sometimes be more challenging than just identifying falsehoods in content [6]. Detecting intent is hard because of the difficulty to uncover ground truth beliefs in people/accounts about the veracity of information content, and the further difficulty in ascertaining their underlying motivations [25]. The current literature states that recognizing the range of motivations for spreading misinformation is valuable, even if the motivations or intentions are hard to disentangle [25]. This is the key motivation behind this study, attempting to quantitatively measure intent and analyze the dynamics of intent and social influence of social media accounts through time.

Most of the existing literature regarding social influence mainly utilized social network centrality, link-topology, and coreness-based measurements to quantify social influence [1,9,13,26]. However, these techinques depend on the underlying network structures of user connectivity, which in turn are typically constructed using the follower-followee network (such as in Twitter) or friendship network (such as in Facebook). But, follower-followee networks or friendship networks represent the users' popularity, and it has been shown that the relation between structural influence and users activities is weak [3]. In addition to these techniques, some studies have used entropy-based measures, which were based upon network structure [4,12] or an information-theoretic approach [2,7,8,17,23]. In this regard, we have utilized the quantification of social influence from our previous work [7,8,17], to calculate *social influence* in this work in order to infer *user intent*.

3 Methodology

We introduce a novel information theoretic approach to the quantification of intent from social media user activity timeseries data, which we applied to a COVID-19 Twitter dataset. We then used two machine learning approaches to classify users as disinformation or non-disinformation actors and used the generated labels to study the importance of social influence and intent on disinformation actor detection.

3.1 Data

We analyzed a dataset of 4,714,617 tweets on the COVID-19 pandemic between January 1st 2021 and May 21st 2021. This data consisted of 14,876 unique users with at least 10 actions (tweets, replies, retweets, and quoted tweets) per month, to ensure meaningful statistical results. The Twitter data was collected as follows. From the GeoCov19 dataset [14], we identified user accounts that have inferred profile- and message- based locations in few countries of interest (Australia, Brazil, Canada, Britain, India, Nigeria, New Zealand, Taiwan, South Africa). Then for these users we collected their tweets, replies, retweets, and quoted tweets, along with those by other users that responded to this activity with replies and retweets, during the time period considered.

3.2   An Information Theoretic Approach to Intent Measurement

We expand on the information theoretic measurement of social influence introduced in our previous studies [7,8,17], which show that given the activity time series of a set of online social media users (say V), the social influence experienced by a user of interest, $u \in V$, due to another user, $v \in V$, can be measured using transfer entropy (say $T_{v \to u}$). $T_{v \to u}$ is defined in the Eq. 1, where t is the current time step, T the entire time period analyzed, and k is history length. In this study, we consider a time step as 1 week, and $k = 1$. Transfer entropy is a directional measure of the information transfer between two random processes. In the case of social networks, it can be utilized to measure the information transfer from the activity time series of v to that of u, acting as an estimator of social influence. If $T_{v \to u} > 0$ a social influence link exists between the two users and v has a certain magnitude of influence over u.

$$T_{v \to u} = \sum_{t \in T} P(u_t, u_{t-1:t-k}, v_{t-1:t-k}) log \frac{P(u_t \mid u_{t-1:t-k}, v_{t-1:t-k})}{P(u_t \mid u_{t-1:t-k})} \quad (1)$$

In this study, we utilized transfer entropy-based estimation of social influence to measure the degree of intent with which users performed actions online. The Shannon entropy of u, H_u, measures the overall information produced by activity of u. We premise that, given sufficient sources of the social influences on u, the information intentionally produced by u would be the Shannon entropy of u minus the sum of all transfer entropy experienced by u, as shown in Eq. 2.

$$I_u = H_u - \sum_{v \in V} T_{v \to u} \quad (2)$$

Similarly, we computed the total influence exerted by the user of interest (u), say T'_u, as the total transfer entropy exerted by a user u on all other users considered, as shown in Eq. 3.

$$T'_u = \sum_{v \in V} T_{u \to v} \quad (3)$$

These two measurements: (ii) degree of user intent (I_u) and (ii) total social influence exerted (T'_u), were used in our analysis to better understand the social influence and user intent dynamics of COVID-19 related discussions on Twitter and disinformation actor detection. Tweets, replies, retweets, and quoted tweets were considered as user actions and the respective action timeseries for each user in the collected data was reconstructed. We test the following *three hypotheses* using these two measurements:

- Hypothesis I: There is a significant correspondence between high intent and high social influence.
- Hypothesis II: The ranking of users by intent and by social influence remains stable over time, i.e. users with high intent and high influence remain so, and vice versa.
- Hypothesis III: There is a significant difference in user intent among disinformation actors from that among non-disinformation actors.

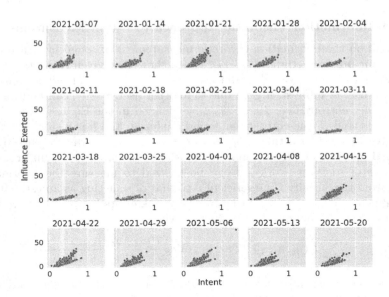

Fig. 1. Distribution of total social influence exerted by users vs intent, by weekly passage of time between Jan 1st and May 21st in 2021. Weeks progress in ascending order from left to right, and from top to bottom.

3.3   Disinformation Classification

We constructed two models to classify each user as either a disinformation actor (i.e., IO - information operative) or a non-disinformation actor (i.e., Real). Specifically, we utilized: (1) a weakly-supervised classification model based on Snorkel [15]; and (2) a logistic regression model.

The weakly-supervised model used Snorkel's labeling function system to encode human cognitive heuristics and fit a weight matrix of conditional probabilities of outputting a particular label. This was based on the label votes of a set of labeling functions provided during training. We used Snorkel labeling functions implemented for detection of IO on Twitter from recent literature [18]. The Snorkel label model classified each user as: *IO*, or *Real*, or *Undecided* (in the case of a tied vote). We replaced Undecided users (approximately 3.65% of the predicted Snorkel labels), with a uniform random choice between *IO* and *Real*, to avoid bias towards either class.

The logistic regression model was trained on features engineered on the collected data. We generated a suite of 32 features, belonging to six broad categories as follows: (i) user social influence and intent; (ii) tweet statistics on emoji, hashtag, mention, character count, etc.; (iii) temporal tweets characteristics; (iv) user profile characteristics; (v) tweets ratio characteristics; (vi) other characteristics like tweet count, date range, etc. Relevant features were selected after an extensive review of existing literature, and also exploratory data analysis on disinformation dataset released by Twitter's Information Operations group [10].

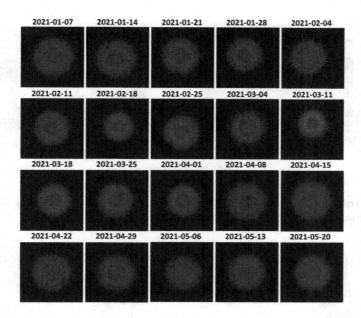

Fig. 2. Visualization of social influence and user intent networks over the passage of time (weeks) between Jan 1st and May 20th. Low intent individuals are colored darker green, higher intent individuals are brighter yellow. Individuals towards the center of the networks have higher connectivity (social influence), and users towards the outer part of the networks have lower connectivity. Weeks progress in ascending order from left to right, and from top to bottom. (Color figure online)

A detailed discussion of the considered features is beyond the of scope of this paper. The logistic regression model was trained to label users as *IO* or *Real*, based on the engineered features, and Snorkel labels (from first model) were used as ground truth for training. We found that the regression model fit the Snorkel labeled data reasonably well (precision $= 0.87$, recall $= 0.86$, f1-score $= 0.86$).

4 Results

We tested Hypothesis I, by examining the correlation between intent and total social influence exerted over time, as shown in Fig. 1. A distinct correlation was seen between intent and total social influence exerted. Furthermore, we observed that the relationship between intent and total social influence exerted, changed with the progression of time (through weeks). Specifically, from 2021-02-04 till 2021-03-25, social influence exerted was strikingly lower even for high intent individuals. Overall, a Pearson correlation test revealed a correlation coefficient of $r = 0.6961$ and $p \approx 0$. Additionally, Fig. 2 displays the snapshots of the social network captured over the progression of time (weeks). Nodes' color intensities signify higher intent, and nodes with higher social influence links are towards

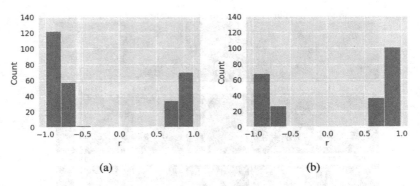

Fig. 3. Distribution of users' Pearson correlation coefficients (r) of: (a) intent and (b) total social influence exerted with time.

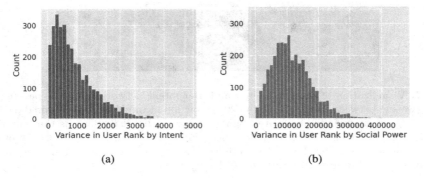

Fig. 4. Distributions of variance in user ranking by: (a) intent and (b) total social influence exerted rank, over a 20 week period.

the center of the network. The brightly colored ring towards the middle of each social network indicates individuals of high intent. There was a slight shift of this ring towards the center of the network starting at week 6 (2021-02-11) until week 13 (2021-03-18). Users with both high intent and high social influence pose high risk for spread of disinformation and likely existed within this band.

To test Hypothesis II, we performed Pearson's correlation tests on both intent and total social influence exerted over time. 3,306 users with at least 5 weeks of activity were tested. A significance level of $\alpha = 0.05$ was assumed and users with $p > \alpha$ were not considered. Figure 3 displays the correlation coefficients of both intent and total social influence exerted among the user population. A strong bi-modality, with many users either having strong positive correlations or negative correlations for both intent and total social influence exerted was observed. However, it is important to note that only 235 out of the 3,306 users had a $p < 0.05$, meaning the rest of the users had insufficient data to produce sufficient confidence in the Pearson correlation test. Within this set of users we find evidence against Hypothesis II, showing that there can indeed be considerable shift in both intent and total social influence exerted over time within the social network.

Furthermore, we measured the change in rank of users based on their intent and total social influence exerted. As shown in Fig. 4, we observed a difference in variance in ranking of users over time changes when considering intent versus total social influence exerted. Particularly, users had much greater variance in ranking by total social influence exerted, than ranking by intent, suggesting that it was more common to see changes in the social network hierarchy, than it was to see changes in ranking by intent. Additionally, the distribution of variance in user rank by intent was highly-skewed, in contrast to that of variance in rank by total social influence exerted, which indicated that while large changes in ranking by total social influence exerted among users may be more normal among the population, it was less common for users to change their ranking by intent.

Finally, in order to test *Hypothesis III*, we examined the correspondence of user intent and total social influence exerted with disinformation actors, as identified by the Snorkel labeling heuristics model and the regression classifier model (both models were described in Sect. 3.3). Figure 5 compares the degree of intent of disinformation actors versus that of non-disinformation actors as classified by the Snorkel heuristics, and Fig. 6 displays the same comparison for total social influence exerted. By conducting Mann-Whitney U tests at 95% confidence, we found support for the alternate hypothesis that intent of non-disinformation actors was significantly less than that of disinformation actors, as classified by both the models: Snorkel weak supervision labels ($U = 408319163.5$, $p = 1.7397 \times 10^{-143} < 0.05$), and regression classifier labels ($U = 428923903.0$, $p = 1.7397 \times 10^{-143} < 0.05$). However, Mann-Whitney U tests at 95% confidence, for the alternate hypothesis that social influence exerted by non-disinformation actors was less than that of disinformation actors, were not supported for both the Snorkel weak supervision labels ($U = 361421379.0$, $p = 0.9990 > 0.05$) and the regression classifier labels ($U = 382374824.5$, $p = 0.2641 > 0.05$).

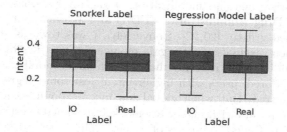

Fig. 5. Comparison the user intent of disinformation actors vs non-disinformation actors as predicted by the Snorkel weak-supervision model.

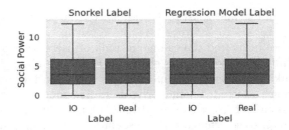

Fig. 6. Comparison total social influence exerted of disinformation actors vs non-disinformation actors as predicted by the Snorkel weak-supervision model.

5   Discussions and Conclusions

In this paper, we introduce a novel entropy-based approach to measure user intent towards posting in online social networks using an entropy-based method. We used this technique to analyze the dynamics of intent and the evolution of social influence on a network of Twitter users discussing COVID-19. The use of our proposed measures for user intent and total social influence exerted led to several interesting and novel findings as elaborated below.

We found that there was a significant correspondence between intent and total social influence exerted, and this relationship changes over time. As shown in Fig. 1, inside the 20 consecutive weeks of analysis, the relationship between the Influence Exerted and the Intent (the slope of a regression line from the scattered data points) remained relatively strong from the week of 2021-01-07 for 4 weeks, after which it remained weak from 2021-02-04 till the week of 2021-03-25. Then the relationship grew again and remained at its initial strength throughout the remaining 9 weeks of our analysis period. This was likely due to an exogenous shock to the influence network during this period. Interestingly, we have observed that during that 8 week period the intensity of news regarding COVID-19 vaccine emergency authorizations and mobilization of vaccine roll-outs by the United States Food and Drug Administration (FDA) and World Health Organization (WHO) heightened greatly [20,22]. Conversely, it was towards the end of the 8 week period when vaccination rates gain momentum for the global low-income population [11,16]. Overall, it seems that when news of mobilization in vaccine deliveries were initiated, users with higher intent lost some degree of the social influence they exerted. But when global low-income population's vaccination gained momentum, users with higher intent likely resumed exerting more social influence like before (before the news of vaccine deliveries started).

We found that the ranking by intent and social influence evolved significantly over time at the microscopic scale, while the distributions remained relatively stable at the macro-scale. Our findings contradicted Hypothesis II, providing evidence that ranking of users by intent and social influence was not necessarily stable over time. We found evidence that a reasonable portion of individuals have high variance in rank by both intent and social influence. Furthermore, we observed that a significant number of individuals have either strong positive or strong negative shifts in intent and social influence over time. This indicated that there was a reasonable amount of evolution in the social hierarchy of the considered population over time.

Most importantly, we found that there was a statistically significant increase in intent among disinformation actors, in comparison to that of non-disinformation actors. This partially supported Hypothesis III, such that disinformation actors can be distinguished by the degree of intent in their activity. Conversely, we found evidence that total social influence exerted may be similar for both disinformation and non-disinformation actors, likely reducing its importance when identifying disinformation actors.

Overall, our findings help further the state-of-the-art in understanding disinformation dynamics and evolution of online social networks. We have shown that intent of user activity has a significant impact on online information dynamics, and is an important feature to be included in the detection of disinformation actors.

References

1. Al-Garadi, M.A., et al.: Analysis of online social network connections for identification of influential users: survey and open research issues. ACM Comput. Surv. **51**(1) (2018)
2. Bhattacharjee, A.: Measuring influence across social media platforms: empirical analysis using symbolic transfer entropy (2019). https://scholarcommons.usf.edu/etd/7745
3. Cha, M., Haddadi, H., Benevenuto, F., Gummadi, K.: Measuring user influence in Twitter: the million follower fallacy. In: Proceedings of the International AAAI Conference on Web and Social Media, vol. 4, no. 1, May 2010. https://ojs.aaai.org/index.php/ICWSM/article/view/14033
4. Chen, X., Zhou, J., Liao, Z., Liu, S., Zhang, Y.: A novel method to rank influential nodes in complex networks based on Tsallis entropy. Entropy **22**(8), 848 (2020)
5. Gottlieb, M., Dyer, S.: Information and disinformation: social media in the COVID-19 crisis. Acad. Emerg. Med. (2020)
6. Guess, A.M., Lyons, B.A.: Misinformation, disinformation, and online propaganda. In: Social Media and Democracy: The State of the Field, Prospects for Reform, pp. 10–33 (2020)
7. Gunaratne, C., Baral, N., Rand, W., Garibay, I., Jayalath, C., Senevirathna, C.: The effects of information overload on online conversation dynamics. Comput. Math. Organ. Theory **26**(2), 255–276 (2020). https://doi.org/10.1007/s10588-020-09314-9
8. Gunaratne, C., Rand, W., Garibay, I.: Inferring mechanisms of response prioritization on social media under information overload. Sci. Rep. **11**(1), 1–12 (2021)
9. Kitsak, M., et al.: Identification of influential spreaders in complex networks. Nat. Phys. **6**(11), 888–893 (2010). https://doi.org/10.1038/nphys1746
10. Operation, T.I.: Insights into attempts to manipulate Twitter by state linked entities. (2022). https://transparency.twitter.com/en/reports/information-operations.html

11. Our World in Data: Global Coronavirus (COVID-19) vaccinations dashboard (2021). https://ourworldindata.org/grapher/cumulative-covid-vaccinations-income-group
12. Peng, S., Li, J., Yang, A.: Entropy-based social influence evaluation in mobile social networks. In: Wang, G., Zomaya, A., Perez, G.M., Li, K. (eds.) ICA3PP 2015. LNCS, vol. 9528, pp. 637–647. Springer, Cham (2015). https://doi.org/10.1007/978-3-319-27119-4_44
13. Peng, S., Zhou, Y., Cao, L., Yu, S., Niu, J., Jia, W.: Influence analysis in social networks: a survey. J. Netw. Comput. Appl. **106**, 17–32 (2018)
14. Qazi, U., Imran, M., Ofli, F.: Geocov19: a dataset of hundreds of millions of multilingual COVID-19 tweets with location information (2020)
15. Ratner, A., Bach, S.H., Ehrenberg, H., Fries, J., Wu, S., Ré, C.: Snorkel: rapid training data creation with weak supervision. VLDB J. **29**(2), 709–730 (2020)
16. Ritchie, H., et al.: Coronavirus pandemic (COVID-19). Our World in Data (2020). https://ourworldindata.org/coronavirus
17. Senevirathna, C., Gunaratne, C., Rand, W., Jayalath, C., Garibay, I.: Influence cascades: entropy-based characterization of behavioral influence patterns in social media. Entropy **23**(2), 160 (2021)
18. Smith, S.T., Kao, E.K., Mackin, E.D., Shah, D.C., Simek, O., Rubin, D.B.: Automatic detection of influential actors in disinformation networks. Proc. Natl. Acad. Sci. **118**(4) (2021)
19. Tagliabue, F., Galassi, L., Mariani, P.: The "pandemic" of disinformation in COVID-19. SN Compr. Clin. Med. **2**(9), 1287–1289 (2020)
20. The American Journal of Managed Care: A Timeline of COVID-19 Vaccine Developments in 2021 (2021). https://www.ajmc.com/view/a-timeline-of-covid-19-vaccine-developments-in-2021
21. Tucker, J.A., et al.: Social media, political polarization, and political disinformation: a review of the scientific literature. Political polarization, and political disinformation: a review of the scientific literature, 19 March 2018 (2018)
22. U.S. DoD: U.S. DoD Coronavirus Timeline (2021). https://www.defense.gov/Spotlights/Coronavirus-DOD-Response/Timeline/
23. Ver Steeg, G., Galstyan, A.: Information transfer in social media. In: Proceedings of the 21st International Conference on World Wide Web. WWW 2012, pp. 509–518. Association for Computing Machinery, New York (2012)
24. Wardle, C., et al.: Information disorder: the essential glossary. Shorenstein Center on Media, Politics, and Public Policy, Harvard Kennedy School, Harvard, MA (2018)
25. Wittenberg, C., Berinsky, A.J.: Misinformation and its correction. In: Social Media and Democracy: The State of the Field, Prospects for Reform, vol. 163 (2020)
26. Zeng, A., Zhang, C.J.: Ranking spreaders by decomposing complex networks. Phys. Lett. A **377**(14), 1031–1035 (2013)

Classifying COVID-19 Related Meta Ads Using Discourse Representation Through a Hypergraph

Ujun Jeong[1][✉][iD], Zeyad Alghamdi[1][iD], Kaize Ding[1][iD], Lu Cheng[1,2][iD], Baoxin Li[1][iD], and Huan Liu[1][iD]

[1] Arizona State University, Tempe, AZ, USA
{ujeong1,zalgham1,kding9,lcheng35,Baoxin.Li,huanliu}@asu.edu
[2] University of Illinois Chicago, Chicago, IL, USA

Abstract. Despite Meta's efforts to promote health information in the COVID-19 pandemic, the growing number of ads is making online content control extremely challenging. To effectively categorize the ads, this work investigates the major discourses shared across Meta ads with various categories related to COVID-19. We propose an interpretable classification model that captures common discourses in the form of keywords and phrases in ads. Particularly, we propose to use hypergraph to connect ads and discourses to capture their high-order interactions. Experiments on a curated Meta Ads dataset show that our model can provide subject-specific discourses and improve classification performance significantly.

Keywords: Meta advertisement · Text classification · Hypergraph

1 Introduction

As COVID-19 continues its global devastation, massive information related to COVID-19 has been seen on social media and other digital platforms. The unfolding of this pandemic has also demonstrated the great impact of this 'infodemic' on the sponsored content in social media. For example, Meta[1] Ads has been trying to promote health-related content by encouraging online campaigns [14]. However, this strategy becomes less effective and confuses the public even more, as advertisers often share controversial opinions such as racist theories about the origin of the virus and conspiracy theories in vaccination[2].

Regarding this issue, narrative theory suggests that identifying the repeated discourse is crucial for characterizing the content, as people tend to use specific phrases for their argument [3]. For example, in Fig. 1, *Ads 1–3* share the vaccination-related phrase "Medical Freedom" with the narrative of political need, and both *Ad 3* and *Ad 4* contain the vaccination-related phrase "Vaccine Mandate" with a negative stance. Based on these discourse relations, we

---

[1] Formerly known as Facebook (www.facebook.com).
[2] This claim is based on the article from Consumer Report (https://bit.ly/3I8xjeY).

© The Author(s), under exclusive license to Springer Nature Switzerland AG 2022
R. Thomson et al. (Eds.): SBP-BRiMS 2022, LNCS 13558, pp. 35–45, 2022.
https://doi.org/10.1007/978-3-031-17114-7_4

may further infer that *Ads 1–4* are related to the policy about treatment and prevention of COVID-19.

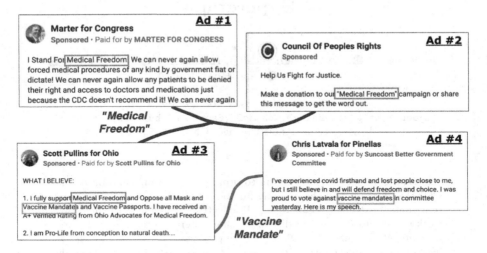

Fig. 1. Example of common discourses in COVID-19 Meta Ads. *Ads 1–3* have the shared phase about medical freedom. *Ads 3–4* are politically against vaccine mandate.

This work aims to help to efficiently classify COVID-19 related Meta ads into a set of pre-defined categories using the discourses repeatedly shared across ads. To achieve this research goal, we first define discourse as a phrase that can consist of one or multiple words shared across ads. However, using discourse for ads classification faces several major challenges: (1) Traditional text classification models are incapable of identifying important discourse during learning phase because they focus on finding an important set of relations at word-level [18]; (2) The importance of discourse cannot be flexibly measured depending on the related category, even though not all discourses are equally useful for classifying the category; and (3) As discourse is shared across the documents, the meaning of discourse should be dependent on the context of documents that contains the discourses. However, existing frameworks do not reflect this relation.

To address these challenges, in this paper, we propose a novel method coined as **DiscourseNet**. It leverages discourses shared in Meta ads for interpretable COVID-19 ads classification. To model these relations across Meta ads, we use hypergraph, an effective method to model the structure of complex relations between objects. Hypergraph is effective in modeling high-order relations [19] via connecting two or more nodes (i.e., ads) by the edge (i.e., discourses). We further integrate attention mechanism into hypergraph to capture important discourses related to specific ads categories.

Our main contributions are summarized as follows:

- Studying a novel classification problem of COVID-19 Meta ads,
- Proposing a hypergraph attention network for Meta Ads, DiscourseNet, to capture the common discourses unique to each category of COVID-19, and
- Curating a new dataset with 1,041 COVID-19 Meta ads for experiments.

2   Related Work

Meta Ad Analysis. This mainly consists of two lines of research: (1) investigating platform transparency and (2) measuring the impact of advertisement. As Meta offers marketing API to its advertisers, it has been questioned whether Meta microtargets users based on their sensitive information, such as race, religion, and sexual orientation [1]. To answer this question, many applications have been developed, such as AdAnalyst [1] and AdObservatory [9], to collect information about Meta's targeting strategies. [15] further showed that it is possible to carry out discriminatory campaigns, even without using sensitive attributes. Another work [14] proposes a classification model to identify the political content in Brazilian elections. This is for increasing the transparency of announcements made during elections with a tool external to Meta. To see the potential impact of Meta ads, Silva et al. [13] has focused on analysis on ads related to COVID-19. By using toxicity and sentiments analyses, they demonstrated the possible impact of political ads on shaping people's opinions.

Text Classification. With the superior performance of deep learning, various neural models have been developed for text classification, such as convolutional neural networks (CNNs) [12] and a series of recurrent neural networks including GRUs [4]. Hierarchical attention networks [17] further improve the model expressiveness by using attention mechanism on both word and sentence level for document classification. BERT [5] uses bidirectional encoding based on the multi-head attention mechanism. Moreover, the advent of graph neural networks has greatly helped to solve the problem of long-term dependence between words. Specifically, TextGCN [18] applies the graph convolutional networks to learn text representations on document-level graphs. HyperGAT [7] uses dual attention mechanism with hypergraphs for document classification, capturing high-order information in inductive manner.

This work aims to classify COVID-19-related Meta ads according to a set of categories, while at the same time identifying the discourses that are discussed within each category. Our framework is inherently different in that we explain the model's decision by keywords and phrases extracted from Meta ads for discourse-level interpretation. Especially, our approach represents the connection between ads and discourses through hypergraph to capture the high-order information across Meta ads while learning the importance of relations by attention networks.

3 Dataset

Data Collection. We use FBAdTracker [11] to collect the ads related to COVID-19 in Meta. FBAdTracker is an application designed to provide an integrated data collection and analysis system for researches on Meta ads. In the program, we begin by querying ads with the keyword *'covid'* for both active and inactive ads on Meta from all available countries. As collecting media content such as videos or images in Meta is not allowed without permission from each advertiser, we only use the text content of ads for our data collection. For this reason, we filter out ads without text content. i.e., we have excluded ads if the field 'ad_creative_body' is empty. Furthermore, we remove ads if the first and last ten words overlap with other ads, as there are many duplicate ads with slightly different choice of words. Finally, we only select those ads written in English. In total, we have collected 1,041 ads covering three months with the time frame from *Nov. 1st, 2021* to *Feb. 1st, 2022*. The statistics show the dataset includes 729 unique advertisers and 559 unique sponsors. Regarding the text in the ad, the average number of sentences in an ad is 6 and the average number of words in a sentence is $\sim$18.

Data Annotation. Following the annotation standard suggested in Lit-Covid [10], we divide the categories into eight different themes: *Prevention, Treatment, Diagnosis, Mechanism, Case Report, Transmission, Forecasting, and General.* We have asked two members of our team to label each sample in a multi-class fashion, which means one sample can be assigned to more or equal to one category. The instructions for the labeling process requires reading only the text content of the ad, and checking every applicable options in the suggested categories. For example, if an ad talks about vaccination and the rising number of cases, the category of both categories *'Treatment'* and *'Case Report'* will be filled with 1 and others will be filled with 0. As shown in statistics of categories in Table 1, there is imbalance between the number of classes. This is because most of the ads include content related to *'General'* as advertisers frequently talk or quote about personal stories to let audience engaged in the message. We publicly release the data by providing the list of IDs of Meta ads and the corresponding annotation in our GitHub[3] according to the terms of service of Meta[4].

Table 1. Number of collected Meta ads per category. The annotation is based on multi-class, and therefore the sum of labels is different from the total number of ads.

Prevention	Treatment	Diagnosis	Mechanism	Report	Transmission	Forecasting	General
187	311	126	18	53	32	18	634

---

[3] https://github.com/ujeong1/SBP22_DiscourseNet.
[4] https://www.facebook.com/terms.php.

4   Methodology

To better classify the COVID-19 related Meta ads, this work proposes to model the relations among different Meta ads based on their discourses to learn high-order representations of each advertisement. This is achieved by using hypergraph [2], a generalization of graph structure in which an edge can connect more than two nodes. In the following, we explain the details about (1) construction of hypergraph for Meta ads (2) learning relational information between nodes and hyperedge using dual attention mechanism [7], and (3) the final layer for multi-class node classification. An overview framework is depicted in Fig. 2.

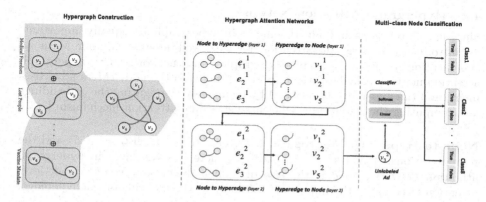

Fig. 2. The overview of the proposed model. It shows an example of node classification using hypergraph where the number of node (advertisement) is 5 and the number of hyperedge (discourse) is 3. The unlabeled ad (3rd node) is classified into eight classes.

4.1   Hypergraph Construction for Meta Ads

In real-world scenarios, relations among the objects are more complex than pairwise relations [19]. Hypergraph has been widely used for modeling high-order relationships in different applications [7,16]. The formal definition of hypergraph is as follows:

Hyeprgraph. A graph $\mathcal{G} = (\mathcal{V}, \mathcal{E})$, where $\mathcal{V} = \{v_1, v_2, \cdots, v_n\}$ denotes the set of nodes in the graph, and $\mathcal{E} = \{e_1, e_2, \cdots, e_m\}$ represents the set of hyperedges. Different from graph, hypergraph connects two or more nodes. The hypergraph $\mathcal{G}$ can be denoted by an incidence matrix $\mathbf{H} \in \mathbb{R}^{|\mathcal{V}| \times |\mathcal{E}|}$, with entries defined as:

$$h(v, e) = \begin{cases} 1 & \text{if } v \in e \\ 0 & \text{if } v \notin e \end{cases} \tag{1}$$

To apply the notion of hypergraph to Meta ads classification task, we use the Meta ads as nodes $\mathcal{V}$ and discourses as hyperedges $\mathcal{E}$. We define discourse as a form of keyword or phrase (a composition of multiple words) which is shared in two or more advertisements. We construct the hypergraph by connecting ads by the common discourse. For example, if the phrase "Lost my family" appears in three ads, we connect them by a hyperedge. To this end, we need to first extract keyword and phrases from Meta ads. We use RAKE[5], which is a tool capable of extracting discourses (keywords and phrases) in a document based on the frequency of co-occurrence. In total, we extract 1,541 of discourses from our Meta Ad dataset after selecting discourses that show at least twice among ads.

4.2 Hypergraph Attention Network

Since not all relations and advertisements in hypergraph are equally important, we introduce a hypergraph attention network well-designed for our Meta ad classification problem. As a family of graph neural networks [6,8], hypergraph attention network calculates the importance between the node (Meta advertisement) and the hyperedge (discourse) by recursively aggregating the embeddings and computing the attention coefficients using dual attention mechanism [7].

Node to Hyperedge Aggregation. Given a hypergraph $\mathcal{G} = (\mathcal{V}, \mathcal{E})$ and the representations of nodes $v^{(l-1)} \in \mathbb{R}^{|\mathcal{V}| \times d}$ where l is the layer in hypergraph attention network and d is the size of hidden dimension. We use node-level attention to compute the importance of nodes to the meaning of the hyperedge. Then, nodes are aggregated to compute the hyperedge representation $e_j^{(l)} \in \mathbb{R}^d$.

$$e_j^{(l)} = ReLU \left(\sum_{v_k \in e_j} \gamma_{jk} \mathbf{W}_1 v_k^{(l-1)} \right), \tag{2}$$

The initial input of hypergraph attention network is defined as $v^{(0)} = v$, and γ_{jk} is the attention coefficient of node $v_k^{(l-1)}$. The attention coefficient is computed based on the trainable weight matrix $\mathbf{W}_1$ and weight vector a_1.

$$\gamma_{jk} = \frac{\exp(a_1^\mathsf{T} u_k)}{\sum_{v_p \in e_j} \exp(a_1^\mathsf{T} u_p)}, u_k = LeakyReLU \left(\mathbf{W}_1 v_k^{(l-1)} \right), \tag{3}$$

Hyperedge to Node Aggregation. Based on the hyperedge representations $e^{(l)} \in \mathbb{R}^{|\mathcal{E}| \times d}$ in layer l and a set of hyperedge $\mathcal{E}_i$ connected to node v_i, we apply edge-level attention mechanism to discover the informative hyperedges. To this end, hyperedge representations are aggregated to compute the next-layer representation of nodes $v^{(l)}$.

$$v_i^{(l)} = ReLU \left(\sum_{e_j \in \mathcal{E}_i} \lambda_{ij} \mathbf{W}_2 e_j^{(l)} \right), \tag{4}$$

---

[5] https://pypi.org/project/rake-nltk/.

$v_i^{(l)}$ is the output representation of the node v_i in layer l and $\mathbf{W}_2$ is λ_{ij} is the attention coefficient of hyperedge $e_j^{(l)}$ on node $v_i^{(l)}$. The attention coefficient is computed based on a weight matrix $\mathbf{W}_2$ and a weight vector a_2 for hyperedges.

$$\lambda_{ij} = \frac{\exp\left(a_2^\mathsf{T} z_j\right)}{\sum_{v_p \in e_q, e_q \in \mathcal{E}_i} \exp\left(a_2^\mathsf{T} z_p\right)}, z_j = LeakyReLU\left(\left[\mathbf{W}_2 e_j^{(l)} \oplus \mathbf{W}_1 v_i^{(l-1)}\right]\right), \tag{5}$$

Node (Meta Ad) Classification. The final vector $v^{(L)} \in \mathbb{R}^{|\mathcal{V}| \times d}$ is a high-level representation resulted from node embedding through hyperedge to node aggregation, where L is the last layer of hypergraph attention network. For the node classification layer, we use a fully connected layer with weight matrix $\mathbf{W}_3$ and bias term b. Furthermore, we add the initial representation of $i-th$ node $v_i^{(0)}$ by skip-connection to maintain the original characteristics of Meta Ads. To train the model, we use BCE (Binary logit Cross Entropy) to optimize the loss using predicted probability p_i and multi-class ground-truths, $\{y_1^k, \ldots, y_C^k\} \in \{0,1\}^C$ where C is the number of the classes.

$$p_i = Softmax(f(\mathbf{W}_3(v_i^{(L)} + v_i^{(0)}) + b)),$$
$$\mathcal{L}_{BCE} = \begin{cases} -\log(p_i{}^k) & if \ y_i^k = 1 \\ -\log(1 - p_i{}^k) & otherwise. \end{cases} \tag{6}$$

5 Experiment

In this section, we present the experiments to evaluate the effectiveness of DiscourseNet. Our experiment design aims to answer the following questions:

- **RQ1:** Can our proposed approach improve the performance of Meta ads classification compared to the baselines in text classification task?
- **RQ2:** Can our model identify meaningful discourses related to the category?

Baseline Settings. We include the following baselines: (1) sequence-to-sequence models, including GRUs [4] and TextCNNs [12]; (2) BERT+MLP, which is a text classification model that applies MLP on BERT [5] pre-trained embeddings from Meta ads; and (3) TextGCN [18] which applies graph convolutional networks for text classification. In the experiments, we set parameters as follows: hidden dimension (128), batch size (128), optimizer (Adam), learning rate (0.001), dropout rate (0.3), and epochs (50). We use Meta ads encoded by BERT [5] with the dimension size of 768. For the evaluation, we use accuracy (exact match) and F1-score (harmonic mean of precision and recall).

5.1   RQ1: Evaluation on Text Classification Task

To answer RQ1, we compare DiscourseNet with representative baselines for text classification task based on 5-fold cross-validation. As shown in Table 2, we observe that the proposed method outperforms all the baselines on both mean accuracy and F1-score. Specifically, DiscourseNet improves accuracy over TextGCN by ∼1% point, and achieves higher F1-score over BERT+MLP around ∼2% points. It is notable TextGCN shows comparable accuracy to DiscourseNet. A possible explanation for this is that TextGCN can leverage the relational information by modeling document-word relation, which helps to find some meaningful correlation between the documents sharing the same words. On the other hand, BERT+MLP shows lower F1-score than DiscourseNet, as it only learns documents individually without any relations between them. Therefore, the experimental result demonstrates that learning relational information in discourse-level works crucially for classifying texts in Meta ads.

Table 2. Evaluation result on the curated Meta ad dataset. We run 5-fold cross-validation and average the results. The results indicate mean ± standard deviation.

Metrics	GRU	TextCNN	BERT+MLP	TextGCN	**DiscourseNet**
Accuracy	33.87 ± 4.58	52.24 ± 2.81	52.72 ± 1.77	56.48 ± 2.27	**57.51 ± 3.33**
F1-score	28.31 ± 5.28	33.16 ± 2.57	33.96 ± 2.42	32.08 ± 2.59	**36.31 ± 3.53**

5.2   RQ2: Discourse Identification in Categories

To answer RQ2, we identify the subject-specific discourses in the curated dataset by investigating the attention scores of the proposed model per category. To this end, we follow three procedures: (1) selecting nodes (Meta ads) corresponding to a certain category (2) getting hyperedges (discourses) connected to the selected nodes (3) ranking the top eight hyperedges based on attention scores.

As shown in Table 3, the top eight discourses are highly related to each category, and not associated with common terms such as stopwords. For example, in 'Prevention' category, we notice that discourses about guidelines suggested by CDC[6], such as mask mandate and wearing mask, and self-isolation. We also observe discourses predominantly used in context of vaccination in 'Treatment' category such as medical freedom, lost people, and federal vaccine. Particularly, the 'General' category shows discourses such as conspiracy theories, human rights, and school closure, which are more common yet controversial subjects.

Furthermore, we examine if the model can highlight the importance of different discourses within a document. We visualize attention scores that measure the importance of discourses in Fig. 3. As shown in the example, discourses closely associated with the category show higher attention scores, while common discourses have lower values. For instance, in the category 'Prevention', the example

---

[6] www.cdc.gov.

Table 3. Top 8 discourses of each category ranked based on the attention scores on hyperedges. Based on the hypergraph construction method suggested in Sect. 4.1, a discourse corresponds to a hyperedge. A discourse is expressed as a keyword or phrase.

Category	Discourses
Prevention	Wear mask, dangerous new policy, self-isolation, help prevent, surviving covid, sending asymptomatic, zero covid, mask mandate
Treatment	Lost people, medical freedom, federal vaccine, anti-vax, second dose, covid jabs, unconstitutional covid, location near
Diagnosis	Get tested, home tests, requiring proof, testing mandate, full covid, completely free, mask except, telescope health
Mechanism	Boosted person, shorter period, increased risk, experience less, unvaccinated, lost several, increase awareness, hospitalized
Case Report	Skyrocketing, infection rates, borders, covid fiscal, covid variant, nursing homes, protect americans, virus safe
Transmission	Transmit, highly transmissible, protect public, spreading, medical experts, omicron variants, guidelines, government mask
Forecasting	Inflation grow, protect small business, relyong on food bank, interest rate, exchange rate, credit card, tax cut, income
General	Covid virus, conspiracy theories, human rights, next governor, school closure, zoom broad cast, covid inquiry, stress

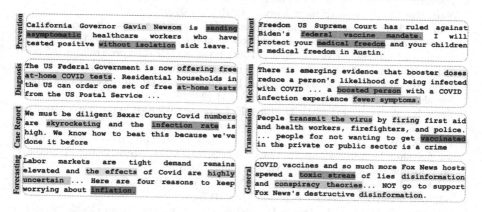

Fig. 3. Visualization of the attention score of discourses in advertisements arranged by each category. The highlighted words and phrases indicate common discourse shared across other documents, and the color represents the attention score (the color is more red when the absolute attention score is higher). The figure is best viewed in color. (Color figure online)

document shows the attention weight for the keyword 'Gavin Newsom' is lower than other phrases such as 'without isolation' and 'sending asymptomatic'.

6   Conclusion and Future Work

We propose DiscourseNet, a hypergaph-based model for text classification and discourse analysis in Meta ads. DiscourseNet outperforms representative baselines in text classification on both accuracy and F1-score by leveraging relational information through shared discourses. Through the experiments, we open a new venue of discourse analysis of Meta ads by quantitatively analyzing the discourses identified by hypergraph attention network. In future work, we focus on dynamically learning the discourses without pre-computation of keywords and phrases.

Acknowledgements. This work was supported by the Office of Naval Research under Award No. N00014-21-1-4002. Opinions, interpretations, conclusions, and recommendations are those of the authors.

References

1. Andreou, A., Silva, M., Benevenuto, F., Goga, O., Loiseau, P., Mislove, A.: Measuring the Facebook advertising ecosystem. In: Network and Distributed System Security Symposium (2019)
2. Berge, C.: Hypergraphs: Combinatorics of Finite Sets. Elsevier, Amsterdam (1984)
3. Bernardi, D.L., Cheong, P.H., Lundry, C., Ruston, S.W.: Narrative landmines. In: Narrative Landmines. Rutgers University Press (2012)
4. Cho, K., Van Merriënboer, B., Bahdanau, D., Bengio, Y.: On the properties of neural machine translation: encoder-decoder approaches. arXiv (2014)
5. Devlin, J., Chang, M.W., Lee, K., Toutanova, K.: BERT: pre-training of deep bidirectional transformers for language understanding. arXiv (2018)
6. Ding, K., Wang, J., Caverlee, J., Liu, H.: Meta propagation networks for graph few-shot semi-supervised learning. In: AAAI (2022)
7. Ding, K., Wang, J., Li, J., Li, D., Liu, H.: Be more with less: hypergraph attention networks for inductive text classification. arXiv (2020)
8. Ding, K., Wang, J., Li, J., Shu, K., Liu, C., Liu, H.: Graph prototypical networks for few-shot learning on attributed networks. In: ACM International Conference on Information and Knowledge Management (2020)
9. Edelson, L., Sakhuja, S., Dey, R., McCoy, D.: An analysis of united states online political advertising transparency. arXiv (2019)
10. Gutierrez, B.J., Zeng, J., Zhang, D., Zhang, P., Su, Y.: Document classification for COVID-19 literature. arXiv (2020)
11. Jeong, U., Ding, K., Liu, H.: FbadtTacker: an interactive data collection and analysis tool for Facebook advertisements. arXiv (2021)
12. Kim, Y.: Convolutional neural networks for sentence classification. Empirical Methods Nat. Lang. Process. (2014)
13. Silva, M., Benevenuto, F.: COVID-19 ads as political weapon. In: Annual ACM Symposium on Applied Computing (2021)
14. Silva, M., Santos de Oliveira, L., Andreou, A., Vaz de Melo, P.O., Goga, O., Benevenuto, F.: Facebook ads monitor: an independent auditing system for political ads on Facebook. In: The Web Conference (2020)
15. Speicher, T., et al.: Potential for discrimination in online targeted advertising. In: Conference on Fairness, Accountability and Transparency. PMLR (2018)

16. Wang, J., Ding, K., Zhu, Z., Caverlee, J.: Session-based recommendation with hypergraph attention networks. In: SIAM International Conference on Data Mining (SDM) (2021)
17. Yang, Z., Yang, D., Dyer, C., He, X., Smola, A., Hovy, E.: Hierarchical attention networks for document classification. In: NAACL (2016)
18. Yao, L., Mao, C., Luo, Y.: Graph convolutional networks for text classification. In: AAAI (2019)
19. Zhou, D., Huang, J., Schölkopf, B.: Learning with hypergraphs: clustering, classification, and embedding. In: NIPS (2006)

A Systematic Approach for Contextualizing Focal Structure Analysis in Social Networks

Mustafa Alassad[(⊠)] and Nitin Agarwal

COSMOS Research Center, UA – Little Rock, Little Rock, AR, USA
{mmalassad,nxagarwal}@ualr.edu

Abstract. Focal Structures are key sets of individuals who may be responsible for coordinating events, protests, or leading citizen engagement efforts on social media networks. Discovering focal structures that can promote online social campaigns is important but complex. Unlike influential individuals, focal structures can effect large-scale complex social processes. In our prior work, we applied a greedy algorithm and bi-level decomposition optimization solution to identify focal structures in social media networks. However, the outcomes lacked a contextual representation of the focal structures that affected interpretability. In this research, we present a novel Contextual Focal Structure Analysis (CFSA) model to enhance the discovery and the interpretability of the focal structures to provide the context in terms of the content shared by individuals in the focal structures through their communication network. The CFSA model utilizes multiplex networks, where the first layer is the users-users network based on mentions, replies, friends, and followers, and the second layer is the hashtag co-occurrence network. The two layers have interconnections based on the user hashtag relations. The model's performance was evaluated on real-world datasets from Twitter related to domestic extremist groups spreading information about COVID-19 and the Black Lives Matter (BLM) social movement during the 2020–2021 time. The model identified Contextual Focal Structure (CFS) sets revealing the context regarding individuals' interests. We then evaluated the model's efficacy by measuring the influence of the CFS sets in the network using various network structural measures such as the modularity method, network stability, and average clustering coefficient values. The ranking Correlation Coefficient (RCC) was used to conduct a comparative evaluation with real-world scenarios.

Keywords: Multiplex networks · Complex network · Focal structures · Entropy · Information gain · COVID-19 · Contextual Focal Structures

1 Introduction

Social media platforms like Twitter, Instagram, and Facebook have become famous for news sharing and consumption, social activities, and hosting commentary on local/global events. These platforms let their users exchange information, links, images, or videos with little restriction on the content. For example, during the recent COVID-19 global pandemic and events such as the 2020 U.S. election, millions of users on Twitter reported

© The Author(s), under exclusive license to Springer Nature Switzerland AG 2022
R. Thomson et al. (Eds.): SBP-BRiMS 2022, LNCS 13558, pp. 46–56, 2022.
https://doi.org/10.1007/978-3-031-17114-7_5

their experiences, shared their thoughts on fighting COVID-19, (dis)agreed with COVID-19 regulations, and discussed elections and related events, which included misinformation about COVID-19 and Black Lives Matter (BLM) movement. Often false information is spread by groups in a coordinated manner. Therefore, it is essential to discover influential groups responsible for a coordinated campaign and weed out the disinformation. Identifying such groups on social networks is the main contribution of this research, where these groups could develop unique structures and act to influence individuals/communities to maximize information dissemination across social networks. Conventional community detection methods focus on larger communities and are oblivious to these influential groups. Moreover, as the social networks exponentially grow, their structure becomes complex, and communities reorganize, making it challenging to identify these influential groups and their information diffusion networks [1–6].

To fill the gap in the analysis, Şen et al. [1] proposed the Focal Structure Analysis (FSA) model to identify the smallest possible influential groups of users that can maximize the information diffusion in social networks. However, this model suffered from certain limitations, such as low-quality focal structure sets (chain groups), limited users' connections to only one set, and no information about the FSA sets' contextual activities. To overcome some of these limitations, Alassad et al. [2] introduced the FSA 2.0 model to enhance the quality of the focal structure sets discovery and to overcome the limits in the activities of the influential users. The authors developed a bi-level decomposition optimization model to identify groups that could maximize the individual's influence in the first level and measures the network's stability in the second level. Nevertheless, the FSA 2.0 model presented in [2] used only a unimodular user-user network in the analysis, where the outcomes were missing the context activities, the users' interests, and overall behavior of the focal structure sets as explained in this paper. To overcome these drawbacks in the state-of-the-art model mentioned in [1] and FSA 2.0 model in [2], this paper introduces the Contextual Focal Structure Analysis (CFSA) model to enhance the discovery and interpretability, reveal the context, and highlight interests of individuals of the focal structure sets.

The rest of the paper is organized as follows: Sect. 2 defines the problem statement and CFSA model in detail. Section 3 uses a real-world Twitter dataset to evaluate the model's performance. The validation procedure confirms the enhancement in the focal structure analysis modeling and real-world datasets; we concluded that the contextual focal structures analysis model (CFSA) outcomes are more interpretable and informative than the FSA 2.0 model. Section 4 reviews the main findings with theoretical and practical implications. Lastly, the conclusion, limitations, and directions for future research are presented in Sect. 5.

2   Research Problem Statement

The proposed research aims to implement the contextual focal structure analysis model into the social network analysis. Given the raw datasets from the online environment, the research problem statement is to implement a systematic model that utilizes the FSA 2.0 model and the multiplex network approach to reveal the users' activities and the focal structure sets behavior in social networks. This approach involves different layers, including users' followers, mentions, retweets, URLs, and contexts in the form of participation layers in the solution procedure.

Moreover, this research presents essential ideas and analysis to study questions like, can traditional community detection methods identify influential groups and reveal the context? How could the CFSA model fill the gap? Furthermore, can the CFSA model help identify activities that explain the activities or interests of an influential set of individuals?

3   Methodology

The CFSA model is designed to consider the multitiered relationships of online users in the social network, like shared topics, links, news, blogs, etc., which can conceptualize the different layers of the multiplex network. The outcomes from the CFSA model are influential sets of users linked to other significant users and, at the same time, connected to the activities and contexts shared by users on social networks.

3.1   Modified Adjacency Matrix for CFSA

In general, the adjacency matrix of an unweighted and undirected graph G with N nodes in an $N \times N$ symmetric matrix $\mathbf{A} = \{a_{ij}\}$, with $a_{ij} = 1$, only if there is an edge between i and j in G, and $a_{ij} = 0$ otherwise. The adjacency matrix of layer graph G_α is $n_\alpha \times n_\alpha$ symmetric matrix $\mathbf{A}^\alpha = a_{ij}^\alpha$, with $a_{ij}^\alpha = 1$ only if there is an edge between (i, α), and (j, α) in G^α.

Likewise, the adjacency matrix of G_β is an $n \times m$ matrix $\rho = p_{i\alpha}$, with $p_{i\alpha} = 1$ only if there is an edge between the node i and the layer α in the participation graph, i.e., only if node i participates in layer α. We call it the participation matrix. The adjacency matrix of the coupling graph G_F is an $N \times N$ matrix $\mathcal{L} = \{c_{ij}\}$, with $c_{ij} = 1$ only if there is an edge between node-layer pair i and j in G_F, i.e., if they are representatives of the same node in different layers. We can arrange rows and columns of $\mathcal{L}$ such that node-layer pairs of the same layer are contiguous, and layers are ordered as shown in the next section. We assume that $\mathcal{L}$ is always arranged in that way. It results that $\mathcal{L}$ is a block matrix with zero diagonal blocks. Thus, $c_{ij} = 1$, with $i, j = 1, \ldots, N$ represents an edge between a node-layer pair in layer 1(user-user layer) and node layer pair in layer 2 (hashtag-hashtag layer) if $i < n_1$ and $n_1 < j < n_2$. The supra-adjacency matrix is the adjacency matrix of the supra-graph $G_\mathcal{M}$. Just as $G_\mathcal{M}$, $\overline{A}$ is a synthetic representation of the whole multiplex $\mathcal{M}$. It can be obtained from the intra-layer adjacency matrices and the coupling matrix in the following way:

$$\overline{\mathbf{A}} = \mathbf{A}^\alpha \oplus_\alpha \mathcal{L} \tag{1}$$

where the same consideration as in $\mathcal{L}$ applies for the indices we also define. $\mathbf{A} = \oplus \mathbf{A}^\alpha$, which we call the intra-layer adjacency matrix.

3.2   Stepwise Description of the CFSA Algorithm

This section provides the technical intuition into our model; it consists of three main components (Data collection, CFS sets discovery, and CFS sets validation and analysis) as presented in Fig. 1. Also, the details on each step of the CFSA model and the solution procedure are explained in this section.

Step 1: A list of contexts was generated to feed the Python API used to collect Tweets from the Twitter Environment, as shown in Fig. 1.

Step 2: The Python API was set to overcome the limitation imposed by Twitter in collecting contexts and running in real-time over different periods.

Step 3: This step is to collect contemporary contexts from the Twitter network over time. The Twitter API was designed to use Python libraries like Scrapy [7] and Tweepy [8] to collect a preset list of co-hashtags related to different events on the Twitter Network. COSMOS research lab at UA Little Rock put lots of effort into a dedicated research group to retrieve a considerable amount of data related to COVID-19 misinformation spread and different social movements on Twitter connected to anti/pro-COVID-19 health regulations. For this research, we used a dataset shown in Table 1 (users-users, hashtag-hashtag, and users-hashtag networks) to evaluate the performance of the CFSA model.

Step 4: The data was retrieved in real-time, stored in different tables, and segmented into columns depending on the content to serve the requirements of this study.

Table 1. Datasets retrieved from Twitter. Users-Hashtags network (UH), Users-Users (UU), Hashtags-Hashtags network (HH), Communities in the network(C), Modularity values (M), Average Clustering Coefficient values (ACC), Nodes (N), Edges (E).

Network	UH		UU		HH		C	M	ACC	Period
	E	N	E	N	E	N	UH	UH	UH	
Domestic Extremist Groups	94706	74764	87273	72746	2976	783	21	0.45	0.163	Nov 2020–March 2021

Step 5: We retrieved the trending hashtags and related features such as retweets, mentions, and any tweets that include related content.

Step 6: This step generates a unimodular hashtag-hashtag network; the co-occurrence hashtags (first layer) in the multiplex network. In this step, we consider the size of the network and the nature of the context used in our case study.

Step 7: This step uses the modularity method to calculate the number of communities in the network [9]; this step would help to harvest those online communities from the database that participated in contexts activities, posted, shared, and retweeted related contexts on Twitter.

Step 8: Based on the features available in the dataset and the communities available in the network, we retrieved a list of users and the hashtags from (Step 6) and (Step 7).

Step 9: This step helps develop the second layer in the multiplex network, the user-user network, where the outcome is a unimodular network, as shown in Fig. 2.

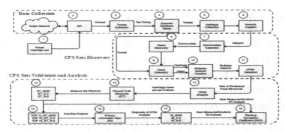

Fig. 1. Overall CFSA model structure. The model is divided into three main steps represented in the research methodology; the first is data collection, the second is CFS sets discovery and multiplex networks, and the third is CFS sets validation and analysis.

Step 10: In this step, we generate the Multiplex network; it is the union of the hashtag-hashtag layer in (Step 6) and the user-user layer as shown in (Step 9). This layer is about the interconnections between users and hashtags. To elaborate, we compare the enhancement achieved on the users' level in the CFSA model versus the FSA 2.0 model, as presented in Fig. 2. Equation (2) shows the objective function used at the user level to maximize the centrality values in the interconnection network.

$$\max \sum_{i=1}^{n} \sum_{j=1}^{m} \left(\delta_i^{UU} \oplus \beta_{ij}^{UH} \hbar_j^{HH} \right) \tag{2}$$

where n is the number of nodes in the user-user layer UU. m is the number of nodes in the hashtag-hashtag layer HH. δ_i^{UU} is the sphere of influence for users i in UU. $\oplus$ is the direct sum. $\hbar_j^{HH}$ is the number of j nodes in HH connected by an edge to user i in UU. Finally, β_{ij}^{UH} represents the interconnection between users and hashtags, where $\beta_{ij}^{UH} = 1$ if and only if node i in UU has a link with node j in HH; otherwise 0.

Step 11: We implemented the user-hashtag network into the CFSA model. This model can accept contexts, users, and user-context links, where this combination represents the coupling matrix $\overline{A}$ shown in Eq. (1).

Step 12: This step is to manually analyze the identified CFS sets, such as the size, number of users, number of edges, and hashtags in each CFS set.

Step 13: To validate the contextual focal sets and quantitatively measure their impacts in social networks, we will use the ablation method to calculate the focal sets' influence and power when each focal set is suspended from the network. For this purpose, we implemented three measures to calculate the changes in the network based on the modularity values [9, 10] (Ground Truth Modularity (GTMOD)), the clustering coefficient method [11] (Ground Truth Clustering Coefficient (GTCC)), and the change in the number of communities (Ground Truth Network Stability (GTNS)) after suspending CFS$_i$ from the entire network.

Step 14: In this step, we sorted the CFSs based on their influence on the network concerning the GT measures (Step 13). This step would narrow down the solutions and provide more flexibility in the analysis to present the GT values of all CFS sets.

Step 15: Select the top ten CFS sets from each GT measure (GTMOD, GTCC, and GTNS), where we measured the changes in the modularity values after suspending all

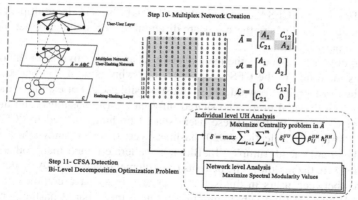

Fig. 2. The CFSA model takes an initial set of user-user Twitter network (1st layer) and hashtag-hashtag (co-occurrence) Twitter network (2nd layer) where $L = 2$. Then, we generate the interconnection network called the user-hashtag layer or the coupling matrix $\overline{A}$.

CFS sets and sorted the results in descending order. The same procedure would apply to the other two GT measures (GTCC and GTNS).

Step 16: Entropy Information Gain theory (IG) is used to measure the originality of the top ten CFS sets, find the differences in the CFS sets' users, links, and context, and calculate how much information a CFS set provides in the solution. Shannon's model defines the entropy for this step.

Step 17: To measure the IG values for the top ten sets identified in (Step 15), IG values based on the Modularity method (IGMOD), IG based on the Clustering Coefficient values (IGCC), and IG based on the Network Stability (IGNS), a Python code used to implement Shannon's model, where the results of the IG values are between $[-1,1]$ for each measure.

Step 18: Ranking Correlation Coefficient (RCC) is used to find the correlation between the outcomes in (Step 13) and (Step 17), respectively. This measure should discover the strength of linear relationship links between the CFS sets based on GT and IG measures. For this step, we implemented three experiments to find the correlated solutions, as shown in the next section.

To summarize, these steps represent the solution procedure of the CFSA model, where three levels containing eighteen steps are considered to complete and enhance the focal structure sets analysis in the social networks.

4   Results

This research is designed to show the benefits of the contextual focal structure analysis model that could increase the quality and enhance the discovery of the focal structure sets in social network analysis.

The case study implemented in the research was related to the Domestic Extremist Groups Network dataset shown in Table 1. These groups spread hateful and radical information about COVID-19 health regulations, wearing masks, and anti-lockdown actions on Twitter. The CFSA model identified 187 CFS sets in the multiplex network (Users-Hashtags layer), where these sets are different in size, number of hashtags, user accounts, and network behavior.

Furthermore, Table 2 shows the manual analysis and the activities of the users and communities identified in the CFS sets, observing "what is going on between online users?" in the most straightforward and smallest possible sets. For example, the CFS14 set contains 40 influential users who shared information (35 hashtags) and influenced thousands of users on Twitter. These users shared hashtags related to "COVID19", "#MAGA", "#trump", "#Elections2020" hashtags were linked to many other influential accounts like "realDonaldTrump", "JoeBiden", "balleralert" and many other users as shown in Fig. 3 (in the middle). The benefits of implementing the CFSA model revealed other desires between users in this set that presents users have completely different opinions and interests (2nd sub-community); where they shared hashtags related to "#StayHome", "#StayHomeStaySafe" and "#WearMask", as shown in Fig. 3. Moreover, to describe the structure of the CFS14 set in-depth, Fig. 3 (left side) shows the spread of users (red dots) and the shared content (dark squares) in the structure of the network. Likewise, this set is considered as one of the top influential sets that include users from different parts of the network and shared popular hashtags.

Table 2. CFS14 set in complex social networks.

CFS Set	Number of User	Number of Hashtag	Number of Edge	Communities (elements of different communities were identified as shown in the annotations)	
CFS14	40	35	129	5	BLM social Movements, COVID-19, India Luck down, Nigeria activities, Far Left
Contexts	#44136, #acab, #antifa, #AppellvonCottbus, #biden, #BlackLivesMatter, #blm, #BLM, #China, #confinementSaison2, #coronavirus, #Covid_19, #COVID19, #covid19, #Election2020, #ElectionDay, #Elections, #Elections2020, #FlattenTheCurve, #Football, #Ghana, #IndiaFightsCorona, #MAGA, #Nigeria, #NorthCarolina, #Police, #StayHome, #StayHomeStaySafe, #StaySafe, #trump, #TrumpCollapse, #TrumpCovidHoax, #TrumpVirus, #Turkey, #WearAMask				

Ground Truth Measures: Three Ground Truth (GT) measures were employed to calculate the influence/importance of the CFS sets in the network. Section 3.2 (step 13) is utilized for actions like GTMOD, GTCC, and GTNS after suspending each CFS set from the network. For example, when the CFS14 set was suspended from the network (G-CFS5) as shown in Fig. 3 (right side), it completely changed the network's structure and maximized the network's modularity values (GTMOD) from 0.6 to 0.78. Likewise, after the CFS14 set was suspended from the network (G-CFS14), this set minimized the stability (GTNS) of the network (maximized number of communities) from 29 communities to 652 communities in the network as shown in Fig. 4.

CFS14   G-CFS14

Fig. 3. CFS sets in social networks. These three CFS sets changed the structure of the network as we can observe the changes before and after suspending these three sets from the network (Color figure online).

Similarly, suspending the CFS14 set from the network (G-CFS14) minimized the average clustering coefficient values (GTCC) from 0.013 to 0.009, as shown in Fig. 4.

In summary, to evaluate the quality of the identified CFS sets, the model employed to suspend each CFS set and measure the changes in the modularity values, the changes in the number of communities, and the changes in the average clustering coefficient values, before and after suspending all CFS set from the network as shown in Fig. 4. Due to the space limit, we will skip presenting other values.

Information Gain Measures (IG): To measure the information gain and determine the amount of information each CFS set can deliver to the overall analysis values as mentioned in Sect. 3.2 (Step 16). We selected the top ten influential sets based on the GT values, where the top ten CFS sets based on GTMOD are (CFS14, CFS7, CFS8, CFS1, CFS26, CFS64, CFS46, CFS73, CFS66, CFS75). The top ten CFS sets based on GTCC are (CFS14, CFS3, CFS22, CFS28, CFS21, CFS70, CFS25, CFS12, CFS7, CFS8). The top ten CFS sets based on GTNS are (CFS14, CFS8, CFS22, CFS1, CFS7, CFS26, CFS4, CFS46, CFS34, CFS30).

The process is to arrange to make a target CFS_i set in the model, then measure each CFS set's uniqueness (information gain) /(distance) concerning the target CFS_i set. Likewise, the model will calculate the information gained alongside the abovementioned top ten sets. Figure 5 right side, shows the IG values when the model arranged the target sets on (CFS14), where CFS14 is highly dissimilar to CFS74. Due to the space limit, we will skip presenting other values.

Ranking Correlation Coefficient values (RCC): We applied three experiments in Sect. 3.2 (Step 18) to find the correlated outcomes based on IG, GT, and IG vs. GT values.

Experiment 1: This step measures the RCC values between values based on (GTMOD, GTCC, and GTNS) and for all 187 CFS sets. This experiment shows that the CFS sets in GTMOD values are correlated with the results in GTNS values, where RCC = 0.161, as shown in Fig. 5 left side.

Experiment 2: This step calculates the RCC values between the top ten sets based on IGMOD, IGCC, and IGNS values. Thus, the correlated results were between the top ten CFS sets based on IGMOD values and the top ten CFS sets based on IGNS values, as presented in Fig. 5 left side.

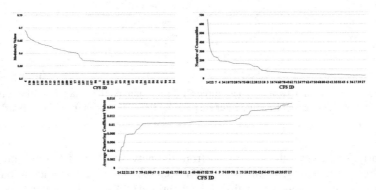

Fig. 4. Changes in the network after suspending CFS sets.

Experiment 3: This experiment measures the RCC values for the results in GT values vs. results in IG values. The outcome of this experiment includes ninety RCC values; we measured the RCC values for the top ten based on IGMOD vs. the three GT measures (GTMOD, GTCC, and GTNS) values. Furthermore, we calculated the average values for each RCC value, and the outcomes from this experiment offer the finest. The correlated solutions between IG and GT values are in dark blue, shown in Fig. 5 left side.

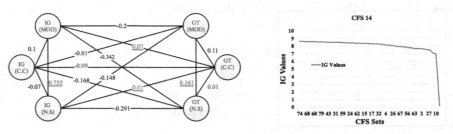

Fig. 5. Left side - the CFS sets' RCC values. Right side - the IG values when CFS14 (target set). (Color figure online)

5   Conclusion and Future Work

This research presents the Contextual Focal Structure Analysis (CFSA) model to reveal influential sets of individuals on social networks and their online contextual activities using multiplex network representation. Multiplex network representation is utilized to capture the communication network among individuals, their content network, and the interconnection between the two layers (viz., through user-hashtag relation). Datasets related to COVID-19, social movements (e.g., "Black Lives Matter"), 2020 U.S. elections, and other events witnessed in 2020–2021 were studied. To evaluate a CFS' influence and impact on network stability, we suspended each CFS one at a time from the network and calculated the changes in modularity, clustering coefficient, and network stability across the network. Next, we used the information gain theory to measure the information we gained from each contextual focal structure and the ranking correlation coefficient factor to highlight the correlated results and find semi-correlated solutions consistent with real-world scenarios.

For future work, to improve the CFS model, we would like to implement different ground truth and information gain methods to validate the results. Another area is in applying the model to dynamic social networks. The third area is implementing CFSA for a cross-platform scenario. This extension would help study contextual focal structure sets that simultaneously span across multiple social media platforms like Facebook, Twitter, Instagram, YouTube, etc.

Acknowledgment. This research is funded in part by the U.S. National Science Foundation (OIA-1946391, OIA-1920920, IIS-1636933, ACI-1429160, and IIS-1110868), U.S. Office of Naval Research (N00014-10-1-0091, N00014-14-1-0489, N00014-15-P-1187, N00014-16-1-2016, N00014-16-1-2412, N00014-17-1-2675, N00014-17-1-2605, N68335-19-C-0359, N00014-19-1-2336, N68335-20-C-0540, N00014-21-1-2121, N00014-21-1-2765, N00014-22-1-2318), U.S. Air Force Research (FA9550-22-1-0332), U.S. Army Research Office (W911NF-20-1-0262, W911NF-16-1-0189), U.S. Defense Advanced Research Projects Agency (W31P4Q-17-C-0059), Arkansas Research Alliance, the Jerry L. Maulden/Entergy Endowment at the University of Arkansas at Little Rock, and the Australian Department of Defense Strategic Policy Grants Program (SPGP) (award number: 2020-106-094). Any opinions, findings, and conclusions or recommendations expressed in this material are those of the authors and do not necessarily reflect the views of the funding organizations. The researchers gratefully acknowledge the support.

References

1. Şen, F., Wigand, R., Agarwal, N., Tokdemir, S., Kasprzyk, R.: Focal structures analysis: identifying influential sets of individuals in a social network. Soc. Netw. Anal. Min. **6**(1), 1–22 (2016). https://doi.org/10.1007/s13278-016-0319-z
2. Alassad, M., Agarwal, N., Hussain, M.N.: Examining intensive groups in YouTube commenter networks. In: Thomson, R., Bisgin, H., Dancy, C., Hyder, A. (eds.) SBP-BRiMS 2019. LNCS, vol. 11549, pp. 224–233. Springer, Cham (2019). https://doi.org/10.1007/978-3-030-21741-9_23

3. Alassad, M., Hussain, M.N., Agarwal, N.: Finding Fake news key spreaders in complex social networks by using bi-level decomposition optimization method. In: Agarwal, N., Sakalauskas, L., Weber, G.-W. (eds.) MSBC 2019. CCIS, vol. 1079, pp. 41–54. Springer, Cham (2019). https://doi.org/10.1007/978-3-030-29862-3_4
4. Alassad, M., Hussain, M.N., Agarwal, N.: Comprehensive decomposition optimization method for locating key sets of commenters spreading conspiracy theory in complex social networks. Cent. Eur. J. Oper. Res. **30**, 1–28 (2021)
5. Alassad, M., Hussain, M.N., Agarwal, N.: Developing graph theoretic techniques to identify amplification and coordination activities of influential sets of users. In: Thomson, R., Bisgin, H., Dancy, C., Hyder, A., Hussain, M. (eds.) SBP-BRiMS 2020. LNCS, vol. 12268, pp. 192–201. Springer, Cham (2020). https://doi.org/10.1007/978-3-030-61255-9_19
6. Alassad, M., Spann, B., Al-khateeb, S., Agarwal, N.: Using computational social science techniques to identify coordinated cyber threats to smart city networks. In: El Dimeery, I., et al. Design and Construction of Smart Cities. JIC Smart Cities 2019. Sustainable Civil Infrastructures, pp. 316–326. Springer, Cham (2021). https://doi.org/10.1007/978-3-030-64217-4_35
7. Scrapy—a fast and powerful scraping and web crawling framework. https://scrapy.org/. Accessed 02 June 2022
8. Tweepy. https://www.tweepy.org/. Accessed 25 June 2022
9. Newman, M.E.J.: Detecting community structure in networks. Eur. Phys. J. B **38**(2), 321–330 (2004). https://doi.org/10.1140/epjb/e2004-00124-y
10. Clauset, A., Newman, M.E.J., Moore, C.: Finding community structure in very large networks. Cond-Mat/0408187, vol. 70, p. 066111 (2004)
11. Zafarani, R., Abbasi, M.A., Liu, H.: Social Media Mining: An Introduction. Cambridge University Press, Cambridge (2014)

Frames and Their Affective Dimensions: A Case Study of Climate Change News Articles

Aman Tyagi[1]($\boxtimes$)(iD), Kenneth Joseph[2](iD), and Kathleen M. Carley[1,3](iD)

[1] Engineering and Public Policy, Carnegie Mellon University,
Pittsburgh, PA 15213, USA
amant@alumni.cmu.edu, kathleen.carley@cs.cmu.edu
[2] Computer Science and Engineering, University at Buffalo,
Buffalo, NY 14260, USA
kjoseph@buffalo.edu
[3] Institute for Software Research, Carnegie Mellon University,
Pittsburgh, PA 15213, USA

Abstract. News articles shared on social media platforms could be framed in ways such that specific points are emphasized or de-emphasized to create confusion on scientific facts. In this work, we use policy frames suggested by Boydstun et al., 2014 to find frames used in over 810k climate change news articles shared on Twitter by news agencies. Moreover, we present a method to find affective dimensions, namely Evaluation (good vs. bad), Potency (strong vs. weak), and Activity (active vs. passive), of the frames. Our results suggest that news articles about climate change are predominantly framed as related to policy issues in the context of a social group's traditions, customs, or values. We also conclude that frames are not reshared based on their *affect*. Lastly, we present implications for the increasingly relevant climate change communication research.

Keywords: Climate change · Framing · Affective dimensions

This work was supported in part by the Knight Foundation. Additional support was provided by the Center for Computational Analysis of Social and Organizational Systems (CASOS), the Center for Informed Democracy and Social Cybersecurity (IDeaS), and the Department of Engineering and Public Policy of Carnegie Mellon University. The views and conclusions contained in this document are those of the authors and should not be interpreted as representing the official policies, either expressed or implied, of the Knight Foundation.

R. Thomson et al. (Eds.): SBP-BRiMS 2022, LNCS 13558, pp. 57–67, 2022.
https://doi.org/10.1007/978-3-031-17114-7_6

1 Introduction

One way to analyze how information is manipulated is by studying *frames* of the presented information, where framing presents certain information in a manner that emphasizes one issue over another. For example, news on Californian wild-fires can be framed either as a natural event causing destruction of property or a human-made disaster causing socio-economic harm. More generally, framing is defined as "selecting certain aspects of a given issue and making them more salient in communication in order to 'frame' the issue in a specific way" [26].

Different approaches have been proposed in Natural Language Processing (NLP)/linguistics research to analyze frames. These approaches are broadly divided into formal/stylistic frames or content-oriented frame [26]. Formal/Stylistic frames concentrate on the structure or formal presentation of text rather than the content (e.g. Iyengar [20]). Content oriented frames focus on the communicative text. Content-oriented frames can further be divided into generic frames or topical frames [9]. Topical frames are issue-specific. In NLP to analyze topical frames, we use computational models such as Latent Dirichlet Allocation (LDA) [4], Latent Semantic Analysis (LSA) [17] and more recently transformer model techniques such as Top2Vec [2]. On the other hand, generic frames are pre-defined sets of categories or patterns that transcend individual issues. For example, Semetko and Valkenburg [28] used frames such as "consequences", "responsibility", "conflict", "human interest", and "morality" on press and television news on European politics. This paper discusses and develops methods to find generic frames on news articles on a crucial socio-economic topic, i.e., climate change.

Topical frames have been used in climate change contexts (e.g. [23] and [19]). However, content framing in articles related to climate change using generic framing techniques is mostly unexplored [26]. Hence, the first research question answered in the present work is, *Which generic frames are predominant in news articles related to climate change?* We answer this research question by using news articles shared on Twitter about climate change. To investigate generic frames in climate change news articles, we discuss and develop a framework to analyze generic frames in large data using a transfer learning approach. We use a pre-trained BERT [10] model to predict sentence level frames. For our analysis, we propose to use frames discussed in the Policy Frame Codebook [6] via a dataset annotated with these frames. The dataset is called Media Frame Corpus (MFC) [8], which is an annotated dataset of Wall Street Journal articles. The articles are annotated as per the Policy Frame Codebook's 15 frames [6] and are commonly used in multiple NLP framing analysis studies [12,25].

Moreover, we develop a method to connect *Affect Control Theory (ACT)* with frames of news articles shared on a social network by news agencies. ACT, initially introduced by Heise [14,15], proposes that individuals maintain their *affective* identities through their actions. The affective identities are operationalized by embedding these in Evaluation (good *vs.* bad), Potency·(strong *vs.* weak), and Activity (active *vs.* passive) (EPA) space. We develop a method to embed frames in the EPA space, assuming that each frame has a particular affective meaning. Although prior work in NLP has identified ways to extract affective dimensions from pre-trained word embeddings, this paper discusses how we can embed and operationalize the affective dimensions of frames themselves. We then use our methodology on climate change news articles shared on Twitter.

Our approach of embedding the policy frames in the EPA dimension helps us determine news articles' emotional valence. In this work, we assume that a person or a news agency sharing the articles on social media with a certain frame would identify with that frame. Therefore, we discuss a mechanism where we can identify an article's emphasis (frame) in the EPA space. To the best of our knowledge, this is the first attempt at connecting computational generic framing research in NLP with ACT. By connecting frames with ACT, we draw implications for climate change communication. Hence, we find frames that are better at communicating climate change urgency as per emotional sociology. Thus, the second research question we address is, *what are the affective dimensions of the frames and which frames are more active and hence suited for communicating climate change urgency?*

Once we have found the frames' affective dimensions, we use the reshare (retweet) count of each frame to find whether each frames' emotional value or *affect* leads to more reshare. ACT states that *affect* drives individual identities and their actions. In this work, we address, *whether or not the frames' affect drive the reshare count on social media?* To answer this research question, we use the reshare count of different frames. We hence conclude which frames in climate change news articles are more likely to be reshared.

2   Data and Method

To collect our dataset, we scraped all the articles shared by news agencies on Twitter using tweets related to climate change between August 26th, 2017 to January 4th, 2019. Our dataset consisted of 38M unique tweets and retweets from 11M unique users. We classified users into news agencies and non-news agencies, thereby collecting 810k articles shared by these news agencies spread across the same timeframe. We will refer to these articles as *news articles* in this paper. Media Frame Corpus [8] (MFC), is an annotated dataset of 22,030 wall street journal articles. The articles are annotated as per the Policy Frame Codebook's [6] 15 frames. The dataset consists of articles related to death penalty, gun control, immigration, samesex marriage, and tobacco. MFC does not cover climate change related annotated articles and is biased towards the Wall Street Journal's articles. Hence, we use decontextualization methods on the corpus. For ACT lexicon, we use the expanded EPA lexicon published by Heise [16][1].

Frame Prediction. We use the information score based classification technique as discussed in Field et al. [12] and propose other transformer-based classifiers for sentence-level prediction of frames.

---

[1] For a more detailed discussion on related work and data collection, refer Tyagi [29].

BERT Based Models: We use a pretrained BERT model to get embeddings of the sentences of different MFC topics. Then we train (1) MLP with one hidden layer of dimension 512 and a softmax layer, (2) 1-D convolution neural network (1D-CNN) similar in dimension to Kim [22].

Information Score Based Prediction: We use the information score based technique as used and validated in Field et al. [12]. In the study, each word is assigned an information score depending upon the frequency of that word occurring in a particular frame. Models evaluated are: (1) PMI-Non Decontextualize: Use information score of unigrams to predict each document's frame similar to Field et al. [12] but without extension of vocabulary, (2) Field et al. [12]: Use information scores but decontextualize by selecting similar words and assigning them the same score using pre-trained continuous bag of words (CBOW) language model embeddings, (3) PMI- Decontextualize (CBOW/FastText): We use the information score lexicons, but instead of adding similar words, we find words during testing which are not in our information score vocabulary. Then we assign these words a score based on a pre-trained language model (CBOW or FastText [5]). The score is assigned for each missing word based on the nearest word in our information score vocabulary.

To check how well the learned models transfer, we train models on four topics and test the model on a different topic. Refer to Tyagi [29] for detailed results of each model. In this paper, we rely on analysis of frames using the validated PMI model [12] which gives reasonable accuracy. Moreover, in Sect. 3 we report a frame as dominant if the frame is in the top 3 of all the frames (accuracy $\sim$80%).

Frame Projection to EPA. Field et al. [12] gives an information score to each word based on the word belonging to one frame over the other. We use the same method to find the information score for each word. Similar to Field et al. [12], Roy and Goldwasser [25], we remove all words occurring in 2% and 98% of the articles. We enriched our lexicon using the decontextualization method used in Field et al. [12] and as benchmarked above (model (2)) with other models. For each frame F, the information score for each word is defined as follows:

$$I(F, w) = \frac{P(F, w)}{P(F)P(w)} = \frac{P(w|F)}{P(w)} \tag{1}$$

where $P(w|F)$ is calculated from the fraction of count of words w and count of all words in sentences annotated with frame F. Similarly, $P(w)$ is calculated from entire MFC training data. We use symbol f to denote set of words with information score associated to frame F.

Next, we use the ACT lexicon (l) to get a $[E_{w'}, P_{w'}, A_{w'}]$ score for each word $w' \in l$. We define EPA score of each frame F as:

$$[E_F, P_F, A_F] = \sum_{c \in l \cap f} \frac{I_{(F,c)} * [E_c, P_c, A_c]}{Z} \tag{2}$$

where Z is the normalization factor equal to the number of words in both EPA lexicon (l) and f. In Eq. 2 each word which is in both the lexicons are weighted by their respective information score in EPA space. We checked the densities of word score distributions ($I_{(F,c)} * [E_c, P_c, A_c]$) for each frame to find no multi modalities. We find that "Capacity and Resources" frame has the least number of common words with 1210 words and "Crime and Punishment" and "Cultural Identity" with the most common words with 1756 words each.

Frame's Average Reshare Count. To find out the mean reshare count for each frame, we use each article's retweet count. For each of the 810k news articles shared via Tweets we scrape the retweet count using Twitter's standard API. We scraped the retweet count of each Tweet in January of 2021, assuming that this retweet count represents the final number of retweets. We believe that this assumption is reasonable since the last Tweet used to collect a news article was on January 4th, 2019. We use the retweet count and average information score calculated from the common words in framing lexicon (f) and each article to find the mean reshare count (R_F) of frame F as:

$$R_F = \frac{\sum_a r_a \frac{\sum_{c \in a \cap f} I_{(F,c)}}{\sum_F \sum_{c \in a \cap f} I_{(F,c)}}}{\#(a)} \tag{3}$$

where r_a is the retweet count of each article a. In Eq. 3, the numerator represents the weighted average of the retweet count for each frame given the information score of an article. This is then summed for each article. The denominator represents the total number of articles[2].

3   Results

3.1   Frame Prediction

We find that the "Cultural Identity" frame is the most dominant frame used in climate change articles. To find the frame of a document, we use all the sentence's average score in that document. In Fig. 1 we report the count of the number of articles with respective dominant frames. We call a frame dominant if the frame is in the top 3 of all the frames. Apart from the "Cultural Identity" frame, we find that "Public Sentiment", "Political," and "Economic" frames are other considerable dominant frames. The "Cultural Identity" frame is defined as "traditions, customs, or values of a social group in relation to a policy issue" [6]. In a manual evaluation of a sample of 100 articles, we find that articles dominant in "Cultural Identity" framing are about changing current practices (eating habits, buying of estate etc.), about protests regarding climate change or changes after a natural disaster[3]. In Fig. 1 we also report the average scores

---

[2] Due to Tweet/user account deletion, we use 700k articles for our average reshare analysis.

[3] Refer https://github.com/amantyag/Framing_Affective_Dimensions for details.

of the information scores used to calculate the dominant frame. There is a high correlation (Pearson Correlation = 0.9) between the top 3 dominant frames and the mean information scores. Frames such as "External Regulation and Reputation" and "Policy Prescription and Evaluation" show the opposite behavior. We conclude that these frames do occur regularly in different climate change articles but are more salient.

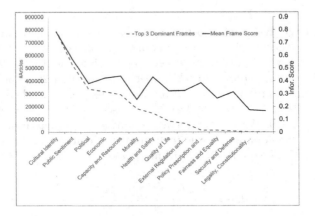

Fig. 1. Number of articles with corresponding top 3 frames and mean of the information score (Eq. 1) for all the articles (blue). (Color figure online)

3.2   Frames in EPA

We project the frames in EPA space to find that "Capacity and Resources", "Quality of Life," and "Morality" score high in the Evaluation (good vs. bad) dimension. "Morality" also scores high in Potency (strong vs. weak). In Fig. 2, we report each frame's EPA dimension and the centered and scaled value to better show contrast between frames. On a manual inspection of top words contributing to high Potency values of "Morality" frame, we find words related to religion such as *jesus*, *christ* and *church*. These words have a higher than usual Potency value. "External Regulation and Reputation" and "Quality of Life" frame score high in the Activity (active vs. passive) dimension. Overall, we find that all the frames are positive (leaning good, strong, and active) with little variation. This is expected as frames are nuanced changes in the presentation of a topic. Moreover, the common words between the EPA lexicon and the frames represent news agencies' neutral emotions. We infer that the highly emotional words in the EPA lexicon are rare or do not occur in our lexicon.

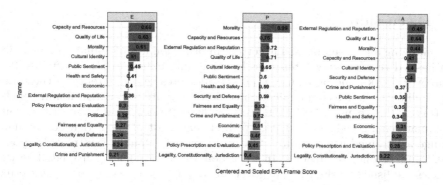

Fig. 2. EPA values centered by mean frame score and scaled by the standard deviation values of frames in each dimension. EPA scores of frames calculated using Eq. 2 are in boldface. EPA dimension range is $[-4.3, +4.3]$.

We also find, that the EPA dimensions of frames used in news articles do not vary greatly with time. For this analysis, we aggregate articles by month to find the average score for each frame and then convert it to the EPA dimension by taking a weighted average using the base EPA dimension score of each frame from Eq. 2. Although the number of articles in each month varies greatly, we find little or no variation with time in all three affective dimensions[4].

3.3   Reshare Count of Frames

The average reshare (retweet) count varies considerably for different frames. The average reshare is less than 1, indicating that a high percentage of articles were not shared. In fact, only 35% of the news articles were shared more than once. We scrape articles from all accounts that exhibit news agency like behavior based on Tweets and user account's metadata. Based on our previous experiments using the classification model, we infer that not many users follow a high percentage of the accounts labeled as news agency accounts. We suspect that some of these accounts could be bot-like. We leave the extended analysis for bot-like accounts for future work. On average, the "Cultural Identity" and "Public sentiment" frame is more than two times more reshared than the "Crime and Punishment" frame.

Next, we find out if *affect* of the frames drive their reshare activity. We find that "Morality", "Quality of Life" and "Capacity and Resources" frames are the most emotional, and "Legality, Constitutionality, Jurisdiction" is the least emotional frame. These results are generally consistent with common perceptions about these frames [29]. We find that there is low correlation (Pearson Correlation = 0.15) between the emotional value of the frames and the average reshare count. This indicates that more emotional (higher *affect*) frames are not necessarily reshared more times.

---

[4] Refer to Tyagi [29] for details on EPA scores for each month.

4   Discussion

Emphasizing and de-emphasizing certain information to manipulate public opinion has led to a growing interest in learning automated frames in articles [25]. Moreover, work done by Kause et al. [21] indicates that difference in the framing of climate change communication could contribute to polarization in beliefs. In this work, we use MFC to find automated frames in an extensive corpus of climate change-related articles. We find that most of the articles on climate change are framed using mainly "cultural identity", "public sentiment", "political," and "economic" frames. In work done by Field et al. [12] related to the articles published by the Russian government news media were mostly "External Regulation", "Political" and "Morality" dominant while using keywords related to the U.S. In a similar work, Roy and Goldwasser [25] also classified news media articles and found the ideological differences in different news media presentation of similar topics. Given our corpus's extensive size, we believe the dominant frame in climate change articles reflects general news articles' nature shared on Twitter. In a manual analysis of 100 articles, we find that news articles about climate change predominantly discuss topics involving changing habits, protests, and the effects of natural disasters. Moreover, the 100 random articles used in our manual evaluation were, for the most part, from local or non-popular news sources. Thus, these news articles either address the population of a specific place or a region or are reposts of national/international news stories.

A perception exists in climate change communication that "considerable competition among (and between) scientists, industry, policymakers and non-governmental organizations (NGOs), each of whom is likely to be actively seeking to establish their particular perspectives on the issues" [1]. Previous studies have described climate change framing in "scientific uncertainty" frame [11,24]. This framing has recently changed to "industry leadership" frame in defeating climate change [18]. Frames have also been shown to differ between countries and over time [13,27]. A recent work done by Badullovich et al. [3] suggests that scientific literature on climate change most commonly use "Scientific, Economic and Environmental" frames and are increasingly using "Public health, Disaster, and Morality/ethics" frames. In our study, instead of focusing on manual analysis, we use computational models to build on climate change communication's rich framing research. Moreover, we focus on news media to decipher perspectives as the media plays a vital role in climate change communication. Using the retweet count of each article shared via Twitter, we calculated the average number of times a frame is reshared. In this work, we show that certain frames are more reshared than others. Moreover, this resharing pattern is not correlated to different frame's emotional valence. This suggests that news stories are reshared based on other factors such as news media popularity, story type, and novelty. We recognize that the online data collected used English language keywords and did not reflect the demographic representativeness necessary to present cross-cultural conclusions.

In this paper, we develop a methodology to project frames in EPA space. We constructed a mechanism where the nuances of the article content are projected to EPA space. We do not make an effort to predict where articles themselves lie in EPA space. By projecting the frames into EPA space, we can now connect the same topic to emotional science research useful for studying group influence and belief change. Work done by Britt and Heise [7] gave clues that more active emotions could be used to incite minority groups by motivating them to participate in more extensive group activities. Our results indicate that frames such as "external regulation", "Quality of Life" and "morality" are more emotionally active (higher activity). As climate change action becomes more urgent and necessary, a more consistent and active framing should be used to convey the policy changes needed. Moreover, multiple previous research studies on climate change discussion on social media have concluded that different belief groups exhibit "echo-chamber" type behavior [30–32]. These different belief groups can be analyzed to find their news sources and align messages with frames that are more likely to be shared by different belief groups.

References

1. Anderson, A.: Media, politics and climate change: towards a new research agenda. Sociol. Compass **3**(2), 166–182 (2009)
2. Angelov, D.: Top2vec: distributed representations of topics. arXiv preprint arXiv:2008.09470 (2020)
3. Badullovich, N., Grant, W., Colvin, R.: Framing climate change for effective communication: a systematic map. Environ. Res. Lett. **15**(12), 123002 (2020)
4. Blei, D.M., Ng, A.Y., Jordan, M.I.: Latent Dirichlet allocation. J. Mach. Learn. Res. **3**(Jan), 993–1022 (2003)
5. Bojanowski, P., Grave, E., Joulin, A., Mikolov, T.: Enriching word vectors with subword information. Trans. Assoc. Comput. Linguist. **5**, 135–146 (2017). https://www.aclweb.org/anthology/Q17-1010
6. Boydstun, A.E., Card, D., Gross, J., Resnick, P., Smith, N.A.: Tracking the development of media frames within and across policy issues, June 2018. https://doi.org/10.1184/R1/6473780.v1, https://kilthub.cmu.edu/articles/journal_contribution/Tracking_the_Development_of_Media_Frames_within_and_across_Policy_Issues/6473780/1
7. Britt, L., Heise, D.: From shame to pride in identity politics. In: Self, Identity, and Social Movements, vol. 5, pp. 252–68 (2000)
8. Card, D., Boydstun, A., Gross, J.H., Resnik, P., Smith, N.A.: The media frames corpus: annotations of frames across issues. In: Proceedings of the 53rd Annual Meeting of the Association for Computational Linguistics and the 7th International Joint Conference on Natural Language Processing (Volume 2: Short Papers), pp. 438–444 (2015)
9. De Vreese, C.H.: News framing: theory and typology. Inf. Des. J. Doc. Des. **13**(1) (2005)
10. Devlin, J., Chang, M.W., Lee, K., Toutanova, K.: BERT: pre-training of deep bidirectional transformers for language understanding. In: Proceedings of the 2019 Conference of the North American Chapter of the Association for Computational Linguistics: Human Language Technologies, Volume 1 (Long and Short Papers), pp. 4171–4186. Association for Computational Linguistics, June 2019. https://doi.org/10.18653/v1/N19-1423

11. Dunlap, R.E., McCright, A.M.: Organized climate change denial. Oxford Handb. Clim. Change Soc. **1**, 144–160 (2011)
12. Field, A., Kliger, D., Wintner, S., Pan, J., Jurafsky, D., Tsvetkov, Y.: Framing and agenda-setting in Russian news: a computational analysis of intricate political strategies. In: Proceedings of the 2018 Conference on Empirical Methods in Natural Language Processing, pp. 3570–3580, Association for Computational Linguistics, October–November 2018. https://www.aclweb.org/anthology/D18-1393
13. Gupta, J.: A history of international climate change policy. Wiley Interdisc. Rev. Clim. Change **1**(5), 636–653 (2010)
14. Heise, D.R.: Affect control theory: concepts and model. J. Math. Sociol. **13**(1–2), 1–33 (1987)
15. Heise, D.R.: Expressive Order: Confirming Sentiments in Social Actions. Springer, New York (2007). https://doi.org/10.1007/978-0-387-38179-4
16. Heise, D.R.: Surveying Cultures: Discovering Shared Conceptions and Sentiments. Wiley, Hoboken (2010)
17. Hofmann, T.: Probabilistic latent semantic indexing. In: Proceedings of the 22nd Annual International ACM SIGIR Conference on Research and Development in Information Retrieval, pp. 50–57 (1999)
18. Ihlen, Ø.: Business and climate change: the climate response of the world's 30 largest corporations. Environ. Commun. **3**(2), 244–262 (2009)
19. Ivanova, A.: Transnationalisierung von Öffentlichkeiten. Springer, Wiesbaden (2017). https://doi.org/10.1007/978-3-658-18356-1
20. Iyengar, S.: Framing responsibility for political issues. Ann. Am. Acad. Pol. Soc. Sci. **546**(1), 59–70 (1996)
21. Kause, A., Townsend, T., Gaissmaier, W.: Framing climate uncertainty: frame choices reveal and influence climate change beliefs. Weather Clim. Soc. **11**(1), 199–215 (2019)
22. Kim, Y.: Convolutional neural networks for sentence classification. In: Proceedings of the 2014 Conference on Empirical Methods in Natural Language Processing (EMNLP), pp. 1746–1751. Association for Computational Linguistics, Doha, October 2014. https://doi.org/10.3115/v1/D14-1181, https://www.aclweb.org/anthology/D14-1181
23. Kirilenko, A.P., Stepchenkova, S.O.: Climate change discourse in mass media: application of computer-assisted content analysis. J. Environ. Stud. Sci. **2**(2), 178–191 (2012)
24. McCright, A.M., Dunlap, R.E.: Defeating Kyoto: the conservative movement's impact on us climate change policy. Soc. Probl. **50**(3), 348–373 (2003)
25. Roy, S., Goldwasser, D.: Weakly supervised learning of nuanced frames for analyzing polarization in news media. In: Proceedings of the 2020 Conference on Empirical Methods in Natural Language Processing (EMNLP), pp. 7698–7716. Association for Computational Linguistics, Online, November 2020. https://doi.org/10.18653/v1/2020.emnlp-main.620, https://www.aclweb.org/anthology/2020.emnlp-main.620
26. Schäfer, M.S., O'Neill, S., Nisbet, M., Ho, S., Markowitz, E., Thaker, J.: Frame analysis in climate change communication: approaches for assessing journalists' minds, online communication and media portrayals. Oxford Research Encyclopedia of Climate Science (2017)
27. Schmidt, A., Ivanova, A., Schäfer, M.S.: Media attention for climate change around the world: a comparative analysis of newspaper coverage in 27 countries. Glob. Environ. Chang. **23**(5), 1233–1248 (2013)

28. Semetko, H.A., Valkenburg, P.M.: Framing European politics: a content analysis of press and television news. J. Commun. **50**(2), 93–109 (2000)
29. Tyagi, A.: Challenges in Climate Change Communication on Social Media, chap. 4. Carnegie Mellon University (2021)
30. Tyagi, A., Babcock, M., Carley, K.M., Sicker, D.C.: Polarizing tweets on climate change. In: Thomson, R., Bisgin, H., Dancy, C., Hyder, A., Hussain, M. (eds.) SBP-BRiMS 2020. LNCS, vol. 12268, pp. 107–117. Springer, Cham (2020). https://doi.org/10.1007/978-3-030-61255-9_11
31. Tyagi, A., Uyheng, J., Carley, K.M.: Heated conversations in a warming world: affective polarization in online climate change discourse follows real-world climate anomalies. Soc. Netw. Anal. Min. **11**(1), 1–12 (2021). https://doi.org/10.1007/s13278-021-00792-6
32. Williams, H.T., McMurray, J.R., Kurz, T., Lambert, F.H.: Network analysis reveals open forums and echo chambers in social media discussions of climate change. Glob. Environ. Chang. **32**, 126–138 (2015)

How Is Vaping Framed on Online Knowledge Dissemination Platforms?

Keyu Chen[1,5], Yiwen Shi[2], Jun Luo[3], Joyce Jiang[3], Shweta Yadav[4],
Munmun De Choudhury[7], Ashique R. Khudabukhsh[6],
Marzieh Babaeianjelodar[1], Frederick L. Altice[1], and Navin Kumar[1,8(✉)]

[1] Yale University School of Medicine, New Haven, CT 06510, USA
navin.kumar@yale.edu
[2] Yale University, New Haven, CT 06510, USA
[3] University of California, Los Angeles, USA
[4] University of Illinois Chicago,Chicago, USA
[5] The University of Edinburgh, College of Arts,Edinburgh, UK
[6] Rochester Institute of Technology, Rochester, USA
[7] Georgia Institute of Technology, Atlanta, USA
[8] National University of Singapore, Singapore, Singapore

Abstract. Studying how vaping is framed on various knowledge dissemination platforms (e.g., Quora, Reddit, Wikipedia) is central to understanding the process of knowledge dissemination around vaping. Such understanding can help us craft tools specific to each platform, to dispel vaping misperceptions and reinforce evidence-based information. We analyze 1,888 articles and 1,119,453 vaping posts to study how vaping is framed across multiple knowledge dissemination platforms (Wikipedia, Quora, Medium, Reddit, Stack Exchange, wikiHow). We use NLP techniques to understand these differences. As an example, regarding question answering results, for the question *What is vaping for?*, we note answers framing vaping as a smoking cessation tool in Quora, Medium, and Stack Exchange. Reddit tended to frame vaping as a hobby. Wikipedia had a mix of answers, some centered on EVALI, and others on vaping as harm reduction. Broadly, results indicate that Quora is an appropriate venue for those looking to transition from smoking to vaping. Other platforms (Reddit, wikiHow) are more for vaping hobbyists and may not sufficiently dissuade youth vaping. Conversely, Wikipedia may exaggerate vaping harms, dissuading smokers from transitioning. A strength of our work is how the different techniques we have applied validate each other. Stakeholders may utilize our findings to design vaping regulation that clarifies the role of vapes as a smoking cessation tool.

1 Introduction

The recent introduction of alternative forms of nicotine products into the marketplace (e.g., e-cigarettes/vapes, heated tobacco products, and smokeless tobacco) has led to a more complex informational environment [4]. The scientific consensus is that vape aerosol contains fewer numbers and lower levels of toxicants than

R. Thomson et al. (Eds.): SBP-BRiMS 2022, LNCS 13558, pp. 68–78, 2022.
https://doi.org/10.1007/978-3-031-17114-7_7

smoke from combustible tobacco cigarettes. Among youth in the USA, adolescent nicotine vaping use increased from 2017 to 2019 but then started declining in 2020. Among adults, a Cochrane review found that nicotine vapes probably do help people to stop smoking for at least six months, working better than nicotine replacement therapy and nicotine-free e-cigarettes [1]. Given that vaping is represented in the public health environment both as a smoking cessation tool and harm to youth health, it is highly controversial and polarizing, with inconsistent messaging across various platforms [2]. For example, manufacturers, retailers, and social media influencers have claimed that e-cigarettes contain only water vapor and are harmless. Such messaging may downplay the risks of vape use and be in part responsible for the youth vaping epidemic. Conversely, there also exists messaging that vapes are just as or more harmful than smoking, perhaps deterring current cigarette smokers who are unable to quit from transitioning to vaping. Similarly, regarding the outbreak of vaping-related lung injury (EVALI), most cases were related to consumption of vitamin E acetate, an additive included in some tetrahydrocannabinol devices. However, news reports have not always differentiated between tetrahydrocannabinol devices and standard nicotine-based vapes, perhaps disproportionately characterizing vaping harms. Such vaping-related news may have triggered national and state-level policy responses, and influenced public perceptions (including misperceptions) regarding the harms of vaping. While there has been research around vaping perceptions on news and social media, there is limited analysis of how vaping is framed on digital knowledge dissemination platforms. By knowledge dissemination platforms, we refer to platforms such as social question-and-answer sites (e.g., Quora), social news aggregation sites (e.g., Reddit), online encyclopedias (e.g., Wikipedia), and online publishing platforms (e.g., Medium). Such platforms are where individuals obtain health information, discuss products (e.g., vapes) and personal health, or get quick answers to health questions. Studying how vaping is framed on these platforms is central to understanding the process of knowledge dissemination around vaping. Such understanding can help us craft tools specific to each platform, to dispel vaping misperceptions and reinforce evidence-based information. For example, findings can lead to tools that buttress accurate vaping information on Wikipedia with peer-reviewed literature, but correct misperceptions on Quora. Such targeted tools may aid in reducing youth vaping and improving smoking cessation rates. Despite the significance of the problem noted above, existing research studying knowledge dissemination platforms' framing of vaping is limited. Most research around vaping on online platforms centers on responses to the 2020 outbreak of vaping-related lung injury (EVALI), or content analysis of vaping. In this paper, we demonstrate how vaping is framed on multiple knowledge dissemination platforms. Our main research question (RQ) is as follows: How is vaping framed in various knowledge dissemination platforms? Our findings suggest that some platforms (Medium, Quora, Stack Exchange) are appropriate for individuals seeking tobacco harm reduction information. Other platforms (Reddit, wikiHow) are more for vaping hobbyists and may not sufficiently dissuade youth vaping. Conversely, Wikipedia may exaggerate vaping harms, dissuading smokers from transitioning. Stakeholders may utilize our findings to design informational tools to reinforce or mitigate vaping (mis)perceptions online.

2   Data and Method

Data. We first selected three content experts who had published at least ten peer-reviewed articles in the last three years around vaping. Given the wide disciplinary focus of vaping research, we sought to select a range of experts across disciplines. We recruited one expert from each of these disciplines: Clinical psychology, medicine, computational social science. Selecting experts from a range of fields allows results to be contextualized to fields where vaping research is concentrated, allowing for findings to be drawn on by stakeholders in psychology, medicine, and computational social science. The context experts separately developed lists of knowledge dissemination platforms most relevant to vaping. Each expert developed a list of ten platforms independently, and we selected only platforms common to all three experts' lists: Wikipedia, Quora, Medium, Reddit, Stack Exchange, wikiHow. Examples of platforms not selected: Facebook, LinkedIn. To capture vaping-related text on these platforms, we used queries based on a related systematic review e.g., electronic-cigarette, electronic cigarette, vape-juice, vape-liquid.

Table 1. Data collected across platforms

Platform	Data collected (e.g., N of posts, articles)	API (N/A if no API)
Wikipedia	50 articles	Wikipedia
Quora	4,890 questions and 31,890 answer posts	N/A
Medium	1,820 articles	N/A
Reddit	129,092 posts and 953,168 comments	Pushshift
Stack exchange	85 questions and 413 answers	N/A
wikiHow	17 articles	N/A

We illustrated the data collection procedures in Table 1. We then removed posts around vaping cannabis (containing terms such as weed, marijuana, cannabis) as this was not relevant to our research question. Examples of removed posts and articles: How much less weed do you guys go through that switched from joints to vape only; Vaping herbs other than cannabis - anyone do this? Does smoking marijuana negatively affect your looks? Is vaping marijuana bad? Why Vaping Weed is Different From Smoking. Two reviewers independently examined 10% of the remaining articles or posts within each dataset to confirm salience with our research question. The reviewers then discussed their findings and highlighted items deemed relevant across both lists. We noted the following relevance proportions: Quora (83%), Reddit (76%), Medium (92%).

Question Answering. Question answering can help us understand how different platforms *answer* the same questions about vaping, perhaps revealing differences in vaping frames. For example, Wikipedia may be more likely to present vaping harms compared to Reddit. We used BERT for answer extraction. The model was applied separately on data from each platform, except wikiHow, which had insufficient data. Questions were developed based on input from content experts. Each content expert first developed a list of ten questions separately. The three experts then discussed their lists to result in a final list of four questions that were broadly similar across all three original lists, and final questions are as follows: What is vaping for? What are the advantages of vaping compared to smoking cigarettes? Why are teens vaping? What is the biggest concern with vaping? We highlighted one question at a time and fed it to the model. While we would have preferred to use more than four questions for our question answering analysis, only four questions were agreed upon by the content experts. This is largely due to disagreement among content experts as to what questions should be included, largely resulting from the controversial nature of vaping, and that academics are in disagreement about the harms and merits of vaping. The model extracts answers for the question leveraging on context information in each article or post. To stay within the admitted input size of the model, we clipped the length of the text (title + body text) to 512 tokens. Each question provided one answer per article or post. We randomly sampled 500, 1000, 1500, and 2000 answers per question. We found that a random sample of 1000 answers provided the greatest range and quality of answers, assessed by two reviewers (80% agreement). Range of answers was determined based on the number of different answers provided by each group of answers (500, 1000, 1500, 2000). Quality was determined by the proportion of sensible and non-repetitive answers to each question compared to total number of answers. Sampling 500 answers provided a limited range of answers and few sensible answers to questions. The 1500 and 2000 group of answers had a large range of answers, but many of these tended to be not useful or relevant to the question, such as stopwords. The 1000 answer selection was found by reviewers to have a good range of answers, comparable to the 1500 and 2000 group of answers, but had a greater proportion of sensible answers compared to other groups of answers. We thus randomly sampled 1000 answers per question. Given space limitations and that several answers were repetitive, with numerous non-useful answers, we are unable to present the 1000 answer selection here. Thus, for brevity and clarity, we decided to present a subsample of the 1000 answer selection, providing an overview of answers, without non-useful and repetitive answers. From the sample of 1000 answers, content experts selected the top 5, 10 and 20 most representative answers per question, for both left-, center-, and right-leaning articles. We found that selecting the top 10 most representative answers provided the least repetition and most sensible answers. We thus randomly sampled 1000 answers per question and content experts then selected the top 10, where possible, most representative answers per question for each platform. The top 10 answers were selected as follows. Content experts first ranked all answers based on their relevance to the corresponding question. Experts were told to put relevant answers at the top of the list and irrelevant answers towards the bottom of the list. For example, for the question *What is vaping for?* relevant answers were *harm reduction* or *smoking cessation aid.* Examples of irrelevant answers were *the, person,* and *coil.* Experts then compared lists to select the top 10 answers which were common across all lists. For clarity, 80% agreement meant that across both reviewers, 80% of answers were considered relevant to the question. As an example, an answer was considered in agreement when both reviewers thought that that answer was relevant to a question. An answer was deemed irrelevant when only a single or neither reviewer deemed it relevant to the question.

Cloze Tests. We used BERT and cloze tests to understand the differences between vaping framing across platforms. Cloze tests represent a fill-in-the-blank task given a sentence with a missing word. For example, *winter* is a likely completion for the missing word in the following cloze task: In the [MASK], it snows a lot. We developed several cloze tests with input from content experts. Each content expert first developed a list of ten cloze tests separately. Then the three experts compared their lists to only retain items appearing in both lists, resulting in a final list of four cloze tests: i) The main issue with vaping is [MASK]; ii) The worst thing about vaping is [MASK]; iii) Teens like vaping because it's [MASK]; iv) Vaping is [MASK] to our health. We applied BERT on each platform's dataset, where possible, to identify the differences in the top five results for each cloze test for Reddit and Quora. There was insufficient data on other platforms to perform similar analyses.

Translation across Platforms through Large-scale Language Models. Next, we use large-scale language models to understand the differences between posts across platforms. Such models serve a range of purposes. We use these models to perform single word translation where the model takes a word in a source language as input and outputs an equivalent word in a target language [3]. For example, in a translation system performing English to Spanish translation, if the input word is hello, the output word will be ola. We build on earlier work [3] and treat platforms as different languages. As our *languages* are actually English from different platforms, on most occasions, translations will be identical. As an example, *food* in English used by the Reddit users (Reddit-English) will likely translate into the same in Quora-English [3]. The interesting cases are pairs where translations do not match. The output is not inherently misaligned, and the algorithm simply produces word pairs. We determine whether there is a misalignment through human review. Most of the time, pairs will match (aligned). However, sometimes the pairs will not match (misaligned) and this is of interest. An example pair that may not match in our context is *ingredients, additives. Ingredients* may be used in favorable contexts in Reddit-English, much like how *additives* may be used in unfavorable contexts within Quora-English. Thus, while both words have different meanings and representations in each platform, they are treated the same by the translation algorithm, creating a mismatch in translation for *ingredients* and *additives*. Such word pairs are misaligned pairs. Such mismatches can provide insights on the differences in how vaping is framed between Reddit and Quora. We fed the models our posts, divided by platform (Reddit, Quora), as two different languages. There was insufficient data on other platforms to conduct similar analyses. We provide a brief technical overview of the technique used, drawing from [3]. Let D1 and D2 be two monolingual text corpora authored in languages L1 and L2 respectively. With respect to D1 and D2, V1 and V2 denote the source and target vocabularies. A word translation scheme that translates L1 to L2 takes a source word (W1) as input and produces a single word translation W2 (more details in [3]). A translation algorithm drives this process. The algorithm requires two monolingual corpora and a bilingual seed lexicon of word translation pairs as inputs. First, two separate monolingual word embeddings are induced using a monolingual word embedding learning model. FastText was used to train monolingual embedding. Next, a bilingual seed lexicon is used to learn an orthogonal transformation matrix, which is then used to align the two vector spaces. Finally, to translate a word from the source language to the target language, we multiply the embedding of the source word with the transformation matrix to align it with the target vector space. Then, the nearest neighbour of the aligned word vector in the target vector space is selected as the translation of the source word in the target language. Two reviewers manually inspected the top 5000 salient translation pairs, ranked by frequency [3], between Reddit and Quora. Reviewers were instructed to independently order the list with most mismatched pairs at the top. By most mismatched we refer to pairs with the greatest difference in meaning, such as *ingredients, additives*. Examples of less mismatched pairs are those which are different words but closer in meaning, such as *got, started*, and *liquids, juices*. The reviewers then compared the top 15 most mismatched pairs in their lists to look for items common to both lists. Two pairs were common to both lists, and are displayed in the results section. Examples of pairs not selected are *combustible, carcinogenic, addicted, pointless*, and *industry, government*. As a clarification, our goal in using techniques described in [3] was not to provide an improvement over an existing technique, but to demonstrate the technique in a different context. While we largely used the work of [3] unchanged, we calculated similarity scores between sentences to find illustrative examples of misaligned pairs between Quora and Reddit where the pairs appear in highly similar contexts - essentially sentences that have similar meanings but with different words. Similarity scores were calculated with Sentence-bert, a modification of the pretrained BERT network that uses siamese and triplet network structures to derive semantically meaningful sentence embeddings that can be compared using cosine-similarity.

3   Results

Overview. We first provide an overview of our data. Reddit posts generally centered on content for vapers and concerns around vaping regulation. Posts catered to vapers, with limited anti-vaping content. Quora seems to focus on vaping as a possible tool for smoking cessation, and deterring youth from vaping. Overall, Quora seems to be the most balanced platform around promoting vaping as a smoking cessation tool and limiting youth use. Medium tends to have a broad scope of vaping viewpoints, with anti-vaping articles, and articles targeted at vaping enthusiasts. It seems that Stack Exchange is primarily for vapers, with some information on vaping as a smoking cessation tool, but limited anti-vaping content. Stack Exchange may not be ideal for dissuading youth from vaping. Overall, Wikipedia pages centered on vape products and major events such as EVALI, detailing that vaping is framed as a consumer product requiring regulation, rather than an alternative to combustible cigarettes - perhaps indicative of Wikipedia's bias against vaping. Broadly, wikiHow seems to cater to vape enthusiasts, with only a single anti-vaping article (*How to Stop Vaping*). wikiHow may thus not present balanced views on vaping and there were no pages on vaping as a tool for smoking cessation.

Table 2. Question-answering results for various platforms.

Question	Reddit	Quora	Medium	Stack exchange	Wikipedia
What is vaping for?	Nicotine, smoking, juice, mods, flavor	Use in quitting smoking, quit smoking, nicotine, harm reduction, lungs	Your wellbeing, to prevent my nicotine addiction from killing me, smoking cessation aids, saving former smokers from smoking, substitute to smoke	Satisfy your craving for a cigarette, smoking cessation aid, personal use, quitting smoking	Use-associated injury, smoking cessation, quitting smoking, nicotine delivery device, harm reduction, giving up smoking
What are the advantages of vaping compared to smoking cigarettes?	Your lungs will probably be a lot happier, you save a ton of money, you don't smell like nasty cigs and have stink, you can do it without reeking	Your health and breath will improve, you don't stink and don't have brown teeth, you can try various flavors, very safe, without burning tobacco, 95% safer, less harmful, cheaper	Without the fire, tars, smells or ash, they are not at all harmful, simpler and is used worldwide, safe and healthier, less harmful, healthier	Reduce your intake of toxins greatly, healthier, fewer long term health effects, much safer,	Smoking cessation, less harmful and more socially acceptable, more efficient
Why are teens vaping?	Trying to fit in, to quit smoking, to save money, to look good, anxiety	Tobacco harm reduction, to show off to their friends, to quit or stay quit from smoking, to help with stress and anxiety, to fit in with their peers	To fit in, marketing, breaks society's rules, believe it's safe, quit smoking	Think they are invincible, quitting smoking	To help them quit, to help them give up smoking, desire to smoke and withdrawal
What is the biggest concern with vaping?	Youth vaping epidemic, your voice, your lungs, your build and voltage, your coils, your current	Your lung, your health, you do not know what you are inhaling, worse on the lungs, vitamin e acetate	Underage smoking, wattage, price, nicotine addiction, severe lung disease, lung injury	Oral health, not safe, fire hazard, harmful vapor, fire and explosion risk,	Underage people obtaining and getting addicted, smoking-related diseases, smoking, severe pulmonary disease, lung illness, lung disease,

Question Answering. We now present answers to four questions and up to 10 most representative answers across each platform in Table 2. Some questions provided less than 10 representative answers due to data availability. For the question *What is vaping for?*, we note answers framing vaping as a smoking cessation tool in Quora, Medium, and Stack Exchange, *harm reduction, to prevent* *my nicotine addiction from killing me, smoking cessation aid.* Reddit tended to frame vaping as a hobby, with answers such as *juice, mods, flavor.* Wikipedia had a mix of answers, some centered on EVALI, *use-associated injury,* and others on vaping as harm reduction *giving up smoking, smoking cessation, quitting smoking.* Regarding *What are the advantages of vaping compared to smoking cigarettes?,* all platforms provide answers around improved health and reduced cost, *your health and breath will improve, cheaper, your lungs will probably be a lot happier, reduce your intake of toxins greatly, less harmful and more socially acceptable.* For *Why are teens vaping?,* all platforms suggest that peer influence is a factor, *to show off to their friends, to fit in with their peers.* We note answers which may indicate that some teens vape as a form of harm reduction, *to quit smoking, to help them give up smoking,* in line with recent work [5]. Finally, for *What is the biggest concern with vaping?,* all platforms except Reddit indicate EVALI-related responses such as *vitamin e acetate, severe lung disease, severe pulmonary disease* or substance use concerns *underage people obtaining and getting addicted, nicotine addiction.* Reddit answers contain such concerns but also

Table 3. The top five candidate words ranked by BERT probability for the cloze test *"The main issue with vaping is [MASK]"*, *"The worst thing about vaping is [MASK]"*, *"Teens like vaping because it's [MASK]"*, *"Vaping is [MASK] to our health."* for Reddit and Quora data.

	Reddit (probability)	Quora (probability)
The main issue with vaping is [MASK]	Cost (0.140)	Safety (0.183)
	Smell (0.053)	Taste (0.144)
	Money (0.044)	Health (0.077)
	Temperature (0.040)	Cost (0.074)
	Flavor (0.039)	Flavor (0.032)
The worst thing about vaping is [MASK]	Money (0.076)	Taste (0.200)
	Smell (0.053)	Stupidity (0.049)
	Smoking (0.041)	Smell (0.036)
	Convenience (0.040)	Safety (0.036)
	Efficiency (0.035)	That (0.032)
Teens like vaping because it's [MASK]	Cool (0.173)	Cool (0.461)
	Safe (0.063)	Safe (0.048)
	Convenient (0.049)	Popular (0.043)
	New (0.035)	Dangerous (0.032)
	Fun (0.034)	Enjoyable (0.025)
Vaping is [MASK] to our health.	Bad (0.479)	Dangerous (0.312)
	Harmful (0.200)	Detrimental (0.229)
	Dangerous (0.068)	Harmful (0.229)
	Detrimental (0.050)	Bad (0.68)
	Important (0.035)	Damaging (0.064)

focused on the hobbyist aspects of vape devices, *your build and voltage, your coils, your current*. We conjecture that Quora, Medium, and Stack Exchange may be appropriate avenues for those seeking information around vaping as an alternative to smoking. Reddit may not be useful for those wanting to make the transition from smoking, and may even provide incorrect information to youth. Wikipedia contains a range of views, and may overemphasize vaping harms. We also note some EVALI-centric answers, which may exaggerate vaping risks.

Cloze Tests. We use cloze tests to gauge the aggregate framing around vaping, across Reddit and Quora. Table 3 shows the cloze test results for several probes using Quora and Reddit data. Broadly, Reddit frames vaping as a hobby, with major concerns such as *cost, smell, money, temperature, flavor*. Quora has a greater focus on the health effects of vaping, with concerns *safety, taste, health, cost, flavor*. We note similar results when detailing *The worst thing about vaping is [MASK]*, where Reddit indicates *money, smell, smoking, convenience, efficiency*, while Quora provides *taste, stupidity, smell, safety, that*. Much like our other findings, Reddit may be ideal for vaping hobbyists, and Quora may be a more appropriate venue for those seeking to transition from smoking to vaping.

Table 4. Misaligned word pairs and illustrative sentence examples for Reddit and Quora regarding vaping framing.

Misaligned Pairs	Reddit	Quora
Illustrative examples		
<fda, propaganda>	Thats why fda says there is no risk with getting addicted to nicotine replacement therapy	Even with all the propaganda about vaping, there is scientific studies that suggest nicotine IS NOT nearly as addictive as it is portrayed to be
	The fda would rather you smoke than vape anyway	Seriously, nearly 20 years of repeated science on the topic of OIL FUMES trashing lungs! Not just vaping and doesn't have a damn thing to do with nicotine! Don't fall for the Reefer Madness propaganda of the anti-vaping stupidity and ignorance!
<ingredients, additives>	Vaping definitely does way less harm than cigarettes, just read the ingredients and the level of formaldehyde has already been proven to be perfectly safe to breathe in	Vaping is shaping up to be significantly more dangerous than cigarette smoking for a number of reasons, largely related to the quality of the stuff you are inhaling, the untested additives, and the concentration of chemicals
	The ingredients that you put inside are Propylene Glycol (PG), Vegetable Glycerin (VG), nicotine by mg increments, and flavorings	It usually contains propylene glycol, glycerin, nicotine, flavorings, additives, and contaminants

Translation across Platforms through Large-Scale Language Models. We demonstrate single word translation results from our large-scale language models to understand differences between Reddit and Quora. Upon manual inspection, we present misaligned pairs for Reddit and Quora posts, and illustrative sentence examples in Table 4. We first indicate the *fda, propaganda* pair which demonstrates how individuals on Reddit frame the FDA, which regulates vaping in the US, similar to how Quora users discuss anti-vaping propaganda. Such evidence may indicate that Reddit users frame the FDA as being anti-vaping, a stance often taken by vaping hobbyists. We then indicate the *ingredients, additives* pair. Reddit tends to use *ingredients*, which has a more neutral connotation, unlike Quora, which uses *additives*, with a more sinister connotation. In the Quora sentence examples, we note that *additives* is often mentioned with *dangerous, untested, contaminants*, unlike the equivalent *ingredients* in Reddit, which is mentioned alongside *safe, less harm*. It seems that Reddit takes a largely pro-vaping stance, possibly not always evidence-based, and perhaps other platforms may provide a more balanced framing for those looking for information on vaping.

4   Discussion

Our RQ was to explore how vaping is framed across online knowledge dissemination platforms. A strength of our work is how the different techniques we applied validate each other as well as reveal differences across platforms. Key to how vaping is framed is the inclusion of vaper viewpoints when writing articles on vaping. Where possible, vapers themselves should be consulted on articles about vaping. For example, a panel staffed by vapers can comment on vaping-related questions and answers on Quora, providing suggestions on how answers can more accurately represent vaper concerns. As the vaping landscape continues to evolve, it is possible that more vaping regulation inimical to smoking cessation is proposed. We suggest vaping regulation that clarifies the role of vapes as a smoking cessation tool. Our findings relied on the validity of data collected with our search terms. We used a range of established techniques to search for all articles/posts relevant to vaping, and our data contained text aligned with how vaping is framed. We are thus confident in the comprehensiveness of our data. We note that the recall of the search string was not tested. We note that our data may not be generalizable to how vaping is framed globally. We also note the limitations of BERT, such as its inability to learn in few-shot settings.

Acknowledgments and Conflict of Interest. This study was pre-registered on the Open Science Framework (osf.io/36j29). This study was funded with a grant from the Foundation for a Smoke-Free World, a US nonprofit 501(c)(3) private foundation with a mission to end smoking in this generation. The Foundation accepts charitable gifts from PMI Global Services Inc. (PMI); under the Foundation's Bylaws and Pledge Agreement with PMI, the Foundation is independent from PMI and the tobacco industry. The contents, selection, and presentation of facts, as well as any opinions expressed herein are the sole responsibility of the authors and under no circumstances shall be regarded as reflecting the positions of the Foundation for a Smoke-Free World, Inc. Navin Kumar and Keyu Chen declare financial support through a grant from the Foundation for a Smoke-Free World. There are no financial relationships with any other organizations that might have an interest in the submitted work in the previous three years; and no other relationships or activities that could appear to have influenced the submitted work.

References

1. Hartmann-Boyce, J., et al.: Electronic cigarettes for smoking cessation. Cochrane Database Syst. Rev. **9**(9), CD010216 (2021). https://doi.org/10.1002/14651858. CD010216.pub6
2. Janmohamed, K., et al.: Interventions to mitigate vaping misinformation: a meta-analysis. J. Health Commun. **27**(2), 84–92 (2022)
3. KhudaBukhsh, A.R., Sarkar, R., Kamlet, M.S., Mitchell, T.M.: We don't speak the same language: interpreting polarization through machine translation. arXiv preprint arXiv:2010.02339 (2020)
4. Kumar, N., et al.: Interventions to mitigate vaping misinformation: protocol for a scoping review (2021). https://doi.org/10.21203/rs.3.rs-417190/v1
5. Sokol, N.A., Feldman, J.M.: High school seniors who used E-cigarettes may have otherwise been cigarette smokers: evidence from monitoring the future (United States, 2009–2018). Nicotine Tob. Res. **23**(11), 1958–1961 (2021). https://doi.org/10.1093/ntr/ntab102

The Missing Link Between User Engagement and Misinformation's Impact on Online Behavior

Daniele Bellutta[✉][iD], Joshua Uyheng[iD], and Kathleen M. Carley[iD]

Carnegie Mellon University, Pittsburgh, PA 15213, USA
{dbellutt,juyheng,kathleen.carley}@cs.cmu.edu

Abstract. By analyzing tweets sent before and after Twitter users' first interactions with known low- or high-credibility information sources, we have observed that people who interacted with low-credibility information tended to be more hateful even before that interaction. Such people seemed to further increase their hatefulness only following particularly engaged interactions with low-credibility content. By demonstrating the importance of a person's level of engagement with misinformation for understanding its impact, these results bridge the gap between studies that detected behavioral effects amongst believers of misinformation and research that instead either failed to detect such effects or concluded that misinformation largely affects small, predisposed audiences. Our analysis also reveals a stronger link between interaction with misinformation and change in what people discuss rather than how they write posts.

Keywords: Social cybersecurity · Misinformation · Fake news

1 Introduction

Social cybersecurity research has focused primarily on detecting and characterizing misinformation and influence campaigns. Much less work has studied misinformation's ultimate impact on people's behaviors and beliefs [2,5,7], and the relatively little research on the matter has reached seemingly conflicting conclusions. Though some studies have found that false stories can influence voter behavior [3,11,21], others have instead concluded that misinformation may have limited impact on small, predisposed portions of the population [9,10].

To investigate this incongruence, we collected the timelines of thousands of Twitter users and tracked changes in their behavior following their first known interaction with sets of low- or high-credibility information sources. Unlike in survey and lab studies [7,9–12,21], our approach allowed us to solely use social media data at the expense of only being able to draw correlational conclusions.

By identifying a neglected link between the level of engagement with misinformation and future changes in user behavior, our results reconcile past findings in this area. People interacting with misinformation already had a small predisposition towards greater hatefulness and only tended to slightly increase that hatefulness following *highly engaged* interactions with misinformation. This work therefore supports past conclusions that misinformation's predominant audience exhibits certain predispositions but also lends credibility to findings of behavioral effects in people who believed (and were presumably highly engaged with) false narratives. Additionally, we observed greater change in *what* people discuss rather than *how* they discuss things after interacting with misinformation.

2   Related Work

Some past research has identified evidence of misinformation impacting personal behaviors and beliefs. In 2006, a German study found that viewers of political debates learned both true and false information from candidates [13]. Later, an American survey revealed that amongst people who voted for Obama in 2012, belief in false stories was strongly tied to not voting for Clinton in 2016 [11]. Similarly, a German survey from 2017 revealed that belief in fake news was tied to an increased likelihood of changing plans from voting for the governing party to instead voting for a right-wing populist party [21]. An online experiment also found that exposure to false statements made by Marine Le Pen swayed participants' intentions towards voting for her in the 2017 French elections [3]. Finally, an Italian analysis of municipal election results in Trentino and Südtirol linked Facebook likes on misinformation pages to increased populist voting [5].

Beyond voting, there is some conflicting evidence of the behavioral impact of COVID-19 misinformation. A 2020 survey found that exposure to misinformation on COVID-19 vaccines reduced stated intentions to get vaccinated [12], but another survey's investigation of this question found that the significance of this effect did not survive Bonferroni correction [7]. Nevertheless, this latter survey did measure a small (but significant) decrease in willingness to download a contact tracing application following exposure to relevant misinformation [7].

Other research has questioned the behavioral impact of misinformation by either failing to detect it or finding that it is limited to small, predisposed audiences. One study found that only 1% of thousands of Twitter users accounted for 80% of misinformation consumption and that interest in politics was strongly tied to exposure to misinformation [9]. Guess *et al.* similarly found that low-credibility sites constituted a small part of participants' information consumption and that people who read more news overall were exposed to more untrustworthy content [10]. Combining their data with voter records further refuted the possibility of large effects on voter choices or turnout [10]. Bail *et al.* tracked survey respondents' interactions with Russian-controlled Twitter accounts in 2017 and did not find a significant effect on participants' feelings towards the opposing political party, independent of whether the interaction was direct or indirect [2].

3   Methods

3.1   Data Collection

To study the behavior of Twitter users who interacted with low- or high-credibility sources of information, we chose corresponding sets of Web sites that

Table 1. The low-credibility sites and accounts used in the data collection.

abovetopsecret.com: @abovetopsecret; activistpost.com: @activistpost; amtvmedia.com: @amtvmedia; barenakedislam.com: @barenakedislam; beforeitsnews.com: @beforeitsnews; breitbart.com: @breitbartnews; chinadaily.com.cn: @chinadailyusa; coasttocoastam.com: @coasttocoastam; dailybuzzlive.com: @dailybuzzlive; dailystar.co.uk: @dailystar; disclose.tv: @disclosetv; english.pravda.ru, pravdareport.com: @engpravda; hangthebankers.com: @hangthebankers; infowars.com: @infowars; lewrockwell.com: @lewrockwell; madworldnews.com: @madworldnews; occupydemocrats.com: @occupydemocrats; presstv.com: @presstv; prntly.com: @prntly; realfarmacy.com: @realfarmacy; rt.com: @rt_com; sgtreport.com: @sgtreport; thecommonsenseshow.com: @thecommonseshow; thedailysheeple.com: @thedailysheeple; theduran.com: @theduran_com; wakingtimes.com: @wakingtimes; worldtruth.tv: @worldtruthtv

Table 2. The high-credibility sites and accounts used in the data collection.

12newsnow.com: @12NewsNow; abc12.com: @ABC12WJRT; abc4.com: @abc4utah; adn.com: @adndotcom; azcapitoltimes.com: @AzCapitolTimes; bismarcktribune.com: @bistrib; bozemandailychronicle.com: @bozchron; bringmethenews.com: @bringmethenews; capecodtimes.com: @capecodtimes; cincinnati.com: @Enquirer; columbian.com: @thecolumbian; concordmonitor.com: @ConMonitorNews; crainsdetroit.com: @crainsdetroit; dailycamera.com: @dailycamera; dailyjournalonline.com: @dailyjournalmo; dailyprogress.com: @DailyProgress; dailyrecord.com: @dailyrecord; desmoinesregister.com: @DMRegister; duluthnewstribune.com: @duluthnews; eastidahonews.com: @EastIDNews; elkodaily.com: @ElkoDaily; floridapolitics.com: @Fla_Pol; fox2now.com: @FOX2now; fox35orlando.com: @fox35orlando; fox40.com: @FOX40; fox59.com: @FOX59; goerie.com: @GoErie; greenbaypressgazette.com: @gbpressgazette; herald-dispatch.com: @heralddispatch; hjnews.com: @HJNews; idahostatesman.com: @IdahoStatesman; journalnow.com: @JournalNow; journalstar.com: @JournalStarNews; kark.com: @KARK4News; kcrg.com: @KCRG; kfor.com: @kfor; kiro7.com: @KIRO7Seattle; kitv.com: @KITV4; kktv.com: @KKTV11News; koamnewsnow.com: @koamfox14; koin.com: @KOINNews; krqe.com: @krqe; kyma.com: @KYMA11; lcsun-news.com: @CrucesSunNews; live5news.com: @Live5News; masslive.com: @masslivenews; missoulian.com: @missoulian; modbee.com: @modbee; myfox8.com: @myfox8; myrecordjournal.com: @Record_Journal; nbc29.com: @NBC29; nbc4i.com: @nbc4i; necn.com: @NECN; news10.com: @WTEN; news9.com: @NEWS9; oanow.com: @oanow; pjstar.com: @pjstar; postandcourier.com: @postandcourier; rapidcityjournal.com: @RCJournal; shreveporttimes.com: @shreveporttimes; silive.com: @siadvance; southbendtribune.com: @SBTribune; stardem.com: @stardem_news; statesmanjournal.com: @Salem_Statesman; sunherald.com: @sunherald; swtimes.com: @TimesRecord; thenevadaindependent.com: @TheNVIndy; timesfreepress.com: @TimesFreePress; trib.com: @CSTribune; valleynewslive.com: @ValleyNewsLive; wabi.tv: @WABI_TV5; wacotrib.com: @wacotrib; walb.com: @WALBNews10; wave3.com: @wave3news; wbay.com: @WBAY; wbko.com: @wbkotv; wbrc.com: @WBRCnews; wcax.com: @wcax; wgno.com: @WGNOtv; wibw.com: @wibw; wifr.com: @23WIFR; wmur.com: @WMUR9; wowt.com: @WOWT6News; wpri.com: @wpri12; wsaz.com: @WSAZnews; wtae.com: @WTAE; wtnh.com: @WTNH; wtoc.com: @WTOC11; wtok.com: @WTOKTV; wtop.com: @WTOP; wusa9.com: @wusa9; wvlt.tv: @wvlt; wyomingnewsnow.tv: @kgwntv

controlled Twitter accounts. To attain the low-credibility sources in Table 1, we took a sample of the sites listed by Media Bias/Fact Check (MBFC) as being of questionable or conspiratorial nature with low or very low factual reporting [14]. For the high-credibility sources in Table 2, we used a sample of local news sources rated by MBFC as being least biased with high or very high factual reporting [14]. This sample spans different media (print, television, etc.) and all states in the U.S. Since these are local news sources, the set needed to be larger to approximately match the low-credibility sites in number of Twitter interactors.

After selecting these sources, we queried Twitter for users who either tweeted or retweeted a link to those sites or replied to tweets from those accounts during the 30 days leading up to 6 January 2021. To shrink our collection size and ensure

Table 3. The number of non-bot users who linked or replied to our selected sources, along with how many tweets they sent within two weeks before or after their interaction.

	Sharer users	Replier users	Sharer tweets	Replier tweets
Low-credibility	3085	5907	297784	785279
High-credibility	8621	1783	971248	171871

we could attain a usable number of tweets from each user, we only considered accounts with at least 400 tweets. Since we wanted to study human behavior, we used the BotHunter machine learning model [4] to attain each account's average bot probability over 40 recent tweets, which recent research has shown to be the optimal amount for producing a stable score [16]. We then filtered out any accounts with mean probabilities of at least 40%, retaining the likely humans.

Using the new Twitter API, we collected the entire public timelines of the human users in our data. We then re-computed each account's average bot score over that timeline and again filtered out accounts with scores of at least 40%. For the remaining users, we searched for the first time they shared links to or replied to the sources in our lists. Table 3 summarizes the resulting data.

3.2 Dependent Variables

Tweet Style. To examine whether people changed how they wrote their tweets after interacting with our selected information sources, we used NetMapper [15] to identify emotional cues and social identities mentioned in each user's tweets. We then computed the proportion of abusive, fearful, angry, happy, sad, disgustful, and explicit words in each tweet. Next, we also calculated the proportion of words mentioning racial, religious, political, and gender identities. Out of concern that misinformation may inspire hate, we fed the NetMapper outputs into a previously developed machine learning model [20] to estimate the probability that each tweet contained hate speech.

User Topic Choices. In addition to studying *how* people wrote their tweets, we also examined *what* people discussed. Specifically, we considered the hashtags people used, the users they mentioned, and the domains of the URLs they shared. For each of these three types of entities, we counted how many times an account used each entity during the two weeks before and the two weeks after the user's interaction with an information source. We then computed the cosine similarity between those two time periods, thereby quantifying the degree to which a user's choice of hashtags, mentions, or URLs changed after interacting with an information source.

3.3 Regression Analysis

Tweet Style. After computing the features on tweet style, we fit separate regression models to each of these tweet-level dependent variables. Since they were formulated as proportions ranging from zero to one, we fit fractional regression models [17] to predictors about each of the tweets authored within two weeks before or after a user's first interaction with an information source.

Our models focused on three independent variables: whether the author of a tweet interacted with a high- or *low-credibility* source, whether the tweet was sent before or *after* that interaction, and whether the user interacted with the source via a link share or a tweet *reply*. To understand whether our dependent variables changed after an individual interacted with a low-credibility source rather than a high-credibility one, we added an interaction term indicating whether a tweet was sent *after* an exposure to a *low-credibility* source. Similarly, to know whether the behavioral variables changed in different ways following different types of exposures, we added an interaction term indicating whether a tweet was sent *after* a *reply* exposure rather than a link share. The remaining interaction term indicating whether a tweet's author *replied* to a *low-credibility* source was also added. Finally, we wanted to analyze the effects of highly engaged interactions with low-credibility sources, so we added the three-way interaction term denoting whether a tweet was sent *after* a *reply* to a *low-credibility* source.

These models also included several control variables: the time between a tweet's writing and the author's interaction with the information source, that time squared, the number of tweets the author sent within the four-week time period considered, the number of characters in the tweet, the season during which the tweet was sent, whether the tweet was sent during a weekend, and the average value of the dependent variable across that particular author's tweets.

For all fitted model coefficients, we performed z-tests with robust standard errors. We then calculated the average marginal effect (AME) [8] of each binary predictor upon the dependent variable by computing the average change in model predictions from when all tweets were assigned a value of *false* for that predictor to when all tweets were assigned a value of *true*. We likewise performed z-tests for the AMEs with robust standard errors estimated using the delta method [8]. To evaluate model fit, we computed each model's root-mean-squared error (RMSE) on the fitted data. Since our dependent variables exhibited ranges narrower than their theoretical range, we standardized each AME and RMSE by dividing by the standard deviation of the dependent variable. This allows for the standardized values to be interpreted in relation to the variability of each dependent variable.

User Topic Choices. To find whether people changed *what* they discussed after interacting with an information source, we constructed separate fractional regression models to estimate the aforementioned similarity of a person's choice of hashtags, mentions, or links using several predictors about that user. Our main independent variables in these models were two binary variables: whether the user had interacted with a high- or a *low-credibility* source and whether that interaction occurred via a link share or a tweet *reply*. To examine highly engaged interactions with misinformation, we also considered the resulting inter-action term denoting whether a user *replied* to a *low-credibility* source. As control variables, we included the number of tweets a user sent in the two weeks before interacting with a source, the number of tweets sent in the two weeks afterwards, and the age of a user's account. Like for the tweet-level regression, we performed z-tests for the model coefficients, computed the associated standardized AMEs, and calculated each model's standardized RMSE.

False Discovery Rate Correction. To control for a false discovery rate of five percent, we applied the Benjamini-Hochberg procedure to all generated p-values.

3.4   Limitations

The main limitations of our methods come from restrictions inherent to Twitter data analysis. First, we cannot guarantee we captured the first time each user was exposed to any low- or high-credibility information online. We can only guarantee we found the first (non-deleted) tweet in which a user linked or replied to one of our selected sources. Second, like for all Twitter data, our sample was not representative of all Twitter users and was biased towards very active users of Twitter, since we had to collect several tweets from each user. Both of these limitations mean that we cannot infer causation in our results and that we cannot generalize them to all Twitter users. Finally, we only analyzed link shares and tweet replies, thereby ignoring other types of Twitter interactions.

4   Results

4.1   Tweet Style

Table 4 shows the standardized results of the tweet style analysis. The first results column reveals a few small but significant changes in style after people interacted with *either* low- or high-credibility information. Instead, the effects of the other two independent variables reveal that some users acted in certain ways even before exposure to our selected sources. The second column shows that people who interacted with low-credibility information tended to already write more hateful, less happy, and more abusive tweets even before that interaction. These people also mentioned more racial, political, and religious identities overall. Sim-ilar results in the third column reveal that users who replied to any of our sources also already tended to mention more racial and political identities and write more hateful, sad, and abusive tweets. Interestingly, the effects of the interaction term in the fourth column show that people who *replied* to low-credibility sources tended to already write happier, less abusive tweets. But, they also mentioned more political identities and wrote angrier tweets.

The remaining results suggest only a few small exposure effects. The fifth results column only shows a small increase in explicit word use following interac-tions with low-credibility sources. Similarly, the sixth column shows that tweets

Table 4. The standardized AMEs from the tweet style models. Each row represents a separate model for which only the standardized RMSE and non-control predictors are shown. Significance: *** for $p < 0.001$, ** for $p < 0.01$, * for $p < 0.05$, · for $p \geq 0.05$.

Dependent variable	After interaction	Interacted with low-credibility	Interacted via reply	Replied to low-cred.	After low-cred.	After reply	After reply to low-cred.	Fit RMSE
% Happy	·	−0.050***	−0.021***	0.039***	·	·	−0.016*	1.019
% Sad	·		0.023***					1.041
% Fearful	·		0.022***					1.001
% Disgustful	−0.006*	−0.013***	0.012**	0.024***				1.025
% Angry	0.011***	·		0.020**				1.054
% Expletives	·	·	0.033***	·	0.016*	0.025***	−0.027***	1.045
% Abusive	−0.010**	0.027***	0.090***	−0.016**				1.020
% Race/Nationality	·	0.021***	0.014**	−0.023***		−0.023***	0.038***	1.038
% Political	0.007*	0.016***	0.013**	0.024***				1.043
% Gender	·	−0.066***	0.026***	−0.023***			0.020*	1.019
% Religion	·	0.030***		−0.020***			·	1.084
Hate Score	−0.007*	0.009**	0.067***	·			0.017*	0.914

Table 5. The standardized AMEs from the topic choice models. Each row represents a separate model for which only the standardized RMSE and non-control predictors are shown. Significance: *** for $p < 0.001$, ** for $p < 0.01$, * for $p < 0.05$, · for $p \geq 0.05$.

Dependent variable	Interacted with low-credibility	Interacted via reply	Replied to low-cred.	Fit RMSE
Hashtags similarity	−0.337***	−0.478***	0.197***	0.952
Mentions similarity	−0.051*	·	0.232***	0.943
Link domains similarity	−0.113***	−0.260***	0.166***	0.949

sent after replying to any source also tended to contain slightly more expletives (and slightly fewer racial identities). The largest exposure effects are instead found for tweets coming after replying to low-credibility sources: the seventh column shows that people tended to be more hateful and mention more political and gender identities after highly engaged interactions with misinformation.

Overall, the regression results show that the models fit our dependent variables within approximately one standard deviation on average. All the effect sizes of our independent variables on the stylistic properties of tweets were exceedingly small, with none of the variables changing the tested properties by even one tenth of one standard deviation. This result may be due to our analysis of only one interaction per user and matches the small effect sizes reported in a study of singular exposures to COVID-19 misinformation [7].

4.2 User Topic Choices

Table 5 shows the standardized results of the user topic analysis. The first results column shows that after interacting with low-credibility sources, people changed their hashtag choices significantly more than those who had interacted with a high-credibility source. People interacting with untrustworthy information also changed the sites they linked to and the people they mentioned in their tweets significantly more than people exposed to trustworthy information. Meanwhile, the second column reveals that people replying to information sources changed their hashtag and link choices to greater degrees than people who simply shared links to such sources, and the magnitude of this difference was even larger than the difference between interacting with low- versus high-credibility sources.

Interestingly, the third column shows that people who replied to low-credibility sources (rather than simply any source) changed their topic choices *less* than other users, implying that they were more likely than other people to continue discussing what they had already been discussing. This may be evidence of a pre-existing interest in topics relevant to misinformation amongst these highly engaged interactors, but further research on this result is warranted.

Like for the tweet style analysis, our models fit users' topic similarities within approximately one standard deviation. However, the magnitudes of the relationships between interactions with information sources and changes in topic choices were much larger than the extremely small relationships with tweet style.

5   Discussion

By highlighting the importance of *how* a person interacts with misinformation for determining its impact, our analysis has identified a factor that is missing from much misinformation research. For example, though prior work investigated the effect of source credibility on intentions to share information, a user's level of engagement with that information was not considered [18]. In studying the propensities towards hate speech of Italian YouTube commenters loyal to either reliable or unreliable COVID-19 content, Cinelli *et al.* similarly did not analyze interactions beyond commenting on videos [6]. Lastly, an ethnographic study's theoretical model for how misinformation might intensify polarization likewise neglects to account for a person's method of interaction with misinformation [1].

Our findings also begin to bridge the gap between past research on the behavioral effects of misinformation. First, our analysis suggests that Twitter users interacting with misinformation may be predisposed to be slightly more hateful. Though this is not the same kind of predisposition as the link between greater interest in news and politics and more exposure to misinformation [9,10], our findings nevertheless support the idea that people who interact with misinformation exhibit certain predispositions that separate them from others. Second, our findings point to small changes in behavior following highly engaged interactions with misinformation, thereby partially supporting studies that have identified behavioral effects from misinformation [7,11,12,21]. However, the small effect sizes we detected do not fit claims that misinformation can sway votes [3,11,21].

It therefore appears that survey and lab studies could be over-estimating the behavioral effects of misinformation. Like Guess *et al.* commented, the study concluding that misinformation had a significant effect on American voter behavior in 2016 [11] relied on self-reporting of voting behavior [10], which may not have always been accurate. In their study detecting changes in the intentions of French voters, Barrera *et al.* even acknowledged that effects on voting *intentions* are generally acknowledged to be stronger than effects on actual voting [3]. Beyond that, lab environments and other "artificial" means of exposing people to false stories can make study participants pay more attention to that misinformation than they normally would "in the wild". The authors of the study on viewers of political debates even cautioned that their work may have over-estimated the resulting effects on participants' beliefs because the study environment may have made them watch the debates more attentively [13].

Moreover, the known predisposition of certain groups to view more misinformation suggests that self-selection may be interfering with several studies. Two of the voting surveys found a relationship between voter choice and *belief* in (not mere interaction with) misinformation [11,21]. Actual belief in false stories may come from deeper engagement with such narratives [5], just as artificially attentive exposure may cause greater contemplation of misinformation. The study of Italian election results even concluded that the causal effect of misinformation represented less than half of the correlation between misinformation exposure and populist voting, with the rest coming from the self-selection of misinformation reaching people who would have voted for populist candidates anyway [5].

Our observation of a slight increase in hatefulness amongst more engaged interactors with misinformation evinces the idea that detecting the behavioral effects of misinformation depends on the level of engagement of the population studied. This distinction likely also explains why our analysis detected some small changes in Twitter user behavior whereas Bail *et al.* [2] did not. Though Bail *et al.* examined the less variable characteristic of personal ideology [2] rather than tweet style or topic choice, they also discriminated between different sets of Twitter interactions than we did. In investigating the difference between direct and indirect interactions with Russian-controlled accounts, Bail *et al.* considered both retweeting and replying to relevant tweets as direct interactions [2]. Our work therefore studied the difference between two direct forms of interaction: tweeting or retweeting links and replying to tweets. Our findings suggest that finer categorization of interaction types may have revealed behavioral changes following highly engaged interactions with Russian-controlled accounts.

Finally, our work also suggests that people interacting with misinformation change *what* they discuss more than *how* they discuss things. This fits with the finding that bots can redirect the focus of online hate [19], suggesting that this distinction may lie at the heart of how misinformation impacts society.

6   Conclusions

Our analysis of tweets before and after people's first known interactions with low- and high-credibility sources of information has revealed a link between a person's level of engagement with misinformation and future changes in personal behavior. Users who interacted with low-credibility sources tended to slightly increase their hatefulness after replying to these sources, not after simply sharing links to such sources. By further finding that users who interacted with misinformation were already slightly more hateful before this exposure, our work also appears to reconcile the seemingly conflicting conclusions of prior research on the behavioral effects of misinformation. Finally, our detection of greater change in people's topic choices rather than in their tweet style points to a significant mode by which misinformation can affect society at large.

Acknowledgements. This work was supported by the Center for Informed Democracy and Social Cybersecurity with funding from the Knight Foundation and Cognizant. Additional support was given by the Center for Computational Analysis of Social and Organizational Systems. The views and conclusions contained herein belong to the authors and should not be interpreted as representing the official policies of the Knight Foundation, Cognizant, or the U.S. government.

References

1. Au, C.H., Ho, K.K.W., Chiu, D.K.W.: The role of online misinformation and fake news in ideological polarization: barriers, catalysts, and implications. Inf. Syst. Front. 1–24 (2021). https://doi.org/10.1007/s10796-021-10133-9
2. Bail, C.A., et al.: Assessing the Russian internet research agency's impact on the political attitudes and behaviors of American twitter users in late 2017. Proc. Nat. Acad. Sci. **117**(1), 243–250 (2019)
3. Barrera, O., Guriev, S., Henry, E., Zhuravskaya, E.: Facts, alternative facts, and fact checking in times of post-truth politics. J. Public Econ. **182**, 104123 (2020)
4. Beskow, D., Carley, K.: Bot-hunter: a tiered approach to detecting & characterizing automated activity on Twitter. In: 2018 International Conference on Social Computing, Behavioral-Cultural Modeling, & Prediction and Behavior Representation in Modeling and Simulation, SBP-BRiMS (2018)
5. Cantarella, M., Fraccaroli, N., Volpe, R.: Does fake news affect voting behaviour? CEIS Working Paper No. 493 (2020)
6. Cinelli, M., Pelicon, A., Mozetič, I., Quattrociocchi, W., Novak, P.K., Zollo, F.: Dynamics of online hate and misinformation. Sci. Rep. **11**, 22083 (2021)
7. Greene, C.M., Murphy, G.: Quantifying the effects of fake news on behavior: evidence from a study of COVID-19 misinformation. J. Exp. Psychol. Appl. **27**(4), 773–784 (2021)
8. Greene, W.: Econometric Analysis, 7th edn. Pearson, Boston (2012)
9. Grinberg, N., Joseph, K., Friedland, L., Swire-Thompson, B., Lazer, D.: Fake news on twitter during the 2016 U.S. presidential election. Science **363**(6425), 374–378 (2019)
10. Guess, A.M., Nyhan, B., Reifler, J.: Exposure to untrustworthy websites in the 2016 US election. Nat. Hum. Behav. **4**, 472–480 (2020)
11. Gunther, R., Beck, P.A., Nisbet, E.C.: "Fake news" and the defection of 2012 Obama voters in the 2016 presidential election. Electoral Stud. **61**, 102030 (2019)
12. Loomba, S., de Figueiredo, A., Piatek, S.J., de Graaf, K., Larson, H.J.: Measuring the impact of COVID-19 vaccine misinformation on vaccination intent in the UK and USA. Nat. Hum. Behav. **5**, 337–348 (2021)
13. Maurer, M., Reinemann, C.: Learning versus knowing: effects of misinformation in televised debates. Commun. Res. **33**(6), 489–506 (2006)

14. Media Bias/Fact Check. https://mediabiasfactcheck.com
15. Netanomics: NetMapper (2021). https://netanomics.com/netmapper/
16. Ng, L.H.X., Robertson, D.C., Carley, K.M.: Stabilizing a supervised bot detection algorithm: how much data is needed for consistent predictions? Online Soc. Netw. Media **28**(1), 100198 (2022)
17. Ramalho, E., Ramalho, J., Murteira, J.: Alternative estimating and testing empirical strategies for fractional regression models. J. Econ. Surv. **25**(1), 19–68 (2011)
18. Suntwal, S., Brown, S.A., Patton, M.W.: How does information spread? a study of true and fake news. In: Proceedings of the 53rd Hawaii International Conference on System Sciences (2020)
19. Uyheng, J., Bellutta, D., Carley, K.M.: Bots amplify and redirect hate speech in online discourse about racism during the COVID-19 pandemic. Soc. Media Soc. **8**(3) (2022). https://doi.org/10.1177/20563051221104749
20. Uyheng, J., Carley, K.M.: Bots and online hate during the COVID-19 pandemic: case studies in the United States and the Philippines. J. Comput. Soc. Sci. **3**, 445–468 (2020)
21. Zimmermann, F., Kohring, M.: Mistrust, disinforming news, and vote choice: a panel survey on the origins and consequences of believing disinformation in the 2017 German parliamentary election. Polit. Commun. **37**(2), 215–237 (2020)

#WhoDefinesDemocracy: Analysis on a 2021 Chinese Messaging Campaign

Charity S. Jacobs[(✉)] and Kathleen M. Carley

CASOS, Institute for Software Research Carnegie Mellon University,
Pittsburgh, PA 15213, USA
{csking,carley}@andrew.cmu.edu

Abstract. China has embraced the social media domain to promote pro-Chinese narratives and stories in recent years. However, China has increasingly been accused of launching information operations using methods such as bot activity, puppet accounts and other forms of inauthentic activity to amplify pro-Chinese messaging. This paper provides a comprehensive network analysis characterization of the hashtag influence campaign China promoted against the US-hosted Summit on Democracy in December 2021, in addition to methods to identify different types of actors within this type of influence campaign.

Keywords: Chinese influence operations · Bots · Network Analysis

1 Introduction

Social media is a critical domain for connecting and promoting ideas and discussion at the international level. China is a relative newcomer to the world of public relations and messaging to the international community, passing domestic legislature as recently as 2007 to increase the country's discourse power by creating a Chinese-controlled media platform Xinhua, capable of shaping narratives about China at the global level [3]. Increasingly, Chinese Communist Party (CCP) officials are using western social media platforms to defend Chinese national interests. These official accounts are not by themselves unique from any other country's use of social media, but have been used to spread disinformation and conspiracy theories such as the origins of COVID-19 [7] and human rights abuse in Xinjiang [8].

Recent research has shown China utilizes Twitter messaging to target western audiences and generally refrains from the use of memes that often take on

This work was supported in part by the Knight Foundation and the Office of Naval Research grant Minerva-Multi-Level Models of Covert Online Information Campaigns (N00014-21-1-2765). Additional support was provided by the Center for Computational Analysis of Social and Organizational Systems (CASOS) at Carnegie Mellon University. The views and conclusions contained in this document are those of the authors and should not be interpreted as representing the official policies, either expressed or implied, of the Knight Foundation, Office of Naval Research, or the U.S. Government.

R. Thomson et al. (Eds.): SBP-BRiMS 2022, LNCS 13558, pp. 90–100, 2022.
https://doi.org/10.1007/978-3-031-17114-7_9

a life of their own [2]. These campaigns are focused on promoting pro-China rhetoric instead of content that destabilizes targeted areas. China has also used extensive bot activity to amplify messaging, such as positive coverage for the 2022 Olympics [5]. Regional analysis on the use of bots has shown that this type of inauthentic activity can perform specific roles within an information campaign [9]. Similar research on Chinese diplomatic Twitter accounts underlined China's centralized censorship policies, but did not explore other elements of information diffusion within the network beyond the diplomatic accounts themselves [4].

The United States hosted a 2021 Summit on Democracy to address democracy-related challenges throughout the world. In response, Chinese state-sponsored Twitter accounts began a hashtag campaign around this event with anti-US sentiment. This particular event presents a time-constrained influence campaign with extensive state-sponsored support. This paper presents novel research on the following research questions to understand how agents within a CCP information campaign propagate narratives using both official state-sponsored accounts, bots, and human influencer accounts:

1. What is the nature of inauthentic and authentic accounts within this network?
2. How is information diffused through a Chinese State-Sponsored campaign?

2 Data and Methodology

2.1 Data Collection and Processing

Twitter networks consist of users and the connections that occur when a user retweets, mentions, or reply to each other. Our data collection using hashtags targets information campaigns that use Twitter's algorithmic approach towards trending topics, which are identified and spread through users by the use of a hashtag sign preceding a topic. Using the Twitter V2 API, we collected tweets using the hashtags #WhoDefinesDemocracy and #WhatisDemocracy, resulting in the collection of 7,798 tweets from September 1 - December 31, 2021. Our second dataset is comprised of over 200 Twitter handles of official Chinese-government affiliated Twitter accounts to include government official, government organization, and media accounts. A node in our dataset may be a Twitter agent or user, hashtag, tweet, or URL. This dataset provided 16 different meta-networks with 12,507 nodes, 79,898 edges, graph density of .0002 and a Newman Modularity score of .453, indicating a high community structure.

Twitter uses three labels for the accounts within our secondary dataset; China Government Official, China Government Organization, or China State-Affiliated Media. However, Twitter currently only labels government accounts that are heavily involved in geopolitics, state-affiliated, or are high profile in 22 countries. Due to the lack of labels across many of our state-sponsored accounts, we report the Twitter label metrics within the Results section for transparency, but make a distinction that our definition of Chinese state-sponsored accounts are any official government accounts and any Chinese media outlets.

2.2   Methods

The analytic workflow for this paper provides both user and network trends within an information campaign by a) labeling Twitter accounts for three different groups; bots, state-sponsored accounts, and all other accounts, b) conducting network analysis to understand network diffusion and echo-chamber qualities between the groups and c) dynamically analyzing the network over three periods to determine how key actors shift or persist.

Agent Labeling. We use a tier-based machine-learning tool Bothunter that classifies Twitter agents as bots using metadata and other account features [1]. To increase certainty around our bot classification for each Twitter account, we use the recommended bot probability score of .7 at which the bot classification label is most stable from flipping from one class to the other for outlying bot activity [6]. Our secondary dataset of Chinese state-sponsored accounts provides a label for agent nodes to determine which parts of our social network are state-sponsored or primarily amplify state-sponsored accounts.

Network Analysis and Echo Chambers. Using the network analysis and visualization software ORA, we use network analysis measurements such as in-degree and out-degree centralities that highlight agents disseminating versus receiving information within the network. For Twitter data, a user with high In-Degree Centrality is generally characterized with high retweet, reply, and quote frequency, whereas a user with high Out-Degree Centrality will have tweets, replies, or quotes that are frequently shared by other users. We also use community structure metrics via an E/I index; a ratio of a Twitter user's internal and external links. We generate these values based on an agent's behavior within a Leiden cluster group to indicate whether an actor is part of an echo-chamber in which beliefs are amplified within a group. We use the Leiden algorithm to generate these clusters based on an efficient local moving heuristic for identifying high modularity communities [10]. We use a non-parametric Kruskal-Wallis test to determine if there is a difference in average E/I index between the three actor groups based on an agent's Leiden group clustering.

Dynamic Network Analysis. Lastly, we analyze the campaign across three periods of equal tweet density to understand how key actors and information diffusion changed throughout the duration of this campaign. This will allow us to better understand the interaction of key actors to include state-sponsored accounts, bots and other accounts across the duration of the campaign.

3   Results

Initial analysis revealed this campaign was predominantly comprised of retweets, with approximately 85% of all tweets disseminated within this network as retweets. Additionally, 54% of all tweets (original and retweets) were created by bot accounts. This section covers the Twitter language metadata analysis of the campaign and the nature of the tweets and messaging to understand bot and state-sponsored account functions for information diffusion.

Fig. 1. Top Retweets within dataset, exhibiting anti-US sentiment

3.1   Campaign Overview

The hashtags #whodefinesdemocracy and #whatisdemocracy were popularized in a 2020 15-part Twitter post by a Chinese influencer on "Chinese-style Democracy" and its merits over western democracy. Prior to November 1, 2021, there were approximately 10 instances of the hashtags, all unrelated to the Democracy Summit. Chinese Diplomat to Lebanon Cao Yi posted five times in October prior to the beginning of the campaign.

The bulk of the campaign occurred within the first two weeks of December before the Democracy Summit, accounting for almost 90% of the total tweets. Using the tweet-level language metadata tags, we found 21 different languages represented in this dataset (see Table 1). The multilingual tweets indicate language diffusion targeting different populations. However, approximately 83% of our tweets are in English, indicating a clear intent to communicate to western and English-speaking audiences.

The top ten retweeted tweets accounts for nearly 25% of all tweets within our network. Of these selected tweets, three tweets discussed Chinese-style democracy and its merits in addition to promoting a Chinese-sponsored "Dialogue on Democracy" event on Chinese-style democracy. The other seven tweets contained anti-US sentiment, discussing US domestic issues such as wealth disparity, gun

Table 1. Top languages and twitter actor ratios in dataset

Language	# Tweets	% Chinese state-sponsored	% Tweets by bots
English	6520	8.2	56.6
Undetermined	324	13.5	57.1
Chinese	219	2.7	47.5
Spanish	195	18.9	51.7
Arabic	140	21.4	29.3
French	126	17.5	52.4
Russian	94	15.9	42.6

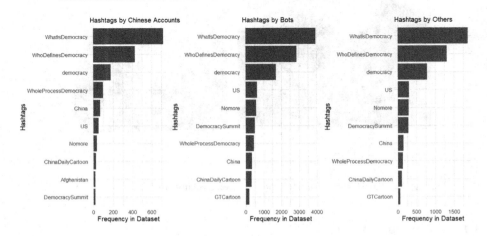

Fig. 2. Comparison of top Hashtags shared by each group.

violence, Black Lives Matter and racism to de-legitimize the United States (see Fig. 1). Lastly, out of the ten top tweets, only one was not created by a state-sponsored account but rather a Chinese youth outreach group.

There is extremely high correlation in hashtags used between the three different groups, indicating that bots, state-accounts and all other accounts are promoting the same messaging (see Fig. 2). By analyzing the top twenty hashtags, we found a perfect correlation in hashtags between Chinese Accounts and "Other" accounts and a .9 correlation between Chinese and Bot accounts. All three groups had the same seven hashtags that are the most widely used with the highest in-degree centrality, indicating this network contains homophilous users that promote similar content.

3.2 State-Sponsored Activity and Bot Amplification

There are 121 state-sponsored accounts within this network, accounting for approximately 3% of user accounts, but nearly half of all original tweets. These accounts also had a 70% rate of being verified through Twitter. However, we discovered that only 17 accounts are labeled as a China Government Official or Organization, 18 accounts are labeled as state-affiliated media, and the remaining 86 accounts had no Twitter label although the account profiles indicated they were either Chinese Embassy, Ambassador, or other official government position accounts.

Of the 17 government accounts, the Chinese Ambassadors to Cuba, France, Pakistan, India, Canada, the United Kingdom, the United States, and Italy, in addition to international organizations such as the EU, UN, and ASEAN all have labels. Twitter also labels the most active and verified accounts such as China Spokepeople Lijian Zhao, Hua Chunying, and the Ministry of Foreign Affairs accounts. Twitter did not label any diplomatic accounts to African or South American countries, indicating that Twitter's initial labeling methodology is centered on a western audience. For this reason, this paper uses the term "state-sponsored" to cover all 121 accounts within this dataset to include state-affiliated media sites and both labeled and unlabeled government accounts. The Chinese state-sponsored accounts within the network accounted for nearly 50% of original Twitter messages (see Table 2). Conversely, bot automation accounted for a smaller subset of original tweets, but the majority of retweets.

Table 2. Twitter Actor description for tweets and retweets

Actor	# Accounts	% Verified accounts	% Original tweets	% Retweets
Chinese state-sponsored	121	70	48.49	3.14
Bots activity	2038	0	16.19	61.42
Other	1420	2.1	34.6	35.44

Network Overview. A visual inspection of our network shows state-sponsored accounts at the center of Twitter user hubs (see Fig. 3). This network visualization supports the activity break-down in Table 2 pertaining to bot automation accounting for the bulk of retweet activity and indicates that the state-sponsored accounts are the main influential actors within this network whereas the bot accounts are primarily not connected to other influential nodes.

Bots and State-Sponsored accounts maintain distinct network properties within this campaign. When we separate total degree centrality into in-degree and out-degree centrality, the state-sponsored accounts generally have higher out-degree centrality paired with a lower in-degree centrality. Our dataset is filled with outliers both for bot accounts and state-sponsored accounts that create long tails within our distributions, such as the top bot account which has the highest in-degree centrality of all accounts within the datset. Our bot retweet distribution has a long tail, with 2,268 retweets or one-third of all retweets coming from Twitter accounts that only retweeted once. This distribution stretches until we hit the outlier accounts for the top two accounts with 70 and 107 retweets.

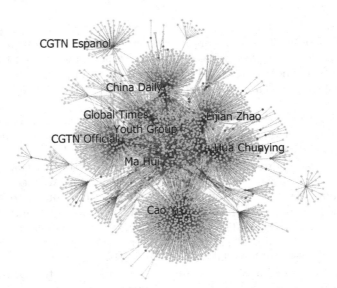

Fig. 3. Agent x Agent Communication Network of the Twitter users, with the top "Superspreaders" labeled. Red nodes are Chinese state-sponsored accounts, green nodes are bots, and gray nodes are all other nodes. (Color figure online)

Similar to the bot accounts, a small amount of State-Sponsored accounts makes up the bulk of original tweets. Of the 711 original Chinese state-sponsored tweets, approximately 50% are from just ten accounts. Additionally, the top ten "Superspreaders" labeled in Fig. 3, or accounts with high out-degree centrality have 5,473 retweets, or account for over 70% of all tweets in this network, indicating clear centralized messaging from a small number of accounts.

Difference in Degree Distributions. If we examine the distributions for indegree and out-degree centrality between our Bot, State-Sponsored Accounts and Other accounts in Fig. 4, the differences are clear regarding who is promoting messages and who is receiving and re-amplifying those messages. For out-degree centrality, the state-sponsored accounts have a wider interquartile range than bots and other accounts, with extreme outliers skewing within the 4th quartile. The outlying Twitter account within the "Other" category is the Chinese Youth group, which we have now seen a few times both as the creator of one of the most widely retweeted messages and a Superspreader in Fig. 3. This account behaves like a state-sponsored account due to its high out-degree centrality and amplification by both bot and other accounts. We see this same trend to a lesser degree regarding in-degree centrality, where bots have many more accounts above the interquartile range than the other two types of accounts with a large skew within the last quartile.

Difference in Echo-Chamber Qualities. We conducted a non-parametric Kruskal-Wallis test to determine if the E/I index scores for Bots, State-

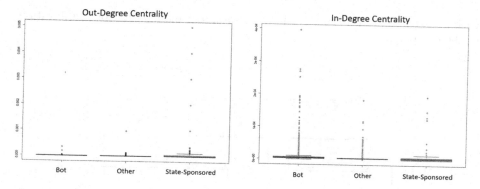

Fig. 4. In-Degree and Out-Degree distributions for State-Sponsored, Bot and Other accounts using the Agent x Agent Communication Network of the Twitter users.

Sponsored, and all other accounts are from the same distribution or if there is on average a difference in scores. We obtained a p-value $< 2.2e-16$, indicating a very statistically significant conclusion that there is a difference in average E/I index scores across the three groups. By analyzing the plot in Fig. 5, we can determine State-Actor accounts have a much lower mean value for E/I index scores, indicating that on average, these accounts participate in communities that are more prone to inner dialogue with other group members. Additionally with the mean E/I index for Bots and Other accounts within the negative value range, we can conclude this information campaign skews more towards an echo chamber environment.

Dynamic Network Analysis. We analyzed how key actors within the network shift throughout the campaign. Across the periods, top out-degree centrality accounts are dominated by state-sponsored accounts, indicating that state-sponsored accounts controlled the messaging. There was considerable consistency in the state-sponsored accounts that maintained a high volume of tweets at least one median above the average for the network across all three periods to include Cao Yi, Hua Chunying, and media account Global Times. The one account not state-sponsored is the China Youth Studio account which was active for the first two periods. Additionally, multilingual media accounts such as CGTN Arabic and CGTN Espanol were active in the second and third periods. This second period also had high out-degree centralities for the accounts to Kenya, Uganda, Cuba and the United States. Diplomatic accounts were not prominent in the third period except for the Cuban Ambassador, mainly dominated by Chinese media outlets and Spokesperson accounts.

Although top accounts for in-degree centrality are primarily bot accounts, there were two state-sponsored accounts that were in the top in-degree category one standard deviation above the mean; Diplomat Cao Yi and the spokesperson account to the United Nations. Cao Yi's account is also the only state-sponsored account with both high in-degree and out-degree centrality measures. This account was the first account to begin tweeting prior to the campaign, indicating that it played a crucial role in maintaining momentum for the duration of the campaign.

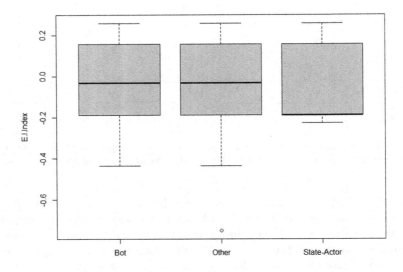

Fig. 5. Inter-quartile distribution of E/I Index scores across groups

3.3 Who Are the "Others" in This Network?

The labeling process leaves approximately 40% of accounts as "Other", indicating they are neither a state-sponsored account nor do they have a bot probability past the .7 threshold (see Table 2). This section seeks to characterize this third group within the network that is responsible for roughly 35% of both original tweets and retweets. Due to only 125 accounts in this category contributing to original tweets, we conducted exploration on this subset to understand the nature of these accounts. We manually annotated the accounts and discovered the tweets fell into approximately three different categories; Pro-China with 132 tweets from 68 accounts, Anti-China with 30 tweets from 20 accounts, and 47 unrelated tweets from 37 accounts. The majority of the Anti-China tweets appeared to be from US-based accounts exhibiting right-wing, anti-Chinese rhetoric. The "unrelated" category contained tweets not related to China's campaign. For example, there were many tweets regarding Myanmar and Nagaland in India that were not associated to the Summit on Democracy.

Pro-China accounts were either state-sponsored accounts that we did not have in our secondary dataset (mislabeled "Other"), Chinese associations, influencers and regular Twitter users. The top accounts in the Pro-China group included the aforementioned Chinese youth group in addition to one more student group with 23 and 12 tweets respectively. There were 8 additional accounts that were labeled by Twitter as either a China government organization or Chinese state-affiliated media, two Russia government organization accounts and one Cuban government account. For individual accounts that could be typically classified as "influencer" accounts, there were 20 accounts by Chinese individuals that typically retweeted many state-sponsored tweets, in addition to about 14 accounts by Twitter users in Ethiopia. This may indicate that apart from potential Chinese diaspora Twitter users, there is also a small contingent of users from other countries (particularly in Africa) participating.

4   Conclusion

This work analyzed a limited information campaign by the Chinese government around the 2021 Democracy Summit, concluding key differences in network measures around State-Sponsored accounts, bots and all other accounts in addition to identifying influencer accounts that behave like state-sponsored accounts. This campaign exhibited strong centralized control of the narrative propagation by select CCP spokespeople and news agencies to promote a distinctly anti-US campaign, with message dissemination to different target populations. A limitation to consider is that our state-sponsored accounts may not capture the entire ground truth as our supplementary data on state-sponsored Twitter accounts is manually created and likely under-capturing the extent of official state-sponsored accounts within the network.

References

1. Beskow, D.M., Carley, K.M.: Bot-hunter: a tiered approach to detecting & characterizing automated activity on twitter. In: Conference Paper. SBP-BRiMS: International Conference on Social Computing, Behavioral-Cultural Modeling and Prediction and Behavior Representation in Modeling and Simulation, vol. 3, p. 3 (2018)
2. Beskow, D.M., Carley, K.M.: Characterization and comparison of Russian and Chinese disinformation campaigns. In: Shu, K., Wang, S., Lee, D., Liu, H. (eds.) Disinformation, Misinformation, and Fake News in Social Media. LNSN, pp. 63–81. Springer, Cham (2020). https://doi.org/10.1007/978-3-030-42699-6_4
3. DiResta, R., Goldstein, J.A.: China's fake twitter accounts are tweeting into the void. Foreign Policy (2021)
4. Huang, Z.A., Wang, R.: Building a network to "tell china stories well": Chinese diplomatic communication strategies on twitter. Int. J. Commun. **13**, 24 (2019)
5. Myers, S.L., Mozur, P., Kao, J.: How Bots and Fake Accounts Push China's Vision of Winter Olympic Wonderland. ProPublica (2022)
6. Ng, L.H.X., Robertson, D.C., Carley, K.M.: Stabilizing a supervised bot detection algorithm: how much data is needed for consistent predictions? Online Soc. Networks Media" **28**, 100198 (2022)
7. Schafer, B.: China Fires Back at Biden with Conspiracy Theories About Maryland Lab. Foreign Policy (2021)
8. TwitterSafety: Disclosing state-linked information operations we've removed (2021). https://blog.twitter.com/en_us/topics/company/2021/disclosing-state-linked-information-operations-we-ve-removed

9. Uyheng, J., Carley, K.M.: Characterizing bot networks on twitter: an empirical analysis of contentious issues in the Asia-Pacific. In: Thomson, R., Bisgin, H., Dancy, C., Hyder, A. (eds.) SBP-BRiMS 2019. LNCS, vol. 11549, pp. 153–162. Springer, Cham (2019). https://doi.org/10.1007/978-3-030-21741-9_16
10. Waltman, L., van Eck, N.J.: A smart local moving algorithm for large-scale modularity-based community detection. Eur. Phys. J. B **86**(11), 1–14 (2013). https://doi.org/10.1140/epjb/e2013-40829-0

Dapping into the Fediverse: Analyzing What's Trending on Mastodon Social

Samer Al-khateeb[✉]

Department of Computer Science, Design and Journalism, Creighton University, Omaha, NE 68178, USA
sameral-khateeb1@creighton.edu

Abstract. Social media has changed the way we consume information daily. Most social media sites are centralized, meaning they are owned by a single entity, e.g., Facebook, Twitter, and YouTube. However, recently other forms of social media sites known as decentralized social networks are getting popular. These platforms are understudied. Hence in this exploratory research, one of the most prominent decentralized social platforms known as Mastodon Social has been studied. A review of what others have focused on when it comes to studying decentralized social networks has been conducted. Scripts to collect data from Mastodon Social are shared and analyses of the collected data with many valuable insights are provided.

Keywords: Mastodon Social · Federated networks · Decentralized social networks · Toxicity analysis · Sentiments analysis · Social network analysis · Bots

1 Introduction

Social media is affecting our daily life tremendously. Some argue it is affecting our life positively, while others argue, it is affecting our life negatively. No matter which side of the coin you pick, social media is affecting the way we consume information (e.g., reading a newspaper vs. reading a news article posted on social media), elect our president (e.g., could motivate you to vote for a specific presidential candidate), or protest to change a government or a regime (e.g., the Arab Spring).

The majority of the known social media sites, e.g., Facebook, YouTube, and Twitter, are owned by a single entity. However, with the advancements in information technology, nowadays, we have social media platforms that are not owned by big tech and instead are owned by the people. These social networks are decentralized networks aka federated networks. A federated network is a network of multiple independent and interconnected servers also known as the Fediverse (short for Federated Universe). It is used for social networking and other activities. It allows users to send and receive messages across platforms/servers/instances using federated/open protocols, e.g., ActivityPub [1] and OStatus [2]. Federated networks are unmoderated and do not have a central authority like Facebook or Twitter. This provides users more freedom (no censorship), personal data ownership, and control over the content generated, e.g., no one can remove or modify content other than the user who created it. Federated networks also provide more privacy to users because it allows them to create accounts without having to link these accounts to real identity via emails or phone numbers which prevent showing users targeted advertisements. Finally, these networks use public-key encryption to protect users' data which makes it more secure because it does not depend on the social media company's security measures [3].

In this research, I investigate one of the most prominent decentralized social networks known as *Mastodon Social*. Other examples of Federated networks are Steemit (social blogging platform, https://steemit.com), DTube (decentralized video platform, https://d.tube) [3], PeerTube (a video sharing site, https://joinpeertube.org), Hubzilla (a platform to create interconnected instances, https://hubzilla.org/) [2], Misskey (microblogging platform, https://join.misskey.page/en-US/), and Pixelfed (image sharing platform, https://pixelfed.social).

Mastodon Social (https://joinmastodon.org) is a microblogging platform (the same category as Twitter but allows 500 characters instead of Twitter's 280 characters limit) first released on March 16, 2016, with a stable release on May 26, 2022 [4]. Currently, it has 4.4M active users, these users can choose from a list of 119 communities (each community set its own policies) that are divided into 10 categories. These categories are General (43 communities), Regional (29), Technology (19), LGBQT+(8), Activism (5), Art (5), Gaming (4), Furry (3), Music (2), and Food (1) [5]. Users on Mastodon Social can pretty much do what users on Twitter can do, e.g., they can post a "Toot", send a direct message, join a list, etc. Mastodon Social is not owned or operated by a single organization like Facebook or Twitter. Many organizations operate it. Its feed is chronological (non-algorithmic) and ads-free, so you can choose what you want to see.

Decentralized social networks, in general, and Mastodon Social, in particular, are understudied. These platforms provide great benefits to their users as stated above, however, they also can be used by malicious actors to do harmful or deviant activities in cyberspace, physical space, or cybernetic space. So, in this research, I am studying the current ecology of Mastodon Social by examining the trending hashtags, the content of the posts that contain these trending hashtags, and the users whose posts become trending. This research provides insightful findings on Mastodon's Social ecology and its users' behaviors. This is accomplished by seeking an answer to the following research questions:

RQ1: What makes a hashtag trend on Mastodon Social?
RQ2: What is the effect of social bots on making a hashtag trend?
RQ3: Is Mastodon Social used in a specific region or used globally? and what are the sentiment and toxicity scores of the posts with trending hashtags?
RQ4: What is the user sharing behavior on Mastodon Social?

The rest of the article proceeds as the following. Section 2 provides a brief review of the literature related to decentralized networks and Mastodon Social. Section 3 explains the methodology followed to collect the data, analyze it, and visualize the results. Section 4 provides the research findings. Section 5 concludes the study with possible future research directions.

2 Literature Review

Social networks have been studied and analyzed in various disciplines such as social science, physics, and computer science. Therefore, in this paper, I focus on reviewing the related research that has been done on decentralized social networks in general and on Mastodon Social in particular. Most of the research conducted on Mastodon Social focused on the structure of the system and its durability; the distribution of users and Toots on instances; the distribution of instances on hosting services or geographic locations; and the release of data about the users, the platform, and Toots to the public. Almost no work focuses on studying what is going on in the platform, in other words, analyzing the content of the toots, the user's type and behaviors, and a bipartite graph.

Research conducted by Raman et al. [2] highlighted the challenges that face Decentralized Web platforms such as Mastodon, PeerTube, and Hubzilla. These challenges are all related to the two key innovations that Decentralized Web platforms depend on. The first concept is *"instance"* which enables anybody to set up their server and people can sign-up to use these servers. The second concept is *"federation"* which enables users to interact across instances/servers [2].

In addition to that, two articles published by Zignani et al. focused on studying Mastodon Social content and social graph growth. In the first research article [6], he focused on studying the inappropriate content shared on Mastodon Social. The author released a dataset containing all public inappropriate English posts (more than 5 million Toots) and presented some statistics about the inappropriate posts' production (e.g., metadata of the servers or instances that share these posts) and characteristics of the textual content (e.g., comparing the length of posts/Toots that deemed "appropriate" and "inappropriate" by the content creator) [6]. The second research was conducted by Zignani et al. [7] focused on studying the growth of followership of Mastodon users (i.e., the social graph). The authors briefly compared Mastodon to other social media platforms (e.g., Twitter) in terms of data confidentiality policies and the effect of recommendation algorithms on other social media platforms. They also released a dataset that contains information about the users and their connections/links/edges, their platform usage, and information about the instances/servers, e.g., the location of these instances and topics allowed per community, among other metadata. Finally, research conducted by Shaw [1] addressed the pros and cons of Mastodon Social by comparing it to the most popular microblogging platform, i.e., Twitter.

3 Methodology

This section provides a description of the methodology used to conduct this research.

3.1 Data Collection

Data were collected for 35 days (March 18, 2022–April 21, 2022), for the purpose of conducting this research, using two Python scripts available at (https://github.com/SamerAl-khateeb/MastodonDataCollection.git). The script *getTrendingHashtags.py* is used to get the top 20 daily trending hashtags on Mastodon Social. While the script *getDataByHashtags.py* is used to collect all associated public data using a hashtag or a list of hashtags. Both scripts were run daily to obtain 682 trending hashtags (412 unique because a hashtag or a post can trend for multiple days) and 13,590 public posts (11,601 unique posts and only 290 (2.5%) of them were marked as "inappropriate" by the users who created the post, i.e., a small percentage as found by [6]) that are posted by 3,831 accounts. These accounts have 3,726 unique account usernames because some accounts have the same username but different account IDs and emails. Next, I explain the analysis conducted.

3.2 Data Analysis

Using the data described above the following analyses were conducted:

- *Correlation Analysis*: to determine what makes a hashtag trend on Mastodon Social (i.e., to answer RQ1). I conducted correlation analysis for the trending *hashtag's attributes, Toot's (containing the trending hashtags) attributes*, and the *account's (that posted the trending Toot with the trending hashtag) attributes*.
- *Posting Accounts Analysis*: to understand the effect of social bots on making a hashtag trend (i.e., to answer RQ2). I analyzed the type of the accounts (bot vs. human) to compare the behaviors of both account types.
- *Content Analysis*: to analyze the content of the trending posts (i.e., to answer RQ3). I applied two sets of analyses, 1) sentiments analysis and 2) toxicity analysis. The sentiment of the post was determined using the *Sentiment Analysis API* provided by *DeepAI* (https://deepai.org/machine-learning-model/sentiment-analysis). This API classifies the given text as *Verynegative, Negative, Neutral, Positive*, and *Verypositive*. The text toxicity score was calculated using Google *Perspective API* (https://perspectiveapi.com). The API returns the probability of a post being toxic, i.e., a score between 0 (most likely not a toxic post) and 1 (most likely a toxic post).
- *Network Analysis*: to understand the user sharing behaviors (i.e., to answer RQ4). Three networks were created, namely *hashtags co-occurrence network, user by hashtag* (a bipartite network), and *user by post network* (another bipartite network).

4   Results

The findings in this section are grouped and presented based on the analysis conducted and the research question it's answering.

4.1   Correlation Analysis and RQ1

To answer the first research question, i.e., what makes a hashtag trend on Mastodon Social? I conducted a correlation analysis for the trending hashtag's attributes, Toot's (containing the trending hashtags) attributes, and the accounts (that posted the trending Toot with the trending hashtag) attributes.

For all the trending hashtags attributes, I found a strong correlation (Pearson Correlation (PC) value = 0.81) between the *number of accounts that used the hashtag* and the *number of times a hashtag was used* (hashtag can be used in multiple posts, e.g., two accounts have seven posts using the same hashtag). So, the accounts tend to use the same hashtag repeatedly in their posts.

For all the trending Toots attributes, I found a correlation (PC value = 0.66) between the *postFravouritedCount* and *postReblogsCount,* so if a post is favorited it will most likely be re-blogged (and vice versa). Re-blogged posts tend to receive more replies than favorited posts (*postReblogsCount* and *postRepliesCount* = 0.45, however, *postFravouritedCount* and postRepliesCount = 0.34).

For the account attributes, I found a correlation of 0.36 between the *accountFollowersCount* and *postFravouritedCount,* so posts posted by accounts with big followership tend to be favorited more, re-blogged more (0.24), and receive more replies (0.11). A positive correlation of 0.28 between the *accountFollowersCount* and *accountFollowingCount,* means accounts that follow more accounts tend to be followed as well. Finally, a weak positive correlation of 0.17 between *accountFollowingCount* and *accountStatusesCount* suggests that accounts that follow others tend to post more. For a complete list of correlations values, see Fig. 1.

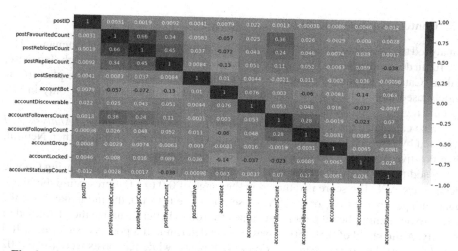

Fig. 1. The Pearson correlation values for all the Toots and accounts numerical attributes.

4.2 Posting Accounts Analysis and RQ2

By analyzing the type of accounts with trending Toots (which include trending hashtags) during the data collection period, I found that out of the 3,831 accounts, 242 accounts (i.e., 6.3%) were marked as bots by the account's creator. These accounts generated 1,864 unique posts out of 11,601 posts (i.e., 16.07%). So, the effect of social bots on making the hashtags trend is not so big (or "marginal" as found by [7]), as exemplified by the small percentage of trending posts created by the social bots. I also found that social bots tend to be most active on Tuesdays and least active on Saturdays (see Fig. 2) and, on average, on weekdays are more active than on weekends.

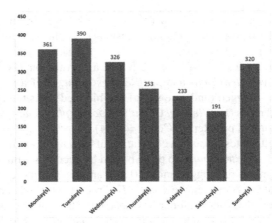

Fig. 2. The number of bot accounts posted with a trending hashtag during the data collection period. The numbers resulted from summing the number of posting accounts for each day.

4.3   Content Analysis and RQ3

I analyzed the post's language of the data collected and found 52 different languages. The top 10 (in descending order) languages are English, German, Spanish, French, Japanese, Italian, Catalan, Russian, Portuguese, and Chinese. This suggests that the platform is widely used in countries speaking the aforementioned languages and not only in one specific region.

I also calculated the sentiments of the posts/Toots using the *Sentiment Analysis API* provided by *DeepAI*. I found most of the posts were marked as Negative, then Neutral, then Positive (see Fig. 3 for the exact number of posts in each class).

In addition to the post sentiments, I calculated the post toxicity score[1] using Google Perspective API. The score is returned in the range of 0.0 to 1.0 representing the likelihood of a post being toxic or not. The closer the score is to 1.0, the more likely that the text is toxic. I multiplied the returned values by 100 to better visualize the likelihood of toxicity. A threshold of 0.50 (50%) was used to determine if a post is toxic or not [9]. I found most of the posts were not toxic (13,088 posts) while few posts were toxic (502 posts have a toxicity score ≥ 50). Out of the 502 toxic posts, only 387 were marked as Negative or Very Negative and out of the 9,576 Negative or Very Negative posts, only 387 posts (4.04%) have a toxicity score ≥ 50. This suggests that even though most of the posts were negative they are not all toxic, i.e., a post can be negative but not toxic, for example, this post "*Shared with Public #Korea 1950, #Guatemala 1954, #Indonesia 1958, #Cuba 1961, #Vietnam 1961, #Congo 1964, #Laos 1964, #Brazil 1964, #Dominicanrepublic 1965, #Greece 1967, #Argentina 1976, #Nicaragua 1981, #Grenada 1984, #Phillipines 1989, #Panama 1989, # Iraq 1991, 2003, #RepublicofSrpska 1995, #Sudan 1998, #Yugoslavia 1999, #Afghanistan 2001, #Yemen 2002, #Somalia 2006, #Libya*

---

[1] Note that toxicity analysis is different from sentiment analysis as the latter usually gives a score ranking the text to be either positive, negative, or neutral [8].

2011, #Syria 2011..... All we are saying is give #PEACE a chance! https://twitter.com/ ****/status/****" was marked very negative but not toxic. The opposite is also true, i.e., there are posts that are marked as "Positive" and toxic, e.g., *"There is a fine line between courage and stupidity. # Philosophy"*.

When it comes to the human and bot posts' sentiments. I found that the posts posted by bots on average are more negative than the posts posted by humans. Humans' posts are more neutral and positive than the bot posts (see Fig. 4 for the normalized number of posts in each class[2]). Finally, humans posted more toxic posts than bots, i.e., out of the 502 toxic posts only 462 (92%) posts were posted by humans while the other 40 (8%) posts were posted by bots.

4.4 Network Analysis and RQ4

To investigate the user sharing behaviors on Mastodon Social, three networks were con- structed and analyzed. These networks are *Hashtags co-occurrence network*, *accountID by Hashtag network* (a bipartite network), and *accountID by postID network* (another bipartite network). The details of each network along with its analysis and findings are presented below.

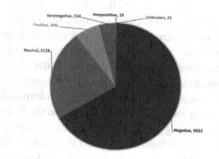

Fig. 3. The post sentiments along with the number of posts per class.

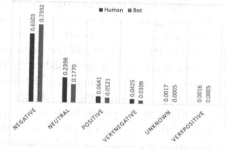

Fig. 4. Human and bot posts sentiments per class. The score is normalized (divided by the total number of posts made by humans and bots) to be in range 0–1.

a) **Hashtags co-occurrence network**

This directed graph was created to investigate the nature of the trending hashtags shared on Mastodon Social. The resulted graph contains 12,256 nodes (divided into 7 connected components: 2 isolates, 1 triad, 1 component with 6 nodes, 1 component with 8 nodes, 1 component with 25 nodes, and 1 giant component with 12,212 nodes) and 69,171 edges. I ignored all the small components as they do not add that much info to the analysis. Instead, I focused on the giant component (shown in Fig. 5) with 12,212 nodes and 68,728 edges. This component has a modularity value of 0.714

---

[2] The *Unknown* class is assigned to posts that the API could not classify.

which means the hashtags co-occurrence network form communities far away from being random. It also contains 21 communities of hashtags used with each other. The network diameter is 10, the average path length is 3.831 (i.e., information can travel fast), and the average clustering coefficient is 0.119 (i.e., close to real-world networks).

By analyzing this graph, I found that most of the hashtags co-occur, i.e., used together in the same post when they are usually related, i.e., discuss the same topic. Also, these hashtags are related to events happenings around the world during the data collection period. For example, I found a community of hashtags that are used together to address the issue of the *Ukraine war* (the green community in Fig. 5), another community of hashtags that are related to *Global warming* (the orange community in Fig. 5), *Information Privacy* (the purple community in Fig. 5), or *Nextcloud* events (the turquoise community in Fig. 5) that were happening during data collection.

b) **accountID by hashtag network**

This directed bipartite graph was created to figure out if users tend to use trending hashtags in their posts. The resulted graph contains 4,243 nodes and 13,590 edges (see Fig. 6). This is divided into 3 connected components: 2 stars (with 7 nodes while the other star contains 27 nodes) and one giant component with 4,209 nodes. This is an interesting graph structure because it means that most of the users (i.e., the ones in the giant component) always use a trending hashtag in their posts. This suggests that either these users look for trending hashtags and use them in their posts or their posts usually contain hashtags that eventually will be trending. I believe the possibility of the first case happening is higher than the latter case. The giant component has a modularity value of 0.746 and contains 33 communities. This means that communities of the giant component are far from being random and users tend to pick hashtags of related topics. For example, in Fig. 7 users in the light green community picked hashtags related to cats, e.g., #cat, #cats, #catsofmastodon, #caturday while users in purple community picked hashtags related to politics and election, e.g., #elections, #debatmacronlepen, #deliveroo, #election2022, #election-presidentielle2022, #elections2022, #vote, etc. This might also suggest that people with specific interests pick a trending hashtag related to their interest and include it in their post to gain the viewership and interaction of people of the same interest, i.e., the community.

c) **accountID by postID network**

This directed bipartite graph was created to find if there exist a set of users who share the same post to make the post trends or to create an echo chamber. The resulted graph contains 15,432 nodes and 13,590 edges. These nodes and edges form 3,830 star-shaped connected components where each account has many posts, but no posts were shared by more than one account. This suggests that there is no attempt to create an echo chamber in the collected data. Also, I found that 5 out of the top 10 accounts that post the most were classified as bots.

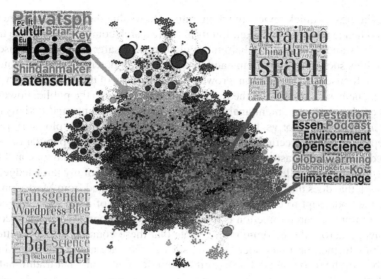

Fig. 5. The giant component of the hashtag co-occurrence network. Nodes are colored based on their modularity class and are sized based on their out-degree. (Color figure online)

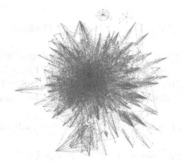

Fig. 6. An accountID X hashtag network resulted from connecting the users to the trending hashtag they included in their post. The graph has three connected components, orange, green, and a giant purple component. (Color figure online)

Fig. 7. The giant component of the bipartite graph (accountID X hashtag) with 33 communities. (Color figure online)

5   Conclusion and Future Work

Decentralized social networks provide users with more control over the content shared as it enables communities to set what is deemed as appropriate and not appropriate. It also lists toots/posts chronologically and hence does not allow sponsored posts to show first. Since this gives more freedom to users, decentralized social networks might gain more popularity in the future as it free people from the central authority imposed by traditional social media sites. A quick review of the literature shows that these platforms are under-studied and hence require more attention from the research community to come up with methodologies and tools that can help these platforms be safer for users because malicious activities such as cyberbullying and hate speech can potentially be present. Many studies have focused on the location, growth, and popularity of the instances/servers and provided some basic statistics on the toots, and released data to the public, however, no studies were focused on content analysis of toots (e.g., sentiments and toxicity), users behavior analysis (e.g., bot vs. human) or network analysis. This exploratory research is one step toward this direction. Its goal is to study one of the most popular distributed social media sites, i.e., Mastodon's Social ecology and its users' behaviors, and to provide a methodology to collect data from Mastodon. To the best of my knowledge, this is the first work that does this. Other studies provided data collected from Mastodon Social but not a method/script to collect data, nor applied this set of analyses to the content. A possible future research direction is to analyze individual communities and compare user behaviors across these communities. Note that these communities are better than communities formed on other social media sites as they are more natural and do not have the bias of the recommendation algorithms implemented on other traditional social media sites.

References

1. Shaw, C.R.: Decentralized Social Networks: Pros and Cons of the Mastodon Platform, p. 6 (2020)
2. Raman, A., Joglekar, S., De Cristofaro, E., Sastry, N., Tyson, G.: Challenges in the decentralised web: the mastodon case. arXiv (2019). http://arxiv.org/abs/1909.05801. Accessed 21 June 2022
3. Decentralized Social Networks: What You Need to Know. Tulane University - School of Professional Advancement (2022). https://sopa.tulane.edu/blog/decentralized-social-networks. Accessed 07 Apr 2022
4. Rochko, E.: Mastodon. Wikipedia.org. https://en.wikipedia.org/wiki/Mastodon_(software). Accessed 22 June 2022
5. Choosing a community. https://joinmastodon.org/communities. Accessed 11 Apr 2022
6. Zignani, M.: Mastodon content warnings: inappropriate contents in a micro-blogging platform. Harvard Dataverse (2019). https://doi.org/10.7910/DVN/R1HKVS
7. Zignani, M., Gaito, S., Rossi, G.P.: Follow the mastodon: structure and evolution of a decentralized online social network, p. 10 (2018)
8. Obadimu, A., Mead, E., Hussain, M.N., Agarwal, N.: Identifying toxicity within YouTube video comment. In: Thomson, R., Bisgin, H., Dancy, C., Hyder, A. (eds.) Social, Cultural, and Behavioral Modeling. SBP-BRiMS 2019. LNCS, vol. 11549, pp. 214–223. Springer, Cham (2019). https://doi.org/10.1007/978-3-030-21741-9_22
9. Al-khateeb, S., Anderson, M., Agarwal, N.: Studying the role of social bots during cyber flash mobs. In: Thomson, R., Hussain, M.N., Dancy, C., Pyke, A. (eds.) SBP-BRiMS 2021. LNCS, vol. 12720, pp. 164–173. Springer, Cham (2021). https://doi.org/10.1007/978-3-030-80387-2_16

Competing State and Grassroots Opposition Influence in the 2021 Hong Kong Election

Samantha C. Phillips$^{(\boxtimes)}$, Joshua Uyheng, and Kathleen M. Carley

CASOS Center, Institute for Software Research, Carnegie Mellon University, Pittsburgh, USA
{samanthp,juyheng,kathleen.carley}@cs.cmu.edu

Abstract. State-led online influence campaigns represent a major frontier in contemporary global politics. Such operations, however, do not take place unopposed and may encounter collective resistance. This study compares two competing influence campaigns during the 2021 Hong Kong Legislative Council (Legco) election: one by the Chinese state seeking to emphasize the legitimacy of local polls, versus pro-democracy activists denouncing Chinese interference in the electoral process. Critically, we discover that the two groups do not directly confront each other online. Rather, both camps appeal to international audiences by leveraging narrative strategies to negatively distort and distract from their opponents, while positively engaging and explaining their own positions regarding the elections. Furthermore, while pro-democracy activists bridge multiple connections to diverse online groups, Chinese state accounts play more specialized, hub-like roles within centralized networked communities. Taking these findings together, we discuss the importance of characterizing online influence campaigns in relation to broader diplomatic objectives. In the Chinese case, success may entail minimizing attention toward critics and an election they had effectively already won.

Keywords: Social cybersecurity · Influence campaigns · Social network analysis

1 Introduction

In January 2021, over 50 pro-democracy legislators and activists in Hong Kong (HK) were arrested for allegedly violating Beijing's National Security Law (NSL)

This work was supported in part by the Knight Foundation and the Office of Naval Research grants N000141812106 and N000141812108. Additional support was provided by the Center for Computational Analysis of Social and Organizational Systems (CASOS) and the Center for Informed Democracy and Social Cybersecurity (IDeaS). The views and conclusions contained in this document are those of the authors and should not be interpreted as representing the official policies, either expressed or implied, of the Knight Foundation, Office of Naval Research or the U.S. government.

by engaging in an informal primary leading up to the Legislative Council (Legco) election.[1] Through mass arrests, the Chinese government showed its ability to silence opposition in HK by preventing many pro-democracy candidates from running in the upcoming election. All but one of the 90 candidates eventually elected were supportive of Beijing's agenda and influence over HK.

Amidst these offline developments, social media discourse featured competing influence campaigns between the Chinese state and HK pro-democracy groups. In this work, we design and apply a social cybersecurity approach to characterize their information maneuvers, and comparatively assess their impact on the broader online conversation surrounding the HK elections [6,8]. We thus shed new light on the nature and objectives of international state-led influence campaigns as well as collective efforts to contest them, specifically in the Asia-Pacific region where Chinese cyber-influence is a core concern to regional geopolitics [4,7,9,13]. We ask: How did Chinese state and HK pro-democracy accounts engage in competing influence campaigns during the Legco election?

2   Related Work

Online social networks have demonstrated vast potential for mobilizing communities to achieve behavioral and social change [8]. State-led influence campaigns have been central in this regard, as they represent well-resourced efforts by high-level actors to utilize social media toward large-scale geopolitical ends [3,13]. Such operations, however, have not transpired in a vacuum. Organized collectives worldwide have likewise harnessed digital platforms to compete for public attention and social influence [1,2]. These collectives even confront powerful nation-states like China.

Multidisciplinary research in social cybersecurity has systematized the study of these phenomena from a socio-computational, multi-methodological standpoint [8]. Competing influence campaigns in the West have been widely studied through this lens, particularly in relation to Russian information operations in the United States and Western Europe [2,3]. This wealth of research has led to the development of general, interoperable pipelines for detecting and characterizing such campaigns and collective resistance to them [14].

Building from this Western base, emerging scholarship on Chinese state influence represents a key frontier in the global social cybersecurity literature. Like Russia, Beijing has used fake accounts and coordinated behavior to shape public opinion outside China [2,12]. However, Chinese tactics are notably different to well-established Russian ones, as are the regional dynamics within which they operate [7,13]. For instance, Chinese control over the internet within various jurisdictions enables their explicit censorship of undesirable messages [4]. While collective action in the region has also been studied, particularly in relation to Hong Kong pro-democracy movements [1], such work has typically employed survey or interview methods, which feature a level of removal from the dynamics of real-time, large-scale information campaigns.

---

[1] https://hongkongfp.com/2021/01/06/breaking-over-50-hong-kong-democrats-arrested-under-security-law-over-2020-legislative-primaries/.

Table 1. Summary of annotated agent types. Shortened labels are given in parentheses.

Agent type	No. of agents	No. of tweets
Chinese state-sponsored accounts (state)	133	855
HK pro-democracy accounts		
Manually labelled (prodem1)	31	1889
Automatically labelled (prodem2)	1372	19596
HK reference group (refhk)	3255	38845
Current HK Legco members (legco)	4	20
Non-Chinese state media (mediaex)	125	649
Non-Chinese government (govex)	144	160
Bot-like users (bots)	2174	5631
Verified (verified)	1165	5242

Contributions of this Work. Our goal in examining the 2021 HK Legco election is thus to not only add to burgeoning understandings of Chinese state influence, but also to compare it meaningfully to pro-democracy resistance movements' efforts in cyberspace. In sum, then, our approach makes the following contributions: first, we empirically demonstrate novel tactical features of state and grassroots information campaigns in the Asia-Pacific region; second, we introduce a general socio-computational methodology for characterizing large-scale state-versus-grassroots information campaigns; and third, we highlight a social cybersecurity perspective that goes beyond single information campaigns to tackle their interactions and relative success in geopolitical context.

3 Data and Methods

3.1 Data Collection

To collect online conversations on the 2021 HK elections, we obtained data from the Twitter API from November 1 thru December 31, 2021. We used the following keywords: Legco, 香港选举 (Hong Kong election), carrielam, 林鄭月娥 (Carrie Lam), bloodycarrie, NationalSecurityLaw, NSL, 国安法 (National Security Law), FreeHongKong, StandWithHongKong, StandwithHK, SaveHK, supportHongKong, hkpolicebrutality, 立会选战 (Legislative Council), and ReleaseMyCandidate. The final dataset consisted of 41,653 agents and 159,081 tweets.

3.2 Data Annotation

Our analysis of competing information campaigns by the Chinese state and Hong Kong pro-democracy activists began with rigorously identifying their accounts on Twitter. We also classified other relevant accounts in the conversation, including current Legco members and non-Chinese government and media accounts, as summarized in Table 1. Below, we define key agent types and the corresponding procedures used to label them.

Chinese State-Sponsored Accounts (state). To label Twitter users as part of the Chinese state influence campaign, referred to as *state* accounts in this work, we curated a list of Chinese government and media figures, including ambassadors, embassies, staff of the Ministry of Foreign Affairs, and diplomats, and state-sponsored media. We then linked these public figures to Twitter accounts. If not labelled by Twitter as "Chinese government official" or "China state-affiliated media",[2] we checked if the accounts were verified. Otherwise, we determined whether the account was followed by at least 5 confirmed state accounts.

Hong Kong Pro-Democracy Accounts (prodem1, prodem2). We identified Hong Kong pro-democracy figures via a stratified classification scheme. The first type, which we refer to as *prodem1*, were entirely manually labelled. We identified established pro-democracy HK organizations and their leaders, previous Legco candidates advocating for democracy in HK, and exiled activists. We then used Twitter usernames and account descriptions to identify corresponding accounts.

The second type, labeled here as *prodem2*, were users identified through an automatic search of user descriptions for key words related to HK pro-democracy efforts or social media campaigns. These key words included variations of "stand with HK", "Release My Candidate", "free HK", and "HK activist". This group was identified to provide an expanded comparison set for the more centralized prodem1 accounts. Prodem1 users were also found to be a subset of prodem2.

HK Reference Group (refhk). We also labelled users whose description referenced Hong Kong in any way as *refhk*. Prodem1 and prodem2 users were likewise found to be subsets of refhk. This provided a reference group against which to compare accounts with more explicit pro-democracy markers on their Twitter accounts.

Current HK Legco Members (legco). Accounts of current members of the HK Legco (as of 2021) are referred to here as *legco*. Using a list of Legco members, we identified accounts based on username, description, and verification.

Media Accounts Excluding Chinese State Media (mediaex). Using a list of known news agencies, we labelled their Twitter accounts using usernames and descriptions. We excluded accounts previously classified as (Chinese) *state* accounts.

Government Accounts Excluding Chinese State Accounts (govex). We identified non-Chinese government accounts by searching account descriptions for keywords such as "state" and "senator". Then we remove non-verified and previously classified (Chinese) *state* accounts.

Bot-Like Users. We also sought to control for potential bot activity in the online conversation, especially given their well-documented use in Western state-sponsored information operations [3]. We used the Tier-1 BotHunter model to designate users as bot or not [5]. We used a validated probability threshold of 0.70 to classify an account as a bot [11].

---

[2] https://help.twitter.com/en/rules-and-policies/state-affiliated.

Verified. Finally, we identified which accounts were designated by Twitter as *verified*.[3] Such accounts are labeled to be of "public interest", and thus we accounted for their behavior relative to unverified users.

3.3   Analysis

Our approach to characterizing competing information campaigns in the 2021 HK Legco election followed a three-stage process. Adopting a social cybersecurity approach [8], we structured our analysis around the comparative measurement of: (a) *who* were targeted in interactions by Chinese state and pro-democracy actors, (b) *what* maneuvers were harnessed by these groups in their competing information campaigns, and (c) *how effective* these maneuvers were in terms of accruing network influence and widespread diffusion of information.

Step 1: Characterization of Information Targeting. We characterized information targeting by measuring the number of times state, prodem1, prodem2, and refhk agents mentioned each other and all the other annotated agent types. This latter category included bots, current Legco members, non-Chinese media and government accounts, and verified accounts. We thus produced a social network represented by a 4×9 targeting matrix with the four mentioning agents of interest and the nine possible target types. Systematic differences in mentioning behavior provided insight into which accounts both state and pro-democracy groups sought to influence during the election.

Step 2: Assessment of Information Maneuvers. We then assessed information maneuvers with the BEND framework. BEND is a transdisciplinary theory to categorize 16 influence operations which positively or negatively impact network structure and narratives on social media [8]. Leveraging previously developed indicators [6,8], we used the ORA software[4] to measure differences in BEND maneuvers between state and HK pro-democracy accounts.

Step 3: Measuring Online Influence. Finally, we assessed the influence and impact of accounts belonging to the competing information campaigns. Alongside standard measures of total degree, betweenness, and eigenvector centrality, we also examined new measures of modularity vitality [10], which quantified accounts' abilities to act as informational hubs or bridges.

4   Results

4.1   Both Camps Target In-Group Members and Verified Accounts

Figure 1 shows the mention network by state, prodem1, prodem2, and refhk accounts directed toward all other account types: state, prodem1, prodem2,

---

[3] https://help.twitter.com/en/managing-your-account/about-twitter-verified-accounts.

[4] https://netanomics.com/ora-pro/.

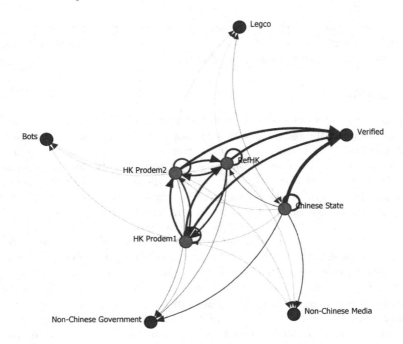

Fig. 1. Network of mentions by Chinese state, prodem1, prodem2, and refhk accounts (red) directed to all other actors in HK election tweets (blue). Edge widths are proportional to the number of mentions. Figure generated with ORA. (Color figure online)

refhk, legco, mediaex, govex, bot-like, and verified. A chi-square test on the targeting matrix revealed significant variation in targeting behavior across agent types ($\chi^2(24) = 2583.8, p < .001$). Closer analysis, however, suggested Chinese state and HK pro-democracy accounts similarly targeted: (a) verified accounts and media outside China and Hong Kong; and (b) their own in-group.

For instance, Chinese state accounts were most likely to mention verified accounts in general (42.17%), followed by other Chinese state accounts (27.71%), then non-Chinese government and media accounts (19.28%). Verified media and foreign government officials were among the top five mentioned by state accounts: @50Trabajadores (a media and news company in Cuba), @MahuiChina (Chinese Ambassador to Cuba), @SecBlinken (U.S. Secretary of State), @CGTNOfficial (Chinese government-affliated media), and @MarisePayne (Australian Senator). Meanwhile, HK prodem1 accounts were most likely to mention prodem1 or prodem2 accounts (43.88%), then the reference HK group (25.65%), followed by verified accounts in general (21.14%). Taken together, these statistics suggest a combination of collaboration within both Chinese state and pro-democracy camps, alongside efforts to interact with influential accounts outside the immediate HK-Chinese geopolitical context, thus indicating a globally targeted audience for their respective campaigns. Cross-camp interactions, meanwhile, were rare.

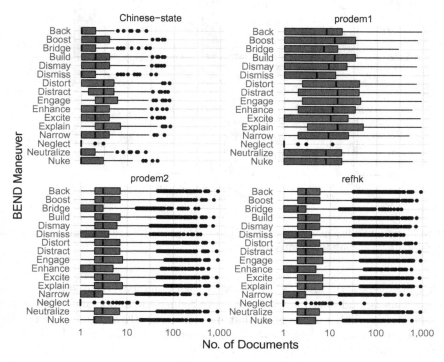

Fig. 2. BEND maneuvers by state, prodem1, prodem2, and refhk accounts. Top 5 most-used BEND maneuvers by group are in red. (Color figure online)

4.2 Parallel Information Maneuvers by Competing Campaigns

Given these targets of Chinese state and HK pro-democracy messaging, Fig. 2 reports the BEND maneuvers used by state, prodem1, prodem2, and refhk users. Notably, Chinese state agents and HK prodem1 accounts featured a nearly identical set of top 5 BEND maneuvers, all of which fell under the narrative category ("E" and "D" maneuvers). Chinese state accounts and HK pro-democracy activists thus sought to influence election narratives in highly similar ways. Both groups detracted from opposing narratives by *distorting* their content or offering *distracting* alternatives. At the same time, they elaborated on their own messages by *engaging* related content and *explaining* their stance on the (il)legitimacy of the election. Crucially, however, prodem1 accounts preferred *excite* maneuvers to trigger positive emotions among their audience, whereas state accounts deployed *enhance* maneuvers to prolong dialogue around their key messages.

Interestingly, prodem2 and refhk accounts also featured highly similar patterns of top used BEND maneuvers. Like prodem1 accounts, they also pursued *engage*, *explain*, and *excite* maneuvers. However, they also notably utilized net-

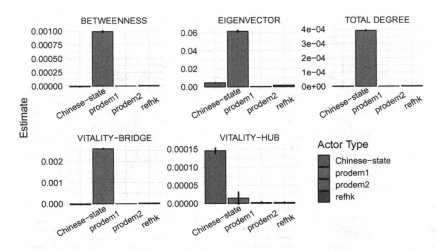

Fig. 3. Mean centrality measures of state, prodem1, prodem2 and refhk accounts. Error bars indicate 95% confidence intervals.

work maneuvers ("B" and "N" maneuvers): *back* maneuvers to support allied opinion leaders, and *neutralize* maneuvers to reduce the importance of opposing opinion leaders. This may suggest that more general HK accounts assisted the prodem1 pro-democracy leaders, an organizational campaign dynamic which the BEND indicators quantitatively capture.

4.3   State Accounts Are Specialized Hubs, Pro-democracy Accounts Are Popular Bridges

Finally, we assessed the types of network influence, if any, both camps had. Figure 3 shows the average betweenness centrality, eigenvector centrality, total-degree centrality, bridge modularity vitality, and hub modularity vitality for each user type. Prodem1 users tended to be the dominant account type across betweenness ($p < .001$), eigenvector ($p < .001$), and total degree centralities ($p < .001$), as well as bridge modularity vitality ($p < .001$). Leaders of the pro-democracy HK movement thus drew indirect connections among other accounts, interacted with highly active groups, and bridged different communities.

Chinese state users, on the other hand, had the highest hub modularity vitality scores ($p < .001$), and thus occupied central roles in the structure of their respective communities, featuring numerous links among a closed set of interactors and few to external users. Although they had lower influence across other centrality measures, Chinese state accounts thus appeared to act as core influencers within a highly centralized network.

5   Discussion

Nation-states have become influential actors on social media, but they do not operate unopposed. How far might online resistance go? By comparing competing Chinese state and HK pro-democracy influence campaigns during the 2021 Legco election, we find that both camps do not seek to influence the online conversation through direct confrontation. Instead, they appeal to the international community through distinct narrative and network maneuvers [6].

On the one hand, by interacting mostly with each other and verified accounts, Chinese state figures engaged in diplomacy efforts "as usual", promoting their agenda towards a non-Chinese audience on Twitter [12]. Given that Legco electoral outcomes favored Beijing's dominance over the political future of HK,[5] state tactics sought to minimize international attention towards critiques of the election's validity amid arrests under the NSL [4,9]. Moreover, by acting as hubs within a curated set of communities, Chinese state actors did not seek to reach all accounts in the online conversation, and instead established a distinct ecosystem within which networked information flow favored their regional interests.

On the other hand, the pro-democracy camp alerted a worldwide audience about jailed Legco candidates, who had been removed from the election under the guise of the NSL. Touting such messages, leaders of the pro-democracy movement in HK (prodem1) appeared to dominate the online discussion about the Legco election, amplified by prodem2 and refhk users. By acting as bridges in the social network, pro-democracy groups further accumulated broad, popular appeal among diverse accounts in the online conversation. Yet while cultivating such a decentralized following, the pro-democracy camp did not break the consensus established by the Chinese state over its core audience.

Overall, we demonstrate the value of quantifying competing information maneuvers [6,8], then situating these measures within geopolitical context [14]. Influence campaigns do not always involve overt, combative behavior. Strategic disengagement may also be a powerful tool in watering down the opposition and avoiding unwanted scrutiny. These observations extend work on Chinese censorship practices [4] and attacks against critics [13], which leverage covert actions or inauthentic accounts. Future work may examine what tactics China and other states combine to advance their agendas and quell resistance. Our analysis of official state-affiliated accounts tackles more formal channels, whereas other, informal tactics may also be in play beyond our present scope.

These insights add to growing work around China's global cyber influence [7,12], and indicate limits in efforts to resist it. Observational social media data does not necessarily indicate the impact of online influence operations on public perception. Yet using recently developed, novel measures of network influence and social-cyber maneuvers [6,10], we present sobering resonance with prior work that suggests pro-democracy activists successfully use social media to extend their reach, but not to persuade offline majorities [1]. This reaffirms the need for

---

[5] https://www.scmp.com/news/hong-kong/politics/article/3157625/hong-kong-elections-only-3-legislative-council-candidates.

enhanced social cybersecurity research not only on state actors and inorganic manipulation [5], but also on competing grassroots collectives [8].

References

1. Agur, C., Frisch, N.: Digital disobedience and the limits of persuasion: social media activism in Hong Kong's 2014 umbrella movement. Soc. Media Soc. **5**(1), 2056305119827002 (2019)
2. Arif, A., Stewart, L.G., Starbird, K.: Acting the part: examining information operations within #blacklivesmatter discourse. Proc. ACM Hum. Comput. Interact. **2**, 1–27 (2018)
3. Badawy, A., Addawood, A., Lerman, K., Ferrara, E.: Characterizing the 2016 Russian IRA influence campaign. Soc. Netw. Anal. Min. **9**(1), 1–11 (2019). https://doi.org/10.1007/s13278-019-0578-6
4. Bamman, D., O'Connor, B., Smith, N.: Censorship and deletion practices in Chinese social media. First Monday **17**(3) (2012). https://doi.org/10.5210/fm.v17i3.3943
5. Beskow, D.M., Carley, K.M.: Bot-hunter: a tiered approach to detecting & characterizing automated activity on twitter. In: Conference paper. SBP-BRiMS: International conference on social computing, behavioral-cultural modeling and prediction and behavior representation in modeling and simulation, vol. 3, p. 3 (2018)
6. Blane, J.T., Bellutta, D., Carley, K.M.: Social-Cyber maneuvers during the COVID-19 vaccine initial rollout: content analysis of tweets. J. Med. Internet Res. **24**(3), e34040 (2022)
7. Bradshaw, S., Howard, P.N.: The global organization of social media disinformation campaigns. J. Int. Aff. **71**(1.5), 23–32 (2018)
8. Carley, K.M.: Social cybersecurity: an emerging science. Comput. Math. Organ. Theory **26**(4), 365–381 (2020). https://doi.org/10.1007/s10588-020-09322-9
9. King, G., Pan, J., Roberts, M.E.: How the Chinese government fabricates social media posts for strategic distraction, not engaged argument. Am. Polit. Sci. Rev. **111**(3), 484–501 (2017)
10. Magelinski, T., Bartulovic, M., Carley, K.M.: Measuring node contribution to community structure with modularity vitality. IEEE Trans. Netw. Sci. Eng. **8**(1), 707–723 (2021)
11. Ng, L.H.X., Robertson, D.C., Carley, K.M.: Stabilizing a supervised bot detection algorithm: how much data is needed for consistent predictions? Online Soc. Netw. Media **28**, 100198 (2022)
12. Schliebs, M., Bailey, H., Bright, J., Howard, P.N.: China's public diplomacy operations: understanding engagement and inauthentic amplifications of PRC diplomats on Facebook and Twitter (2021)
13. Uyheng, J., Cruickshank, I.J., Carley, K.M.: Mapping state-sponsored information operations with multi-view modularity clustering. EPJ Data Sci. **11**(1), 25 (2022)
14. Uyheng, J., Magelinski, T., Villa-Cox, R., Sowa, C., Carley, K.M.: Interoperable pipelines for social cyber-security: assessing Twitter information operations during NATO Trident Juncture 2018. Comput. Math. Organ. Theory **26**(4), 465–483 (2019). https://doi.org/10.1007/s10588-019-09298-1

Modeling and Simulation

Revisiting Linus' Law in OpenStreetMap: An Agent-Based Approach

Aylin McGough[1](✉), Hamdi Kavak[1], and Ron Mahabir[2]

[1] George Mason University, Fairfax, VA 22030, USA
{amcgough,hkavak}@gmu.edu
[2] University of Liverpool, Liverpool L69 3BX, UK
Ron.Shane.Mahabir@liverpool.ac.uk

Abstract. OpenStreetMap, a wiki-style map of the world, has become a popular source of free and open geospatial data by leveraging the power of an immense community of volunteers. Much like other collaboration-based peer production projects such as Wikipedia, OpenStreetMap is decentralized and participant-driven, so questions of data reliability are frequent. Within these participant-driven projects, the assumption known as Linus' Law suggests that data quality increases with the number of contributors. In this paper, we evaluate Linus' Law as applied to the co-production of volunteered geographic information using an agent-based model and examine the effects of knowledge level, variability, and prioritization on emergent production patterns and overall data quality. We demonstrate how diminishing returns limit Linus' Law and that, in the end, data quality is dependent more on the experience of contributors, rather than the number of contributors.

Keywords: Volunteered geographic information · OpenStreetMap · Linus' Law · Spatial data quality · Agent-based model

1 Introduction

Crowdsourcing projects such as OpenStreetMap (OSM), a freely editable global map, represent an invaluable source of geographic information and a platform for citizen engagement [11,20]. Started in 2004, OSM has since grown to be one of the largest collections of volunteered geographic information (VGI), where it has given visibility to previously unmapped communities [21,22], and its geospatial data has been relied upon to support critical humanitarian aid and crisis response efforts [28]. Currently, the OSM platform has more than 8.5 million registered users globally, with the number of users continuing to grow [1]. As a commons-based peer production effort, OSM is developed through the collaboration of many individuals who work cooperatively to produce data. However, compared to more formal systems, such as commercial and government organizations, these activities are typically less structured [7]. The process is also decentralized, with participants largely acting independently, resulting in generated

R. Thomson et al. (Eds.): SBP-BRiMS 2022, LNCS 13558, pp. 123–133, 2022.
https://doi.org/10.1007/978-3-031-17114-7_12

content that reflects the various individual skills and motivations of volunteers. Correspondingly, the reliability of the data produced through such means has been an important area of concern [10,16].

One possible method for evaluating the quality of VGI projects is to use Linus' Law, a mantra within the software development community. Linus' Law asserts that given enough eyes on an open-source project, almost every issue can be identified and fixed [27]. Applied to open source mapping projects, this would suggest that as the number of contributors increases, there is a resulting increase in the quality of the map as well [18]. However, some researchers dispose of this law as a fallacy, citing a lack of evidence and that data quality does not scale linearly with the number of users [15,18].

To better understand the mechanisms behind emergent patterns of data creation and to assess the validity of Linus' Law as applied to open source mapping projects, we simulate the co-production of spatial data using an abstract agent-based model (ABM). Collaborative knowledge production is a complex process, and an ABM is apt for simulating the heterogeneous interaction between populations required to produce such dynamic spatial content [12,30]. This paper explores mechanisms that include the level and variability of knowledge within a community of mappers and how prioritizing editing affects data production and quality.

2   Related Works

Data quality as it applies to VGI has been studied along various dimensions, including spatial coverage [23], positional [17], and attribute accuracy [9]. However, the results of these measurements depend largely on good quality reference datasets, which are not always accessible [23]. Further, results can vary from one location to another due largely to the heterogeneous nature of VGI [10]. This has prompted the need for intrinsic measures of data quality to assess VGI [6]. These include measures that leverage user behavior, data trust, and data history [16,19,33], among others.

Linus' Law, in particular, has been viewed as a possible indicator for intrinsically evaluating VGI quality. Although a high number of contributors and versions (i.e., updates to data) can be a positive indicator of feature trustworthiness [19], the implication of Linus' Law can be misleading. Haklay et al. [18], for example, empirically tested the validity of Linus' Law in OSM and found little improvement in the positional accuracy of road networks mapped in England beyond 15 contributors. Further, other sources suggest that Linus' Law does not apply well to VGI because errors in obscure features are naturally more likely to go unnoticed [10,16].

Most current works that study contributors' impact on the spatial data quality of VGI use a top-down approach. Given the complexity of this system and the prevalence of interactions between users and their environment, a bottom-up approach using an ABM can provide important insights for understanding the underlying processes and the various factors that drive emergent production patterns. Regarding the use of ABM, Panchal [26] represents one of few works that study contribution patterns in commons-based production projects. Other representations include multi-agent simulations of the evolution of contribution patterns in GitHub based on historical data [8], and simulations of co-production activities within Wikipedia and community reaction to vandalism [32]. However, these works are not specific to VGI projects. Concerning VGI, Arsanjani et al. [4,5] predicted contributions in OSM using cellular automata models, stressing the need for a better understanding of the behavioral patterns of OSM mappers as a part of a collaborative project. Overall, there is a need to combine components of previous work to explore contribution patterns in VGI projects using an ABM approach, as the present research addresses.

3 Model Design

The model's design is based on an environment of mappable cells that a set of agents can choose to interact with and edit over multiple time steps. The model is relatively simple, with an abstracted environment and agents. We implemented a pattern-oriented modeling approach to optimize the model in terms of complexity and to help ensure a balance between simplicity and explainability [12]. This entailed testing the model's sensitivity to parameter uncertainties and comparing resulting patterns with similar OSM data and contributor behavior.

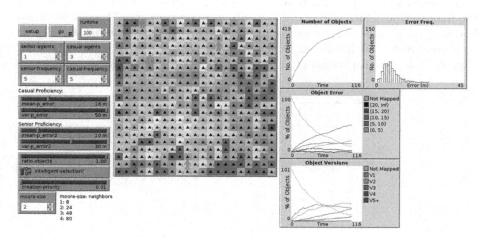

Fig. 1. Model layout and example of the final state of a run with 3 casual agents (blue). (Color figure online)

3.1 Environment

The model environment is a grid composed of A x A cells (see Fig. 1), where each cell represents a mappable geographic object in a given space. Cells have two attributes, error and version number, to track the quality and quantity of agents' interactions with each cell. The *error* represents the positional error in meters of a geographic object. This metric, and its range, were chosen to correspond to the work of Haklay et al. [18], where they define a positional error as the offset between OSM road segments and an authoritative data source. In this case, 0m represents a perfect agreement, while larger values represent less accurate OSM data. This definition of error is arbitrary, but since our goal is to come to a qualitative agreement with empirical observations, the approach used to assess error in this study was suitable. A cell's error is visualized by a gradient of white (offset of 0 m) to red (offset of 40 m). A number in each cell represents its current *version*. At initialization, all cells begin at version 0. Any cells with version 0 are greyed out, indicating that the cell has yet to be mapped.

3.2   Agents

Throughout the simulation, agents react to a changing environment, where their agent-environment interactions lead to indirect agent-agent interactions. Agents represent the contributors of OSM (i.e., mappers) who create and edit geographical features. They are initialized at random start locations within the gridded environment, and at each time step, they select a cell within their Moore neighborhood of 24 cells to move to and edit (see Fig. 2). A smaller Moore Neighborhood size was chosen to reduce the computational needs required to run simulations and does not impact the results. The user specifies the number of agents and the frequency at which they move and edit within a time step. Agents' behavior is described in probabilistic terms to account for the distribution of different volunteers and their likelihood of choosing where and how to contribute VGI. Blythe et al. [8] and Dawson et al. [13] used similar probabilistic approaches.

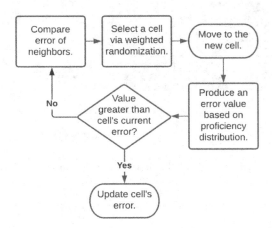

Fig. 2. Flow diagram of agents' decision-making within a time step.

If *priority-based selection* is toggled **ON**, agents move to new cells based on a weighted randomization of the attractiveness of all cells in their neighborhood. The attractiveness of a cell is computed using a power law of its error, $0.01^{(1-err/40)}$, where unmapped cells are by default weighted at 1.0 given a maximum error of 40 m. The *creation priority* parameter allows the user to set unmapped cells' attractiveness (0 to 1.0) in the weighted randomization. Overall, this selection prioritization emulates geographic features' absence or obvious positional inaccuracies may tend to attract more attention from contributors.

Once an agent moves to a new cell, they have the option to edit and update its error. In this model, an agent will only update the error and version of a cell if it is an improvement. The quality of an agent's contribution is determined by their *proficiency*, a randomized gamma distribution characterized by the parameters, mean and variance, set by the user. A gamma distribution was chosen as it most closely approximated the distribution of positional error in OSM derived by Haklay et al. [18].

3.3 Model Implementation and Output

The ABM was built using NetLogo [31], a multi-agent programmable modeling environment that provides a framework to incorporate agent transitions and interactions, widgets for user interactivity, adjustable model parameters, and various options for visualizing model outputs. Model outputs include a distribution of mapped cell errors, and time series of the number of cells (geographic objects), average cell error, and cell versions. The model environment is also used to help visualize the dynamic distribution of spatial data created and its changing quality. Our experiments focus on the final values for the number of cells mapped, their average error, and average version number.

4   Experiments and Results

We conducted two experiments using our ABM to assess the applicability of Linus' Law as it relates to VGI projects. These evaluated how contributors' behavior and knowledge, in terms of prioritization and proficiency, impact the relationship between the final average error and the number of contributors. The run time, frequency of edits, and the number of cells are kept constant in the experiments. This decision was based on the results of prior sensitivity tests (results not presented), which showed that while these parameters affect the rate of convergence of error vs. the number of contributors, they do not impact the final qualitative results. Their values were determined based on the best fit with the positional error vs. the number of contributors result from Haklay et al. [18]. Our study area is a 20×20 gridded region, representative of a local community, with a run time of 100 and frequency of 5. The final output values were recorded as the average of ten runs, with the number of initialized casual agents ranging from 1 to 33. Error bars in the results represent the standard deviation of ten runs.

4.1   Experiment One: Influence of Prioritization

In the first experiment, we observed the impact of prioritization on the relation-ship between error and the number of contributors by varying the value of the creation priority parameter and toggling priority-based selection. Agents' pro-ficiency distributions were set to a mean of 16m and a variance of 50m. When testing the impact of priority-based selection, the creation priority parameter was set to 1% (or 0.01). Figure 3 shows the experiment results.

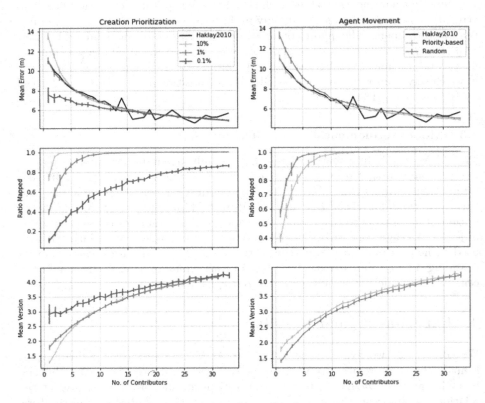

Fig. 3. Impact of prioritization on the relationship between error and the number of contributors. Change in the weight given to creating objects (left) and whether cell selection is prioritized at all (right).

With priority-based selection and a creation priority of 1%, our results match the trend from Haklay et al. [18], $R^2 = 0.93$, although our model does not capture the same variability. Based on sensitivity tests, our variability was impacted by run time and frequency. The agreement between our model and empirical data suggests that the nonlinearity between spatial data quality and the number of contributors can be explained by the simple mechanisms driving the ABM. In particular, as the positioning of geographic objects becomes more accurate, or at least meets the standard accuracy expected for a specific application, it is less likely to be noticed by contributors and further positionally corrected. Additional tests (results not presented) using a uniform distribution to describe the proficiency of agents also result in nonlinearity between spatial data quality and the number of contributors.

Priority-based selection has little impact on the results except when incorporating prioritization for creating cells. Varying creation priority impacts the trend of the results, where a lower creation priority results in greater linearity. With a higher creation priority, agents will focus on mapping the entire environment before returning to edit and improve existing data. Therefore, the extent to which agents prioritize creating data has a more significant impact on environments with few contributors. Essentially, when provided with a limited number of actions, agents trade-off between improving data expansiveness or quality. It may be necessary then to empirically investigate how the number of contributors impacts the completeness of VGI and whether trends for completeness and positional accuracy negatively correlate. Further, our model correlates average version numbers with average error. Although feature version is a positive indicator of trustful VGI [19], the actual relationship may not be obviously one-to-one as presented here.

4.2 Experiment Two: Influence of Proficiency

In the second experiment, we observed the impact of contributors' proficiency on data quality, given the number of contributors. This was accomplished by independently varying the mean and variance parameters that describe the proficiency distribution. For this experiment, the creation priority parameter was set to 1%.

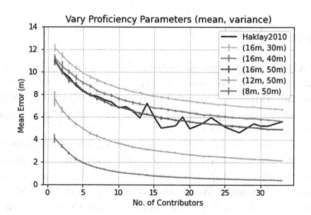

Fig. 4. Impact of the mean (blue) and variance (orange) of agent proficiency on the relationship between error and the number of contributors. (Color figure online)

The results from experiment two suggest that the number of contributors alone is insufficient for determining data quality within a region. Instead, we must also consider other intrinsic measures, such as the experience of contributors. Figure 4 shows that both improved mean and greater variance in proficiency result in a lower error. From a practical perspective, improved mean can be achieved by providing training to OSM contributors in organizations and volunteer communities. Greater variance in proficiency relates to greater diversity in a mapping community, where contributors may have specific knowledge of certain features in an area to provide higher quality contributions. Similarly, a diverse community of reviewers in open source software projects is paramount to Linus' Law's effectiveness in improving code quality [29].

5   Discussion

Overall, we found that OSM data production patterns of quality vs. the number of contributors can evolve from simple agent-environment interactions using an ABM. In the process, we corroborated previous research on the validity of Linus' Law that suggests that the relationship between the quality of VGI and the number of contributors is not linear. Using the model allowed an exploration of the processes underlying this nonlinearity. Our analysis is consistent with the hypothesis that contributors to VGI are more likely not to notice obscure or subtle errors as with bug catching in open source software projects, thus limiting the effectiveness of Linus' Law in VGI. Incorporating analysis of completeness and versions along with the positional accuracy of OSM objects can help understand the impact of the number of contributors on VGI quality. Additionally, we show that, although the number of contributors can be a positive indicator of data quality, it is not a replacement for greater proficiency and diversity in contributors.

6   Conclusion

In this paper, ABM was used to understand how co-editing amongst volunteers impacts the overall quality of spatial data. To this end, we corroborate that Linus' Law is a limited method for intrinsic quality assurance of VGI that cannot substitute for contributor experience, and we produced suggestions for future empirical studies of Linus' Law in VGI.

This study also identified several limitations, which provide opportunities for future work. First, while the ABM results were comparable to findings of prior work, many factors affect mapping quality, such as contributors' socio-economic and demographic backgrounds [3]. A more advanced model should take these into account. Second, OSM features such as buildings, roads, and green areas should be investigated instead of generic spatial features used in this work. We also suggest that these features mirror existing land cover/land use for the specific study area. Third, similar to prior work [24,25], the different types of OSM mappers and their editing dispositions should be investigated. Finally, future work may also incorporate more complex collaboration between agents such as competition [14] and social networks [2].

In all, we show that there is a great need and capability to apply agent-based modeling to gain insight into the behavior underlying collaboration and knowledge production in VGI projects such as OSM. Especially given the complexity of collaborative knowledge production, we expect that advances in this regard can help inform the development of ideal conditions to foster reliable and quality crowdsourced geographic information.

Notes: Additional information, code, and data sets for this paper are freely available at https://github.com/a-mcgough/LinusLaw-OSM.

References

1. Stats. https://wiki.openstreetmap.org/wiki/Stats
2. Anderson, T., Dragićević, S.: Neat approach for testing and validation of geospatial network agent-based model processes: case study of influenza spread. Int. J. Geogr. Inf. Sci. **34**(9), 1792–1821 (2020)
3. Antoniou, V., Skopeliti, A.: Measures and indicators of VGI quality: an overview. In: ISPRS Annals of Photogrammetry, Remote Sensing and Spatial Information Sciences vol. II-3/W5, 345–351 (2015)
4. Arsanjani, J.J., Helbich, M., Bakillah, M., Loos, L.: The emergence and evolution of OpensSreetMap: a cellular automata approach. Int. J. Digit. Earth **8**(1), 76–90 (2015)
5. Arsanjani, J.J., Mooney, P., Helbich, M., Zipf, A.: An exploration of future patterns of the contributions to OpenStreetMap and development of a contribution index. Trans. GIS **19**(6), 896–914 (2015)
6. Barron, C., Neis, P., Zipf, A.: A comprehensive framework for intrinsic OpenStreetMap quality analysis. Trans. GIS **18**(6), 877–895 (2014)
7. Benkler, Y., Nissenbaum, H.: Commons-based peer production and virtue. J. Polit. Philos. **14**(4), 26 (2006)
8. Blythe, J., et al.: The DARPA SocialSim challenge: massive multi-agent simulations of the github ecosystem. In: Proceedings of the 18th International Conference on Autonomous Agents and MultiAgent Systems, pp. 1835–1837 (2019)
9. Borkowska, S., Pokonieczny, K.: Analysis of OpenStreetMap data quality for selected counties in Poland in terms of sustainable development. Sustainability **14**(7), 3728 (2022)
10. Calazans Campelo, C.E., Bertolotto, M., Corcoran, P.: Volunteered geographic information and the future of geospatial data. IGI Global (2017)
11. Cochrane, L., Corbett, J., Evans, M., Gill, M.: Searching for social justice in GIScience publications. Cartogr. Geogr. Inf. Sci. **44**(6), 507–520 (2017)
12. Crooks, A.T., Heppenstall, A.J.: Introduction to agent-based modelling. In: Heppenstall, A., Crooks, A., See, L., Batty, M. (eds.) Agent-Based Models of Geographical Systems, pp. 85–105. Springer, Dordrecht (2012). https://doi.org/10.1007/978-90-481-8927-4_5
13. Dawson, R.J., Peppe, R., Wang, M.: An agent-based model for risk-based flood incident management. Nat. Hazards **59**(1), 167–189 (2011)
14. Girres, J.F., Touya, G.: Quality assessment of the French OpenStreetMap dataset. Trans. GIS **14**(4), 435–459 (2010)

15. Glass, R.: Facts and fallacies of software engineering. Addison-Wesley, Boston (2003)
16. Goodchild, M.F., Li, L.: Assuring the quality of volunteered geographic information. Spat. stat. **1**, 110–120 (2012)
17. Haklay, M.: How good is volunteered geographical information? a comparative study of OpenStreetMap and ordnance survey datasets. Environ. Plann. B. Plann. Des. **37**(4), 682–703 (2010)
18. Haklay, M., Basiouka, S., Antoniou, V., Ather, A.: How many volunteers does it take to map an area well? the validity of Linus' law to volunteered geographic information. Cartogr. J. **47**(4), 315–322 (2010)
19. Keßler, C., de Groot, R.T.A.: Trust as a proxy measure for the quality of volunteered geographic information in the case of OpenStreetMap. In: In: Vandenbroucke, D., Bucher, B., Crompvoets, J. (eds.) Geographic Information Science at the Heart of Europe. Lecture Notes in Geoinformation and Cartography, pp. 21–37. Springer, Cham (2013). https://doi.org/10.1007/978-3-319-00615-4_2
20. Lauriault, T., Mooney, P.: Crowdsourcing: a geographic approach to public engagement. Available at SSRN: https://ssrn.com/abstract=2518233 (2014)
21. Mahabir, R., Croitoru, A., Crooks, A.T., Agouris, P., Stefanidis, A.: A critical review of high and very high-resolution remote sensing approaches for detecting and mapping slums: trends, challenges and emerging opportunities. Urban Sci. **2**(1), 8 (2018)
22. Mahabir, R., Crooks, A., Croitoru, A., Agouris, P.: The study of slums as social and physical constructs: challenges and emerging research opportunities. Reg. Stud. Reg. Sci. **3**(1), 399–419 (2016)
23. Mahabir, R., Stefanidis, A., Croitoru, A., Crooks, A.T., Agouris, P.: Authoritative and volunteered geographical information in a developing country: a comparative case study of road datasets in Nairobi, Kenya. ISPRS Int. J. Geo Inf. **6**(1), 24 (2017)
24. Mooney, P., Corcoran, P.: Analysis of interaction and co-editing patterns amongst open street map contributors. Trans. GIS **18**(5), 633–659 (2014)
25. Neis, P., Zipf, A.: Analyzing the contributor activity of a volunteered geographic information project-the case of OpenStreetMap. ISPRS Int. J. Geo Inf. **1**(2), 146–165 (2012)
26. Panchal, J.H.: Agent-based modeling of mass-collaborative product development processes. J. Comput. Inf. Sci. Eng. **9**(3), 031007 (2009)
27. Raymond, E.: The cathedral and the bazaar. Knowl. Technol. Policy **12**(3), 23–49 (1999)
28. Soden, R., Palen, L.: From crowdsourced mapping to community mapping: the post-earthquake work of OpenStreetMap Haiti. In: Rossitto, C., Ciolfi, L., Martin, D., Conein, B. (eds.) COOP 2014 - Proceedings of the 11th International Conference on the Design of Cooperative Systems, 27-30 May 2014, Nice (France), pp. 311–326. Springer, Cham (2014). https://doi.org/10.1007/978-3-319-06498-7_19
29. Wang, J., Shih, P.C., Carroll, J.M.: Revisiting Linus's law: benefits and challenges of open source software peer review. Int. J. Hum. Comput. Stud. **77**, 52–65 (2015)
30. Whitenack, L., Mahabir, R.: A tool for optimizing the efficiency of drive-thru services. In: 2022 Systems and Information Engineering Design Symposium (SIEDS), pp. 151–156. IEEE (2022)
31. Wilensky, U.: NetLogo. Tech. Rep., Center for Connected Learning and Computer-Based Modeling. Northwestern University, Evanston, IL (1999). http://ccl.northwestern.edu/netlogo/

32. Xu, J., Yilmaz, L., Zhang, J.: Agent simulation of collaborative knowledge processing in wikipedia. In: Proceedings of the 2008 Spring simulation multiconference, pp. 19–25. CiteSeer (2008)
33. Zhou, Q.: Exploring the relationship between density and completeness of urban building data in OpenStreetMap for quality estimation. Int. J. Geogr. Inf. Sci. **32**(2), 257–281 (2018)

OSIRIS: Organization Simulation in Response to Intrusion Strategies

Jeongkeun Shin[(✉)], Geoffrey B. Dobson, Kathleen M. Carley, and L. Richard Carley

Carnegie Mellon University, Pittsburgh, PA 15213, USA
jeongkes@andrew.cmu.edu, {gdobson,kathleen.carley}@cs.cmu.edu
LRC@cmu.edu

Abstract. OSIRIS, Organization Simulation In Response to Intrusion Strategies, is an agent-based simulation framework that models virtual organization composed of end user agents with complex and realistic behavior patterns. The purpose of OSIRIS is to predict and analyze the scale of cyberattack damage on the organization once targeted by cybercriminals with a consideration of organization members' properties, behavior patterns, and social relations. In this paper, we detail how we reflect real world organization environments and cyberattack scenarios to OSIRIS by illustrating our organization and cybercriminal design.

Keywords: Agent-based modeling and simulation · Human behavior modeling · Organization studies

1 Introduction

As the Internet is universally supplied and innovative information technologies emerge, the number of cybercrimes consistently increase year by year. Cybersecurity Ventures predicts that "global cybercrime costs will grow by 15% per year over the next five years, and it will reach $10.5 trillion USD annually by 2025" [13]. It is surprising that over 95% of security incidents come from "human error", and the most common human error is "Double Clicking" a malicious attachment or unsafe URL [8]. Thus, it is essential to analyze what causes end users to make human errors to reduce cybercrime incidents. However, vulnerabilities caused by human factors are often overlooked, partly because human tests are expensive and very difficult to repeat [1]. Moreover, conducting a human test in the real organization is often not welcomed by organization members. For example, when Rizzoni and his team ran a phishing simulation campaign, they sent custom phishing emails that asked employees to click the malicious link to receive a Christmas bonus. Disappointed that the bonus was not real, some employees complained about the campaign, and it was eventually terminated [14]. To analyze human errors and their impacts without conducting actual human tests, we introduce OSIRIS, an agent-based simulation framework that models a virtual organization and end user agents with realistic

© The Author(s), under exclusive license to Springer Nature Switzerland AG 2022
R. Thomson et al. (Eds.): SBP-BRiMS 2022, LNCS 13558, pp. 134–143, 2022.
https://doi.org/10.1007/978-3-031-17114-7_13

human behavior patterns. Carley stated, "the human organization has long been used as a metaphor for the organization of computational process" [2]. Thus, if computational model of human behaviors, organization settings, and cyberattack scenarios is appropriately designed, simulations of virtual human tests against cyberattacks can not only be cost-effective, faster, and more comprehensive, but also allows systematic examination of various complicated outside-the-box scenarios [3]. The ultimate goal of OSIRIS is to provide a testbed where a client can build a custom virtual organization, and then simulate cyberattack scenarios on that organization to predict potential cyberattack damage and to test the effectiveness of various cyber-defense strategies to minimize human errors.

2   Related Works

There have been various attempts to implement models to simulate cyberattacks on virtual end users. Schultz proposed a framework that predicts and detects insider attack using end users' behaviors and symptoms including deliberate markers, meaningful errors, preparatory behaviors, correlated usage patterns, verbal behavior and personality traits [15]. Kotenko implemented multi-agent simulation of cyber-attacks and a multi-level cyber-defense system where defense agents can cooperate to counter cyber-attacks [11]. Blythe et al. developed the agent community systems to test cyber security systems by modeling human behaviors, physiology, and emotion [1]. Vernon-Bido et al. introduced a model that examines factors that make a user become an attacker by leveraging rational choice theory, routine activity theory, social learning theory, and planned behavior theory [17]. Dobson and Carley introduced Cyber-FIT framework [4], an agent-based cyber warfare simulation framework that models and simulates military cyber forces that defend cyber terrains against adversaries. Dobson et al. expanded this framework by adding more realistic adversary behaviors to explore the cyber defense teams' defensive efforts in the organization [5] and then modeled the agents' ability to perceive cyber situational awareness [6].

Unlike previous works, OSIRIS builds an *organizational-behavior-centric* simulation framework, which implements human agents' entire daily routine and social relationships in the organization. We modeled end user's commonly observed behaviors and software usage patterns in the organization in addition to abilities to respond to the cyberattacks. OSIRIS will provide a testbed to observe how changing one or several human factors will impact the overall cyberattack damage to the entire organization.

3   OSIRIS Simulation Framework

In this section, we introduce our simulation framework, OSIRIS, in detail. OSIRIS is implemented with NetLogo [19]. Its simulation time is counted in ticks. We assume that one tick corresponds to one minute in the real world. While a simulation is running, we keep track of ticks and translate it to real world time. Figure 1 displays OSIRIS in NetLogo [19] user interface.

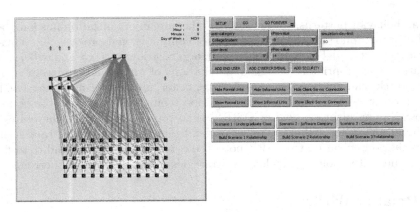

Fig. 1. OSIRIS in NetLogo environment.

3.1 End User Agent

End user agents represent people working at the organization. Similar to humans in the real world, end user agents arrive at the organization early morning or in the afternoon, work 6 to 10 hours, and then leave work. In OSIRIS, an end user class can be defined by distributing daily work time to 13 different behavior categories. While the simulation is running, each end user agent's daily behavior pattern is determined by its own predefined time allocation. We predefined 7 different end user classes that are commonly observed in various organizations. How each end user class spends time at organization is summarized at Table 1.

Table 1. How each end user class spends their time in the organization.

	Email	Messenger	Social Network	Software Development	Business Communication	Data Cleaning
College Student	15%	9%	9%	0%	0%	3%
Software Engineer	15%	3%	4%	48%	5%	10%
Engineering Manager	13%	2%	1%	34%	10%	5%
Human Resource Team	12%	4%	4%	0%	10%	0%
General Office Worker	34%	4%	3%	0%	16%	10%
Blue Collar Worker	5%	5%	5%	0%	0%	0%
Data Scientist	15%	4%	3%	0%	5%	28%

	Data Analysis	Human Resource	General Administration	Social Media	Study	Meeting	Work Outside
College Student	0%	0%	0%	14%	45%	5%	0%
Software Engineer	0%	0%	0%	5%	0%	10%	0%
Engineering Manager	0%	0%	10%	5%	0%	20%	0%
Human Resource Team	0%	36%	8%	4%	0%	22%	0%
General Office Worker	0%	0%	19%	4%	0%	10%	0%
Blue Collar Worker	0%	0%	0%	0%	0%	0%	85%
Data Scientist	30%	0%	0%	5%	0%	10%	0%

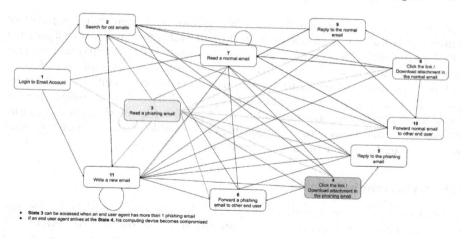

Fig. 2. Behavior flow diagram of the 'Email' behavior category.

While the simulation is running, deployed end user agents' remaining time in 13 behavior categories is monitored every tick, and behavior change is made when necessary. Each behavior category is composed of a set of specific behaviors. For example, Fig. 2 illustrates the shape of the 'Email' behavior category, which is composed of 11 specific behaviors. Each specific behavior has a list of next specific behavior candidates, and an end user agent selects the next specific behavior every tick. In total, we defined 92 specific behaviors in 13 behavior categories, and 3 specific behaviors are causal factors of "human errors": 1) Read a phishing email, 2) Read a phishing message from the messenger, 3) Read a phishing message from the business communication software. These behaviors can only be accessed when an end user agent has more than 1 phishing email or message. According to the recent survey [7], 2.94% of employees eventually click on a link in the malicious email. However, this value should vary from person to person depending on an individual's level of cybersecurity knowledge. We defined the property 'Cybersecurity Expertise Level', where level 1 represents cybersecurity novice and level 5 represents cybersecurity expert. Each level has a different probability value to eventually click the phishing link or download the malware: Level 1 = 11.76%, Level 2 = 5.88%, Level 3 = 2.94%, Level 4 = 1.47%, and Level 5 = 0.735%. This property is assigned to the end user agent when it is deployed. When an end user agent's current specific behavior is one of three causal factors of human error, its computing device can become compromised with a probability corresponding to its cybersecurity expertise level.

In the real world, people build a human network at organizations. Similarly, end user agents in OSIRIS are intertwined with each other formally or informally. Formal relationships are formulated among end user agents who work together to achieve a certain goal while informal relationships are structured based on friendships or personal relationships. The survey [7] states that there is a 0.78% probability that an end user eventually forwards a phishing email to another end user. Reflecting this in OSIRIS, when an end user agent reads a phishing content, it is forwarded to one or more formal and informal relationships with 0.78% probability. Moreover, while a cybercriminal agent is exploiting an end user's computing device, it can deliver phishing contents to the end user's formal and informal relationships using the end user's personal account (Lateral Movement). Reflecting the fact that phishing contents delivered by a credible person seems more persuasive, the probability to be deceived by phishing contents forwarded by formal or informal relationships is a double of the probability value corresponding to the recipient's cybersecurity expertise level.

3.2 Cybercriminal Agent

In OSIRIS, one cybercriminal agent can be deployed. It conducts a phishing attack on end user agents in the organization based on MITRE ATT&CK [16], the collection of adversary tactics and techniques based on real-world observations, which covers almost all types of cyberattacks. Among all tactics and techniques, Korea Internet & Security Agency (KISA) sorts out ones involved in a phishing attack [9,10]. The cybercriminal agent uses these selected cyberattack tactics and techniques in its phishing attack scenario. Broadly, the attack scenario is divided into two phases. If no compromised computing device exists in the organization, a cybercriminal agent is at the Attack Phase 1, attempting phishing through several delivery methods. As soon as one computing device becomes compromised, the cybercriminal moves on to the Attack Phase 2, exploiting compromised computing devices.

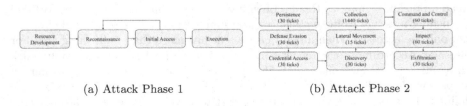

(a) Attack Phase 1   (b) Attack Phase 2

Fig. 3. Cybercriminal agent's phishing attack scenario.

Figure 3(a) illustrates Attack Phase 1. During this phase, the cybercriminal agent builds an infrastructure, prepares a malware software, collects end users' personal information, and attempts phishing through various delivery methods until an end user agent's computing device becomes compromised. According to the Verizon's Data Breach Investigation Report [18], 96% of phishing attacks are delivered using email. Reflecting this, our cybercriminal agent's phishing attacks are delivered through 96% email, 2% messenger, and 2% business communication software.

As described in Fig. 3(b), during Attack Phase 2, a cybercriminal agent sequentially leverages nine different MITRE ATT&CK [16] tactics to exploit an end user's compromised computing device. Each tactic is composed of a set of attack techniques, and the cybercriminal agent randomly chooses one technique every tick to damage computing devices. Each technique produces one of five adverse effects on compromised computing devices for a tick: None, Slowdown, Data Loss, Data Modification, and Data Leakage. In total, a cybercriminal agent uses 46 attack techniques, and we assign the most relevant adverse effect to every attack technique. An end user agent with a compromised computing device suffers from one of five adverse effects every tick until the security agent fixes the computing device, or the cybercriminal agent finishes exploitation.

3.3 Security Agent

In OSIRIS, security agents monitor end user agents' computing devices and repair them if a virus is found. In every 15 ticks, each security agent randomly selects one computing device and inspects whether it is virus-infected or not. The probability to successfully detect and repair the compromised computing device during the inspection should be assigned before starting the simulation (1–100%). As soon as the security agent successfully detects and fixes the virus, the cybercriminal agent immediately loses the access to that computing device. If the last compromised computing device becomes fixed, the cybercriminal agent has no computing device to exploit. Then, it is immediately transferred to Attack Phase 1, and should deliver phishing contents to end user agents again until another computing device in the organization becomes compromised.

4 Virtual Experiment

We conducted virtual experiments to observe how three factors, 1) organization size, 2) cybersecurity expertise level, and 3) proportion of communication, impact on the scale of the cyberattack damage once the organization is targeted by cybercriminals.

The simulation setting for this experiment is summarized in Table 2. We deployed one cybercriminal agent and three security agents. Each end user agent is asked to randomly build 1 or 2 bidirectional formal relationships and informal relationships with other end user agents in the organization. Considering the Krebs' experiment result that antivirus software successfully detects computer viruses with average 24.47% and median 19% [12], we set the security agent's inspection success rate as 20%. Then, we built 80 different simulation settings with 4 different values of organization size, 5 different values of cybersecurity expertise level, and 4 different values of end user agent's proportion of communication. The communication includes three behavior categories: Email, Messenger, and Business Communication. To conduct these experiments, we declared four different types of end user agents that respectively spend 10%, 20%, 40% and 80% of their daily work time on the communication. The remaining time is equally distributed to 10 remaining behavior categories. For each case, we run 10 simulations (800 simulations in total). Each simulation is played

Table 2. Simulation summary

Number of cybercriminal agents	1
Number of security agents	3
Number of formal relationship of each end user agent	1 or 2
Number of informal relationship of each end user agent	1 or 2
Inspection success rate	20%
Organization Size	10, 20, 40, or 80
Cybersecurity Expertise Level	1, 2, 3, 4, or 5
Proportion of Communication	10%, 20%, 40%, or 80%
Simulation period	90 days (129,600 ticks)
Number of simulations for each case	10

for 129,600 ticks, which corresponds to 90 days in OSIRIS. After running simulations of each case, we record the average cyberattack damage of 10 simulations, which are summarized in Table 3 and Table 4.

Simulation results in Table 3 illustrate that the number of overall virus infection in the organization tends to increase as the organization size increases, end user agents' cybersecurity expertise level decreases, and the proportion of communication increases. Table 4 illustrates that the magnitude of 4 different cyberattack damage increases as organization size increases, end user agents' cybersecurity expertise level decreases, and the proportion of communication increases. One noticeable thing is the 'Data Loss' adverse effect. It tends to be close to 0 when the organization size is small, but rapidly increases as the organization size increases. Data Loss damage occurs during 'Impact' MITRE ATT&CK [16] tactic, which is located at the latter part of Attack Phase 2. This implies that when the organization size is small, three security agents succeed to detect and fix the virus before the cybercriminal agent reaches the endpoint, but cannot manage to do so as the organization size gets bigger.

5　Discussion and Future Works

Although not represented in this paper in detail, the OSIRIS can be used to test the effectiveness of cybersecurity strategies to mitigate cyberattack damage. For example, one common strategy to keep end users cautious is to intermittently pop up the warning message at the end user agent's computing device. If an end user agent's cybersecurity expertise level becomes maximum for a while after an end user agent sees the warning message, running two different simulations, one with the strategy and the other without it, will show how much this strategy is effective to mitigate the overall damage from phishing attacks.

There are still limitations in the OSIRIS. Currently, end user agents cannot directly report and ask for inspection to security agents when they recognize

Table 3. Projected number of virus infections and standard deviation.

Organization size	CyberSecurity Expertise Level	Proportion of communication							
		10%		20%		40%		80%	
		Infections	SD	Infections	SD	Infections	SD	Infections	SD
10	1	5.7	2.263	12.1	3.573	24.9	5.971	38.9	10.34
	2	2.8	1.989	4.6	1.955	12.5	3.689	17.3	6.129
	3	1.4	1.075	4.5	2.068	5.6	2.366	9.1	2.424
	4	1.4	0.966	1.8	1.135	2.8	2.201	4.3	2.002
	5	1.2	0.919	1.3	1.059	1.4	1.265	2.5	1.08
20	1	9	3.266	21.8	3.853	49.3	8.166	81.3	10.199
	2	5.1	1.969	10.6	2.797	21.1	5.087	33.4	8.488
	3	1.6	1.173	5.4	2.459	10.5	4.836	17.4	4.526
	4	1.3	0.949	3.8	1.135	5.3	2.908	6.1	2.807
	5	0.7	0.823	1.5	1.08	3.1	1.912	3	1.563
40	1	21.1	4.28	47.6	13.689	101.7	16.687	246.6	22.897
	2	10.9	3.573	20.4	3.718	37.3	7.675	74.1	10.796
	3	4.3	1.494	11.1	3.035	17.6	3.748	30.2	5.77
	4	2.6	2.17	4.5	1.841	8.4	2.319	15.5	4.743
	5	0.9	0.876	2.3	1.567	4.3	2.359	7.2	2.573
80	1	37.4	6.398	106.4	20.14	333.7	35.393	680.1	41.72
	2	16.6	5.103	33.9	6.082	81.5	10.32	243	25.373
	3	7.2	3.765	15.2	5.959	33.2	8.162	63.6	9.046
	4	4.1	2.331	8.2	3.824	13.8	4.872	25.5	7.322
	5	2.4	1.897	4.5	2.121	9.8	4.211	12.6	3.239

Table 4. Projected overall cyberattack damage in the organization.

Organization size	Proportion of communication	Expertise level	Data modification	Slow down	Data leakage	Data loss	Proportion of communication	Expertise level	Data modification	Slow down	Data leakage	Data loss
10	10%	1	61.3	193.6	900.9	0	20%	1	125.4	408.5	2571.9	6
		2	26.6	94.9	429.9	0		2	45.7	154.9	828.2	0
		3	13.7	44.9	167.4	0		3	42.6	153	770.7	0
		4	16.5	54.1	321.7	0		4	17.6	60.7	289.3	0
		5	12.2	43.1	251.7	0		5	12.8	40.7	186.6	0
	40%	1	257.6	844.2	4456	0	80%	1	393	1293.3	6605.6	0
		2	120.6	424.3	2193.9	0		2	174.5	573.9	2941.8	0
		3	55.4	186.6	919.7	0		3	99.8	320	2072.8	0
		4	30.2	99.8	581.9	0		4	43.3	139.6	632.8	0
		5	16.7	50.8	309.3	0		5	23.9	83.3	371.3	0
20	10%	1	105.7	318.3	3542.3	18	20%	1	252.4	791.7	8485.7	30
		2	59.3	178.9	1684.9	1.3		2	133	378.1	4546.1	24
		3	28.8	60.2	749.3	0		3	63.2	187.2	2191.8	10.9
		4	12.6	46.5	272.7	0		4	52.1	137.3	2140.2	12
		5	8.7	25.7	249.8	0		5	20.7	53.9	731.1	0
	40%	1	587.9	1726.4	20663.7	114.8	80%	1	966.7	2776.9	35186.4	225.3
		2	247.1	740.9	8296.8	20.8		2	387.1	1149.4	13864.5	47.7
		3	136	392.9	4199	40.4		3	204.9	593.7	6096	32.3
		4	64	188.6	2282.9	18		4	80.8	215.4	2771.5	18
		5	33.6	105.8	1227.9	0		5	32.2	104.1	1078.4	0
40	10%	1	324.5	743.8	14437.9	221.7	20%	1	767.1	1664.9	33740	538.9
		2	167.2	388	7878.8	108		2	337.6	734.3	15780.8	258.6
		3	69.8	151.9	3145.9	47.3		3	188.2	409.3	8307.1	134.2
		4	36.9	94.4	1781.5	18		4	76.8	167.9	3097.8	58.9
		5	15.5	33.7	763.6	12		5	34.9	82.4	1671.7	18
	40%	1	1601.2	3569.8	72001.9	1110.1	80%	1	3660	8350.7	169237.2	2481.2
		2	583.3	1336.8	24692	384.7		2	1162.2	2587.2	52278.3	809.6
		3	283.6	631.8	13044.1	199.1		3	482.3	1093.5	22451	315.7
		4	154.7	308.4	7388.9	149.1		4	260.4	549.2	12478.4	215.3
		5	73.7	152.9	3599	63.8		5	109.1	263.4	5003.6	54
80	10%	1	848.9	1361.4	38490.8	1026.3	20%	1	2315	3795.4	99661.8	2682.1
		2	385.9	604.6	17778.9	468		2	759.8	1240.5	35672.5	892.7
		3	156.3	263.4	7317.7	177.2		3	334.4	558.4	16089	367.6
		4	102.1	153.1	4605.1	133.4		4	192.4	299.6	8315.1	237.5
		5	50.6	90.9	2328.9	48		5	105.3	171.2	4938.4	126
	40%	1	6994.6	11340.4	323031.2	8210.2	80%	1	13271.5	21533.6	611702.1	15602.6
		2	1739.8	2908.4	79772.3	1988.9		2	5054.9	8382.3	235521.8	5811
		3	754.5	1229.9	34730	875		3	1399.5	2306.6	64276.9	1641.4
		4	326.9	515.7	15014.2	392.3		4	575.5	932	26184.3	657
		5	232.4	360.7	10197.6	281		5	295.2	458.3	13087.9	366

abnormal symptoms in its computing device. They cannot learn from the mistakes in the past. Also, only one type of cyberattack, phishing, can be simulated. Lastly, the end user agent's emotional states such as hunger, fatigue, or the motivation, which influence its performance level, are not fully implemented.

In the future, as we implement these functionalities, OSIRIS can be used in more diverse analysis such as calculating the optimal number of security agents in the organization to minimize the damage, observing organization's vulnerabilities from various types of cyberattacks, and analyzing the impact of end users' emotional states against cyberattacks.

6   Conclusion

In this paper, we introduced OSIRIS, and illustrated how three factors, organization size, cybersecurity expertise level, and proportion of communication affect the scale of overall cyberattack damage on the organization. OSIRIS will provide a testbed that clients can replicate real world organizations, and conduct various cyberattack simulations to observe and analyze potential cyberattack damage started from human errors without conducting actual human tests. It is cost effective, easy to repeat, and allows various outside-the-box experiments without any constraints. In the future, for more realistic simulation, we will improve the model with various human factors, social interactions, and various types of cyberattacks.

Acknowledgement. The author(s) disclosed receipt of the following financial support for the research, authorship, and/or publication of this article: This research was supported in part by the Minerva Research Initiative under Grant #N00014-21-1-4012, and by the center for Computational Analysis of Social and Organizational Systems (CASOS) at Carnegie Mellon University. The views and conclusions are those of the authors and should not be interpreted as representing the official policies, either expressed or implied, of the Office of Naval Research or the US Government.

References

1. Blythe, J., et al.: Testing cyber security with simulated humans. In: Twenty-Third IAAI Conference (2011)
2. Carley, K.M.: Organizational adaptation. Annal. Oper. Res. **75**, 25–47 (1997)
3. Carley, K.M., et al.: BioWar: scalable agent-based model of bioattacks. IEEE Trans. Syst. Man Cybern.-Part A: Syst. Hum. **36**(2), 252–265 (2006)
4. Dobson, Geoffrey B.., Carley, Kathleen M..: Cyber-FIT: an agent-based modelling approach to simulating cyber warfare. In: Lee, Dongwon, Lin, Yu.-Ru., Osgood, Nathaniel, Thomson, Robert (eds.) SBP-BRiMS 2017. LNCS, vol. 10354, pp. 139–148. Springer, Cham (2017). https://doi.org/10.1007/978-3-319-60240-0_18
5. Dobson, G.B., Rege, A., Carley, K.M.: Informing active cyber defence with realistic adversarial behaviour. J. Inf. Warfare **17**(2), 16–31 (2018)
6. Dobson, Geoffrey B.., Carley, Kathleen M..: A computational model of cyber situational awareness. In: Thomson, Robert, Dancy, Christopher, Hyder, Ayaz, Bisgin, Halil (eds.) SBP-BRiMS 2018. LNCS, vol. 10899, pp. 395–400. Springer, Cham (2018). https://doi.org/10.1007/978-3-319-93372-6_43

7. Flouton, M.: Threat Spotlight: Post-Delivery Email Threats. Journey Notes, 21 October 2021. https://blog.barracuda.com/2021/06/02/threat-spotlight-post-delivery-email-threats/. threat-spotlight-post-delivery-email-threats
8. IBM: IBM security services 2014 cyber security intelligence index (2014)
9. Korea Internet & Security Agency (KISA): TTP #2 Analysis of the Bookcodes RAT C2 framework starting with spear phishing (2020). https://www.boho.or.kr/krcert/publicationList.do
10. Korea Internet & Security Agency (KISA): TTP #4 Phishing Target Reconnaissance and Attack Resource Analysis (2021). https://www.boho.or.kr/krcert/publicationList.do
11. Kotenko, I.: Multi-agent modelling and simulation of cyber-attacks and cyberdefense for homeland security. In: 2007 4th IEEE Workshop on Intelligent Data Acquisition and Advanced Computing Systems: Technology and Applications. IEEE (2007)
12. Krebs, B.: A Closer Look: Email-Based Malware Attacks. Krebs Secur., 21 June 2012. krebsonsecurity.com/2012/06/a-closer-look-recent-email-based-malware-attacks/
13. Morgan, S.: Cybercrime to Cost the World $10.5 Trillion Annually by 2025. Cybercrime Mag., 27 April 2021. https://cybersecurityventures.com/cybercrime-damage-costs-10-trillion-by-2025/
14. Rizzoni, F., Magalini, S., Casaroli, A., Mari, P., Dixon, M., Coventry, L.: Phishing simulation exercise in a large hospital: a case study. Digital Health **8**, 20552076221081716 (2022)
15. Schultz, E.E.: A framework for understanding and predicting insider attacks. Comput. Secur. **21**(6), 526–531 (2002)
16. Strom, B.E., Applebaum, A., Miller, DP., Nickels, K.C., Pennington, A.G., Thomas, C.B.: Mitre att&ck: Design and philosophy. Technical report (2018)
17. Vernon-Bido, D., Padilla, J.J., Diallo, S.Y., Kavak, H., Gore, R.J.: Towards modeling factors that enable an attacker. In: SummerSim, p. 46 (2016)
18. Widup, S., Hylender, D., Bassett, G., Langlois, P., Pinto, A.: Verizon data breach investigations report (2020)
19. Wilensky, U.: NetLogo (1999). http://ccl.northwestern.edu/netlogo/. Center for Connected Learning and Computer-Based Modeling, Northwestern University, Evanston, IL

Detection of Coordination Between State-Linked Actors

Keeley Erhardt[✉][iD] and Alex Pentland[iD]

MIT Media Lab, Cambridge, MA 02139, USA
{keeley,pentland}@mit.edu

Abstract. Powerful actors have engaged in information control for centuries, restricting, promoting, or influencing the information environment as it suits their evolving agendas. In the Digital Age, information control has moved online, and information operations now target the online platforms that play a critical role in news engagement and civic debate. In this paper, we use a discrete-time stochastic model to analyze coordinated activity in an online social network, representing the behaviors of accounts as interacting Markov chains. From a dataset of 31,521 tweets posted by 206 accounts, half of which were identified by Twitter as participating in a state-linked information operation, we evaluate the coordination, measured by the apparent influence, between pairs of state-linked compared to unaffiliated accounts. We find that the state-linked actors exhibit more coordination amongst themselves than with the unaffiliated accounts. The degree of coordination between the state-linked accounts is also much higher than the observed coordination between the unaffiliated accounts. Additionally, we find that the account that represented the most coordinated activity in the network *had no followers*, demonstrating the power of our modeling approach to unearth hidden connections even in the absence of explicit network structure.

Keywords: Coordinated activity · Influence modeling · Markov chains

1 Introduction

The rate of online media consumption has dramatically increased and individuals' online social networks (OSNs) are an ever more popular source for news content. State and non-state actors desiring to manipulate the information environment have adapted to this trend, launching information operations targeted at a range of online platforms. Since October 2018, Twitter has publicly identified more than 40 state-linked information operations attributed to over 20 countries targeted at its platform [15]. From 2017 through mid-2021, Facebook similarly took down and reported over 150 information operations originating from more than 50 countries [7]. An information operation can be characterized as coordinated activity aimed at a strategic objective that is fundamentally deceptive in nature [6]. This deception may not necessarily imply explicitly false information (e.g., out-of-context images, agenda-setting, or flooding the information environment with superfluous messaging to confuse and distract [8,14]).

R. Thomson et al. (Eds.): SBP-BRiMS 2022, LNCS 13558, pp. 144–154, 2022.
https://doi.org/10.1007/978-3-031-17114-7_14

Much of the literature in this space focuses on detecting information operations through content-based features [1, 13], or network-based approaches [16]. Other studies examine the temporal patterns of post activity [9, 10]. In this paper, we choose to instead revisit the "Influence Model", first proposed in [2]. This model is most similar to the temporal approach in [10] but has the advantage of being able to distinguish the directionality of apparent influence rather than producing an undirected account to account coordination graph. The influence model describes the dynamics of networked, interacting Markov chains. A Markov chain is a method for generating a sequence of random variables in which the current value is always probabilistically dependent on only the most recent past value.

In this context, we choose to model individual social accounts as Markov chains with random variables representing post activity for a given user. With the influence model, we can measure the coordination between pairs of accounts based on post activity alone. From these coordination measures, it is possible to quantify hidden connections between accounts and, potentially, inauthentic activity. We focus on the coordination aspect of information operations for a few reasons. First, it alleviates some privacy and bias concerns associated with moderation. Second, an influence modeling approach is more language and media agnostic than content-based alternatives. Third, unlike network-based methods, this approach does not require access to the underlying network structure.

Our contributions are as follows. First, we present a novel application of the influence model for detecting accounts engaged in an information operation. Second, we demonstrate how state-linked accounts can be distinguished from other accounts in a network based on their coordinated post activity alone. And third, we have published an open-source Python library that efficiently implements the influence model and supports the learning of its parameters from sequences of observations.

2   The Influence Model

The "Influence Model" describes the relationships between networked Markov chains in terms of the "influence" chains have on one another. The model is made up of a network of interacting Markov chains each associated with a node in a network. At the network level, nodes are referred to as sites and their connections are described by the stochastic network matrix D. At the local level, each site has an internal Markov chain $\Gamma(A)$ and assumes one of the statuses of $\Gamma(A)$ at any given discrete-time instant. These statuses are represented by a length-m status vector s, an indicator vector containing a single 1 in the position corresponding to the present status and 0 everywhere else:

$$s_i'[k] = [0...010...1]. \tag{1}$$

Each chain evolves according to its own status and the statuses of its neighbors. Updating the status of the ith site in the influence model takes place in three stages:

1. The ith site, site_i, randomly selects one of its neighbors to be its determining site; site_j is selected with probability d_{ij}.
2. The status of site_j at time k, $\boldsymbol{s}_j[k]$, fixes the probability vector $\boldsymbol{p}_i[k+1]$ that is used in (3) to randomly select the next status of site_i.
3. The next status $\boldsymbol{s}_i[k+1]$ is realized according to $\boldsymbol{p}_i[k+1]$.

A state-transition matrix A_{ij} describes how the state-transition probabilities of site_j depend on the previous status of site_i. A_{ij} is an $m_i \times m_j$ non-negative matrix with rows summing to 1. A is a matrix with A_{ij} in its (i,j)th block. From the stochastic network matrix D and the state-transition matrix A, one can compute the influence matrix H that describes the "influence" exerted by and on each site in the network. H is given by the generalized Kronecker product of D' and $\{A_{ij}\}$:

$$H = D' \otimes \{A_{ij}\}. \tag{2}$$

The influence model has been applied to a number of problems, ranging from modeling failures in a power grid to recognizing functional roles in meetings [3,5] For more detail on the model, its properties, and applications, we refer readers to [3] and [11].

2.1　The influence Library

In conjunction with this paper, we have published an open-source Python library that provides an efficient implementation of the influence model. The library supports defining new influence models and generating observations through applying the model's evolution equations. We also implement methods to reconstruct an influence model from observations, learning the parameters D, A, and H. Additionally, the project implements the basic, simulated example presented in [4] to familiarize new users with the core concepts of the model.

```python
import numpy as np

leader = Site("leader", np.array([[1], [0]]))
follower = Site("follower", np.array([[0], [1]]))
D = np.array([
    [1, 0],
    [1, 0],
])
A = np.array([
    [.5, .5, 1., 0.],
    [.5, .5, 0., 1.],
    [.5, .5, .5, .5],
    [.5, .5, .5, .5],
])
model = InfluenceModel([leader, follower], D, A)
initial_state = model.get_state_vector()
next(model)
next_state = model.get_state_vector()
```

3   Data

In this paper, we analyze an information operation targeted at Twitter and attributed to the People's Republic of China (PRC). The operation focused on promoting Chinese Communist Party (CCP) narratives related to the treatment of the Uyghur population in Xinjiang. In December 2021, Twitter published a representative sample of accounts and tweets associated with this state-linked information operation, including 31,269 tweets from 2,016 unique accounts [15]. The tweets begin April 20, 2019 and end April 5, 2021. We augment this dataset with "unaffiliated" accounts and tweets, defined as accounts and tweets still permitted on the Twitter platform as of March 2022. Tweets from unaffiliated accounts were collected using the Twitter Search API v2, selecting for tweets posted between April 20, 2019 and April 5, 2021 with at least one of the keywords or hashtags: "xinjiang", "uighur", "uighurs", "uyghur", "uyghurs", "uygur", "uygurs", "uigur", or "uigurs". This search query returned a total of 14,728,582 tweets from 2,665,001 unique accounts.

To ensure a reasonable number of observations (tweets) for each account, we only consider tweets from accounts in the top one percent of accounts by total number of tweets. This means that an account must tweet at least 60 times over the two-year period to be included in the analysis. After downselecting tweets to only those posted by the most prolific accounts, we are left with 10,889 tweets from 103 state-linked accounts and 6,231,955 tweets from 27,003 unaffiliated accounts. From these unaffiliated accounts, we randomly select 103 accounts (corresponding to the number of state-linked accounts) and their associated tweets to analyze. Our final dataset then includes 31,521 tweets from 206 accounts (50% state-linked and 50% unaffiliated).

4   Methodology

Each account in our dataset is represented as a site in a network graph. The two classes of accounts (state-linked and unaffiliated), as well as the true network structure (the follower-following relationships), are not known a priori. Our goal is to quantify the "influence" that determines the status of each site in the network using observed behaviors.

4.1   Constructing Observations

Sites interact by posting messages (tweets), the observed behavior. If a site posts a message at discrete-time instant k, we consider the site "active" at time k. At any given time, a site can be in one of two states, *Active* or *Inactive*. We choose to discretize tweets into 1-h time blocks to ensure enough granurity to differentiate explicitly coordinated behavior from topics that begin to trend, while still ensuring a reasonable number of accounts are likely to be *Active* at any given time. The sequence of observations for each account represents the account's status over time.

Algorithm 1: Constructs a sequence of observations for each site

---

1 <u>function GetObservations</u> (*posts, accounts, start, end*)
    Input : All posts, accounts, and the time range of interest
    Output: Mapping from accounts to observations
2 delta $\leftarrow$ 1 hour
3 **foreach** *account* $\in$ *accounts* **do**
4   **while** *start* $<$ *end* **do**
5   k $\leftarrow$ time range from start to delta
6   **if** *account posted at time k* **then**
7   status $\leftarrow$ 1
8   **else**
9   status $\leftarrow$ 0
10   AddToObservations (account, status)
11   start $\leftarrow$ start + delta

Given we expect coordinated actors to collectively promote similar narratives, we are less interested in overall post activity and more interested in post activity by topic. We choose a simple definition for "topic": any entity is a topic. Each message contains zero or more entities, defined as hashtags, URLs, or user mentions. We first extract all entities from posts and then construct observation sequences for each entity individually, across all sites. For example, for the entity #hashtag, we only consider an account *Active* if the account posts a message that includes #hashtag. We exclude any entities that were used as search terms in collecting accounts from the Twitter API. And, we normalize URLs by stripping the protocol, subdomain(s), and any query parameters.

4.2 Learning the State-Transition Matrices

In the influence model, the status of each site varies over time based on the "influence" of the other sites in the network. This influence is represented in part by the state-transition matrices covered previously. Given sequences of observations for each site, we can reconstruct the state-transition matrices using a maximum-likelihood estimate, similar to the approach in [4]. Each state-transition matrix is 2×2 representing the two possible statuses, *Active* and *Inactive*. If $site_j$ perfectly follows the behavior of $site_i$ (positive coordination), then A_{ij} is the identity matrix. To obtain a scalar coordination measure for each state-transition matrix, we compute the Frobenius inner product of A_{ij} and the identity matrix. The coordination measure can range $[0, 2]$. Zero represents maximum positive coordination, $site_i[k-1] = site_j[k] \, \forall \, k$, and two represents maximum negative coordination, $site_i[k-1] \neq site_j[k] \, \forall \, k$. By averaging these coordination measures across all entities, we can determine the master state-transition matrix for each pair of sites.

5   Results

We find that the accounts engaged in the most coordinated activity are over-whelmingly the accounts controlled by state-linked actors. Additionally, we dis-cover that the accounts at the center of networks of coordination would not have been identifiable through analysis of the more traditional follower-following rela-tionship network (even if it were available), as these accounts predominantly had few to no followers.

5.1   Account Clusters

To assess clusters of accounts with high-levels of coordinated activity, we con-struct a coordination network from the pairwise coordination measures. A directed edge (i, j) in the coordination network represents that $site_i$ exhibits apparent influence on $site_j$ with an edge weight equal to one minus the coordi-nation measure. We are primarily interested in positive coordination—when an account mimics the behavior of another account—so only create an edge if the coordination measure is less than one (recall that zero corresponds to maximum positive coordination). This filtering means that not all accounts are represented in the coordination network. If an account does not positively "influence" another account and is not itself "influenced", it will be absent. We find that the clusters of accounts with high degrees of coordination are primarily controlled by state-linked actors, and that each cluster is typically made up of all state-linked or all unaffiliated accounts. This corresponds to our intuition that accounts will exhibit differences in the accounts that they coordinate with based on class membership.

We observe differences in how coordination is expressed when we examine the three entity types individually. In all cases, state-linked accounts make up the majority of the accounts engaged in coordinated activity and almost exclusively coordinate with other state-linked accounts. The unaffiliated accounts are most represented in the network through URL shares, potentially due to the rapid rate at which emerging news stories can diffuse through an OSN.

5.2   Coordinated URL Sharing

For the state-linked accounts, an English-language article from Xinhua News Agency, the official state press agency of the PRC, revealed the most coordinated activity. The story condemned sanctions imposed by the United States (US) for alleged human rights violations in Xinjiang. For the unaffiliated accounts, a Chinese-language Facebook post from the Photographic Society Of Hong Kong Media Limited (PSHK Media) describing the "sinicization" of the Uyghur pop-ulation in Xinjiang by CCP officials revealed the most coordination. The post accused CCP officials of coercing the ethnic, Muslim minority into celebrating a traditional Chinese holiday and consuming pork. Interestingly, Facebook blocks redirects to PSHK Media's official site from its platform and, as of the writing of this paper, the site appears to have been suspended by its hosting provider.

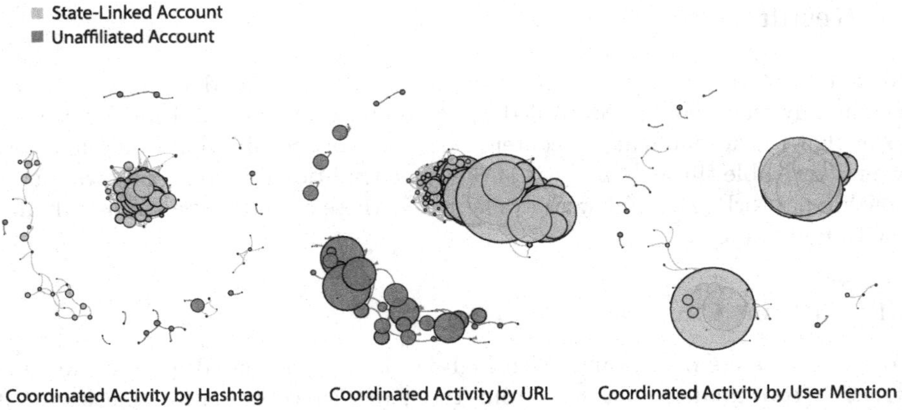

■ State-Linked Account
■ Unaffiliated Account

Coordinated Activity by Hashtag   Coordinated Activity by URL   Coordinated Activity by User Mention

Fig. 1. The coordination between accounts. An edge is colored yellow if it represents coordinated activity between a state-linked account and another state-linked account, blue if the coordination is from an unaffiliated account to an unaffiliated account, and gray if the edge connects accounts from different classes. The size of a node is scaled by the total "influence" the account exerts. (Color figure online)

5.3   Top Influencer

Averaging across the hashtag, URL, and user mention coordination networks produces a new network consisting of 81 accounts, 75 state-linked accounts and six unaffiliated. In this network, we find that one account exhibits a much higher degree of coordination than any other account. This "top influencer" is state-linked, and exclusively coordinates with other state-linked accounts. Interestingly, this account did not follow any other users and *had no followers*.

The account posted 87 times during the two-years of the PRC information operation. 59 tweets included a hashtag, the most popular being "xinjiang", "xinjiangonline", and "stopxinjiangrumors". 28 included URLs, referencing stories from eight news or informational sites owned by the Chinese government in addition to the People's Daily, a newspaper of record for the CCP. 71 of the user's tweets contained user mentions. The tweets range from argumentative, countering allegations of state-mandated sterilizations and forced labor in Xinjiang, to upbeat, describing the happy, peaceful, and productive lives of people in the region.

5.4   Spike in State-Linked Tweets

On January 19, 2021, Mike Pomepo's last day as US secretary of state, he released a press statement accusing China of "ongoing" genocide perpetuated against the Uyghur population in Xinjiang [12]. The statement appears to have triggered a dramatic increase in tweet activity from state-linked accounts (Fig. 2).

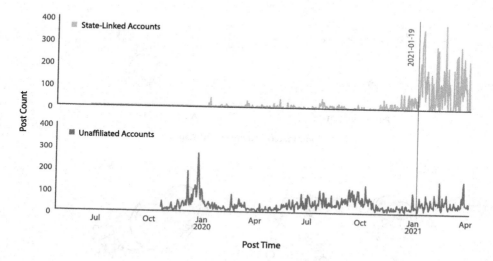

Fig. 2. The tweet count per day across state-linked and unaffiliated accounts.

Given the high volume of state-linked tweets between January and April 2021, we were curious how the coordination network compared between low-activity and high-activity periods. We computed the same networks as in Fig. 1, this time subdividing tweets into two groups: tweets posted before January 19, 2021, and tweets posted after. We find similar results as when we considered the entire two-year period, though the detected coordination between the state-linked accounts is more prevalent following Pompeo's public statement when state-linked tweet volume is highest (Fig. 3).

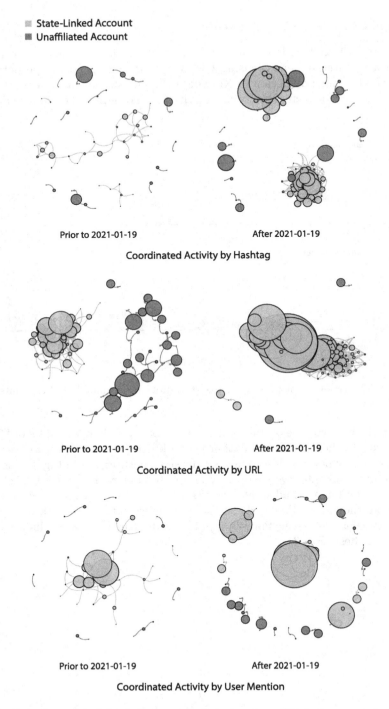

Fig. 3. Coordinated activity between state-linked and unaffiliated accounts before and after Mike Pompeo publicly accuses the PRC of genocide.

6 Discussion and Future Work

We believe that this work represents a unique approach to detecting coordinated information operations, rooted in a well-studied model with broad utility. As an immediate next step, we would like to re-run the analysis on the entirety of the unaffiliated accounts and tweets that we collected, rather than a sample. This will require exploring approaches to minimize the number of sites for which to compute pairwise coordination measures. N sites will always have $N!$ ordered pairs, resulting in a high runtime for large networks. As another area of research, it would be interesting to consider behaviors beyond post activity. And finally, we are interested in exploring how our method performs on additional information operations. Twitter has released dozens of datasets containing accounts and tweets from over 40 state-linked information operations. We would like to see how our model performs on this wide-range of campaigns.

References

1. Alizadeh, M., Shapiro, J.N., Buntain, C., Tucker, J.A.: Content-based features predict social media influence operations. Sci. Adv. **6**(30), eabb5824 (2020)
2. Asavathiratham, C.: The Influence Model: A Tractable Representation for the Dynamics of Networked Markov Chains. Ph.D. thesis, Massachusetts Institute of Technology (2001)
3. Asavathiratham, C., Roy, S., Lesieutre, B., Verghese, G.: The influence model. IEEE Control Syst. Mag. **21**(6), 52–64 (2001)
4. Basu, S., Choudhury, T., Clarkson, B., Pentland, A.: Learning human interactions with the influence model. NIPS (2001)
5. Dong, W., Lepri, B., Cappelletti, A., Pentland, A., Pianesi, F., Zancanaro, M.: Using the influence model to recognize functional roles in meetings. In: Proceedings of the 9th International Conference on Multimodal Interfaces, pp. 271–278 (2007)
6. Erhardt, K., Pentland, A.: Disambiguating disinformation: Extending beyond the veracity of online content. Workshop Proceedings of the 15th International AAAI Conference on Web and Social Media (2021)
7. Facebook: Threat report the state of influence operations 2017–2020. https://about.fb.com/wp-content/uploads/2021/05/IO-Threat-Report-May-20-2021.pdf. Accessed 24 Jun 2022
8. King, G., Pan, J., Roberts, M.E.: How the Chinese government fabricates social media posts for strategic distraction, not engaged argument. Am. Polit. Sci. Rev. **111**(3), 484–501 (2017)
9. Luceri, L., Giordano, S., Ferrara, E.: Detecting troll behavior via inverse reinforcement learning: a case study of Russian trolls in the 2016 us election. In: Proceedings of the International AAAI Conference on Web and Social Media, vol. 14, pp. 417–427 (2020)
10. Magelinski, T., Carley, K.M.: Detecting coordinated behavior in the twitter campaign to reopen America. In: Center for Informed Democracy & Social-Cybersecurity Annual Conference, IDeaS (2020)
11. Pan, W., Dong, W., Cebrian, M., Kim, T., Fowler, J.H., Pentland, A.: Modeling dynamical influence in human interaction: Using data to make better inferences about influence within social systems. IEEE Signal Process. Mag. **29**(2), 77–86 (2012)

154 K. Erhardt and A. Pentland

12. Pompeo, M.: Determination of the secretary of state on atrocities in xinjiang. https://2017-2021.state.gov/determination-of-the-secretary-of-state-on-atrocities-in-xinjiang/index.html. Accessed 24 Jun 2022
13. Rheault, L., Musulan, A.: Efficient detection of online communities and social bot activity during electoral campaigns. J. Inf. Technol. Politics **18**(3), 324–337 (2021)
14. Starbird, K., Arif, A., Wilson, T.: Disinformation as collaborative work: Surfacing the participatory nature of strategic information operations. In: Proceedings of the ACM on Human-Computer Interaction 3(CSCW), pp. 1–26 (2019)
15. Twitter: Transparency report: Information operations. https://transparency.twitter.com/en/reports/information-operations.html. Last accessed 24 Jun 2022
16. Vargas, L., Emami, P., Traynor, P.: On the detection of disinformation campaign activity with network analysis. In: Proceedings of the 2020 ACM SIGSAC Conference on Cloud Computing Security Workshop, pp. 133–146 (2020)

Counteracting Filter Bubbles with Homophily-Aware Link Recommendations

Robert Warton[1], Cupcake Volny[1], and Kevin S. Xu[1,2](✉) (iD)

[1] Department of Electrical Engineering and Computer Science, University of Toledo, Toledo, OH 43606, USA
robert.warton@rockets.utoledo.edu, cvolny@gmail.com, ksx2@case.edu
[2] Department of Computer and Data Sciences, Case Western Reserve University, Cleveland, OH 44106, USA

Abstract. With the prevalence of interaction on social media, data compiled from these networks are perfect for analyzing social trends. One such trend that this paper aims to address is political homophily. Evidence of political homophily is well researched and indicates that people have a strong tendency to interact with others with similar political ideologies. Additionally, as links naturally form in a social network, either through recommendations or indirect interaction, new links are very likely to reinforce communities. This serves to make social media more insulated and ultimately more polarizing. We aim to address this problem by providing link recommendations that will reduce network homophily. We propose several variants of common neighbor-based link prediction algorithms that aim to recommend links to users who are similar but also would decrease homophily. We demonstrate that acceptance of these recommendations can indeed reduce the homophily of the network, whereas acceptance of link recommendations from a standard common neighbors algorithm does not.

Keywords: Polarization · Political homophily · Link prediction · Common neighbors · Modularity reduction

1 Introduction

The Internet, particularly social media platforms, enables unprecedented opportunities for individual expression and the global exchange of thought. As social platforms vie for users and their engagement, significant gains have been made in positive link suggestions and curated content feeds. Activist and author Eli Pariser describes an emergent phenomenon that individualized content feeds and search results effectively filter conflicting viewpoints and promote isolated intellectual and information bubbles [15]. Filter bubbles can have negative impacts

---

R. Warton and C. Volny—Contributed equally to this work.

© The Author(s), under exclusive license to Springer Nature Switzerland AG 2022
R. Thomson et al. (Eds.): SBP-BRiMS 2022, LNCS 13558, pp. 155–164, 2022.
https://doi.org/10.1007/978-3-031-17114-7_15

on a community by excluding potential links outside the bubble while promoting isolation within. This also leads to disrupting the spread of information through a social network. One instance of this isolation of particular interest is the divisive political climate leading up to the 2020 United States presidential election.

Many approaches for link recommendation in online social networks (OSNs), e.g. friend or follow suggestions, are functions of reciprocity (this person follows you), common neighbors (friends of friends), preferential attachment (popular page), or a composite of these strategies (your friends follow this page). Consequently, these strategies often yield recommendations that promote filter bubbles. In particular, methods based on common neighbors can give recommendations that are likely to be accepted; however, the nature of recommendations based on a person's direct neighbors are unlikely to give recommendations outside of a network's isolated communities. These recommendation systems are likely not inherently maligned and do fulfill a desirable outcome of using OSNs: to connect with like-minded peers or information sources. However, simply selecting the best match in similarity often encourages filter bubbles due to homophily—the tendency for a person to form links with similar people.

A direct approach to this problem of recommendations that encourage filter bubbles would be to give recommendations that seek to directly break up communities. This is relatively easy in principle; for instance, if a network is categorized by many small communities, accepting random link recommendations would result in successfully breaking up the communities. However, this is entirely counterintuitive to the purpose standard social network link recommendations serve in the first place. Random recommendations would be unlikely to be accepted and would be seen as poor recommendations; therefore, this is not a good solution to filter bubbles. It would instead be desirable to generate recommendations that are likely to be accepted while simultaneously breaking up the insulated communities within the network.

In this paper, we consider a Twitter network that exhibits political homophily, with nodes labeled as left, right, or neutral depending on their political affiliation. Our main contributions are as follows:

- We define a *polarization index* for a node that indicates the tendency of a node to form edges with other nodes with the same or different affiliation.
- We propose 3 homophily-aware common neighbors-based scores with the goal of providing relevant link recommendations that can reduce homophily.
- We demonstrate that our proposed homophily-aware link recommendation scores can indeed produce relevant link recommendations that, if accepted, would reduce political polarization on a Twitter network.

2   Related Work

McPherson et al.'s work in homophily in social networks [9] lays out the sociological phenomenon from which the filter bubble emerges: people's attraction to similarity in their social network. Moeller and Helberger survey the domains, scopes, and causes of filter bubble works and describes a contrast in polarization concerns between the US (political) and European (news audiences) [11]. Geschke et al. [5] proposes a three-leveled filtering process; individual, social, and technological; and uses an Agent-Based Model to study the contributions of each filter layer to content filtering and possible strategies to remediate filtering. Various works have studied the effects of content diversity over time [13] and strategies to counteract bubbles in recommendation systems [14]. Garimella et al. have studied quantifying controversy in social networks and proposed a strategy to visualize, inform, and counter polarization on controversial issues [3,4].

Mehrabi et al.'s survey on bias and fairness in machine learning [10] provides an excellent introduction into the problem domain Pariser describes in his book [15]: algorithms having unforeseen consequences in promoting bias in a system. Of the types of bias described, the problem domain of political homophily can most aptly be categorized as historical and emergent biases: networks of high assortative mixing will yield recommendations that reinforce that trend.

Masrour et al.'s work in fairness-aware network link prediction [8] discusses a novel approach to link prediction while maintaining fairness to a protected attribute such as gender. They utilize the modularity [12] with respect to the protected attribute as a measure of homophily and provide a model for adversarial learning to train "fair" link predictions.

3   Data Description

We consider the data collected by Conover et al. [2] from Twitter, a social network with high political community homogeneity still featuring cross-community connections. This is a dataset of mentions and retweets recorded during the Fall 2010 United States midterm election via the Twitter "gardenhose" stream into three networks: retweets, mentions, and the combination of those two.

In the retweet network, retweet events recorded a directed edge from the subscriber who retweeted to the original poster. The retweet network showed remarkably high polarization characterized as the vast majority of retweet edges occurring between politically aligned nodes. The mentions network, however, shows more lax community insulation and shows evidence that user-to-user communication tended to publish across political lines more often than with retweeting. This aligns with the findings of Majmundar et al.'s "why we retweet scale" [7] categories of to "show approval" and "showing support" users retweeting content are intentionally expanding the audience of a tweet to their own followers (implying support for the views or opinions of that entry).

Nodes within these networks were labeled as left, right, or neutral based on political affiliation using hashtag co-occurrence with the seed tags #p2 (progressive 2.0) and #tcot (top conservative on Twitter): both popular and polarized hashtags for the election cycle studied. When other hashtags co-occurred with these, they were studied and, if confirmed to be politically aligned, were included in their node categorization effort. The resultant networks published are the largest connected components of each graph with the aforementioned node labels applied; this is the dataset used in this paper. A visualization of the retweet network with nodes colored by political affiliation is shown in Fig. 1.

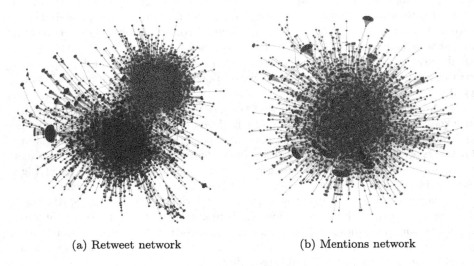

(a) Retweet network   (b) Mentions network

Fig. 1. Force-directed layouts of (a) retweet and (b) mentions networks. Red nodes denote right-leaning users, and blue nodes denote left-leaning users. Community structure is strong in the retweet network and weak in the mentions network. Figure credit: [2].

Table 1. Network properties after conversion to undirected network

Network type	Nodes	Edges	Avg. degree	Modularity
Retweet	18,470	48,053	5.20	0.475
Mentions	7,175	11,681	3.26	0.109
Combined	22,405	59,926	5.35	0.417

This dataset serves as a reasonable size of network labeled by a divisive topic. This clearly demonstrates the tendency to form isolated communities, and is a good target for trying to avoid the filter bubble phenomenon. Encouraging fairness in the flow of information is beneficial to a divided political climate where each party is likely to have an agenda.

4   Methodology

We convert the 3 networks from directed to undirected based on the norm of the Twitter platform: both users are aware of these interactions, and therefore, it can be argued this constitutes a reciprocated network connection of peer awareness. Some basic summary statistics of the networks are shown in Table 1, where the modularity is computed with respect to the political affiliation as a measure of assortative mixing [12]. Each of the three political affiliations (left, right, and neutral) is treated as its own group when computing modularity. The high modularity of the retweet network suggests that there is a lot of assortative mixing, i.e. users mostly retweet from other users with the same political affiliation.

Many of the polarizing qualities of the retweet network carried over into the combined network; albeit, dampened by cross community connections of the mentions network. We use the combined network as the main target of further analysis because it draws from both retweets and mentions and averages out some of the assortative and disassortative features of both networks.

4.1 Polarization Index

A common approach to measure homophily at the level of an individual ego node is the External-Internal (EI) homophily index [6]. The EI index is given by (1).

$$\mathrm{EI}(u) = \frac{N_{\mathrm{external}} - N_{\mathrm{internal}}}{N_{\mathrm{external}} + N_{\mathrm{internal}}} \in [-1, 1], \tag{1}$$

where N_{external} and N_{internal} denote number of edges the ego node forms to external and internal nodes, respectively. Here, a node is considered to be internal to another node if it has the same political affiliation, and external otherwise. This gives a metric that indicates if a node has a strong tendency to form links with nodes of the same political affiliation (-1) or the opposite affiliation (1). Nodes close to 0 have little tendency to prioritize links based on political affiliation. Using the EI index, neutrals would normally be considered as external to both the left and right.

However, for our purposes since the aim is to split up the more polarized groups, it is beneficial to treat neutrals as neither external nor internal to any nodes. This approach was chosen so that neutrals are considered favorably. This is a modification of the EI homophily index, which we will refer to as the *polarization index (PI)* (2).

$$\mathrm{PI}(u) = \frac{N_{\mathrm{opposite}} - N_{\mathrm{same}}}{N_{\mathrm{opposite}} + N_{\mathrm{same}} + N_{\mathrm{neutral}}} \in [-1, 1] \tag{2}$$

The distribution of polarization indices in the combined network is shown in Fig. 2. We also make use of the absolute value of the polarization index, which can be thought of as a measure of a node's general tendency to form links based on political affiliation.

4.2 Homophily-Aware Common Neighbors

We propose 3 homophily-aware based link recommendation scores that attempt to extend common neighbor-based recommendations in a different way using political alignment.

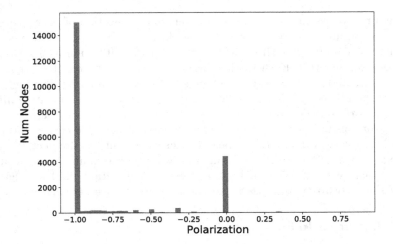

Fig. 2. Polarization index of nodes in the combined network. Most nodes have a polarization index close to −1, indicating strong political polarization.

Common Neighbors of Opposite Alignment: The first is nearly identical to common neighbors, but only considering nodes of opposite political alignment to recommend. For neutral ego nodes, we consider nodes of either left or right alignments. Recommending common neighbors of opposite alignment is a direct way of breaking up the two polarized communities while keeping the score rooted in common neighbors.

Ego Score: Our second score directly uses the polarization from a node's ego network, so we refer to it as the *ego score*. Inspired by Adamic and Adar's approach of inversely weighting common neighbors by degree to give higher weight to low-degree nodes [1], we consider weighting common neighbors with respect to polarization index. We weight common neighbors with polarization index close to 0 more strongly because they are more neutral and weight more insulated common neighbors (with polarization index close to −1 or 1) less, as shown in (3):

$$\text{Ego Score}(u, v) = \sum_{w \in \text{CN}(u,v)} \left[1 - |\text{PI}(w)|\right], \tag{3}$$

where $\text{CN}(u, v)$ denotes the set of common neighbors between nodes u and v. This favors recommendations with a high number of common neighbors, but also offers the added effect that the polarization index of the common neighbors is a major determining factor in the recommendation. Additionally, there is the benefit that the recommendations are not forced to be of opposite alignment.

Adjacent Score: The last score directly includes the number of common neighbors, but weights it by the difference of the absolute polarization of each of the nodes. The absolute value of the polarization index is in $[0, 1]$ and can be thought of as the level of insulation, regardless of whether the node prefers to connect with internal or external nodes. Nodes close to 1 will have a strong preference to connect to one type of node (either internal or external), while nodes close to 0 do not have a strong preference. We call this score the *adjacent score*, as it only includes polarization of each of the two nodes. The adjacent score shown in (4) will have a strong preference to connect nodes of high and low absolute polarization, while still factoring in the number of common neighbors $|CN(u, v)|$ between u and v:

$$\text{Adjacent Score}(u, v) = |CN(u, v)| \, \big||PI(u)| - |PI(v)|\big|. \tag{4}$$

Each of these scores gives insight into how the inclusion of homophily can affect recommendations but incorporates it in a different manner.

5 Experiments

We use the homophily-aware common neighbor scores proposed in Sect. 4.2 to generate a ranked list of recommendations for each node u. We then accept the best recommendation for node u (call this node v) by adding the edge (u, v) to the network. However, edge (u, v) may have already been added if node u was the best recommendation for node v, and node v was considered before node u.

We consider two different approaches to handle these duplicate recommendations. The first is to *allow duplicate recommendations* by not adding any new edge for node u. This results in less total edges added to the network. The second approach is to *avoid duplicate recommendations* by choosing the second best recommendation (call this node w) by adding (u, w) if the edge (u, v) for the best recommendation already exists. (If an edge with the second best recommendation already exists, then we choose the third best, and so on.)

By accepting the best recommendation for each node, we can get a direct comparison of how each of the methods is changing the network[1].

5.1 Evaluation Metrics

An effective homophily-aware link recommendation should have two qualities:

1. *Link recommendation quality:* The user should be likely to accept the recommendation.
2. *Polarization reduction:* If accepted, the polarization of the network should decrease.

The polarization reduction can be measured by comparing the polarization of the network before and after accepting the recommendation. We compute the *modularity change* to be the difference in modularity from the original network to the new network after accepting the best recommendation for each node. We

---

[1] Code to reproduce experiments is available at https://github.com/IdeasLabUT/Homophily-Aware-Link-Recommendation.

use the modularity change as the evaluation metric for change in polarization due to recommendation.

To measure the link recommendation quality, one would likely have to deploy the homophily-aware link recommendation algorithm onto an online social network and then compare acceptance rates of recommendations compared to a baseline recommendation algorithm that does not consider political homophily, e.g. common neighbors (CN). In the absence of such a deployment, we consider an alternative approach. We assume that CN-based recommendations will give good recommendations (i.e. likely to be accepted). With this in mind, we can investigate the similarity between the recommendations given by our scores with the potential CN recommendations.

We consider 3 evaluation metrics for these similarities. First, for each ego node, we examine the rank of the top recommendation in the ranked list of CN recommendations. A lower rank indicates that the recommendation is better matched with CN recommendations, with the best possible rank of 1 indicating that our recommendation aligns with CN. We consider the *mean rank* over all ego nodes in the network. Since the mean rank may be prone to outliers due to a small number of recommendations having very high ranks, we also consider the *median rank* over all ego nodes.

Additionally, for each ego node, we compute the number of CNs that our top recommendation has with the ego node. We divide by the maximum number of CNs that any node may have with the ego node to get a proportion of maximum CNs. A higher proportion indicates better agreement with CN recommendations, with the best possible proportion of 1 indicating that our recommendation has the same number of CNs as the recommendation by the CN score. We consider the *mean proportion of maximum CNs* over all ego nodes in the network.

All 3 of these metrics give us an idea of how well matched our top recommendation is with CN, which we use as a proxy for how likely our top recommendation is to be accepted.

6   Results

The results of our experiments are shown in Table 2. First, notice that accepting the top recommendation from the baseline common neighbors (CN) score barely changes the modularity of the network—in other words, it is not increasing polarization but also not decreasing polarization. On the other hand, each of the 3 homophily-aware scores reduces modularity, with the highest reduction achieved by simply recommending the node of the opposite political alignment with the most CNs, denoted by CN (opposite). Thus, all the homophily-aware link recommendations do indeed decrease the political polarization of the network, although the decrease is very small for the Ego Score (3).

Next, we consider the similarity of the recommendations to CN recommendations. CN (opposite) generally achieves the worst link recommendation quality of the 3 homophily-aware scores, with the lowest mean proportion of maximum CNs. The Ego Score (3) achieves the best link recommendation quality, which is not much lower than that achieved by the baseline CN score.

Table 2. Link recommendation results assuming top recommendation is accepted (with different ways of handling duplicate top recommendations as described in Sect. 5). Median rank, mean rank, and mean proportion of maximum CNs measure link recommendation quality. Modularity change measures polarization reduction. Best result for each metric is shown in bold.

(a) Allowing duplicate recommendations				
Evaluation Metric	Common Neighbors	CN (opposite)	Ego Score (3)	Adjacent Score (4)
Modularity change	−0.008	**−0.173**	−0.017	−0.082
Median rank	1	6	1	6
Mean rank	1	17.38	8.93	19.42
Mean proportion of maximum CNs	1	0.831	0.946	0.906
# of added edges	21,868	19,076	21,816	**21,909**
(b) Avoiding duplicate recommendations				
Evaluation Metric	Common Neighbors	CN (opposite)	Ego Score (3)	Adjacent Score (4)
Modularity change	−0.009	**−0.175**	−0.018	−0.084
Median rank	1	6	1	6
Mean rank	**1.02**	17.38	9.28	19.28
Mean proportion of maximum CNs	**0.999**	0.831	0.944	0.906
# of added edges	22,261	19,322	22,254	**22,356**

Between the 3 homophily-aware recommendation scores, we can observe different trade-offs. CN (opposite) is forced to recommend a node on the opposite end of the political spectrum, even when no such node with many CNs exist, so accepting its recommendation will always reduce modularity. For about 3,000 ego nodes, no such node with *any* CNs exist, so it cannot even make a recommendation! This is why the number of added edges for CN (opposite) is about 3,000 lower than for the other methods. Thus, the evaluation metrics for link recommendation quality for CN (opposite) may even be too favorable, since it avoids making recommendations for ego nodes that don't have any CNs with any nodes of the opposite political affiliation. Of the 3 homophily-aware scores, the Adjacent Score seems to offer the best balance between the recommendation quality and polarization reduction.

7 Conclusion

This paper provides evidence and methods for how the use of homophily-aware link recommendation could decrease political polarization on social media. We proposed 3 approaches to provide relevant link recommendations while also potentially reducing homophily, if accepted. These approaches are all based on common neighbors. The main limitation in our study is the evaluation of link recommendation quality, which we performed by comparing our recommendations to those of a common neighbors score. To better evaluate the recommendation quality and impact of our homophily-aware approaches, they would need to be deployed onto an online social network to evaluate how they change acceptance rates of recommendations.

Acknowledgements. We thank the anonymous reviewers for their suggestions to improve this paper. This material is based upon work supported by the National Science Foundation grants IIS-1755824 and IIS-2047955.

References

1. Adamic, L.A., Adar, E.: Friends and neighbors on the Web. Soc. Networks **25**, 211–230 (2003)
2. Conover, M., Ratkiewicz, J., Francisco, M., Gonçalves, B., Menczer, F., Flammini, A.: Political polarization on Twitter. In: Proceedings of the 5th International AAAI Conference on Web and Social Media, pp. 89–96 (2011)
3. Garimella, K., De Francisci Morales, G., Gionis, A., Mathioudakis, M.: Mary, mary, quite contrary: Exposing Twitter users to contrarian news. In: Proceedings of the 26th International Conference on World Wide Web Companion, pp. 201–205 (2017)
4. Garimella, K., Morales, De Francisci Morales, G., Gionis, A., Mathioudakis, M.: Quantifying controversy on social media. ACM Trans. Soc. Comput. **1**(1), 1–27 (2018)
5. Geschke, D., Lorenz, J., Holtz, P.: The triple-filter bubble: Using agent-based modelling to test a meta-theoretical framework for the emergence of filter bubbles and echo chambers. Br. J. Soc. Psychol. **58**(1), 129–149 (2019)
6. Krackhardt, D., Stern, R.N.: Informal networks and organizational crises: an experimental simulation. Soc. Psychol. Quart. **51**(2), 123–140 (1988)
7. Majmundar, A., Allem, J.P., Boley Cruz, T., Unger, J.B.: The why we retweet scale. PLoS ONE **13**(10), e0206076 (2018)
8. Masrour, F., Wilson, T., Yan, H., Tan, P.N., Esfahanian, A.: Bursting the filter bubble: Fairness-aware network link prediction. In: Proceedings of the 34th AAAI Conference on Artificial Intelligence, pp. 841–848 (2020)
9. McPherson, M., Smith-Lovin, L., Cook, J.M.: Birds of a feather: homophily in social networks. Ann. Rev. Sociol. **27**(1), 415–444 (2001)
10. Mehrabi, N., Morstatter, F., Saxena, N., Lerman, K., Galstyan, A.: A survey on bias and fairness in machine learning. ACM Comput. Surv. **54**(6), 1–35 (2021)
11. Moeller, J., Helberger, N.: Beyond the filter bubble: Concepts, myths, evidence and issues for future debates. Tech. rep., University of Amsterdam (2018). https://dare.uva.nl/search?identifier=478edb9e-8296-4a84-9631-c7360d593610
12. Newman, M.: Networks. Oxford University Press, 2nd edn. (2018)
13. Nguyen, T.T., Hui, P.M., Harper, F.M., Terveen, L., Konstan, J.A.: Exploring the filter bubble: the effect of using recommender systems on content diversity. In: Proceedings of the 23rd International Conference on World Wide Web, pp. 677–686 (2014)
14. Oku, K., Hattori, F.: User evaluation of fusion-based approach for serendipity-oriented recommender system. In: Proceedings of the Workshop on Recommendation Utility Evaluation: Beyond RMSE, pp. 39–44 (2012)
15. Pariser, E.: The filter bubble: What the Internet is hiding from you. Penguin UK (2011)

Mutual Information Scoring: Increasing Interpretability in Categorical Clustering Tasks with Applications to Child Welfare Data

Pranav Sankhe[✉], Seventy F. Hall, Melanie Sage, Maria Y. Rodriguez, Varun Chandola, and Kenneth Joseph

University at Buffalo, Buffalo, NY, USA
{pranavgi,sfhall,msage,myr2,chandola,kjoseph}@buffalo.edu

Abstract. Youth in the American foster care system are significantly more likely than their peers to face a number of negative life outcomes, from homelessness to incarceration. Administrative data on these youth have the potential to provide insights that can help identify ways to improve their path towards a better life. However, such data also suffer from a variety of biases, from missing data to reflections of systemic inequality. The present work proposes a novel, prescriptive approach to using these data to provide insights about both data biases and the systems and youth they track. Specifically, we develop a novel categorical clustering and cluster summarization methodology that allows us to gain insights into subtle biases in existing data on foster youth, and to provide insight into where further (often qualitative) research is needed to identify potential ways of assisting youth.

Keywords: Categorical data · Clustering · Foster care youth

1 Introduction

There are over 420,000 children currently in foster care across the United States [2]. Current and former Foster youth face a number of adverse outcomes in adolescence and early adulthood. For example, we know that of the roughly 25,000 foster youth who are never adopted or reunited with their families, 46% are unemployed, one in four are homeless— a rate around 200 times higher than the general population— and one in three have dropped out of high school [9,15,22].

Scholars in the field of Social Work have spent decades identifying the factors that lead to poor life outcomes for foster youth, from systemic inequalities [10, 12,21] to funding challenges [4]. As in many social policy settings, one common source of data in these analyses are administrative data. Specifically, myriad studies leverage the annually reported *Adoption and Foster Care Analysis and Reporting System* (AFCARS) [1] foster care file, which contains individual-level data on foster youth across all 50 states, DC, and Puerto Rico who received services from government-funded agencies during that year. However, there are a number of well-documented challenges that come with the use of such data [8]. In particular, they are 1) often missing critical information, 2) potentially difficult-to-work-with high dimensional categorical data, and 3) are biased by both systemic and individual-level factors [4,10,12,21].

In the present work, written jointly by computer scientists and social work scholars, the high-level *technical* question is, *(how) can we help Social Work scholars to use AFCARS data to help advance research that improves the lives of foster youth, while still accepting the shortcomings and difficultiees of the data?* Our solution is to develop a novel clustering and cluster summarization approach that can be applied to high-dimensional categorical data to rapidly identify distinct and explainable clusters, or youth profiles, from coarse but large-scale administrative data. Our goal, then, is to use administrative data to *inform future qualitative and/or experimental work*, rather than to try, as in most other technical work surrounding the foster care system, to make claims or predictions about youth based solely on lacking administrative records [9,10,12,21].

More specifically, we propose an information-theoretic approach, using a mutual-information based scoring criteria to 1) identify and 2) summarize clusters. Our approach, unlike most other clustering methods for categorical data, does not require the number of clusters as an input, and also provides a novel approach to identify more easily explainable clusters. We evaluate our method in two ways. First, we show that the proposed method produces clustering performance superior to existing methods for categorical data [3,19] on a suite of benchmark data sets. Second, we conduct a case study in the utility of our method on foster care data from AFCARS in 2018. This case study, while brief, presents an example of how our method can be used to draw insights into real-world administrative data.

Our work, available here, thus presents three primary contributions:

- We propose a novel approach to clustering and cluster summarization for large-scale administrative data that outperforms state-of-the-art methods on benchmark datasets.
- We identify novel and informative clusters of foster youth that we argue can help to shape future qualitative studies of foster care worker decision-making.
- Finally, we identify several systematic biases in the AFCARS dataset—the most widely used for studying foster youth—that warrant a careful consideration of which data are used, and how, if valid conclusions are to be drawn.

2   Related Work

The vast majority of data mining applications within the context of child welfare has focused on the use of predictive risk modeling. These models were designed, for example, to predict maltreatment substantiation [11,25,28], or to inform child welfare workers' actions in response to screened-in maltreatment reports (e.g., removal, home-based support services) [27]. Nearly all of these studies rely on administrative data of some kind, including the use of the datasets discussed here [6]. Our work offers a prescriptive, unsupervised method to help Social Work scholars understand potential patterns and data biases, rather than making (often biased) predictions about youth.

To do so, we build on work focused on the clustering of categorical data. We do so because our data, and many other administrative datasets, are largely categorical in nature, and categorical data present unique challenges that have been addressed by these methods. Methods for clustering categorical data can be grouped into three categories. Methods in the first category mimic the k-means algorithm by first randomly assigning the data instances into clusters and then iteratively redefining the clusters and reassigning the instances to the most appropriate cluster. COOLCAT [5], k-ANMI [19], and G-ANMI [13] are examples of this approach, and use information-theoretic measures to assign an instance to a cluster. However, they rely on knowledge of the optimal number of clusters. The second category of methods operates in a bottom-up agglomerative fashion, starting with individual data instances as clusters, and use a dissimilarity measure to recursively merge smaller clusters [16,18]. For instance, CACTUS [16] uses the overlap between two attribute vectors, while ROCK [18] uses the Jaccard coefficient.

The method proposed in this paper falls in a third category of top-down agglomerative methods, which recursively split the data into partitions starting from a single cluster. The splitting process of this top-down approach can be used as an explanatory insight into the clustering process, which is a desirable feature for the domain analysts. Most similar to the present work is the MGR method [24], which selects an attribute with the maximum mean gain ratio and then chooses the partitions with the minimum entropy. Our work differs from MGR in the choice of the information theoretic measure.

3   Data

Our analysis uses two types of data. First, in order to show that our method identifies meaningful clusters, we use seven publicly available and widely used data sets from the UCI repository [14]. We select a diverse array of data sets with varying sizes - from 101 to 12960 data samples, which have also been used as benchmark data sets by other methods to evaluate performance. No changes are made to the data sets; even the samples with missing entries are used as-is.

Second, to show that our method has real-world utility, we conduct a case study on data from AFCARS. Although AFCARS is a national data set and all agencies are required to report on the same variables for all of the youth they serve, there are differences between states in how these variables are operationalized and recorded [17]. Here, we therefore focus our case study on data from two states that represent different models of child welfare administration: New York (NY) and Texas (TX) [17]. These two states represent a more decentralized and a more centralized approach to administration, respectively, and we thus expect them to differ in interesting and important ways.

The AFCARS data set contains over one hundred variables providing details about foster youth. In the present work, we restricted our analysis to a specific set of variables of theoretical interest to the Social Work scholars on our team. Specifically, our analysis included three sociodemographic, five clinical diagnostic, and 19 child welfare and family-related variables. Sociodemographic characteristics included sex , race and ethnicity , and a nine-category the rural-urban (R-U) continuum code representing the urbanization of the county in which the youth is located. We also included five dichotomous variables that captured whether or not the youth had been diagnosed as intellectually disabled, visually/hearing impaired, physically disabled, emotionally disturbed, or as having any other medical condition requiring special care.

Child welfare-related variables included the manner in which youth were removed from their homes (voluntary, court-ordered, or not yet determined), whether parental rights had been terminated (yes or no), and the youth's current placement setting (pre-adoptive home, relative foster family, non-relative foster family, group home, institution, supervised independent living, runaway, or trial home visit). The reasons for removal are separated into 15 dichotomous variables, each of which are coded as either applicable or non-applicable to the youth's situation, full details on these variables are provided in our replication materials. Finally, we included one variable describing the structure of the family from which the youth was removed.

Administrative data often suffers from missing data problem, AFCARS data is no exception. Commonly used methods to handle missing data are data imputation techniques such as mean substitution, regression imputation, maximum likelihood [20]. These methods require making parametric assumptions regarding data generating process; which for our purpose of analysis isn't required as the task in hand is to study the data itself rather than using data for downstream tasks like prediction. We impute the missing data with a separate missing data category labeled '?'. This has key advantages; 1) does not require any parametric assumptions 2) provides us a way to uncover, if any, non-random missing data.

4   Method

4.1   MIS Clustering Method

Our approach is a top-down clustering method that clusters the data using a mutual information-based scoring metric. Formally, our goal is, given a set of data samples $O = \{o_1, ..., o_n\}$ (e.g. foster youth), described by a set of attributes $A = \{a_1, ..., a_r\}$ (sociodemographics, etc.), to partition O into a set of clusters $C = \{C_1, ..., C_k\}$ such that the samples (youth) within each cluster 1) share at least one attribute and 2) are similar to one another. We argue (and show) that this leads to effective, interpretable clusters. Note that each attribute is characterized by two or more *categories* (e.g. the attribute placement setting has categories pre-adoptive home, group home, etc.).

Our algorithm recursively creates clusters via a two step procedure. First, it identifies a *significant attribute*, which we define intuitively as the attribute that *provides the most information about the structure of the data to be clustered.* To identify the significant attribute, we must define a measure of which attribute provides the "most information." We do so using a modified mutual information score. We first define mutual information:

Definition 1 (Mutual Information). *For attributes $a_i, a_j \in A$ with domain sizes (number of categories in an attribute) of l and m respectively, and which define a partition $O/a_i = \{P_1, \cdots, P_l\}$ and $O/a_j = \{Q_1, \cdots, Q_m\}$ respectively on O, the mutual information between these two attributes is written as follows, where the probability $P(P_s) = \frac{|P_s|}{|O|}$ and the joint probability $P(P_s, O_t) = \frac{|P_s \cup Q_t|}{|O|}$; $P_s, Q_t \subseteq O$.*

$$MI(a_j, a_i) = \sum_{s=1}^{l} \sum_{t=1}^{m} P(P_s, Q_t) \log_2 \frac{P(P_s, Q_t)}{P(P_s)P(Q_t)}, \qquad (1)$$

Using this definition, we then define the *mutual information score* (MIS) of each attribute as follows, where $l|O/a_i|$ is the number of partitions defined by a_i on O also referred to as domain size of a_i:

Definition 2 (Mutual Information Score). *For an attribute $a_i \in A$ which defines a set of partition $O/a_i = \{P_1, \cdots, P_l\}$ on O. The mutual information score is defined as*

$$MIS(a_i) = \frac{\sum_{j=1, j \neq i}^{|A|} MI(a_j, a_i)}{|l|}, \qquad (2)$$

Note that in the definition of MIS above, the standard definition of mutual information is divided by the number of partitions defined by significant attribute. We do so in order to offset known biases in mutual information, where mutual information is generally greater for attributes with more categories and lower for fewer data samples [26]. Bias towards fewer data samples does not affect our method as we compare attribute columns, and each of these columns has the same number of samples. However, we do need to offset the bias introduced due to the differences in the number of categories in each attribute.

Having identified the significant attribute, we then create data partitions based on categories of the significant attribute. For example, if the significant attribute was *manner in which youth was removed*, partitions are created based on its categories: voluntary, court-ordered, or not yet determined. Data samples that are similar when grouped together result in low entropy [5]. Thus, the partition with the least entropy is selected to form a new cluster, P_i. The entropy H of a partition P_i can be written as the joint entropy of set of attributes $A = \{a_1, \cdots, a_r\}$, that is, as $H(P_i) = H(a_1, \cdots, a_r) = \sum_{a \in A} H(a)$ if and only if attributes are statistically independent. Independence of the attributes cannot always be guaranteed and therefore our measure of *partition entropy* is rather an approximation, defined as:

Definition 3 (Partition Entropy). *Given set of attributes* $A = \{a_i, \cdots, a_r\}$ *and a partition* $O/a_i = \{P_1, \cdots, P_l\}$ *induced by a significant attribute* $a_i \in A$

$$H(P_i) = \sum_{i=0}^{r} \sum_{x \in P_i} - p(x) \log_2 p(x) \tag{3}$$

4.2   Cluster Summarization

Our MIS clustering approach identifies clusters that share a single attribute and are similar along other attributes. Initial use of the tool with Social Work scholars suggested, however, that it would be most useful if we also were able to explain, or summarize, *how these clusters were similar*. To do so, we construct a method based on KL-divergence. Specifically, let $A = \{a_1, \cdots, a_k\}$ be the set of attributes associated with all the data samples O, we refer to this as *global attributes*. Let $A_c^i = \{a_1^i, \cdots, a_k^i\}$ be the set of attributes associated with data samples belonging to the cluster $p_i \in P$, where $P = \{p_i, \cdots, p_k\}$. We measure the KL-divergence between the probability distribution q_j, p_j of the cluster attributes a_j^i and a_j; with a set of states X and global attributes as

$$D(q_j, p_j) = \sum_{x \in X} q_j(x) \log_2 \frac{q_j(x)}{p_j(x)}, \tag{4}$$

5   Comparison with Other Methods

Table 1 shows that our MIS algorithm either outperforms or has comparable performance to other state-of-the-art methods on 4 out of 6 standard data sets from the UCI repository. We compare our proposed method to five other state of the art categorical clustering methods introduced in Sect. 2: MMR, MGR, k-ANMI, G-ANMI, COOLCAT, and K-modes. The K-modes algorithm was evaluated using an available implementation [29], and the results for the remaining methods are reported from the original papers. Finally, our proposed algorithm MIS can operate with or without providing the number of clusters. In order to make fair comparisons, we set the number of clusters to the number of real classes for the respective data set, similar to the evaluation of the other methods we analyze. We also have provided results for clusters obtained without specifying number of cluster as MIS-auto.

We use purity to evaluate the performance of each method. Purity is an external evaluation metric that measures the extent to which a cluster overlaps with a class. For a set of clusters $C = \{C_1, \cdots, C_k\}$ and classes $D = \{D_1, \cdots, D_d\}$, purity is defined as $\frac{\sum_{i=1}^{k} \max_{j=1}^{d} |C_i \cap D_j|}{N}$, where N is the total number of data samples. Purity is bounded between 0 and 1, wherein 1 indicates perfect clustering, i.e. all data samples in a cluster belong to the same class.

MIS performs exceedingly well on the Mushroom data set, which contains 22 attributes describing each of the 8124 mushrooms. Out of 22 attributes, 'odor', which has 9 different categories, is the attribute with the highest total mutual information (MI). However, since the MI is artificially boosted for attributes with greater domain size, MIS counters this and determines 'bruises' to be a more suitable significant attribute. MIS's performance is on par with MMR and MGR on the Balance data set and otherwise outperforms these methods. G-ANMI has the best purity score for the Vote data set when the number of clusters is specified, however, MIS-auto outperforms G-ANMI. In general, the performance of MIS-auto is greater than or equal to performance of MIS with specified number of clusters, which in part is due to the bias discussed in Sect. 4.1.

Table 1. Purity of categorical clustering algorithms on UCI data sets.

Algorithm	Zoo	Vote	Cancer	Mushroom	Balance	Chess	Average
MGR	**0.930**	0.827	0.864	0.677	**0.635**	0.533	0.744
MMR	0.911	0.687	0.669	0.518	**0.635**	0.523	0.657
K-MODES	0.860	0.852	0.651	0.560	0.587	0.503	0.668
k-ANMI	0.733	0.869	**0.978**	0.587	0.506	0.547	0.703
G-ANMI	0.874	0.871	0.966	0.547	0.518	0.543	0.719
COOLCAT	0.785	0.839	0.650	0.531	0.506	0.533	0.640
MIS	0.891	0.828	0.882	0.743	**0.635**	0.533	0.752
MIS (auto)	0.891	**0.949**	0.927	**0.828**	**0.635**	**0.558**	**0.80**

6   Case Study

We applied our MIS algorithm and cluster summarization approach to AFCARS data for youth in New York (N=23,676), resulting in 10 clusters, and in Texas (N=52363), resulting in 6 clusters. As is typical in unsupervised modeling, some clusters offered clear insights, others did not. This brief case study is organized around three main insights that were gleaned via analyses of cluster summaries produced by our method by Social Work scholars:

1. Clear patterns of non-randomness in (non-)missing data: Many of the clusters in our data were, surprisingly, largely defined by the *absence of missing values*. That is, the salient factor which differentiated these clusters from all others were that they had significantly more complete data on certain attributes than one would expect by chance. The high percentage of missing values overall is not unexpected in administrative data. However, the patterns our clustering algorithm identifies in where data was *not* missing offered our team new insights into the nature of *how* data were missing, and thus informed our understanding of the ways in which data seem to have been collected.

For example, we identified two clusters of youth in New York which had both a) no youth with missing values for various Clinical Diagnosis attributes (e.g. "Clinically Diagnosed with an Emotional Disability"), compared to a base rate of around 12% in the general population, and b) were heavily characterized by particular Placement Settings. In one of the clusters, 69% had a Placement Setting of *Pre-adoption home*, meaning a home into which they were likely to be adopted, compared to only 12% of all youth. And in the other, youth were almost twice as likely as the base rate to be in a Foster Care setting. These findings suggest differences in the accessibility or completeness of information about youths' medical histories across different placement settings.

These non-random patterns of missing values are particularly critical because they vary along youth Placement Setting, perhaps the most important variable in understanding the trajectory of a youth through the foster care system [7]. While such patterns of missing values can potentially be remedied, our analysis presents the first evidence that we are aware of to identify these non-random patterns of missing values in the widely-used AFCARS data set.

2. The importance of viewing the data that represent youth holistically: Because our cluster summarization approach allows us to construct profiles of youth that are unique (from a mutual information perspective) across many attributes, we are able to better study more general patterns of differences across profiles of youth rather than focusing on differences in specific levels of specific attributes. For example, in Texas, we identified one cluster representing a small subset of children in voluntary placements. High percentage of these youth were in trial homes (22%) and relative foster care (36%). The number of youths placed back into their homes in this cluster skewed lower relative to the overall sub-sample. In contrast, a second cluster in Texas had significantly higher percentages of youth in pre-adoptive placements (40%) and non-relative foster homes (30%) and placement disruptions that skewed higher relative to the overall sub-sample.

The implication of this is that there is an inextricable relationship between these different kinds of placement types and the extent to which a youth "bounces around" in the system. There are many possible reasons why this linkage between placement types and number of placement settings might exist; for example, youth who have been in care for longer periods of time often experience many placement disruptions and lose connections to relatives. However, to the best of our knowledge, this linkage has not been previously identified in the literature, thus showing the utility of our method in identify new pathways for future work.

3. State-level funding decisions may have influenced the structure of the clustering results, at least in New York: Some clusters we identified seemed to reflect patterns related to different funding eligibility criteria, which overlaps with the placement type attribute. For example, we identified one cluster of youth in New York who were predominantly in pre-adoptive placements (23%) or relative foster homes (44%). There were far fewer youth in non-relative foster homes (3%), group homes (12%), supervised independent living programs (14%), and institutions (4%). Some of these placements may not have been approved as licensed foster homes [23]. Youth may live with a relative who does not have legal custody for several months before the relative petitions the court and becomes a certified foster caregiver or pursues adoption, or may have a criminal history or safety issue in the home that precludes licensure.

These youth, and those with whom they are placed, might therefore not have been eligible for certain services or subsidies, which in turn may have influenced their outcomes that are reflected in AFCARS. These clusters that seem to be driven in part by the ways in which state policies revolve around funding decisions suggest critical future work in understanding the relationship between state-level policy and administrative data.

7 Conclusions

We have described a novel clustering algorithm for categorical data which uses an information-theoretic splitting criterion. The algorithm is significantly better (See Table 1) than other state of art algorithms on several benchmark data sets. At the same time, the KL-divergence based interpretability strategy offers an explainable summary of the clusters, which is a highly desirable feature when presenting the results to domain researchers. In particular, the algorithm, when applied to the AFCARS data, revealed new potential insights that suggest the need for further (social) theory, and both qualitative and quantitative work into better understanding the impact of the youth's characteristic on outcomes.

However, it is crucial to remember, as we begin to apply machine learning to high-stakes child welfare decision-making, that tools like this clustering exercise can aid in understanding, and perhaps help guide policy and practice decisions, but data always tells an incomplete story. Even if a child is well-represented by clustered attributes, personal knowledge of the child will always be important when making decisions about that child's needs.

References

1. AFCARS foster care annual file user's guide (2019). https://www.ndacan.acf.hhs.gov/datasets/pdfs_user_guides/afcars-foster-care-users-guide-2000-present.pdf
2. The AFCARS report. Tech. Rep. 27, Administration on Children Youth and Families, Children's Bureau, US Department of Health and Human Services (2020)
3. Andreopoulos, B., An, A., Wang, X., Schroeder, M.: A roadmap of clustering algorithms: Finding a match for a biomedical application. Briefings in bioinformatics
4. Bald, A., Doyle, Joseph J, J., Gross, M., Jacob, B.: Economics of foster care. Working Paper 29906, National Bureau of Economic Research, April 2022
5. Barbará, D., Li, Y., Couto, J.: Coolcat: an entropy-based algorithm for categorical clustering. In: Proceedings of the Eleventh International Conference on Information and Knowledge Management, pp. 582–589 (2002)
6. Camasso, M.J., Jagannathan, R.: Conceptualizing and testing the vicious cycle in child protective services: the critical role played by child maltreatment fatalities. Child Youth Serv. Rev. **103**, 178–189 (2019)

7. Connell, C.M., Vanderploeg, J.J., Flaspohler, P., Katz, K.H., Saunders, L., Tebes, J.K.: Changes in placement among children in foster care: a longitudinal study of child and case influences. Social Service Review **80**(3), 398–418 (2006)
8. Connelly, R., Playford, C.J., Gayle, V., Dibben, C.: The role of administrative data in the big data revolution in social science research. Social Science Research 59
9. Courtney, M., Dworsky, A., Brown, A., Cary, C., Love, K., Vorhies, V.: Midwest evaluation of the adult functioning of former foster youth: Outcomes at age 26. Tech. Rep. 9, University of Chicago, Chapin Hall Center for Children (2011)
10. Cusick, G., Courtney, M.: Offending during late adolescence: How do youth aging out of care compare with their peers?, January 2007
11. Daley, D., Bachmann, M., Bachmann, B.A., Pedigo, C., Bui, M.T., Coffman, J.: Risk terrain modeling predicts child maltreatment. Child Abuse & Neglect 62
12. Day, A.G., Dworsky, A., Fogarty, K.J., Damashek, A.: An examination of post-secondary retention and graduation among foster care youth enrolled in a four-year university. Child Youth Serv. Rev. **33**, 2335–2341 (2011)
13. Deng, S., He, Z., Xu, X.: G-anmi: a mutual information based genetic clustering algorithm for categorical data. Knowl.-Based Syst. **23**(2), 144–149 (2010)
14. Dua, D., Graff, C.: UCI machine learning repository (2017)
15. Dworsky, A., Napolitano, L., Courtney, M.: Homelessness during the transition from foster care to adulthood. American Journal of Public Health 103(S2)
16. Ganti, V., Gehrke, J., Ramakrishnan, R.: CACTUS-clustering categorical data using summaries. In: SIGKDD, pp. 73–83 (1999)
17. Green, B.L., et al.: It's not as simple as it sounds: Problems and solutions in accessing and using administrative child welfare data for evaluating the impact of early childhood interventions. Children Youth Serv. Rev. **57**, 40–49
18. Guha, S., Rastogi, R., Shim, K.: Rock: a robust clustering algorithm for categorical attributes. Inf. Syst. **25**(5), 345–366 (2000)
19. He, Z., Xu, X., Deng, S.: k-anmi: a mutual information based clustering algorithm for categorical data. Inf. Fusion **9**(2), 223–233 (2008)
20. Jadhav, A., Pramod, D., Ramanathan, K.: Comparison of performance of data imputation methods for numeric dataset. Appl. Artif. Intell. **33**(10)
21. Martin, E.: Hidden Consequences: The Impact of Incarceration on Dependent Children, March 2017
22. Matta Oshima, K.M., Narendorf, S.C., McMillen, J.C.: Pregnancy risk among older youth transitioning out of foster care. Children and Youth Services Review 35(10)
23. NYS Office of Children and Family Services.: Eligibility manual for child welfare programs (2018)
24. Qin, H., Ma, X., Herawan, T., Zain, J.M.: MGR: an information theory based hierarchical divisive clustering algorithm for categorical data. Knowl.-Based Syst. **67**, 401–411 (2014)
25. Rodriguez, M.Y., DePanfilis, D., Lanier, P.: Bridging the gap: Social work insights for ethical algorithmic decision-making in human services. IBM J. Res. Dev. **63**(4/5), 8:1–8:8 (2019)
26. Romano, S., Bailey, J., Nguyen, V., Verspoor, K.: Standardized mutual information for clustering comparisons: one step further in adjustment for chance. Proc. Mach. Learn. Res. **32**, 1143–1151 (2014)
27. Schwartz, I.M., York, P., Nowakowski-Sims, E., Ramos-Hernandez, A.: Predictive and prescriptive analytics, machine learning and child welfare risk assessment: The broward county experience. Children Youth Serv. Rev. **81**, 309–320

28. Vaithianathan, R., Maloney, T., Putnam-Hornstein, E., Jiang, N.: Children in the public benefit system at risk of maltreatment: Identification via predictive modeling. Am. J. Prev. Med. **45**(3), 354–359 (2013)
29. de Vos, N.J.: kmodes categorical clustering library (2015–2021). https://github.com/nicodv/kmodes

Imitation Learning for Social Simulation

Justin Downes$^{(\boxtimes)}$ and Hamdi Kavak

George Mason University, Fairfax, VA 22030, USA
jdownes4@gmu.edu

Abstract. Modeling the behavior of complex agents is challenging. In social systems, agents have different motivating factors and goals that drive each decision. In some situations, though, we can observe the agent behavior and the outcomes while being at a loss on how to quantify the decision-making process. Imitation learning is a powerful tool to learn behavior without understanding reasoning. In this paper, we explore modern machine learning techniques to train models that imitate agents' behavior in social environments. This work continues and builds off of emerging work that merges social simulation and modern machine learning. We have shown that such surrogate models can learn heuristically-driven agent behavior. We note that, however, these models do show fragility to changes in environmental dynamics.

Keywords: Agent-based modeling · Imitation learning · Computer vision · Social science · Surrogate models · Direct policy learning

1 Introduction

As social simulations get increasingly complex, it becomes more and more challenging to enumerate all of the parameters and dynamics we want to explore. With agent-based models, this includes how the environment is structured, the agent's interactions with that environment, and the heuristics that drive agent interactions. This leads to a couple of challenges for social scientists to overcome. First, when modeling agent behavior from scratch, how do we know we are crafting the correct parameters to simulate the target of interest? And second, how do we prevent our biases from being introduced to guide the agent's behavior towards the target behavior? These complications are not new, and they are not unique to the social sciences.

In this paper, machine learning is used to learn the underlying behaviors of social agents in order to replicate an observed social dynamic. The use of learning models that can operate in complex environments is a well-worn path in the areas of self-driving cars [16], robotics [17], and flying [5], among others. While many of these tasks replicate human behavior, the goal, regardless of the human's actions, is measurable. For instance, safely navigating from point A to point B is a measurable task even if a human does not make the decisions. It is a bit different for the social sciences since we are seeking to replicate human behavior

© The Author(s), under exclusive license to Springer Nature Switzerland AG 2022
R. Thomson et al. (Eds.): SBP-BRiMS 2022, LNCS 13558, pp. 176–185, 2022.
https://doi.org/10.1007/978-3-031-17114-7_17

as much as possible to model and predict actions they will take. Therefore, this line of research aims not to achieve some optimal performance for a task that humans currently do but to replicate how humans do a particular task.

Much of the current work in this area focuses on replicating the model's overall behavior [3,6], but not necessarily with an emphasis on an individual agent's specific behavior. Efforts replicating agent behaviors tend to focus on data mining techniques or hand-crafted methods to identify features to learn on [4,12]. Additional work in this area has used machine learning models as a surrogate in order to perform sensitivity analysis [9,20]. The contribution of this work is that it is meant to explore how to learn agent behavior solely through observation while evaluating the model through the imitation agents' collective behavior's ability to replicate the observed model.

Agent based models are ideal for solutions based in Reinforcement Learning (RL) techniques and its method of learning through long term rewards seems perfect for the social sciences. Yet the lack of an a priori reward function and the limited ability to observe social dynamics often precludes this method. Imitation learning techniques such as behavior cloning offer similar solutions that work nicely with these constraints and there is ongoing debate as to when each method should be used [14]. Behavior cloning's method of learning from historical examples that have been recorded allows the model to directly learn the policy that drives the agent's actions [5,8] and is the method we have chosen for this set of experiments.

2   Case Study: Schelling's Model of Segregation

We aim to choose a case study to test out mechanisms and complications that may arise from learning social dynamics. To this end, a model was chosen such that the underlying driver of agent behavior was known a priori. In practical use, if the underlying behavior were already known, then one would not need to construct a model to learn it. This type of solution would be more suitable for situations when one could observe complex behavior in dynamic environments. Situations such as evacuation [15] and traffic [21] simulations would be ideal for ABMs that have learned agent behavior through imitation. Since this experiment is about understanding the techniques that can be useful in this type of problem, a predefined model of agent behavior as the target is sufficient.

The specific social simulation chosen for this paper to imitate was Schelling's model of segregation [18]. The behavior of self-segregating agents is easy to measure both in individual agent decision-making as well as a final measure of outcome. The Schelling model, as originally specified, had agents moving randomly around a grid world until some segregation threshold was achieved in that agent's field of view and its type. This model demonstrated how even slight desires for segregation, i.e. the agent's threshold, can lead to systemic segregation in that world. A complication of the Schelling model is that the agent's moves are random, this means that the decision space for an agent is the entire grid world and the determination of that decision is random. This can introduce unnecessary complications when training models and does not reflect the intended goal of learning underlying decision making motivations.

The Sert *et al.* [19] variation of the Schelling model modifies the agent behavior such that it is modeled as a reinforcement learning problem that has been trained to behave in a way that maximizes future segregation of the system. The individual decisions that an agent makes are no longer driven by rules as the Schelling model but instead learned through this goal maximization process. This reinforcement learning modification provides two advantages for our problem. First, it makes an agent's decisions tractable and based on the environment instead of randomly moving. And second, it defines the goal-seeking that drives the agent's behavior, which can be used to define those behaviors in this experiment explicitly. With these modifications, an environment can be constructed where a model can learn to imitate an agent's actions in a dynamic environment.

3 Methods

In order to conduct this experiment we created two separate models. The heuristic model which sought to replicate the results of Schelling's model [18] by utilizing some of the advancement's made in Sert *et al.* [19], and the imitation model, which is a machine learning model that learns to imitate the actions that those agents take in different segregation environments.

3.1 The Grid World

The grid environment used in this paper is a replica of the Sert *et al.* [19] environment. It is a 50×50 grid with wrapping in both horizontal and vertical directions. There are two types of agents that are randomly placed in the environment targeting a desired population ratio of each type to number of cells (default of 5%). Each agent has an observable window size of 11×11 cells, with the agent at the center of that window, as illustrated in Fig. 1.

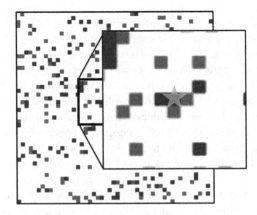

Fig. 1. The grid world with focus on the visible window for an agent.

The metric of how much an environment is segregated is calculated through a multi-scale entropy formulation [19], which calculates Shannon's entropy at multiple scales for 2 agent types in a window. It works by first calculating the entropy (see eq. (1)), for each patch E_n of size n, in this experiment 6×6, 12×12, and 25×25, where A is the number of type A agents and B is the number of type B agents in that patch. The final segregation score for an environment S_e is 1 minus the average of all of the patch entropy scores (see eq.(2)).

$$E_n = -\left(\frac{A}{A+B} log_2 \frac{A}{A+B} + \frac{B}{A+B} log_2 \frac{B}{A+B} \right) \tag{1}$$

$$S_e = 1 - \frac{1}{|N|} \sum_{n \in N} E_n \tag{2}$$

3.2 The Heuristic Model

This model acts as the baseline agent behavior for which the imitation model will learn from. Agents in this model move in a direction towards the maximum segregation patch in their visual window, with the expectation that the emerging segregated state of agent positions is in line with the original Schelling and Sert models.

A model can choose to move in direction d from a choice of directions D which is defined as a vector of x and y step sizes from a choice of three possible steps $\{-1, 0, 1\}$, or simply as the permutation of all 2 choices from that set of 3 movement steps $\{-1, 0, 1\}$, $D = P^r(\{-1, 0, 1\}, 2)$. This gives us 8 directions of movement and 1 choice to stay still, for a total decision space of 9 for each agent. Given an agent a_i, its optimal movement decision d_{opt} is defined as the maximum segregation score $s(w_i, d)$ for a window $w_{i,d}$ in a given direction $d \in D$ from an agent a_i's coordinates a_{xi}, a_{yi}, given compactly here.

$$d_{opt} = \max_{d \in D} s(w(a_i, d)), \text{ where } D = P^r(\{-1, 0, 1\}, 2) \tag{3}$$

The window $w_{i,d}$ for an agent a_i in direction d is simply the x and y coordinate vector of the agent's location added to the direction d vector multiplied by a look distance l_{dist}, and then getting the bounds of that window by adding and subtracting the observation window's dimensions, $[o_{width/2}, o_{height/2}]$, to get the upper left and lower right coordinates of the window (4). While the movement vector d has a magnitude of 1 the look distance l_{dist} magnitude is 3, this is done so that the segregation values for patches is more cleanly separated and, by moving 1 cell at a time, the agent can move more smoothly. In this experiment the look distance is set to 3 and the observation window is 5.

$$w(a_i, d) = w_{i,d} = [a_{xi}, a_{yi}] + l_{dist}[d_{xi}, d_{yi}] \pm [o_{width/2}, o_{height/2}] \tag{4}$$

The score for a window $w_{i,d}$ is simply $1 - the\ entropy\ score$, which is described in (1). Since the entropy score of a patch is defined as the negative entropy it is simplified here in (5) as $1 + the\ entropy\ score$.

$$s(w_{i,d}) = 1 + \left[\frac{A}{A+B} log_2 \frac{A}{A+B} + \frac{B}{A+B} log_2 \frac{B}{A+B} \right] \quad (5)$$

For each step this model calculates the segregation score for all agents in all directions. The simulation may stop at some fixed step count or until some threshold ratio of non-moving agents to moving agents is reached. In practice, both methods were used depending on whether the imitation model was being trained (threshold stopping was used) or evaluation was being conducted (fixed length run time was used).

3.3 The Imitation Model

The imitation model seeks to replicate the heuristic agent's decisions by observing an agent's action given its current state (observation window). The selected model architecture was a simple convolutional neural network (CNN) trained in a supervised fashion, shown in Fig. 2. It consists of multiple convolutional layers, topped with dense, fully connected layers and a classification layer that determines the direction for the agent to move. Trainable layers utilized Rectified Linear Unit (ReLU) activations with the final classification using a Softmax activation. The model used Adam optimization [13] and categorical cross-entropy as its loss.

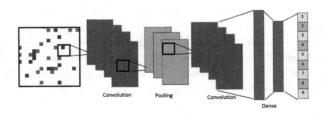

Fig. 2. The CNN model architecture.

We trained the model using two different methods. A static dataset of 100 simulations was generated from which a model was trained from in different batches. A separate model was trained off of simulations that were created on demand. This dynamically trained model was trained for a total of 50k simulation steps. Each input into the model is a single agent's viewable window, where the label is the direction of movement as determined by the heuristic model. Batches are sampled by shuffling multiple agent's windows and actions from across the available scenarios. All simulations had an early stopping mechanism once an entropy threshold was met (default .15). This early stopping mechanism was implemented to yield better agent action distribution, as at higher entropy levels most agents remain still. The static dataset of 100 simulations equates to roughly 6k simulations steps, yeilding approximately 10x difference between the static and dynamic dataset sizes. These two different methods of training were developed to simulate the different real world scenarios where you may have limited observed data due to safety constraints or other complications of generating observations and scenarios where you could realistically have an abundance of observed data, e.g. the stock market. The goal is to identify performance degradations between these different scenarios.

4   Results

The imitation model was evaluated on how well it was able to replicate the segregation score of the heuristic model at each step in a simulation run. Simulation runs were capped at 25 steps since at this point all observed simulations had ceased to have any significant movement. For evaluation, 10 simulations were run with both the statically and dynamically trained model, where each of these simulations had the same starting state. They were each compared to the heuristic model which also started in the same environment state.

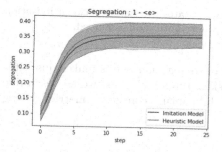
(a) Model trained on static dataset.

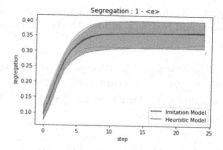
(b) Model trained on dynamic dataset.

Fig. 3. Mean segregation score for imitation models and heuristic model, with min and max bands. Run on the same 10 starting environments for 25 steps. The segregation score is 1 - the hierarchical entropy score $<e>$, described in Eq. 2.

As can be seen in Fig. 3, both models were able to achieve roughly the same mean growth of segregation scores with similar min/max bands for the same simulations. This means that the imitation model is segregating generally at the same pace as the heuristic says it should for a given starting environment and ends with approximately the same metric. The displayed bands are not error bands but show the entire range of segregation scores for a given step during the 10 runs. The comparison should be in how well the mean line and border of the bands line up.

Another question to ask though is whether the end states look the same. If one expects for each agent's observable world the imitation model can make the same decision most of the time, then the end state should look approximately similar between the heuristic and imitation models. Figure 4 shows the end state of each imitation model overlaid with the end state of the heuristic model from the same starting state, broken down into the end state for the model trained on a static dataset in Fig. 4a and the dynamically trained model in Fig. 4b.

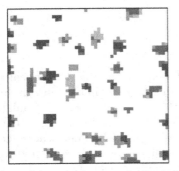
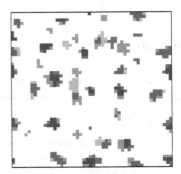

(a) Model trained on static dataset.   (b) Model trained on dynamic dataset.

Fig. 4. Overlay of end states from same starting states compared between imitation models and heuristic model. Darker areas are where both models agreed.

The stochastic nature of the evolution of segregation states makes quantitative analysis a constant battle of sample size. Ten simulations were chosen due to computation timeliness constraints but did capture consistent metrics during the multiple runs.

4.1 Impact of Agent Density

One reason to train an agent to imitate another agent is to run simulations where the environment is too novel, or agent behavior is too difficult to enumerate. For instance, in evacuation scenarios where one wants to test new floor plans and would like to predict behavior from a set of real observations. To set up that type of situation with these models, new environments were constructed that had higher densities of agents than what had been observed and therefore trained on. For the heuristic model, this change in density is not a problem, as decisions are deterministic and can be anticipated and corrected. For the learned agents, though, this may demonstrate a weakness in the model where it is not robust to the environment changes one would expect and desire from a social model. In this experiment, fragility in the learned model is determined by deviation from the expected behavior of the heuristic model.

These experiments were run at increasing agent densities starting at 5%, which was the agent density for the preceding experiments, going up to 45% with steps of 2.5%. Of note is that this density percentage is for each agent type, and since there are two types of agents, the actual agent density is two times the displayed percentage. These experiments also followed the format of the other experiments in that the same ten starting states were used for all models, but each set of 10 starting states would be different for each density setting.

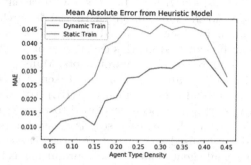

Fig. 5. Plot of Mean Absolute Error in segregation scores between dynamic and static model compared to the heuristic model at different agent densities. Since there are two agent types the overall density is approximately twice the displayed agent density.

As can be seen in Fig. 5, we start to see an increase in error of segregation scores as agent density increases. This may be an artifact of the stochastic states, but the trend is fairly clear that the model starts to deviate from expected behavior. We do also see a reversion to expected behavior as the density approaches maximum. Intuitively this appears to show a weakness in the model to replicate decisions where the environment starts to have many similar options, i.e. it easy when it's not dense because the attractive options are obvious and its easy when it's very dense as it can be best to stay still. This implies that even though creating agent models through machine learning can seem to simplify the features we want to model, one still must be aware of the biases they are introducing. In future simulations with learning based agents, holding out certain environmental dynamics may be warranted.

5   Discussion and Conclusion

This research investigated a method of learning an agent's behavior through observation. While we knew the correct choice an agent should make at each step, as defined by the target model, the model's behavior was evaluated on its holistic ability to replicate model metrics instead of individual agent decisions. The target agent in this scenario was driven heuristically, but in practical applications would be agents behaving in real-world situations under observation. These situations would be such that manually defining their behavior would be prohibitive to developing accurate models. We can unlock simulations of highly complex behaviors and environments by developing systems that can learn agent behavior. Also, by utilizing machine learning models as surrogates for heuristic agents, we can simplify computation, easily expand model sensitivity analysis, and create agents that are reusable across different environments.

The method implemented here utilized a computer vision model that was trained in a supervised fashion. It was able to know the agent's observable state and which action was taken. This simplified the model architecture that was required and the training mechanism utilized. There are other methods of imitation learning that can be explored for this exact type of problem [11,17], which may be more robust to more complex environments. Many problems exist where the state is not entirely observable, or the action taken at each step may not be known. Methods such as Reinforcement Learning (RL) [1] and Generative Adversarial Networks (GANs) [10] have been developed to work in just these types of scenarios. When the action taken at each step is noisy or missing, the end goal or a periodic reward can be used as a substitute for supervision. Future research in using RL to learn social agent behavior looks promising as it is already widely used to learn how to take actions in many environments [7], but still generally requires hand crafted rewards which this method we present operates through observation alone. Along with traditional RL, Inverse Reinforcement Learning could be especially useful for these types of experiments as it may allow for more ease in transportability for agent behavior to new environments [2] as the reward function can be more abstract than the visual features.

References

1. Abbeel, P., Ng, A.Y.: Apprenticeship learning via inverse reinforcement learning. In: Proceedings of the Twenty-first International Conference on Machine Learning. ACM Press (2004)
2. Adams, S., Cody, T., Beling, P.A.: A survey of inverse reinforcement learning. Artif. Intell. Rev. **55**(6), 4307–4346 (2022). https://doi.org/10.1007/s10462-021-10108-x
3. Angione, C., Silverman, E., Yaneske, E.: Using machine learning as a surrogate model for agent-based simulations. PLoS ONE **17**(2), 1–24 (2022). https://doi.org/10.1371/journal.pone.0263150, https://doi.org/10.1371/journal.pone.0263150, publisher: Public Library of Science
4. Bell, D., Mgbemena, C.: Data-driven agent-based exploration of customer behavior. SIMULATION **94**(3), 195–212 (2018). https://doi.org/10.1177/0037549717743106
5. Bratko, I., Urbančič, T., Sammut, C.: Behavioural cloning: phenomena, results and problems. IFAC Proc. Vol. **28**(21), 143–149 (1995). https://doi.org/10.1016/S1474-6670(17)46716-4, https://www.sciencedirect.com/science/article/pii/S1474667017467164, 5th IFAC Symposium on Automated Systems Based on Human Skill (Joint Design of Technology and Organisation), Berlin, Germany, 26-28 September
6. ten Broeke, G., van Voorn, G., Ligtenberg, A., Molenaar, J.: The use of surrogate models to analyse agent-based models. J. Artif. Soc. Soc. Simul. **24**(2), 3 (2021). https://doi.org/10.18564/jasss.4530, http://jasss.soc.surrey.ac.uk/24/2/3.html
7. Charpentier, A., Élie, R., Remlinger, C.: Reinforcement learning in economics and finance. Comput. Econ. (2021). https://doi.org/10.1007/s10614-021-10119-4
8. Chemali, J., Lazaric, A.: Direct policy iteration with demonstrations. In: Twenty-Fourth International Joint Conference on Artificial Intelligence (2015)

9. Edali, M., Yücel, G.: Automated analysis of regularities between model parameters and output using support vector regression in conjunction with decision trees. J. Artif. Soc. Soc. Simul. **21**(4), 1 (2018). https://doi.org/10.18564/jasss. 3786. http://jasss.soc.surrey.ac.uk/21/4/1.html

10. Ho, J., Ermon, S.: Generative adversarial imitation learning. In: NeurIPS (2016)

11. Hussein, A., Gaber, M.M., Elyan, E., Jayne, C.: Imitation learning: a survey of learning methods. ACM Comput. Surv. **50**(2) (2017). https://doi.org/10.1145/ 3054912

12. Kavak, H., Padilla, J.J., Lynch, C.J., Diallo, S.Y.: Big data, agents, and machine learning: towards a data-driven agent-based modeling approach. In: Proceedings of the Annual Simulation Symposium. ANSS 2018, San Diego, CA, USA. Society for Computer Simulation International (2018)

13. Kingma, D.P., Ba, J.: Adam: A method for stochastic optimization (2014). https:// doi.org/10.48550/ARXIV.1412.6980, https://arxiv.org/abs/1412.6980

14. Kumar, A., Hong, J., Singh, A., Levine, S.: When should we prefer offline reinforcement learning over behavioral cloning? In: Proceedings of the International Conference Learning Representations (2022)

15. Liu, Q., Lu, L., Zhang, Y., Hu, M.: Modeling the dynamics of pedestrian evacuation in a complex environment. Phys. A: Stat. Mech. Appl. **585**, 126426 (2022). https://doi.org/10.1016/j.physa.2021.126426, https://www.sciencedirect. com/science/article/pii/S0378437121006993

16. Muller, U., Ben, J., Cosatto, E., Flepp, B., Cun, Y.: Off-road obstacle avoidance through end-to-end learning. In: Weiss, Y., Schölkopf, B., Platt, J. (eds.) Advances in Neural Information Processing Systems, vol. 18. MIT Press (2005). https:// proceedings.neurips.cc/paper/2005/file/fdf1bc5669e8ff5ba45d02fded729feb-Paper. pdf

17. Osa, T., Pajarinen, J., Neumann, G., Bagnell, J.A., Abbeel, P., Peters, J.: An algorithmic perspective on imitation learning. Found. Trends Robot. **7**(1-2), 1–179 (2018). https://doi.org/10.1561/2300000053, https://ieeexplore.ieee.org/ document/8620668

18. Schelling, T.C.: Dynamic models of segregation. J. Math. Sociol. **1**(2), 143–186 (1971)

19. Sert, E., Bar-Yam, Y., Morales, A.J.: Segregation dynamics with reinforcement learning and agent based modeling. Sci. Rep. **10**, 11771 (2020)

20. van Strien, M.J., Huber, S.H., Anderies, J.M., Grêt-Regamey, A.: Resilience in social-ecological systems: identifying stable and unstable equilibria with agent-based models. Ecol. Soc. **24**(2) (2019). https://doi.org/10.5751/ES-10899-240208, https://www.ecologyandsociety.org/vol24/iss2/art8/, publisher: The Resilience Alliance

21. Zhao, B., Kumar, K., Casey, G., Soga, K.: Agent-Based Model (ABM) for city-scale traffic simulation: a case study on San Francisco, pp. 203–212 (2019). https://doi. org/10.1680/icsic.64669.203, https://www.icevirtuallibrary.com/doi/abs/10.1680/ icsic.64669.203

Modeling Memory Imprints Induced by Interactions in Social Networks

James Flamino[1]([⊠]), Ross DeVito[2], Omar Lizardo[3],
and Boleslaw K. Szymanski[1]([⊠])

[1] Network Science and Technology Center, RPI, Troy, NY 12180, USA
{flamij2,szymab}@rpi.edu
[2] University of California, San Diego, CA 92093, USA
[3] University of California, Los Angeles, CA 90095, USA

Abstract. Memory imprints of the significance of relationships evolve over time. This evolution is driven by these imprints, gaining strength during interactions between the people involved, and weakening between such events. Despite the importance of understanding this evolution, few research papers explore how long-term interactions in social networks correlate with the memory imprints of relationship importance. In this paper, we represent memory dynamics by adapting a well-known cognitive science model. Using two unique longitudinal datasets, we fit the model's parameters to maximize agreement of the memory imprints of relationship strengths of a node predicted from call detail records with the ground-truth list of relationships of this node ordered by their strength. We find that this model, trained on one population, predicts not only on this population but also on a different one, suggesting the universality of memory imprints of social interactions among unrelated individuals. This paper lays the foundation for studying the modeling of social interactions as memory imprints, and its potential use as an unobtrusive tool to early detection of individuals with memory malfunctions.

Keywords: Social network · Cognitive modeling · Memory model

1 Introduction

Interactions among people in social networks drive their temporal evolution. Yet, the underlying mechanics of mapping interaction patterns to the evolution of relationships, and consequently to personal memory imprints, are not clear. A primary reason is the paucity of data providing comprehensive information on both interactions (such as Call Detail Records) and relationship characteristics (such as ego network surveys). Previous work using such data focuses instead on machine learning and natural language processing models, or more "black box" approaches [5–7]. While this work may accurately predict surface-level correlations among interactions and people's memory imprints, they lack any analytical, explanatory value. An individual's memory recall reflects their perception of the impact of interactions, each leaving a temporally evolving imprint. But how can such longitudinal phenomena in social networks be directly modeled in analytical form?

In a recent paper [8], Michalski et al. implement a cognitive model of memory recall (CogSNet) and evaluate its accuracy at "nominating" significant relationships between individuals from dyadic communication records. This research provides insight into how patterns of communication map to strengths of memory recall of interacting members of the network. However, the authors formulate their model with a parameter which is not a part of the established, well-known memory model, ACT-R [2]. This added parameter represents the threshold value of a memory imprint at which such imprint vanishes from memory. Yet, unexpectedly, optimal values of this parameter are high and are unlikely to correspond to human memory processes. In this paper, we modify CogSNet, improving its compatibility with ACT-R. CogSNet uses three parameters to represent memory imprints. Our adapted model, the Memory Imprint Model (MIM), inherits two CogSNet parameters based on the ACT-R model that is applied to the entire population. We replace the third CogSnet parameter with a new one that defines, for each individual, a threshold for the significance of relationships with their partners. This change is significant since we discovered that the optimal fit for the MIM parameters are actually universal for populations of peoples with healthy memories. Provided that individuals with malfunctioning memory will recall past interactions and relationships differently than healthy ones, we hypothesize that MIM could be an unobtrusive tool for diagnosing memory malfunction in humans.

In the rest of the paper, Sect. 2 outlines the datasets used to evaluate MIM. Then, in Sect. 3, we explain how MIM differs from CogSNet, and how we map interactions among individuals into an evolving memory imprint. We compare the performance of MIM to a standard Hawkes model and three baseline models. Section 4 discusses our evaluation process in detail. In Sect. 5, we assess the universality of model parameters and find that parameters learned on a population of healthy subjects are valid for other populations of similar individuals. Finally, Sect. 6 summarizes all our results and hypotheses, discusses their implications, and proposes some avenues for future research.

2 Datasets

Testing the mechanisms of memory imprints arising from interactions in social networks requires longitudinal data containing objective records of communications among individuals within a social network, as well subjective data on relationship characteristics, such as those obtained using ego network surveys. The former is used to provide dyadic events that can be fitted by the model to simulate the memory imprint left by interactions between the two involved individuals. The latter is used to provide actual empirical measures of significance between the two people involved as they see it. Unfortunately, data fitting these requirements is scarce. Of the past works mentioned above, most of those having data meeting these requirements are cross-sectional, thus only capable of testing their models on snapshots of social networks but unable to explore the evolution of those networks. One exception is the already mentioned CogSNet model that uses data collected in the NetSense study [11]. The data were voluntarily collected from randomly selected first-year students entering the University of Notre Dame in 2011. From Fall 2011 to Spring 2013, the participating students had Call Detail Records of their phones continuously recorded. In addition, the participants were required to fill out ego network surveys at the end of each semester. The NetSense study followed 196 students at its peak. We also use data from the follow-up NetHealth study [10] involving first-year students arriving in Notre Dame in 2015 and leaving in 2019 using a similar approach as used by NetSense. NetHealth followed 594 students at its peak.

2.1 Communication Records

Communication records for both studies were formatted to conform to the standard CDR format that includes for each call a timestamp, sender, receiver, type, and length. While there are auxiliary digital communication channels in NetSense (such as WhatsApp), these are sparse, so we keep only the text and phone calls, which provided us with $7,465,776$ events. We filter similarly for NetHealth, extracting $41,677,368$ calls and text messages generated by the participants in that study.

2.2 Ego Network Surveys

Each study contains ego network surveys collected once a semester to complement communication records. Ego network surveys in these studies essentially capture student perceptions on their interactions, which characterizes their subjective rapport with those involved. These surveys were prefaced with a question (the name generator) asking the survey-taker (the ego) to list individuals (the alters) with whom they spend a significant amount of time communicating or interacting. Each ego can list up to 20 alters, including people not participating in the study. Thus, ego-alter connections can involve a variety of relationship types such as friends, parents, coworkers, and romantic partners. Each ego was subsequently asked about the history of contact with these alters and their shared interests and activities (the name interpreter). Importantly, the surveys also asked the ego to subjectively rate similarity and closeness with the alters. The NetSense study includes four ego network surveys over four semesters, and the study participants listed on average 15.9 alters per survey. The NetHealth study includes eight ego network surveys over eight semesters, and the study participants listed on average 8.4 alters per survey.

2.3 Quantifying Relationship Significance

To model the significance of interactions using memory imprinting, we need an empirically-based measure of the significance of relationships that acts as ground truth. Previously, in [8], the authors establish their ground truth as the list of alters nominated by the ego. According to the authors: "These nominations are based on students' perception of the corresponding relations as one of the top twenty most interacting peers in the surveys administered to participants." However, while the set of the alters themselves can be considered significant to the ego as a whole, there is additional information from the surveys that provide information on the significance of individual alters, as perceived by the egos, in even greater detail. This allows us to produce a finer measure of significance from which we can more thoroughly test the capabilities of the models in this paper.

In the previous section, we mentioned that there are "name interpreter" questions asked about the alters that are listed by the ego. The answers to these questions are mostly selected from a set of modalities that grade the magnitude of an attribute of the alter or the relationship. For example, when asking about an ego's perceived closeness with a listed alter, the choices include "Especially close", "Close", "Less than close", or "Distant". There are also a few questions requiring open answers in the form of a rational number (like self-reported tie duration). In this paper, we focus on a subset of the inputs from the surveys: closeness, history duration, subjective similarity, emotional significance (for the NetSense surveys only), and perceived communication frequency (for the NetHealth surveys only). With these question sets, we convert the list of alters into a ranked list, where the higher the rank of an alter, the more significant they are to the ego.

To determine an ordering from the mixed inputs without assuming the importance of any one input over another, we use a pairwise comparative tournament selection process. Consider one ego network survey. Every alter listed by this ego is compared on each question against all the other listed alters. An alter whose assigned answer to a question is considered "closer to the ego" compared to their counterpart, is awarded a point. If the answers of both competitors are of the same value, they are both awarded a point. These points are aggregated across all the questions and then a ranked list is created by ordering everyone by their score in descending order. If there is a tie in the aggregate score between two alters, the duration attribute is used to break the tie, as it is the only considered input with a rational number answer. After all comparisons are complete for that ego network survey, we are left with our rankings for the top-k significant dyadic relations between the ego and each of its listed alters. The higher the alter is on the list, the more significant relations this alter has with the ego. We run this process for all egos for every survey, yielding our ground truth for this paper.

Given a model and CDR data between an ego and an individual, who interacted with this ego, we fit our model to predict not only if this individual should be listed on the ego survey list, but also what rank, if any, this individual should have on this list. This allows us to assess the model's ability to determine finer levels of significance from the memory imprint from events, not just if the considered relationship has perceived significance.

3   Models

3.1   Hawkes Model

The Hawkes process is a natural choice for simulating the significant relations between two individuals as determined by communication, since the frequency and volume of communication is central to determining the significance of the relationship. Furthermore, past work directly uses this method to understand relationship dynamics [9]. Here, we use a univariate Hawkes process with an exponential kernel for alter nomination and ranking, as defined by the Eq. 1.

$$\lambda(t) = \lambda_0(t) + \sum_{t_i < t} \beta e^{-\beta(t - t_i)} \tag{1}$$

where λ is the Hawkes event intensity at time t (the event time at which the function is being evaluated), t_i is a set of event times before the event time t, and β is the decay rate (which in this scenario represents the decay rate of the memory imprint of an event). We set the arrival rate of immigrant events $\lambda_0(t)$ to 0. Given this function, at survey time t, we consider the communication history of all individuals who have communicated with the ego (as at this point we do not know who is an alter). We feed this data into the Hawkes process up to time t, producing a corresponding λ value for each candidate alter. We then sort these candidate alters in order of descending magnitude of their associated λ value, producing an ordered list of who is significant to the ego according to Hawkes event intensity. We discuss tuning the Hawkes model parameters in Subsect. 4.1.

3.2   Memory Imprint Model

Our next model, the Memory Imprint Model (MIM), is a variant of the CogSNet model introduced in [8]. Unlike Hawkes, CogSNet uses a recursive piecewise function (cf. Eq. 3) and produces a signal that is normalized to the range [0, 1]. We made several adjustments to CogSNet to improve its compatibility with the ACT-R model, and to reduce its computational complexity. First, we define the MIM recall function:

$$r_{ij}(t) = w_{ij}(t_{ij}^b)e^{-(t - t_{ij}^b)\frac{\ln(2)}{L}} \tag{2}$$

where $t_{i,j}^b$ is the time of the last communication event between nodes i and j in the considered social network before the evaluation time t, and L is the parameter that controls the half-life of node i's memory imprint of their interactions with j. Given this, we define the strength of the MIM memory imprints of interactions between i and j to be

$$w_{ij}(t) = s_{ij}(t) + \begin{cases} r_{ij}(t)(1 - s_{ij}(t)) & \text{when } t > t_{ij} \\ \mu + (1 - \mu)r_{ij}(t)(1 - s_{ij}(t)) & \text{otherwise} \end{cases} \tag{3}$$

where μ is the MIM second parameter that defines the memory imprint strength between i and j. We list alters j's of ego i at each survey time t in the descending order of their $w_{i,j}(t)$. The length of the list is limited to 20, to mimic the limit for the list length in surveys, and by the threshold defined by the third MIM parameter θ, which limits eligible for listing alters to those whose value of $w_{i,j}(t)$ exceeds θ. Ultimately, MIM introduced here is simpler than CogSNet, and fully compliant with ACT-R. We discuss tuning the MIM parameters in Subsect. 4.1.

3.3 Baseline Models

Previous research has often used frequency of communication to predict significance of relations [4–7]. Following this established approach, we specify the frequency model in the baseline class that calculates frequency (this model's value that is used to nominate significant alters and rank them) by dividing the number of communication events between two individuals by the elapsed time since they first communicated at the timestep for which it is being evaluated. In addition, we create a recency model using the elapsed time since the last communication between two people as an inversely related estimate of frequency of contact, as is done in [5]. This produces a recency value that we use to nominate significant relationships and generate the corresponding rankings. Finally, we create a random model that just randomly orders all individuals that the target ego has communicated with, prior to the considered time, into an arbitrary ranking.

4 Results

4.1 Evaluation Process

Given our two datasets are longitudinal, each with its own set of egos, list of alters, and ego-alter CDR, we designed a comprehensive evaluation process that provides training data for the models to fit their parameters and testing data for the models to test their fit. In the process, we avoid any overlap between training and testing data or accessing in learning the future CDR or ground truth data.

Initially, for a given dataset, we use the standard three-fold cross validation to shuffle and then equally split the involved egos into three mutually exclusive groups. Then, for each fold, let N_s be the number of semesters within the target dataset. Within a fold, we separate the training and testing data into N_s subsets, split by semesterly survey time. At each survey time, the training and testing subset includes only the surveys and communication data from before that time (therefore the later subsets contain the earlier subsets). We stagger the communication training data, such that the models only fit their parameters with communication data up to the survey time that precedes the survey time against which the models are being tested. This design ensures that the models cannot use any of the training surveys administered at the same time as the current target testing surveys. Subsequently, we start with the second semester for rankings in each fold. After models have fit their parameters with the current training subset and have produced rankings for the current testing subset, the process is then advanced one subset forward, allowing more training and testing data to be released with each following survey time.

Note that the training and testing data are kept completely separate at all times. Testing data, even from previous semesters, is never used to fit the models' parameters, and test-fold ground-truth from surveys is only used to score a model's rankings. The order of the training and testing data used in each fold is kept the same for all models to ensure training and testing consistency. Once all predictions for a fold are complete, we compute the fold's overall score: the weighted average ranking prediction accuracy of the predicted rankings across all available surveys for testing egos.

For ranking accuracy when comparing rankings generated by a model against the top-k ground truth, we use Ranked Biased Overlap (RBO) [12]. We chose it because of its use of an indefinite rank similarity measure for the similarity of two ranked lists. Moreover, RBO handles items being present only in one ranking, weights the agreement of top ranking items higher than that of lower ranking items, and works with any given ranking length. This makes RBO a better measure of accuracy for our models' rankings than Jaccard Similarity or Kendall's τ. We set the RBO's weight parameter p to 0.98.

The average of the RBO scores for all available testing ego surveys is weighted by the length of the corresponding top-k ground truth lists, accentuating accurate predictions of larger lists. The final score is computed as the average fold score over all folds. This setup allows our models to show if they can continuously predict rankings over extended periods.

When fitting the models using the training data, we use a proven, established framework for optimized parameter fitting: Optuna [1], which uses an efficient approach to parameter sweeping and critical parameter identification when tuning models. Optuna is used to tune β for Hawkes, and L, μ, and θ for MIM each time a new chunk of training data is released during the evaluation process.

4.2   Model Performance

We evaluate the performance of each model on NetSense and NetHealth data and present the results in Table 1. The random model sets the lowest bar for performance, followed by recency and the frequency. The tunable models, Hawkes and MIM, outperform the baselines to a statistically significant degree but these two are statistically equivalent. Both models are promising, considering the fact that these models are not only nominating significant relationships for the fit of their interactions, but are also assigning accurate levels of significance of each relationship.

Table 1. Average RBO scores (variances) for NetSense and NetHealth.

Model	RBO Scores	
	NetSense	NetHealth
Random	0.03022 (0.002)	0.03299 (0.004)
Recency	0.28295 (0.029)	0.27508 (0.033)
Frequency	0.29526 (0.030)	0.29526 (0.030)
MIM	0.36058 (0.031)	0.35833 (0.036)
Hawkes	0.36497 (0.031)	0.37117 (0.038)

5   Cross-Dataset Modeling

In this section, we evaluate the generalizability of our models by using Hawkes and MIM tuned on data from one study to nominate and rank alters in the other study. Successful cross-dataset ranking performance serves as an indicator that a model is picking up on transferable cognitive mechanisms that should be universal across populations. In this comparison, we need to consider the different sizes of NetSense and NetHealth datasets. Tuning models on NetHealth to test on NetSense will give them an overt advantage over the time series models because of the size of the training data compared to the testing data. As mentioned in Sect. 2, NetHealth has 594 egos, while NetSense only has 196. Therefore, we randomly remove 6 egos from the NetHealth dataset and then evenly split the remaining egos into three subsets, resulting in three subgroups of 196 egos, equal to the number of available egos in NetSense. Then to equalize the number of social tie rankings, we repeat the splitting twice, with the egos first keeping their first four semesters of data, and then the last four semesters of data. This results in six NetHealth subgroups that can be used independently for training and testing with NetSense.

Here, we evaluate only the memory models, since they have parameters that can be tuned, and since the two datasets were collected during entirely different times, we do not need to worry about staggering the training and testing process as done previously. When training on NetHealth to test on NetSense, we tune the models on one of the six NetHealth subgroups and then test it against all the NetSense data, then repeat for all subgroups. When training on NetSense to test on NetHealth, we tune the models just once on NetSense and then test on each NetHealth subgroup. For both approaches, the average of all RBOs weighted by top-k list length gives us the subgroup scores, the average of which creates the final score. The results of this evaluation process are shown in Table 2.

Importantly, the cross-dataset modeling yields results similar to those obtained on within-dataset. This suggests that these tuned models are picking up on memory imprint mechanisms that are universal across datasets. The universality of these mechanisms implies that while communication patterns and overall behavior within populations may change, the way individuals process and perceive them in memory over time does not. Our models are trained on subjects

Table 2. The dataset on the left of the arrow is the dataset on which the models were exclusively trained. The dataset on the right of the arrow is the dataset the models were tested on after training. The score is average RBO with the variance in parentheses.

Model	Training dataset → testing dataset	
	NetHealth → NetSense	NetSense → NetHealth
MIM	0.35970 (0.0005)	0.33063 (0.0021)
Hawkes	0.36293 (0.0006)	0.35071 (0.0016)

with healthy memories. Hence, we can hypothesize that they are effective not only at modeling memory imprints within single social networks, but also on social networks with healthy members.

6   Conclusions

Our results show that the Memory Imprint Model and the Hawkes model are capable of effectively capturing memory imprints of interactions. This process allows us to not only identify significant relationships from interactions, but also assign levels of significance to the relationship, giving us a finer degree of explanatory power when evaluating connections between people in social networks. Importantly, our results on the cross-dataset modeling shows that these models, when fit on the memory imprint dynamics of one dataset, can be used to accurately nominate and rank significant relationships of the other dataset. Based on these results, we hypothesize the MIM and Hawkes models capture the dynamics of a healthy memory, as we are studying the cognitive dynamics of populations of young adults starting college. Consequently, the participants whose mechanics of memory imprint we are modeling will be, generally, in their prime health-wise. Hence, the accuracy of the results for cross-dataset modeling confirms the two models' efficacy in representing the mechanics for the memories of young, healthy adults.

In future work, we will attempt to more directly evaluate the hypothesis that the models and the process we have designed for evaluating said models can be considered a viable standard for representing memory imprint of interactions for healthy memories that can ultimately be used as a comparative tool for diagnosing malfunctioning memory imprint patterns in humans. We believe that perception of healthy and malfunctioning memories differ. Unlike current indirect methods for diagnosing memory ailments [3], modeling perception similar to what was done with student perception in this paper allows us to explicitly measure the strength of distortion of perception. Specifically, if we tune our models to nominate significant relationships using a population of healthy adults and then test it against a population where some individuals have malfunctioning memory (e.g., Alzheimer's, Dementia, Mild Cognitive Impairment), the model performance will be negatively affected, as the memory imprints of the ailing individuals would not match the memory imprints of the healthy population.

The easily and unobtrusively obtainable differences in memory import distortion may indicate the type and level of advancements of illnesses, like Alzheimer's or dementia.

Acknowledgments. JF and BKS were partially supported by the Army Research Office (ARO) under Grant W911NF-16-1-0524 and by DARPA under Agreements W911NF-17-C-0099 and HR001121C0165. Data collection for the NetHealth project was supported by National Institutes of Health grant #1 R01 HL117757-01A1 (OL Investigator). Data collection for the NetSense project was supported by National Science Foundation grant #0968529 (OL Co-PI).

References

1. Akiba, T., Sano, S., Yanase, T., Ohta, T., Koyama, M.: Optuna: A next-generation hyperparameter optimization framework. In: Proceedings of the 25rd ACM SIGKDD International Conference on Knowledge Discovery and Data Mining (2019)
2. Anderson, J.R., Bothell, D., Lebiere, C., Matessa, M.: An integrated theory of list memory. J. Mem. Lang. **38**(4), 341–380 (1998)
3. Bayat, S., et al.: GPS driving: a digital biomarker for preclinical Alzheimer disease. Alzheimer's Res. Therapy **13**(1), 1–9 (2021)
4. Bulut, E., Szymanski, B.K.: Exploiting friendship relations for efficient routing in mobile social networks. IEEE Trans. Parallel Distrib. Syst. **23**(12), 2254–2265 (2012)
5. Conti, M., Passarella, A., Pezzoni, F.: A model for the generation of social network graphs. In: 2011 IEEE International Symposium on a World of Wireless, Mobile and Multimedia Networks, pp. 1–6. IEEE (2011)
6. Flamino, J., DeVito, R., Szymanski, B.K., Lizardo, O.: A machine learning approach to predicting continuous tie strengths. arXiv preprint arXiv:2101.09417 (2021)
7. Gilbert, E., Karahalios, K.: Predicting tie strength with social media. In: Proceedings of the SIGCHI Conference on Human Factors in Computing Systems, pp. 211–220 (2009)
8. Michalski, R., Szymanski, B.K., Kazienko, P., Lebiere, C., Lizardo, O., Kulisiewicz, M.: Social networks through the prism of cognition. Complexity 2021 (2021)
9. Nurek, M., Michalski, R., Rizoiu, M.A.: Hawkes-modeled telecommunication patterns reveal relationship dynamics and personality traits. arXiv preprint arXiv:2009.02032 (2020)
10. Purta, R., et al.: Experiences measuring sleep and physical activity patterns across a large college cohort with fitbits. In: Proceedings of the 2016 ACM International Symposium on Wearable Computers, pp. 28–35 (2016)
11. Striegel, A., Liu, S., Meng, L., Poellabauer, C., Hachen, D., Lizardo, O.: Lessons learned from the netsense smartphone study. ACM SIGCOMM Comput. Commun. Rev. **43**(4), 51–56 (2013)
12. Webber, W., Moffat, A., Zobel, J.: A similarity measure for indefinite rankings. ACM Trans. Inf. Syst. (TOIS) **28**(4), 1–38 (2010)

Theory and Methods

Theory and Method

Unleashing Computational Organization Theory with Quantum Probability Theory

David Mortimore$^{(\boxtimes)}$ ⓘ and Mustafa Canan ⓘ

Naval Postgraduate School, Monterey, CA 93943, USA
{dbmortim1,anthony.canan}@nps.edu

Abstract. Since its nascence, computational organization theory has predominantly relied on classical probability theory to model and simulate organizational properties. However, key assumptions of classical probability theory conflict with empirical studies of organizational behaviors and processes, thereby raising the question if an alternate theoretical basis for probabilistic modeling of organizations might improve the relevancy of computational organization research. In the context of the garbage can model of organizational decision-making, this paper provides two examples—path dependency and system measurement—to illustrate the inadequacy of classical probability theory and to stimulate discussion on the merits of incorporating quantum probability theory in computational models. This paper recommends that future work explore the sensitivity of computational models to probability theories, the impacts theoretical assumptions might have on modeling and simulating dynamic organizational interdependencies, and the implications to methods.

Keywords: Computational organization theory · Probability theory · Quantum theory · Decision-making

1 Introduction

For nearly thirty years, computational organization theory (COT) models have contributed to understanding and theorizing about organizational properties. Scholars and practitioners alike employ COT intellective, agent-based, emulative, social networking, and mathematical and logic models to simulate decision-making and other behaviors [1]. Despite the remarkable nature of contributions by Burton and Obel, Carley, Levitt, and others, the use of classical probability theory (CPT) in modeling and simulating organizational behaviors limits the accuracy of COT studies and, by extension, their contributions to knowledge and practice. Moreover, experimental research findings contradict axioms on which CPT relies, thereby raising the question if a supplemental theoretical basis for probabilistic modeling of organizational behaviors might improve the relevancy of organizational models and simulations based on those models [2–4].

Incorporating quantum probability theory (QPT) and its associated axioms into computational models of organizational behaviors offers the potential to address incongruencies between CPT and organizational properties—both theoretical and empirical.

© The Author(s), under exclusive license to Springer Nature Switzerland AG 2022
R. Thomson et al. (Eds.): SBP-BRiMS 2022, LNCS 13558, pp. 199–208, 2022.
https://doi.org/10.1007/978-3-031-17114-7_19

QPT offers a framework to resolve anomalies associated with CPT, particularly path dependency, non-unicity, measurement impacts, and the irreducibility of system-level behaviors. Unfortunately, there is a relative paucity of research in this area [5].

The purpose of this paper is to stimulate discussion regarding the CPT employed in COT models and simulations, and to propose theoretical and computational exploration of QPT constructs, which might strengthen experimental validity. This paper provides an overview of the axioms and principles upon which CPT relies and the associated implications to COT. Then, QPT and six characteristics particularly relevant to COT are summarized. The garbage can model of organizational decision-making is described next, along with an elementary example to illustrate how QPT might better accommodate empirically demonstrated organizational behaviors. Finally, recommendations for future research are offered.

1.1 Classical Probability Theory

Computational models and simulations of organizational behaviors predominantly use CPT, even though some foundational assumptions conflict with organizational behaviors. Based on Kolmogorov's axioms and set-theoretical principles, CPT assigns probabilities to random events as sets in a two-dimensional statistical sample or probability space [6].[1] Additionally, CPT is based on Boolean logic axioms [6, 7]. Consistency should exist, therefore, between organizational behaviors, foundational axioms, and theoretical and computational models.

Commutative Axiom. According to the commutative axiom, the order in which operations are performed has no consequence on subsequent events. As Boole asserts, the commutative axiom "is *indifferent* [emphasis added] in what order two successive acts … are performed" [7, p. 17]. In the context of COT, the commutative axiom implies the sequence in which individuals and organizations learn and experience phenomena, known as "path dependency," should not affect outcomes. Path dependency is problematic for CPT because event conjunction is the intersection of commutable events [8]. More simply, the commutative axiom contradicts a commonly observed organizational behavior—path dependency—that influences empirically observed outcomes [2, 8, 9]. For theorists and modelers, alike, this means investigating the impacts the order of events might have on outcomes is necessary.

Unicity Principle. The principle of unicity implies every conceivable event is part of the sample or probability space, which can be an issue when comparing dramatically different scenarios. The unicity principle refers to the assumption that there exists a unique and exhaustive sample or probability space for each experiment; if an event is not in the space, it does not exist [8, 10]. This assumption becomes problematic when a system is unable to be in a single, definite state regarding two decision options; a definite state for one option might be an indefinite state for another option, a condition referred to as "incompatibility." Consider, for example, a manager evaluating the

---

[1] The terms "occurrences" and "outcomes" are used synonymously for the term "events" in classical probability theory.

likelihood of success of two dramatically different strategic plans. One plan continues the organization's existing services and set of clients, while the other involves wholesale change of both. It is unlikely there exists a single sample or probability space that adequately supports comparative analysis of probabilities associated with the strategic plans; therefore, the manager must try to compare two disparate sets of options. More colloquially, the principle of unicity requires the manager to compare apples to oranges *with* a shared basis (i.e., both are fruit). For theorists and modelers, this CPT limitation means operationalizing models with disparate bases likely sacrifices accuracy.

Law of Total Probability. A consequence of the Law of Total Probability is the total probability of an event occurring cannot be different than the sum of its disjoint probabilities; however, empirical studies document natural and organizational phenomena that violate this law. Based on the distributive axiom and the principle of unicity, the Law of Total Probability enables the determination of an event's likelihood using disjoint conditional probabilities. Simply put, the total probability of an event cannot be less than any of its parts. In the context of CPT, the Law of Total Probability is supposedly inviolable; however, studies demonstrate both natural and social phenomena do violate it. The double-slit experiment in physics demonstrates systemic violations of the Law of Total Probability [8]. The conjunction fallacy demonstrates how individual behaviors when assessing a situation and deciding the likelihood of potential outcomes can violate the Law of Total Probability [11]. CPT does not accommodate decision-making outcomes in which knowledge workers, for example, determine less probable events are more likely outcomes contrary to the foundational axioms and probability theory used. Computational models might be particularly sensitive to this discrepancy because of the inherent uncertainty it adds, a factor theorists and modelers might need to consider.

Definite State Condition. Contrary to empirical study findings, there exists an assumption in CPT that measurements neither disturb a system nor affect outcomes. Supposedly, measurements only record the system state [5] and the system is insensitive to such interactions. In a stochastic simulation, for example, an agent is assumed to be in a definite state at the start with respect to possible outcomes then moves deterministically between definite states during the simulation. In a Markov simulation, mixed states represent different outcomes, each with a probability assigned based upon the observer's uncertainty, and the system moves deterministically from one state to a subsequent one during the simulation [8]. Findings from the 1928–1932 Hawthorne Studies, for example, contradict the assumption of a definite state condition; measurements generated significant system behaviors [3, 12]. Although the definite state condition might assist theorists and modelers describe the system status, it ignores the impacts measurement has on the system and, by extension, outcomes lessening study relevancy.

Although the use of CPT as the foundational probability theory to model and simulate systems is ubiquitous, foundational axioms are inconsistent with empirical descriptions of organizational behaviors. Such discrepancies limit the experimental validity of COT studies. Incorporating QPT into computational models of organizational behaviors addresses conflicts between CPT and organizational properties—both theoretical and empirical—thereby strengthening experimental validity.

1.2   Quantum Probability Theory

Alternatively, QPT might provide a more comprehensive and coherent foundation than CPT to explore organizational behaviors. QPT assigns probability amplitudes to events, and a vector space construct replaces the set-theoretical construct of CPT. Events conform to Dirac [13] and von Neumann [14] axioms that treat events, sequences, and system interactions differently than CPT [8]. This section summarizes six interrelated QPT principles particularly relevant to modeling organizational behaviors, like decision-making [8]. More comprehensive descriptions are beyond the scope of this paper.

The Logic of Subspaces. Dirac-von Neuman axioms provide the foundational logic of subspaces, therefore, QPT is not constrained by Boolean and Kolmogorov's axioms, or the set-theoretical construct of CPT. QPT accommodates CPT and its underlying axioms, however, it is neither bound to nor constrained by those axioms [8]. Conceptually, QPT relies upon a vector space representation of events and probabilities that includes the set-theoretical representation of CPT [5, 8]. This means organizational behaviors might be reasonable QPT-wise while appearing unreasonable from a CPT perspective [5]. Theorists and modelers should consider the axiomatic implications of QPT and CPT in determining which probability theory is more appropriate for a study.

Order Effects. Event order matters, and QPT recognizes the sequence of events impacts outcomes. Such "order effects," or non-commutability, introduce uncertainty [8], which is the difference between information needed for decision-making and information the organization possesses [15], into the system. The sequence in which natural and artificial agents experience events can impact individual and organizational information gathering, processing, and sharing operations [5, 16]. Decision-making outcomes, for example, are contingent upon the information, experience, and expertise individuals possess; future outcomes are not independent of past events. Thus, theoretical and computational models need to account for order effects to represent organizational behaviors more accurately.

The Superposition State. QPT assumes systems start and remain in an indefinite state, known as the superposition state, until the act of measurement transiently "collapses" or "fixes" some part of the system to a definite state. In the superposition state, precise probabilities for potential outcomes remain ambiguous explaining violations of CPT axioms observed in cognitive systems. In decision-making, for example, all decision options remain feasible while the cognitive system is in a superposition state; the option selected remains indeterminate until the decision is made, which is a form of measurement. Therefore, theorists and modelers should balance the consequences of anchoring a system to an intermediate decision, for example, with permitting artificial and natural systems to operate unfixed.

Measurements Generate System Behaviors. In QPT, measurements affect system properties; the act of observing a system induces irrevocable changes to its behaviors. Not only does a measurement affect system behaviors, it also generates potentially new system properties and outcomes [5]. This phenomenon is consistent with the findings of 1928–1932 Hawthorne studies [3, 12] and subsequent studies that observing behaviors resulted in dramatic changes to outcomes [10, 16][2] Although measurements might not affect computational agents to the same degree as humans, theorists and modelers should consider how measurements might create deviations between computational models and the systems the models represent.

Non-unicity. QPT permits decision-makers, for example, to consider a broader range of questions and potential outcomes than CPT because QPT is not constrained by the principle of unicity. QPT allows for a non-Boolean combination of multiple Boolean sample and probability spaces [5, 8]. Such a construct allows for the assignment of event probabilities without exhaustive identification of joint probabilities of events, which permits consideration of what might be incompatible questions in a CPT framework. In other words, QPT enables decision-makers to compare apples to oranges, even if they were *not* both fruit. This is an important feature of QPT for theorists and modelers. Freedom from the assumption of unicity provides the opportunity to model and simulate a broader range of events and outcomes than CPT allows. Non-unicity likely impacts modelers more than theorists because it necessitates operationalizing a framework connecting potentially disparate event spaces to allow exploration of incompatible options.

Irreducibility. Some systems and behaviors might be irreducible, or non-decomposable, to subsets of random variables contrary to methods that reduce organizational properties to micro-behaviors for experimentation. The *Virtual Design Team*, for example, uses micro theory to emulate individual-level behaviors before aggregating results to describe macro-level, or system-level, behaviors [17]. Interdependencies between decision-making participants, for example, might mean behaviors, and sets of behaviors, cannot be decomposed contrary to the reductionist perspective. In contrast, QPT supports the phenomenon in which multiple agents and entities exhibit behaviors consistent with others, which is described by the mathematical construct explaining quantum entanglement [8]. Intuition suggests this construct might mean modeling and simulation activities below the quantum entanglement level lessen experimental validity.

Fundamental assumptions and principles of QPT appear to address shortcomings of CPT assumptions and resulting impacts to models and simulations of organizational behaviors. QPT encapsulates CPT, therefore, QPT axioms and principles are not as restrictive as those used predominantly in COT today [8]. Using the framework of a well-established decision-making model, an elementary example further describes the potential implications of incorporating QPT into organizational models.

2 The Garbage Can Model

The garbage can model of organizational decision-making [18] provides a useful framework to describe ways in which QPT addresses organizational behaviors that conflict

---

[2] The 1928–1932 Hawthorne studies were instrumental in the development of the neo-classical, or Human Relations, school of organization theory approximately ten years later. Thus, the organization sciences community has had access to empirical evidence for nearly 75 years that CPT might not comprehensively describe organizational properties and behaviors.

with assumptions of CPT. Rejecting the view that organizational decision-making is a purely rational activity in which knowledge workers enjoy access to complete and accurate information, and exhaustively explore every option before making the optimal decision, the garbage can model characterizes decision-making as an intrinsically irrational activity. According to the model, non-uniform preferences, ambiguity regarding how the organization accomplishes its tasks, and varying knowledge worker participation intersect with decision opportunities [18]. Furthermore, individuals and organizations are cognitively limited regarding the amount of time and processing capabilities available for cognitive tasks [9, 19]. Such limitations result in *satisficing* behaviors in which individuals make boundedly rational decisions that are good enough, not optimal [19, 20]. Instead, organizational decision-making is a confluence of: (a) problems, which require resolution; (b) solutions, which are answers available to be matched to problems; (c) participants, who are decision-makers looking for problems to solve; and (d) choice opportunities, which are discrete points in time when an organization is to render a decision [18]. Expressed more colloquially, organizational decision-making is "a collection of choices looking for problems, issues and feelings looking for decision situations in which they might be aired, solutions looking for issues to which they might be the answer, and decision makers looking for work" [18, p. 2]. This paper provides two examples—path dependency and system measurement—to illustrate the inadequacy of classical probability theory and the merits of QPT in computational models.

2.1 Example Scenario

Consider a scenario in which an organization needs to modernize its capabilities. A typical process involves a manager in the organization soliciting proposals and deciding in which ones to invest. In the framework of the garbage can model of decision-making:

- the problem is the need to develop capabilities in response to stakeholder requirements and organizational priorities;
- the solution involves the information sharing mechanisms (ISMs) by which proposals are solicited and obtained;
- the participants (knowledge workers) include managers, proposal submitters, reviewers, and others; and
- the choice opportunity is in what proposals and, by extension, capabilities to invest.

2.2 Path Dependency Impacts

A simple example refutes axiomatic assumptions of CPT that do not recognize the existence of order effects and demonstrates how QPT addresses path dependency. Path dependency, or order effects, in decision-making refers to the change in outcomes based solely on the sequence of definite states, or operations, through which the decision-making process progresses. More simply, the sequence in which questions are asked, or supporting decisions are made, influences outcomes [8, 9].

Consider, for example, the order in which the solution and participants come together in the decision-making process. If a manager determines the ISMs to be used (i.e., the solution) before the set of individuals and organizations from which proposals will be solicited (i.e., the participants), the set of decision options (i.e., the proposals) might be different than if the manager determines the participants before the solution. A solution limited to an intra-organization e-mail distribution list limits participants to individuals on the list and to whom the call for proposals is forwarded. If the set of participants includes individuals internal and external to the organization, then the solution will involve ISMs that reach the broader set of participants. The difference in decision options available to the manager can result in different decision-making outcomes reflecting path dependency, or order effects, in organizational behaviors (See Fig. 1).

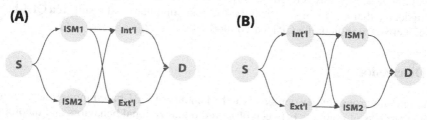

Fig. 1. Using a revised illustration of the double-slit experiment [8, p. 9], the two graphics depict the initial system state, S, the order of decisions involving potential solutions and participants, and the outcome state, D, in which the decision in what proposals to invest is made. Potential solutions include two ISMs and potential participants include individuals internal (Int'l), and internal and external (Ext'l) to the organization. The graphic on the left, (A), depicts the case in which the manager determines the solution before the participants, and the graphic on the right, (B), depicts the selection of the participants before the solution.

Path dependency can introduce or exacerbate additional phenomena that impact system outcomes. One example is "structural interference," which describes phenomena that undermine communications between individuals and organizations in which expertise is distributed [21]. Structural interference negatively impacts organizational behaviors, like decision-making, and performance [22] by limiting accessible information. In addition to impacting the decision options available, the path dependency in organizational decision-making can impact system performance.

2.3 System Measurement Impacts

An assumption of CPT-based models is that measuring a system only records the system state immediately prior to the measurement without influencing subsequent states [5, 8]. In contrast, QPT holds the system state is "constructed from the interaction between the superposition state and the measurement taken" [5, p. 235]. A system remains in a superposition of possible outcomes until measured; the outcome is uncertain. System measurements, like project reviews, change the system permanently. The act of measuring a system necessarily generates irrevocable changes to its properties and behaviors that can dramatically influence outcomes. A simple example is illustrative.

Consider, for example, a situation in which the manager wants to check the number of proposals received and general distribution of proposed topics before the official cutoff date for proposal submission. Essentially, the manager is investigating the extent to which the solution addresses the problem at-hand; the act of retrieving such information constitutes a measurement of the system. Even though the manager might not intend to act based on the measurement, a new state is constructed based on the interaction permanently altering the system [5, 8, 16]. The irrevocable change to the system would be more apparent and relevant to COT in the case wherein the manager acts based upon the measurement, perhaps to solicit additional proposals. The manager's actions might change the participant make-up, the solution employed, the choice opportunity, or a combination thereof. Notwithstanding the scope of the disturbance to the system, measurement irreversibly altered it. Furthermore, the disturbance to the system might be to a degree that results in significantly different computational results if a QPT-based model were used in lieu of a CPT-based model.

3 Discussion

Although numerous studies demonstrate the benefits of CPT-based models and simulations regardless of conflicts between observed organizational behaviors and theoretical assumptions, the discrepancies might become problematic in future research. Intuition suggests computational power formerly available to theorists and modelers constrained the scope of experiments thereby limiting the effect theoretical discrepancies had on results. Also, the aggregation of micro-behaviors to approximate macro-level behaviors [17] might mask any disagreement between actual organizational behaviors and CPT-based models. COT studies generally emphasize interactions within a single organization and a unidirectional set of interactions between organizational levels, like micro-level to macro-level, therefore, conflicts between the actual behaviors of modeled organizations and the models themselves might not significantly affect results. Nevertheless, the inherent disagreement between organizational behaviors and assumptions of CPT-based models might impact the accuracy of future studies.

In contrast, QPT accommodates observed and non-observed organizational behaviors, and address discrepancies between such behaviors. Empirical studies, such as the 1928–1932 Hawthorne studies [3, 12], are consistent with the QPT assumption that measurement generates system-level properties [5]. QPT is well-suited for studying processes involving, for example, information allocation, retrieval, processing, and sharing; and varying requirements, such as decision-making [5]; micro-, meso-, and macro-level interdependencies [8, 10]; and properties of multi-organization communities. Furthermore, QPT accommodates behaviors that might seem irrational and contradictory in a CPT framework, like the conjunction fallacy and boundedly rational decision-making [19, 20], and might strengthen the experimental validity of COT studies.

The issue, therefore, seems to center around the extent to which: (a) QPT-based models might better support research activities, particularly in more complex systems and nested complex systems; (b) future studies emphasize dynamic interdependencies within and between organizational levels; and (c) the merits of incorporating QPT exceed the investment to do so. In the future, theorists and modelers should deliberately consider which probability theory provides a stronger foundation for their studies.

Future studies should empirically explore the extent to which results from QPT-based and CPT-based models differ, and if there exist contexts in which the use of more restrictive CPT-based models is appropriate. Three recommended focus areas for studies include: (a) the sensitivity of COT models to the assumptions of QPT and CPT, and associated sensitivity ranges; (b) impacts to computationally modeling organizational interdependencies between the micro-, meso-, and macro-levels; and (c) impacts to modeling and simulation practices and tools.

4 Conclusion

Intellective and computational models of organizational properties have provided useful insights for scholars and practitioners for decades. Those models, and the simulations employing them, generally rely on CPT and its underpinning axioms. Some empirically determined organizational behaviors conflict with CPT tenets, thereby raising questions about the accuracy with which the models describe organizational properties. Using the framework of the garbage can model of decision-making, this paper presented two elementary examples that illustrate potential issues if CPT serves as the sole probability theory framework for organization theorists. The inability of CPT and its foundational axioms to recognize demonstrated organizational behaviors seems to limit COT's impact on knowledge and practice. QPT, and its associated assumptions, seem to address weaknesses of CPT and might serve to strengthen the experimental validity of COT studies. Furthermore, QPT encompasses CPT and its axioms; incorporating QPT into models and simulations should expand and strengthen COT community members' contributions.

Acknowledgements. This research is supported by America's Sea Land Air Military Research Initiative (SLAMR) at the Naval Postgraduate School and the Naval Undersea Warfare Center Division, Keyport. We are indebted to Professor Raymond Buettner, Jr. For his mentorship and to LtCol Scott Humr, USMC, for his continued support.

References

1. Frantz, T.L., Carley, K.M., Wallace, W.A.: Computational organization theory. In: Gass, S.I., Fu, M.C. (eds.) Encyclopedia of Operations Research and Management Science, pp. 246–252. Springer, Boston (2013). https://doi.org/10.1007/978-1-4419-1153-7_143
2. Koch, J., Eisend, M., Petermann, A.: Path dependence in decision-making processes: exploring the impact of complexity under increasing returns. Bus. Res. 2(1), 67–84 (2009). https://doi.org/10.1007/BF03343529
3. Mayo, E.: The Social Problems of an Industrial Civilization. Andover Press, Andover (1945)
4. Pierson, P.: Increasing returns, path dependence, and the study of politics. Am. Polit. Sci. Rev. 94(2), 251–267 (2000). https://doi.org/10.2307/2586011
5. White, L., Pothos, E., Busemeyer, J.: Insights from quantum cognitive models for organizational decision making. J. Appl. Res. Mem. Cogn. 4(2015), 229–238 (2015). https://doi.org/10.1016/j.jarmac.2014.11.002
6. Kolmogorov, A.: Foundations of the Theory of Probability, 2nd edn. Chelsea Publishing Company, New York (1956)
7. Boole, G.: The Mathematical Analysis of Logic: Being an Essay Towards a Calculus of Deductive Reasoning. Philosophical Library Inc., New York (1948)

8. Busemeyer, J., Bruza, P.: Quantum Models of Cognition and Decision. Cambridge University Press, Cambridge (2012)
9. Carley, K., Gasser, L.: Computational organization theory. In: Weiss, G. (ed.) Multiagent Systems: A Modern Approach to Distributed Artificial Intelligence, pp. 299–330. MIT Press, Cambridge (1999)
10. Griffiths, R.: Consistent Quantum Theory. Cambridge University Press, Cambridge (2003)
11. Tversky, A., Kahneman, D.: Extensional versus intuitive reasoning: the conjunction fallacy in probability judgment. Psychol. Rev. **90**(4), 293–315 (1983)
12. Landsberger, H.: Hawthorne Revisited: Management and the Worker, its Critics, and Developments in Human Relations in Industry. Cornell University, Ithaca (1958)
13. Dirac, P.: The Principles of Quantum Mechanics, 4th edn. Oxford University Press, London (1958)
14. von Neumann, J.: Mathematical Foundations of Quantum Mechanics. Princeton University Press, Princeton (1955)
15. Galbraith, J.: Organization Design. Addison-Wesley Publishing Co., Menlo Park (1977)
16. Lord, R., Dinh, J., Hoffman, E.: A quantum approach to time and organizational change. Acad. Manag. Rev. **40**(2), 263–290 (2015)
17. Levitt, R., Orr, R., Nissen, M.: Validation of the Virtual Design Team (VDT) Computational Modeling Environment. CRGP Working Paper Series #25. Stanford University, Stanford (2005)
18. Cohen, M., March, J., Olsen, J.: A garbage can model of organizational choice. Adm. Sci. Q. **17**(1), 1–25 (1972). https://doi.org/10.2307/2392088
19. Simon, H.: The Sciences of the Artificial. MIT Press, Cambridge (1996)
20. Campitelli, G., Gobet, F.: Herbert Simon's decision-making approach: investigation of cognitive processes in experts. Rev. Gen. Psychol. **14**(4), 354–364 (2010)
21. Wegner, D., Erber, R., Raymond, P.: Transactive memory in close relationships. J. Pers. Soc. Psychol. **61**(6), 923–929 (1991)
22. Arrow, K.: The Limits of Organizations. W. W. Norton & Company Inc., New York (1974)

Cultural Value Resonance in Folktales: A Transformer-Based Analysis with the World Value Corpus

Noam Benkler[✉], Scott Friedman, Sonja Schmer-Galunder, Drisana Mosaphir,
Vasanth Sarathy, Pavan Kantharaju, Matthew D. McLure,
and Robert P. Goldman

Smart Information Flow Technologies, 319 N. 1st Avenue, Suite 400, Minneapolis,
MN 55401, USA
{nbenkler,sfriedman,sschmer-galunder,dmosaphir,vsarathy,pkantharaju,
mmclure,rgoldman}@sift.net
https://www.sift.net

Abstract. Although implicit cultural values are reflected in human narrative texts, few robust computational solutions exist to recognize values that resonate within these texts. In other words, given a statement text and a value text, the task is to predict the label that resonates, conflicts or is neutral with respect to the value. In this paper, we present a novel, annotated dataset and transformer-based model for *Recognizing Value Resonance* (RVR). We created the World Values Corpus (WVC): a labeled collection of [statement, value] pairs of text based on the World Values Survey (WVS), which is a well-validated, comprehensive survey for assessing values across cultures. Each pair expresses whether the value resonates with, conflicts with, or is neutral to the statement. The 384 values in the WVC are derived from the WVS to assure the WVC's cross-cultural relevance. The statement pairs for each value were generated by a pool of six annotators across genders and cultural backgrounds. We demonstrate that off-the-shelf *Recognizing Textual Entailment* (RTE) models perform unfavorably on the RVR task. However, RTE models trained on the WVC achieve substantially higher accuracy on RVR, serving as a strong, replicable baseline for future RVR work, advancing the study of cultural values using computational NLP approaches. We also present results of applying our baseline model on the "World of Tales" corpus, an online repository of international folktales. The results suggest that such a model can provide useful anthropological insights, which in turn is an important step towards facilitating automated ethnographic modeling.

Keywords: Recognizing values resonance · World Values Corpus ·
Folktales value analysis

1   Introduction

The study of implicit values embedded in language has been a long-standing research focus of linguists, political scientists, social scientists, and cultural anthropologists. Graeber defines value as the importance of social action through which people demonstrate their belief in what is the good life [8]. Although values are dynamic and changing over time, cultures create different standards of value, and cross-cultural analysis have shown distinct patterns of values relating to well-being [6], trust [11], political support [2], gender gaps and biases [7], and other factors. Despite recent advances in NLP and computational social science, we lack widespread computational methods for recognizing cultural values that resonate in cultural texts. By *resonate*, we mean the degree to which texts amplify, exemplify or embody certain values. For example, we can understand the concept of value resonance on analogy to the sentence "the siren resonated across the harbor." Our approach automatically predicts whether "cultural value X resonates in this text." Importantly, this approach identifies values not explicitly mentioned in the text. It is an open question whether human readers also engage in value resonance reading. To date, cultural values are assessed at different scales - quantitatively (e.g. survey statistics) and qualitatively (e.g. fieldwork, interviews, etc.). However, new methodological approaches combining qualitative and quantitative methods allow us to better understand implicit values in text across languages and cultures.

This paper introduces the NLP problem of *Recognizing Value Resonance* (RVR): given a *statement* text (e.g., sentence(s) from a narrative or utterance) and a *value* text, predict the *label* for whether the value (a) resonates with, (b) conflicts with, or (c) is neutral with respect to the statement. In support of RVR, we present the World Value Corpus (WVC) dataset that includes labeled ⟨*statement, value, label*⟩ examples, and show a proof-of-concept application of RVR to a novel domain, using RVR to depict values that resonate or conflict with sentences of three folktales from different cultural origins. We formulate this problem analogous to the Recognizing Textual Entailment (RTE) problem [13], though our results (Sect. 3) show that state-of-the-art RTE models cannot predict RVR problems with higher than 60% accuracy (chance is 33%). Our RVR-trained model exceeds 90% accuracy, and we believe that future work can improve upon these results. We continue with a brief overview of background materials, describing the World Value Survey (WVS) in Sect. 2.1 and RTE models in Sect. 2.2. We then describe our approach in Sect. 2, including the problem statement, our labeled World Value Corpus (WVC) for RVR, and an initial, specialized RTE model for RVR. We present encouraging RVR results in Sect. 3 using a pre-trained RTE model with additional WVC training. We then present a preliminary application (Sect. 4). This provides early evidence for the applicability of RVR to a new domain (non-Western folktales) without training in the new domain, and shows plots relating to various values across cultures. These plots can be viewed as a distance metric across cultural narratives. We conclude with a discussion (Sect. 5) of limitations and future work. Our WVC datasets are publicly available at OSF [3].

2 Approach

Our approach to *Recognizing Value Resonance* involves the creation of a novel corpus based on the WVS, recognizing RVR as a *Recognizing Textual Entailment*-proximal task re-targeted from factual implication to sentimental implication, and tuning a baseline RTE model on WVC data.

2.1 Background: World Value Survey

The World Value Survey [9,14] is a global research project focused on people's values and beliefs, how they change over time, and how values impact social and political life in different countries of the world. The WVS's central research instrument is a representative comparative survey conducted every 5 years and consists of 290 standard questions. These questions cover 14 distinct thematic domains: social values, attitudes and stereotypes, societal well-being, social capital and trust, economic values, corruption, migration, post-materialistic values, science and technology, religion, security, ethics and norms, politics, and demography.[1] The breadth and depth of value coverage, extensive geographical scope, and open data accessibility make the WVS one of the most authoritative, widely-used cross-national surveys in social science research today.[2]

Previous work has used the WVS to explore determinants of well-being [6], social trust [11], support for democracy [2], gender gaps [7], and more. This paper extends the existing literature to provide a dataset—and preliminary NLP model—to help identify WVS values that resonate within narrative or ethnographic text.

2.2 Problem Statement: Recognizing Value Resonance

The NLP task of *Recognizing Textual Entailment* is: given a premise (statement) and a hypothesis (value), predict whether the facts in the premise necessarily imply the facts in the hypothesis. We define *Recognizing Value Resonance* as the task of, given a statement and a value, predicting whether the value resonates with, conflicts with, or is neutral to the statement. This is a distinctly different, yet proximal task to that of *Recognizing Textual Entailment*. Where RTE focuses on factual implication of a value given a statement, RVR expands this definition to cover endorsement or rejection of a value given a statement. While RVR and RTE are similar in nature we believe RTE models will not perform well when directly applied to the task of RVR and present a few reasons why.

First, RTE (and related NLI) notions cover concepts of entailment and contradiction. The associated datasets (SNLI, SICK, MNLI, etc.) generally contain examples that are inherently propositional in nature. For example, "two dogs are running through the field" from SNLI, is derived from a scene description

---

[1] In certain nations, additional questions or value domains are covered under the World Values Survey, such as gender norms and family planning.
[2] https://www.worldvaluessurvey.org/WVSContents.jsp.

Table 1. Value Resonance Examples Difficult for RTE models, suggesting "resonance" may possess distinct characteristics, different from textual entailment. RVR labels are coded as R (Resonant), N (Neutral) and C (Conflicted). RTE labels are coded as E (Entailment), N (Neutral) and C (Contradict)

Statement (Premise)	Value (Hypothesis)	True RVR Label	Primary RTE Label
It's foul that no one is allowed to perform abortions in this town!	Women should have access to free and safe abortions	R	N
We live in a monarchy	Democracy is very important to me	N	C
We, the faithful will not be harmed by the incursion of science into our lives for science is but the pursuit of God's truth, as is religion	We depend too much on science and not enough on faith	C	N

of an image. The propositional nature of this example allows models to determine if another propositional sentence, say "there are animals outdoors" is true (entailed), might be true (neutral), or is definitely false (contradicted) given the original sentence. By contrast, in RVR, neither the statement nor the value are generally propositional. For example, the sentence "we live in a monarchy" in Table 1 is at best "epistemically" propositional in that "the speaker believes they live in a monarchy." This suggests the examples in RVR might have a different distribution from those in RTE-related datasets.

Second, the notion of resonance is inherently different from that of entailment. One might be able to argue that a narrative text epistemically entails a value; but, one might just as easily argue that a value is an implicit social concept presupposed by the speaker in their narrative texts. We believe (and demonstrate) that entailment models, although not sufficient alone, can serve as useful starting point for learning and recognizing value resonance.

2.3   Dataset: The World Value Corpus

We constructed the World Values Corpus as a comprehensive dataset covering all questions in the World Values Survey and its Gender module that met two central criteria: a) the question was not inherently numeric[3] b) the question was easily framed to allow for binary restatement/negation annotation.[4] 335 WVS questions met both of these criteria.[5] Of the 335 questions included in the WVC, 27 required segmentation to ensure comprehensive WVS coverage under the strict binary (restatement/negation) WVC annotation framework. Each question was then converted to a directed value statement while staying as true to the underlying question as possible. These statements acted as parent prompts for annotation. The final list of WVC prompts consists of 384 prompts.

---

[3] e.g. "What is your age?", "What is your income level?".

[4] This includes questions easily split into sub-questions that comprehensively cover the response spectrum.

[5] 266 questions from the standard WVS questionnaire and 69 questions from the WVS Gender module.

Following prompt generation, 6 annotators reviewed each prompt in the WVC and submitted annotations in one of 4 categories: direct restatement, direct negation, narrative restatement, and narrative negation. Restatements reaffirm the central message of the parent prompt and negations oppose the central message of the parent prompt. Direct annotations simply reword the prompt (or negate the prompt) whereas narrative annotations are episodic statements that convey the underlying parent prompt (or the negation of that prompt). For complete, single-level coverage we ensure every parent prompt in the WVC is matched to at least one narrative restatement.

Finally, all annotations and prompts were collected in [statement, value, label] sets with annotations as statements, parent prompts as values, and the relation[6] between the two as labels. Each label was re-coded such that restatements became 'resonant' and negations became 'conflicted.' Next, we randomly paired each unique statement with two unrelated values and each unique value with at least two unrelated statements. Our researchers examined each of these [statement, value] pairs to ensure neutrality with respect to the value. This process was repeated until each statement and value was part of at least two true neutral pairs. These pairs were appended to the WVC RVR dataset as sets coded: [statement, value, 'neutral']. Before modeling, we split the WVC RVR dataset into a training set (1114 examples), validation set (275 examples), and testing set (275 examples). The distribution of labels under each split was not significantly different from the underlying WVC according to a 2-sample Kolmogorov-Smirnov Test ($p - val > 0.99$).

2.4   Preliminary Model for Recognizing Value Resonance

We selected an RTE model to use as a baseline for text embedding and finetuning through a preliminary performance evaluation of the top 5 performing RTE models from AllenNLP [5,13,15,17] at the task of RVR. Model performance was evaluated by mean overall accuracy averaged over 5 random splits of our WVC training set, and we chose the transformers [16] implementation of RoBERTa MNLI [13], roberta-large-mnli, as our baseline for finetuning a RVR model. We trained Resonance Tuned RoBERTa, our RVR tuned model, over the WVC training set, evaluating every epoch, and tuning hyperparameters to maximize accuracy over the WVC validation set. We tuned the following hyperparameters: learning rate (1.4e−05), alpha (0.708), momentum (2.16e−2), # training epochs (4), seed (87), batch size (8)[7]. This method was implemented using transformers [16] for training and ray-tune [12] for hyperparameter optimization. Each hyperparameter setting was run on a single machine with population based hyperparameter refinement and resource allocation using a Population Based Training scheduler [10] and stochastic gradient descent for optimization.

---

[6] Relation meaning: direct restatement, direct negation, narrative restatement, narrative negation.

[7] Final optimal values in parentheses.

3   Results: Evaluation on WVC

Here we describe the results of applying multiple RTE NLP models, including our value-resonance trained model (Sect. 2.4) on the problem of recognizing value resonance in statements and narratives.

Table 2 displays the comparative performance results of each RTE and RVR model explored in this paper against our WVC derived test set. We find our Resonance-Tuned RoBERTa outperforms all the top performing RTE models from AllenNLP in all performance metrics covered. Resonance Tuned RoBERTa outperformed all RTE baseline models by an accuracy margin of 0.914 over 0.672 and an F1 margin of 0.912 over 0.666.

Table 2. Comparative Model Performance on RVR, evaluated against WVC test-set. (Precision, Recall, and F1 scores are calculated as a weighted average by support for each label <resonant, neutral, conflicted>)

Model	Accuracy	Precision	Recall	F1
Resonance Tuned RoBERTa	0.914	0.92	0.914	0.912
roberta-large-mnli [13]	0.672	0.721	0.672	0.666
RoBERTa MNLI [13]	0.664	0.741	0.664	0.661
RoBERTa SNLI [13]	0.477	0.488	0.477	0.465
Adversarial Binary Gender Bias-Mitigated RoBERTa SNLI [17]	0.477	0.502	0.477	0.476
Binary Gender Bias-Mitigated RoBERTa SNLI [5]	0.445	0.447	0.445	0.431
ELMo-based Decomposable Attention [15]	0.438	0.445	0.438	0.42

Table 3. Breakdown of accuracy with respect to individual class in RVR <Resonant, Neutral, Conflicted>.

Model	Entailment	Neutral	Contradiction
Resonance Tuned RoBERTa	0.938	0.969	0.922
Adversarial Binary Gender Bias-Mitigated RoBERTa SNLI [17]	0.836	0.555	0.562
roberta-large-mnli [13]	0.828	0.695	0.82
RoBERTa MNLI [13]	0.82	0.672	0.836
Binary Gender Bias-Mitigated RoBERTa SNLI [5]	0.805	0.531	0.555
RoBERTa SNLI [13]	0.797	0.57	0.586
ELMo-based Decomposable Attention [15]	0.633	0.672	0.57

Table 3 shows the accuracy for each of the models tested by individual class. Per-class results from Table 3 shows Resonance Tuned RoBERTA continues to outperform all the tested competitors on a class by class basis. Confusion matrices (not shown here) indicate that three of the RTE models made fewer False Entailment mistakes than Resonance Tuned RoBERTA, though all three performed worse on scoring True Entailments. Roberta-large-mnli outperformed

Resonance Tuned RoBERTA at the task of scoring True Contradictions, though also made many more False Contradiction mistakes than Resonance Tuned RoBERTA.

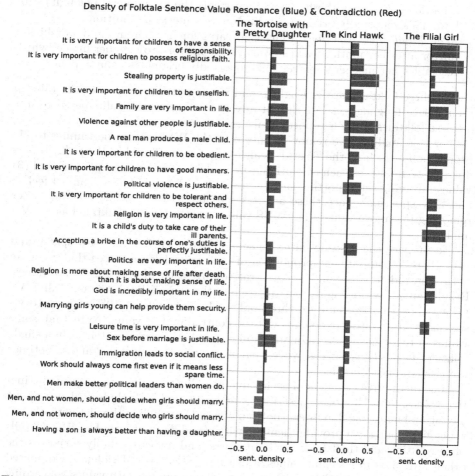

Fig. 1. WVS values resonating (blue, to right of axis) and conflicting (red, to left of axis) with sentences of three folktales, predicted by a RVR NLP model, from 242 possible WVS values. (Color figure online)

4 Preliminary Results: Resonance in Folktales

We next present a proof-of-concept application of RVR in a novel domain, to provide early evidence of RVR NLP applicability without any training in the novel domain. For this experiment, we selected folktales from the "World of Tales" online repository of international folktales [1] as a novel domain:

1. *"The Tortoise with a Pretty Daughter"* describes a poor tortoise who had an attractive daughter that is married by a prince and thereby brings wealth to her family. This story reportedly originates from Nigeria.
2. *"The Kind Hawk"* describes a boy who is kidnapped by another tribe, and a hawk then rescues the boy and then steals the kidnappers' belongings for him. This reportedly originates from Native American tradition.
3. *"The Filial Girl"* describes a girl who cares for her parents and worships a mirror after her mother passes away, as the mirror projects her image, which resembles her mother's image. This reportedly originates from Japan.

All three folktales are in English, and we do not have access to the tales in their native languages, so we do not advise attributing the value-based results of these folktales to their reported cultural origins.

For this analysis, we remove a subset of the WVS values pertaining to (1) proper nouns such as the "World Health Organization" and "AIDS," (2) procedures or technologies such as "euthanasia" and "modern contraceptives," and (3) values involving self-reporting such as "I'm often..." and "I have..." and "I feel..." and "My spouse..." since these are less relevant to the folktale domain. After removing the above values, 242 WVS values remain for this folktale-based RVR analysis.

To prepare the folktale data, we sentencized each folktale with spaCy and used RVR to compute the proportion of each folktale's sentences that resonate with, contradict with, and are neutral toward each of the 242 WVS values. Results are shown in Fig. 1, plotting each of the three folktales against all WVS values above a 10% sentence threshold, such that at least 10% of any story's sentences must either resonate with or contradict the value. Note that some values in Fig. 1 have *both* resonance and contradiction from sentences in a single folktale. This is because, e.g., violence may sometimes be justified and sometimes unjustified, and so-forth.

The distinctive elements of each value plot illustrates the narratives' distinctive values. The "Tortoise" describes a marriage and so includes valence about having and marrying daughters (bottom of Fig. 1), including the distinctive "marrying girls young can provide them security" (middle/bottom). The "Hawk" tells of retribution and theft from the kidnappers, and understandably surpasses the other narratives in resonant values of justifying stealing and violence. Compared to the other two, "The Filial Girl" distinctively resonates with values concerning children caring for their parents and concerning life after death.

Some of the common value resonance detected by RVR was unexpected. The possession of religious faith and the importance of religion were both detected in multiple narratives, though religion itself was not mentioned in any of the three folktales. Further, some of the higher-density values detected by RVR in Fig. 1 (e.g., responsible children, unselfish children, obedient children) may be prominent in many folktales about children (as are these three folktales), or they may be areas where RVR is over-sensitive. We expect that training RVR in this domain will substantially improve its performance, but these early results are encouraging in a novel domain.

5   Conclusions

This paper has presented a NLP problem of Recognizing Value Resonance (RVR) in text, trained on a World Value Corpus (WVC) dataset derived from human contributions and annotations over the World Value Survey.

We demonstrated that training large RTE language models on RVR data improves their RVR performance over untrained RTE models, suggesting that RTE is related to, and can be repurposed for, the problem of RVR, but RTE alone is not sufficient for RVR.

We present preliminary out-of-domain results applying RVR on international folktales in a small comparative analysis to help characterize distinctive values and shared values. The folktale values detected by RVR cohered with central plot elements and character relationships in each folktale, but importantly, folktales about violence and theft do not necessarily *condone* or *promote* said violence and theft; consequently, applying RVR to folktales requires that we interpret it as a summary of the relationships and issues addressed by (or relevant to) the narrative.

We believe that automation of value recognition in cultural texts and statements will benefit anthropology, sociology, political science, and the social science community. However, as shown in our initial out-of-domain results, RVR models may misidentify cultural values and may contain suboptimal biases, so we do not believe this system is yet ready for large scale deployment for predicting or characterizing human cultures or values.

The WVC includes sentences comprising restatements, negations, narrative restatements and narrative negations of the WVS values, but these are not themselves cultural texts. Consequently, the results reported in this paper—even the folktale results—should not be interpreted as RVR performance on real cultural texts or as values held by human cultures.

Important ethical issues of consent from cultures to having their language and texts digitized, or analyzed in this way should be addressed on a case by case basis, and in equitable consultation with these cultures, e.g., [4].

While our initial results are encouraging, important work remains. Extending the WVC to new domains–folktales, ethnography, and social media–will improve its coverage, reduce error rates and increase its applicability.

As RVR can produce a value vector over a text, story, or corpus (see Fig. 1), it might be usable as a value-based distance metric over texts or corpora.

Finally, as with previous work on RTE, RVR models and RVR datasets should be extensible, including (1) new (non-WVS) value statements and (2) new narrative sentences that are assessed with respect to WVS and non-WVS values. The present work uses the WVS as a source of vetted cross-cultural values, but we do not believe the WVS to be complete over all cultures or over time with respect to any single culture.

References

1. Andonov, V.: World of tales - stories for children, folktales, fairy tales and fables from around the world! https://www.worldoftales.com/
2. Ariely, G., Davidov, E.: Can we rate public support for democracy in a comparable way? cross-national equivalence of democratic attitudes in the world value survey. Soc. Indic. Res. **104**(2), 271–286 (2011)
3. Benkler, N.: Recognizing value resonance with the world values corpus, August 2022. osf.io/wpu8r
4. Cormack, D., Kukutai, T. (2022). Indigenous Peoples, Data, and the Coloniality of Surveillance. In: Hepp, A., Jarke, J., Kramp, L. (eds.) New Perspectives in Critical Data Studies. Transforming Communications – Studies in Cross-Media Research, pp. 121–141. Springer, Cham (2022). https://doi.org/10.1007/978-3-030-96180-0_6
5. Dev, S., Li, T., Phillips, J.M., Srikumar, V.: On measuring and mitigating biased inferences of word embeddings. In: Proceedings of the AAAI Conference on Artificial Intelligence, vol. 34, no. 05, pp. 7659–7666 (2020). https://doi.org/10.1609/aaai.v34i05.6267
6. Fleche, S., Smith, C., Sorsa, P.: Exploring determinants of subjective wellbeing in OECD countries: evidence from the world values survey. Organization for Economic Co-Operation and Development (2012)
7. Friedman, S., Schmer-Galunder, S., Chen, A., Goldman, R., Rye, J.: Relating linguistic gender bias, gender values, and gender gaps: an international analysis. In: BRiMS Conference, Washington, DC, July (2019)
8. Graeber, D.: Toward an Anthropological Theory of Value: The False Coin of Our Own Dreams. Springer, New York (2001). https://doi.org/10.1057/9780312299064
9. Inglehart, R., Basanez, M., Diez-Medrano, J., Halman, L., Luijkx, R.: World values surveys and European values surveys, 1981–1984, 1990–1993, and 1995–1997. Ann Arbor-Michigan, Institute for Social Research, ICPSR version (2000)
10. Jaderberg, M., et al.: Population based training of neural networks (2017)
11. Jen, M.H., Sund, E.R., Johnston, R., Jones, K.: Trustful societies, trustful individuals, and health: an analysis of self-rated health and social trust using the world value survey. Health Place **16**(5), 1022–1029 (2010)
12. Liaw, R., Liang, E., Nishihara, R., Moritz, P., Gonzalez, J.E., Stoica, I.: Tune: a research platform for distributed model selection and training. arXiv preprint arXiv:1807.05118 (2018)
13. Liu, Y., et al.: Roberta: a robustly optimized Bert pretraining approach. arXiv:abs/1907.11692 (2019)
14. Minkov, M.: What makes us different and similar: a new interpretation of the World Values Survey and other cross-cultural data. Klasika i Stil Publishing House Sofia, Bulgaria (2007)
15. Parikh, A.P., T"ackstr"om, O., Das, D., Uszkoreit, J.: A decomposable attention model for natural language inference. arXiv:abs/1606.01933 (2016)
16. Wolf, T., et al.: Huggingface's transformers: state-of-the-art natural language processing (2020)
17. Zhang, B.H., Lemoine, B., Mitchell, M.: Mitigating unwanted biases with adversarial learning. In: Proceedings of the 2018 AAAI/ACM Conference on AI, Ethics, and Society (2018)

Transition to Adulthood for Young People with Intellectual or Developmental Disabilities: Emotion Detection and Topic Modeling

Yan Liu[1]([⊠]) [iD], Maria Laricheva[2], Chiyu Zhang[2], Patrick Boutet[2], Guanyu Chen[2], Terence Tracey[2], Giuseppe Carenini[2], and Richard Young[2]

[1] Carleton University, Ottawa, ON, Canada
yanz.liu@carleton.ca
[2] The University of British Columbia, Vancouver, BC, Canada

Abstract. Transition to Adulthood is an essential life stage for many families. The prior research has shown that young people with intellectual or development disabilities (IDD) have more challenges than their peers. This study is to explore how to use natural language processing (NLP) methods, especially unsupervised machine learning, to assist psychologists to analyze emotions and sentiments and to use topic modeling to identify common issues and challenges that young people with IDD and their families have. Additionally, the results were compared to those obtained from young people without IDD who were in transition to adulthood. The findings showed that NLP methods can be very useful for psychologists to analyze emotions, conduct cross-case analysis, and summarize key topics from conversational data. Our Python code is available at https://github.com/mlaricheva/emotion_topic_modeling.

Keywords: Transition to adulthood · Intellectual or development disabilities · Emotion detection · Sentiment analysis · Topic modeling · Natural language processing

1 Introduction

Transitioning to adulthood is an essential life stage for many families. It requires advanced planning and preparation, especially for families with a child who has intellectual or developmental disabilities (IDD). Youth with disabilities often experience more challenges than their peers when transitioning into adult roles, e.g., independent living, work, and engagement in social life [1, 2]. Additionally, some services and supports come to an end when the person with IDD turns 18 years old, and parents need to identify new support resources for a growing adult.

Researchers have been trying to help young people with IDD to transition to adulthood in the past two decades [3]. Unfortunately, many young people with IDD still have been struggling in this process [4]. There is a need to understand more about what essential issues and concerns the youths and their families have and how their emotions

R. Thomson et al. (Eds.): SBP-BRiMS 2022, LNCS 13558, pp. 219–228, 2022.
https://doi.org/10.1007/978-3-031-17114-7_21

are affected. Contextual action theory [5, 6] has been used to study adulthood transition and other career development issues. With a social constructionist approach, this framework helps people understand their own and others' thinking and behaviors in the joint actions. Because researchers need to understand actions in certain contexts, a pair of participants, also called dyads, are usually required to attend the study.

The conversational data obtained from this approach have been analyzed by psychologists using qualitative methods [4, 7]. However, the data analysis process is complex. Pairs of researchers are usually assigned to conduct the initial analysis. The conversations are segmented minute by minute first, then analyzed line by line, and labeled according to a pre-established coding list. After the narrative summaries are developed from the initial analysis, the research team will review the analysis and summaries. One common strategy for psychologists is to conduct a cross-case analysis to understand the commonalities and differences among participants. It is usually conducted by grouping two or three cases at a time until the common themes and key information is extracted.

Recently, NLP methods, a combination of linguistics and machine learning techniques, have been developed rapidly for analyzing text data. The NLP methods have been shown to be a promising approach for analyzing conversational data [8, 9]. Several studies have explored how NLP methods can be applied to large scale counselling conversational data. For example, Imel et al. [10] and Althoff et al. [11] analyzed the language of counselors to evaluate counsellor performance. Using online counseling conversations, Park et al. [12] analyzed client utterances to evaluate the therapy outcome.

However, the prior research focused on text counselling in mental health, so it is unknown whether NLP methods can work well for other psychological areas. Very few studies have investigated emotion issues and have not paid attention to cross-case analysis. Additionally, supervised machine learning with large scale data were used in these studies. However, many psychological studies have relatively small data as it is impossible to get large scale data due to limited funding and personnel. This study tries to bridge the gaps discussed here and explores how NLP methods, especially unsupervised machine learning methods, can be used for adulthood transition research.

2   Study Purpose

With a focus on adulthood transition research, especially for young people having IDD, this study aims to explore how to use NLP methods examine (1) common emotions and emotion intensity among all the dyads, (2) sentiment distributions across multiple transcripts, and (3) common topics and important issues discussed among all the dyads. Additionally, we compared the results to those obtained from young people without IDD to have a better understanding on emotions and essential issues for young people having IDD. More specifically, this study is to address three research questions:

RQ1: What common emotions can be identified from conversations made by all dyads whose family had a young person with IDD? Do the conversations made by young people without IDD have the same emotion distributions and intensities as compared to those made by families with a young person having IDD?
RQ2: How do dyads differ on their affects (positive vs. negative)?

RQ3: What common topics can be identified from conversations made by all dyads whose family had a young person with IDD? Do young people without IDD discuss the same topics as compared to those obtained from families with a young person having IDD?

3 Methods

3.1 Data Source

The present study is a secondary analysis of data that were collected from several studies related to adulthood transition between 2013 and 2016 [4, 13, 14]. The purposes of original studies were to understand joint actions and career goals of young people with IDD as well as those without IDD in their transition to adulthood. All dyads were invited to the lab for two meetings. Less than half of the dyads came back for the second meeting with 3–6 months apart. We pulled the conversations collected from both meetings for the final analysis because we found slight differences in the results of the two meetings. All the conversational data were labeled according to a pre-established coding list by researchers in the original studies.

Final dataset for the data analysis consisted of 63 text transcripts, with the duration about 10–20 min per transcript. The data included conversations between parents or a parent and an old sibling (29 transcripts), a parent and a child (9 transcripts), and two friends (25 transcripts). Friends, also called peers in this paper, were young people without IDD who were used as a reference to compare to young people having IDD.

3.2 Data Preprocessing

For emotion and sentiment analysis, we only used utterances related to emotions classified by the original studies, which is a small subset of the original data. A total of 1,552 utterances were included in our analysis. Most of original classifications were consistent with Plutchik's eight-emotion wheel, but some were more refined categories. To evaluate the results obtained from lexicon analysis, researchers pulled some original categories together to fit to the eight-emotion wheel. For example, "expresses gratitude", "expresses joy", "expresses like", and "express love" were all considered as "joy". We cleaned the data using the part-of-speech (POS) tagging provided in NLTK python package to remove digits, conjunctions, prepositions, modals, pronouns and particles. To simplify the work with the lexicon, an utterance was transformed to the list of words. However, we kept some words that would be considered as stop words in existing python packages because they expressed certain emotions. For example, word "aaaah" is associated with fear.

Different from emotion and sentiment analysis, all utterances were used for topic modeling analysis. In addition to the stop words provided by NLTK python package [15], we added 48 stop words. The words in the data were transformed to their numeric representations using term-frequency inverse-document-frequency (TF-IDF). Each transcript was split into sets with 25 utterances per set, which was identified to be an optimal document size by manual inspection of individual transcripts.

3.3 Analytical Methods

Emotion Detection with NRC Lexicon. We adopted National Research Council (NRC) lexicon [16] for emotion detection. Plutchik's eight-emotion wheel is utilized in NRC, including anger, anticipation, sadness, fear, trust, joy, surprise and disgust [17]. NRC lexicon provides a list of key words and their associations with eight emotions. Each word may be assigned to more than one emotion. For example, "money" has an association score of 0.586 with anticipation, 0.531 with joy, and 0.359 with trust. The association score can be used as an index of emotion intensity, i.e., a higher intensity score indicates a higher level of emotion.

We examined the distribution of emotions, i.e., the predicted proportion of each emotion, average emotion intensity, and the top common words related to each emotion. The average intensity score was obtained from the average of association scores from all utterances. When utterances were assigned to multiple emotions, the emotion with the highest association score was chosen for the emotion analysis.

To improve the quality of classification, we followed the recommendations by Mohammad and Turney [16] and adapted the lexicon to our study purpose. We removed the association between some keywords and emotions that we considered irrelevant. For instance, we removed the association between "kind" and joy because participants frequently treated it as adjective in a sentence, such as "It is kind of …".

Sentiment Analysis with Bing Lexicon. We used the Bing lexicon [18] to compare the positive and negative sentiment across 24 transcripts. This demonstration is to show readers that sentiment analysis can be used for cross-case analysis.

Topic Modeling. Non-Negative Matrix Factorization (NMF) method was used for the topic modeling analysis and was shown to perform better than other methods when analyzing short documents [19]. NMF topic modeling decomposes the higher dimensional vectors of document-word representation, i.e., TF-IDF in this study, into a topic-document matrix with lower dimensional vectors and a word-topic matrix. We also used the combination of L1 and L2 norms for regularization in the NMF analysis.

4 Results

4.1 Emotion Detection with NRC Lexicon

Table 1 shows the predicted distribution of emotions using NRC lexicon, which was compared to the original classification made by researchers. Three types of emotions, i.e., *anticipation*, *joy*, and *trust*, were identified by NRC with a proportion above 0.2 for the families with young people having IDD. Similarly, *joy* and *trust* were identified for peers. However, peers had a relatively higher proportion on *disgust*, but lower on *anticipation*.

The results were consistent to most of researchers' classification. However, *trust* (0.277) was identified using NRC lexicon, but researchers did not include this class. It should be noted that *apprehension* (0.294), which is a subclass of *fear* based on the eight-emotion wheel, was included as an independent class by researchers because it was constructed by several psychological statuses (e.g., "expresses worry", "express confusion") that were semantically different from *fear*. We expected that the utterances originally classified as *apprehension* would be identified as *fear* by NRC. However, it was not shown in the NRC results.

Table 2 shows the results of the average emotion intensity scores across two time points. Figure 1 visualizes the results and clearly shows that the overall emotion intensity levels for families with young people having IDD were much higher than their peers regardless the time changes. The top three emotions identified in the emotion distribution analysis, i.e., *anticipation, joy,* and *trust,* also showed high emotion intensity scores, all above 0.65 for families with young people having IDD. The same top emotions were identified for peers, but the intensity levels were lower, ranging from 0.325 to 0.537.

Table 1. Distributions of emotions compared to researchers' classification (IDD vs. peers)

Emotion	IDD		Peers	
	Original	Lexicon	Original	Lexicon
Apprehension	0.294	–	0.204	–
Anger	0.048	0.043	0.063	0.065
Anticipation	**0.237**	**0.204**	0.098	0.163
Disgust	0.081	0.023	0.151	0.058
Fear	0.103	0.043	0.043	0.067
Joy	**0.201**	**0.308**	**0.349**	**0.288**
Sadness	0.014	0.084	0.024	0.076
Surprise	0.022	0.018	0.068	0.037
Trust	-	**0.277**	-	**0.288**

Table 2. The average emotion intensity scores across time (IDD vs. peers)

Emotion	IDD		Peers	
	Time-1	Time-2	Time-1	Time-2
Anger	0.187	0.079	0.158	0.141
Anticipation	**0.654**	**0.579**	**0.377**	**0.325**
Disgust	0.105	0.059	0.114	0.145
Fear	0.300	0.147	0.186	0.155
Joy	**0.690**	**0.678**	**0.537**	**0.452**
Sadness	0.309	0.237	0.171	0.159
Surprise	0.163	0.145	0.156	0.095
Trust	**0.709**	**0.739**	**0.491**	**0.396**

The emotions showed some changes over time for both populations although the changes were not in a large magnitude. For families with young people having IDD, the intensity level of positive emotions (*joy* & *trust*) was either remained around the same level or increased to a small degree over time, whereas the intensity level of negative emotions (*anger, disgust, fear,* & *sadness*) decreased over time. On the contrary, the results for peers suggested that the intensity of negative emotions (*disgust*) were increased slightly over time, whereas the intensity of positive emotions were decreased to some degree, *joy* (from 0.537 to 0.452) and *trust* (from 0.491 to 0.396).

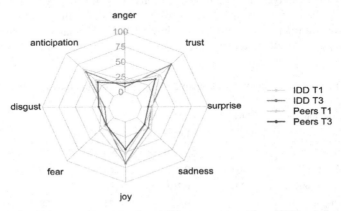

Fig. 1. The average emotion intensity scores across Time (IDD vs. peers)

We also provided the top common words here to help researchers understand the connection of the emotion to the top common words used in the conversation. Table 3 provides a demonstration using data from families with young people having IDD, including *joy* and *trust*, and *fear*. We removed some words, e.g., "pretty", "good", because they are too generic. The results showed that "home, friends, money, love, family, happy, fun, hope, and independent" were related to people's *joy* and "school, money, love, happy, hope, doctor, friend, teacher, and mother" were associated with *trust*.

Table 3. Common words related to emotions for families with young people having IDD

Fear		Joy		Trust	
Word	Count	Word	Count	Word	Count
Worry	25	Home	41	School	37
Bad	10	Friends	21	Money	20
Feeling	7	Money	20	Love	16
Nervous	6	Life	18	Happy	10
Hate	5	Love	16	Hope	9

(continued)

Table 3. (*continued*)

Fear		Joy		Trust	
Word	Count	Word	Count	Word	Count
Concerned	4	Special	12	Doctor	7
Scared	3	Family	11	Feeling	7
Stealing	3	Happy	10	Friend	6
Mad	3	Fun	9	Safe	6
Government	3	Hope	9	Teacher	6
Therapist	3	Independent	8	Mother	5

In general, the common words of positive emotions were more frequently appeared than those associated to negative emotions. The most frequently appeared common word related to *fear* is "worry". Additionally, "government" and "therapist" were shown in the conversations. It should be noted that "government" was more frequently appeared in the full transcripts, but it was only shown three times in this small subset of data. This common word reflected one common worry when parents talked about the government policy on the support to young people having IDD.

4.2 Sentiment Analysis with Bing Lexicon

To demonstrate how sentiment analysis can be used for a cross-case analysis, we only randomly selected 24 transcripts from the conversations made by families with young people having IDD. Each transcript represents one case (two dyads). Figure 2 shows the distribution of the sentiment of the conversation on each transcript. The X-axis is the number of lines of utterances and each unit represents 20 lines; Y-axis is the frequency of utterances with positive sentiment above zero and negative below zero.

The sentiment was found to be different across cases. Some participants were more positive, some were more negative, and others had equally distributed positive and negative emotions. For example, case #7 was positive in the beginning and negative towards the end. Case #5 appeared to be negative over the whole conversation. Case #23 showed positive sentiment most of the time. This can be an easy tool for researchers to organize the transcripts before they conduct further in-depth qualitative analysis.

4.3 Topic Modeling with Non-negative Matrix Factorization (NMF)

Five main topics were identified by NMF from the conversations of families with young people having IDD (Fig. 3). The final number of topics was chosen based on the best interpretation. These topics were also shown in the original studies [4, 13], including family, job search and work, financial issues (e.g., money management, eating, buying stuff), commuting and housing arrangement, and schooling. Additionally, the results showed that "independent" living may be a more concern for families with young people having IDD.

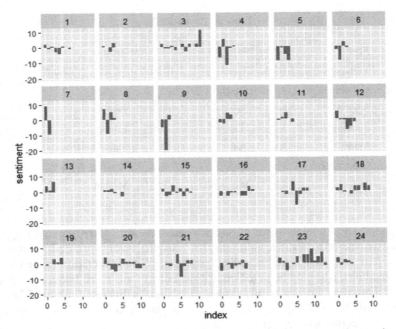

Fig. 2. Frequency distribution of utterances relative to positive and negative sentiment

More topics were appeared in the conversations made by peers. Similarly, schooling (topic 4), family (topic 6), and financial issues (topic 7) were identified for peers. However, job interview was separated (topic 5) from work (topic 2); three new topics appeared, including functional communication (topic 1; e.g., help, feel, guess), communication for fun or social communication (topic 8), and driving car (topic 3) (Fig. 4).

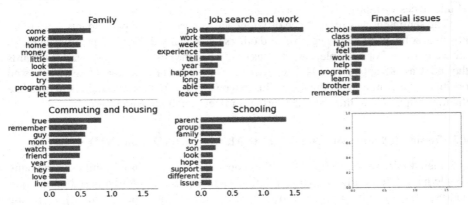

Fig. 3. Topic modeling on conversations of families with young people having IDD

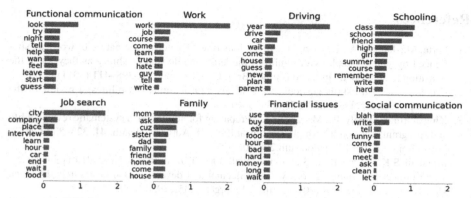

Fig. 4. Topic modeling on conversations of young people without IDD

5 Conclusion and Discussion

This study investigated how NLP methods can be applied to adulthood transition research with relatively small conversational data. More specifically, this study explored how to use unsupervised machine learning methods to investigate emotions, sentiments, and topics in adulthood transition research, especially for families with youths having IDD. The results were also compared to young people without IDD.

The emotion and sentiment analysis have been neglected in earlier NLP applications. Our study showed that emotion detection and sentiment analysis can be reliable tools for psychologists to study participant emotions. Our results obtained from lexicon analysis were consistent with researchers' classification on emotions. Three top emotions were detected, including *joy, anticipation*, and *trust* for families with young people having IDD. Similar results were found for young people without IDD except *anticipation*. However, regardless of time changes, families with young people having IDD showed an overall higher level of emotion intensity than young people without IDD.

Sentiment analysis can be an efficient and quick tool for cross-case analysis, which allows researchers to compare the participant affects across multiple transcripts. This may help researchers quickly categorize the transcripts for further qualitative analysis. Future studies are encouraged to make more use of this method.

Topic modeling identified five key topics for families with young people having IDD, including family, job search and work, financial issues, commuting and housing, and schooling, which echoed the findings from the original studies. Three more topics were identified for young people without IDD, i.e., functional communication, communication for fun, and driving. This may reflect the difference in essential issues between young people with and without IDD. Topic modeling is an efficient tool to exact key topics. However, this method may bring limitations to psychologist who want to extract deeper meaning from the conversation.

In general, our study has shown that NLP methods are useful for adulthood transition research and can be a practical tool for psychologists. Unsupervised machine learning methods work well with relatively small sample data. More research is encouraged to explore how NLP methods can be used for other research topic areas in psychology.

References

1. Forte, M., Jahoda, A., Dagnan, D.: An anxious time? Exploring the nature of worries experienced by young people with a mild to moderate intellectual disability as they make the transition to adulthood: an anxious time? Br. J. Clin. Psychol. **50**, 398–411 (2011)
2. Cronin, M.E.: Life skills curricula for students with learning disabilities: a review of the literature. J. Learn. Disabil. **29**, 53–68 (1996)
3. Kingsnorth, S., Healy, H., Macarthur, C.: Preparing for adulthood: a systematic review of life skill programs for youth with physical disabilities. J. Adolesc. Health. **41**, 323–332 (2007). https://doi.org/10.1016/j.jadohealth.2007.06.007
4. Marshall, S.K., Young, R.A., Stainton, T., Wall, J.M.: Transition to adulthood as a joint parent-youth project for young persons with intellectual and developmental disabilities. Intellect. Dev. Disabil. **56**, 263–304 (2018). https://doi.org/10.1352/1934-9556-56.5.263
5. Young, R.A., Valach, L., Collin, A.: A contextual explanation of career. In: Brown, D. (ed.) Career Choice and Development, Jossey-Bass, San Francisco, CA (2002)
6. Young, R.A., Valach, L., Domene, J.F.: The action-project method in counseling psychology. J. Couns. Psychol. **52**, 215–223 (2005). https://doi.org/10.1037/0022-0167.52.2.215
7. Valach, L., Young, R.A., Lynam, M.J.: Action Theory: A Primer for Applied Research in the Social Sciences. Greenwood Publishing Group (2002)
8. Carenini, G., Murray, G.: Methods for mining and summarizing text conversations. In: Proceedings of the 35th International ACM SIGIR Conference on Research and Development in Information Retrieval - SIGIR 2012, Portland, Oregon, USA, p. 1178. ACM Press (2012)
9. Goldberg, Y.: Neural network methods for natural language processing. Synth. Lect. Hum. Lang. Technol. **10**, 1–309 (2017). https://doi.org/10.2200/S00762ED1V01Y201703HLT037
10. Imel, Z.E., Steyvers, M., Atkins, D.C.: Computational psychotherapy research: scaling up the evaluation of patient–provider interactions. Psychotherapy **52**, 19–30 (2015). https://doi.org/10.1037/a0036841
11. Althoff, T., Clark, K., Leskovec, J.: Large-scale analysis of counseling conversations: an application of natural language processing to mental health. Trans. Assoc. Comput. Linguist. **4**, 463 (2016)
12. Park, S., Kim, D., Oh, A.: Conversation model fine-tuning for classifying client utterances in counseling dialogues. Paper Presented 2019 Annual Conference of the North American Chapter of the Association for Computational Linguistics (2019)
13. Young, R.A., et al.: Transition to adulthood as a peer project. Emerg. Adulthood. **3**, 166–178 (2015). https://doi.org/10.1177/2167696814559304
14. Young, R.A., et al.: The transition to adulthood of young adults with IDD: parents' joint projects. J. Appl. Res. Intellect. Disabil. **31**, 224–233 (2017). https://doi.org/10.1111/jar.12395
15. Bird, S., Klein, E., Loper, E.: Natural Language Processing with Python, Analyzing Text with the Natural Language Toolkit. O'Reilly Media, Beijing (2009)
16. Mohammad, S.M., Turney, P.D.: Crowdsourcing a word-emotion association lexicon. Comput. Intell. **29**, 436–465 (2013). https://doi.org/10.1111/j.1467-8640.2012.00460.x
17. Plutchik, R.: Chapter 1 - A general psychoevolutionary theory of emotion. In: Theories of Emotion, pp. 3–33. Elsevier Inc. (1980)
18. Liu, B.: Sentiment Analysis and Opinion Mining: Synthesis Lectures on Human Language Technologies. Morgan & Claypool (2012)
19. Lee, D.D., Seung, H.S.: Learning the parts of objects by non-negative matrix factorization. Nature **401**, 788–791 (1999). https://doi.org/10.1038/44565

Optimizing Pharmaceutical and Non-pharmaceutical Interventions During Epidemics

Nitin Kulkarni[✉], Chunming Qiao, and Alina Vereshchaka

Department of Computer Science and Engineering, State University of New York at Buffalo, Buffalo, USA
{nitinvis,qiao,avereshc}@buffalo.edu

Abstract. Controlling the spread of infectious diseases is a major challenge. Understanding the dynamics between human behavior and the spread of infection is essential for policymakers. Evolving contagion dynamics make it difficult to develop an efficient mitigation strategy. In this paper, we develop an epidemiological model to forecast the epidemic and use an offline reinforcement learning framework that adapts to the evolving dynamics of disease spread to optimize the mitigation strategy. We demonstrate that our framework can produce efficient mitigation strategies for the COVID-19 pandemic based on data collected from New York, USA.

Keywords: Optimization · SEIHRD model · Pandemic · COVID-19 · Reinforcement learning · Epidemiological model · Mitigation regulations

1 Introduction

Throughout history, humanity has encountered several pandemics such as the Spanish flu, the Hong Kong flu (H3N2), and recently the COVID-19 pandemic. If appropriate measures are not taken to curb the spread of infection it can spread exponentially [1]. These pandemics have adverse effects on numerous aspects of society as evident from the recent events. They can disrupt the public health infrastructure [2], cause long-term supply chain issues [3], and disrupt the economy and public well-being.

Understanding the dynamics of disease spread is essential to forecast the epidemic curve and take the appropriate mitigation strategy. Thus, developing an accurate epidemiological model is essential. Additionally, due to the stochasticity, evolving dynamics of disease spread, and uncertain public resistance to harsh regulations, policymakers face difficulties to find the most efficient mitigation strategy.

In this paper we present a new epidemiological model called SEIHRD^v (Sect. 3.1) for the COVID-19 pandemic. This is a compartmental epidemiological model [4] related to the commonly used SIR model [5]. Compartmental

© The Author(s), under exclusive license to Springer Nature Switzerland AG 2022
R. Thomson et al. (Eds.): SBP-BRiMS 2022, LNCS 13558, pp. 229–240, 2022.
https://doi.org/10.1007/978-3-031-17114-7_22

epidemiological models have been used to model the spread of various diseases [6,7].

We also present our method for estimating model parameters based on real-world data using the Levenberg-Marquardt algorithm [8] (Sect. 3.2). This algorithm is widely used for curve fitting [9] and was successfully applied in domains such as nuclear physics [10], spectroscopy [11], and electron optics [12].

The ultimate objective of this work is to tackle the challenge of introducing an efficient mitigation strategy to curb the spread of infection while also minimizing the impact on the economy and positive public perception. To this end, we have developed a reinforcement learning (RL) framework that uses the SEIHRD^v model to simulate how the epidemic evolves under various non-pharmaceutical and pharmaceutical interventions (Sect. 3.3), thus integrating epidemic forecasting and control into a decision-support tool for policymakers. RL is a powerful tool that has been successfully applied to solve problems in complex domains such as robotics [13], navigation [14], and optimizing lockdown policies [15,16].

We demonstrate the empirical performance of our solution under different government priorities based on the COVID-19 data for the State of New York, USA collected from April 1, 2021 to April 30, 2022. (Sect. 4.2).

The rest of the paper is organized as follows: Sects. 2.1 and 2.2 provide the background on the existing SEIRD epidemiological model and RL respectively. In Sect. 2.3 we discuss related work, in Sect. 3.1 we present our SEIHRD^v epidemiological model, in Sect. 3.2 we present our method for estimating the model parameters, in Sect. 3.3, we present our RL framework which derives the optimal policy to assist policymakers, in Sect. 4.1 we present the datasets used, in Sect. 4.2 we discuss the results of our framework, finally in Sect. 5 we conclude our work.

2   Background

2.1   SEIRD Epidemiological Model

Compartmental epidemiological models divide the population under study into different groups (compartments) with underlined transition dynamics describing the transition of individuals in the population between the compartments [4,5].

The SEIRD epidemiological model divides the population under study (N) into five compartments: susceptible (S): individuals susceptible to infection; exposed (E): individuals exposed to infection; infected (I): infected individuals; recovered (R): individuals who have recovered from the infection; deceased (D): individuals who have died as a result of infection [6,17]. An individual can only belong to a single compartment at any given time.

The number of people in the epidemiological compartments evolves over time as given by the following differential equations:

$$\frac{dS}{dt} = -\beta \frac{S}{N} I, \quad \frac{dE}{dt} = \beta \frac{S}{N} I - \zeta E, \quad \frac{dI}{dt} = \zeta E - \gamma I - \mu I, \quad \frac{dR}{dt} = \gamma I, \quad \frac{dD}{dt} = \mu I \quad (1)$$

where, β is the exposure rate, ζ is the rate at which exposed individuals become infected, γ is the recovery rate and μ is the mortality rate.

We discuss related work in Sect. 2.3 and describe our $SEIHRD^v$ epidemiological model as an extension in Sect. 3.1.

2.2 Reinforcement Learning

Reinforcement learning is a mathematical formalism for learning-based decision making. RL problems are usually formulated as a Markov decision process defined as a tuple $(\mathcal{S}, \mathcal{A}, r, p, \gamma)$, where $\mathcal{S}$ denotes the set of states $s \in \mathcal{S}$, $\mathcal{A}$ is the set of actions $a \in \mathcal{A}$, $r : \mathcal{S} \times \mathcal{A} \rightarrow \mathbb{R}$ is a reward function, p defines the conditional probability $P(s_{t+1}|s_t, a_t)$ describing the system dynamics, $\gamma \in (0, 1]$ is a scalar discount factor. The objective is to learn a policy $\pi : \mathcal{S} \rightarrow \mathcal{A}$ mapping states to actions.

The RL objective, $J(\pi)$ can be written as an expectation under the trajectory distribution:

$$J(\pi) = \mathbb{E}_{\tau \sim p_\pi(\tau)} \left[\sum_{t=0}^{T} \gamma^t r(s_t, a_t) \right] \quad (2)$$

Using neural networks as powerful function approximators RL algorithms can learn policies that maximize $J(\pi)$ to learn how to achieve the required goal even in complex domains. We apply RL to derive an optimal policy for assisting policymakers.

2.3 Related Work

Previous works have modeled the COVID-19 pandemic using the SEIRD epidemiological model [6,17]. These early works were published at a time when a vaccine for COVID-19 was not developed. Later works considered the effects of vaccination through an additional 'Vaccinated' compartment.

In their excellent works, Fawaz [18] and Amona [19] developed a SEIRDV model which takes into consideration the vaccine efficacy as a means to account for vaccinated individuals getting infected. The papers concluded that the basic reproduction number R_0 declines drastically as the population gets vaccinated.

Previous works have also evaluated the effect of various interventions on the epidemic spread. Giordano [20] and Reiner [21] evaluated the effects of interventions such as lockdowns, mask mandates, population-wide testing, and contact tracing. Their superlative works provide policymakers a tool to assess the impact of various mitigation strategies.

Note that while the previous works considered the efficacy of the vaccines, they did not consider the impact of vaccination on the severity of symptoms developed after infection leading to significantly different mortality and hospitalization rates [22,23]. Additionally, while previous works allowed policymakers to assess the impact of various mitigation strategies, they did not provide a way to find an optimal mitigation strategy.

We extend the SEIRD model with an additional 'Hospitalized' compartment which would help public health authorities be better prepared based on model forecasts. Additionally, we consider the effect of vaccination on the infection, hospitalization, and mortality rates thereby developing a model reflecting today's reality more accurately. Finally, we develop a RL framework to assist policymakers find an optimal mitigation strategy.

3   Methodology

In this section, we present: (1) the proposed extension to the SEIRD epidemiological model; (2) the method used for calibrating the model parameters; and (3) the reinforcement learning framework to optimize government regulations.

3.1   SEIHRD^v Epidemiological Model

We extend the SEIRD epidemiological model (described in Sect. 2.1) to include an additional 'Hospitalized (H)' compartment for individuals hospitalized as a result of infection. This allows hospitals and public health authorities to be better prepared (e.g., to estimate needs for COVID-19 treatments and hospital beds) based on the model forecasts. In addition, we divide each compartment into subcompartments based on an individual's vaccination status, since the infection, hospitalization, and mortality rates differ significantly based on vaccination status [22,23]. We also consider that not all individuals exposed to infection (contact with an infected individual) get infected, thus allowing exposed individuals to become susceptible again [24].

Transition dynamics between the compartments of the proposed SEIHRD^v epidemiological model are shown in Fig 1.

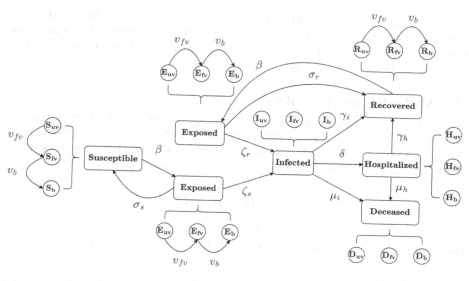

Fig. 1. Flow chart of the SEIHRD^v epidemiological model describing the transition dynamics of disease spread. The Susceptible (S), Exposed (E), Infected (I), Hospitalized (H), Recovered (R), and Deceased (D) compartments are divided into sub-compartments by vaccination status; subscripts uv, fv, and b represent the unvaccinated, fully vaccinated, and booster vaccinated sub-compartments respectively.

The evolution of the population in the compartments of the SEIHRD^v model over time is given by the ordinary differential equations (ODEs) (3).

$$
\begin{aligned}
\frac{dS}{dt} &= -\beta \frac{S}{N} I^\alpha + \sigma_s E & \frac{dE}{dt} &= \beta \frac{S+R}{N} I^\alpha - (\zeta_s + \zeta_r)E - (\sigma_s + \sigma_r)E \\
\frac{dI}{dt} &= (\zeta_s + \zeta_r)E - \gamma_i I - \delta I - \mu_i I & \frac{dH}{dt} &= \delta I - \gamma_h H - \mu_h H \\
\frac{dR}{dt} &= -\beta \frac{R}{N} I^\alpha + \sigma_r E + \gamma_i I + \gamma_h H & \frac{dD}{dt} &= \mu_i I + \mu_h H
\end{aligned} \tag{3}
$$

where, N is the size of the population under study, β is the exposure rate to infection, α is the mixing coefficient to account for the imperfect mixing of population, ζ is the rate at which individuals exposed to an infected individual become infected, σ is the rate at which individuals exposed to an infected individual do not develop an infection, δ is the rate at which infected individuals get hospitalized, γ is the recovery rate, and μ is the mortality rate. We also compute v_{fv}; the rate at which the population is getting fully vaccinated and v_b; the rate at which the population is getting the boosters from the vaccination data[1] collected from Centers for Disease Control and Prevention (CDC).

---

[1] https://covid.cdc.gov/covid-data-tracker.

$\zeta, \sigma, \delta, \gamma$, and μ differ based on an individual's vaccination status. ζ and σ also differ based on whether an individual has been previously infected as a previous infection provides some immunity [25]. γ and μ also differ based on whether the individual is hospitalized or not.

3.2   Model Parameter Estimation

To estimate the model parameters α, β, ζ, σ, δ, γ and μ we fit the solution of (3) to the COVID-19 data for 2021–2022 collected from the state of New York (NY), USA. We set the problem as an initial value problem (IVP) for the system of ODEs (3) ($\mathbf{y}'(t)$) with initial values ($\mathbf{y_0}$) based on NY data.

$$
\begin{aligned}
\mathbf{y}'_i(t) &= f_i(t, y_1(t), y_2(t), ...)\\
\mathbf{y(t_0)} &= \mathbf{y_0}
\end{aligned}
\tag{4}
$$

We solve the IVP using the Explicit Runge-Kutta method of order 5(4).

$$
y_{n+1} = y_n + h \sum_{i=1}^{5} b_i k_i
$$

where,

$$
\begin{aligned}
&k_1 = f(t_n, y_n); k_2 = f(t_n + c_2 h, y_n + h(a_{21}k_1)); \ldots ;\\
&k_5 = f(t_n + c_5 h, y_n + h(a_{51}k_1 + a_{52}k_2 + \ldots + a_{54}k_4))
\end{aligned}
\tag{5}
$$

The estimation of the population in different compartments based on model parameters can be denoted by the vector $\hat{\mathbf{e}}$ while the actual values that we get from NY State data can be denoted by the vector $\mathbf{a}$. The estimation vector $\hat{\mathbf{e}}$ is parameterized by $\{t, \alpha, \beta, \zeta, \sigma, \delta, \gamma, \mu\}$. We calibrate the model parameters by solving the following non-linear least squares optimization problem using the Levenberg-Marquardt algorithm [9] with positivity and bound constraints on the parameters based on CDC statistics:

$$
\underset{t,\alpha,\beta,\zeta,\sigma,\delta,\gamma,\mu}{\text{minimize}} \|\hat{\mathbf{e}} - \mathbf{a}\|_2^2
\tag{6}
$$

The model parameters are estimated in four week intervals to accurately represent the changes associated with the advances in treatments, public health interventions, and public behavior.

3.3   Reinforcement Learning for Optimization of Regulations

We use the SEIHRD^v model proposed in Sect. 3.1 to simulate the spread of the infectious disease using the parameters $\{\alpha, \beta, \zeta, \sigma, \delta, \gamma, \mu\}$ estimated in Sect. 3.2. We scale β based on the action of government authorities, e.g., a lockdown would see β decreasing. To model the stochasticity in pandemic spread we add a small Gaussian noise to the parameters. We adapt the epidemic mitigation strategy algorithm using offline RL [15] for our framework.

Initial: To initialize the SEIHRD^v model simulator, we pass the initial values of the population in all the compartments based on data for COVID-19 from NY State. This is the point from which we simulate the pandemic and optimize government regulations.

Observations: At each time step, the RL agent receives information about the proportion of exposed (E), infected (I), deceased (D), unvaccinated (uv), fully vaccinated (fv), and booster vaccinated (b) individuals in the population (N), and the economic and public perception rate η_t for the last 14 days. The state at time step t is:

$$\text{state}_t = \{ \frac{E_{t-14}}{N}, \frac{I_{t-14}}{N}, \frac{D_{t-14}}{N}, \frac{uv_{t-14}}{N}, \frac{fv_{t-14}}{N}, \frac{b_{t-14}}{N}, \eta_{t-14}, \cdots \\ \frac{E_{t-1}}{N}, \frac{I_{t-1}}{N}, \frac{D_{t-1}}{N}, \frac{uv_{t-1}}{N}, \frac{fv_{t-1}}{N}, \frac{b_{t-1}}{N}, \eta_{t-1} \}$$

(7)

Actions: Actions represent the policy-maker's response to the current state. Our framework considers both non-pharmaceutical and pharmaceutical interventions (NPIs and PIs) in the form of five actions $\mathcal{A}$: {no_NPI/PI, lockdown, social distancing mandates, mask mandates, vaccination mandates}. The exposure rate β is scaled depending on the action taken. It is assumed that regulations which limit the interaction among the population such as lockdowns and social distancing mandates (SDMs), or which limit the spread of the virus, such as mask mandates will result in lower exposure rates. If no NPI or PI interventions are taken it is assumed that the exposure rate will be higher. Some actions can be taken simultaneously such as imposing SDMs and mask mandates while others cannot as they are mutually exclusive such as no_NPI/PI and any other action. Policymakers can specify their preferences for the maximum duration an action might be taken.

Rewards: We design our reward function to motivate the agent to minimize the number of infections and deaths while keeping the economy operating and maintaining the freedom and happiness of citizens. Policymakers define the priorities by $\boldsymbol{\rho} = [\rho_0, \rho_1, \rho_2]$. For certain regions some of the parameters can be omitted by setting $\rho_i = 0$. We aim to maximize the following objective function:

$$r_t = \rho_0 \frac{\eta_t}{\eta_0} - \rho_1 \frac{I}{N} - \rho_2 \frac{D}{N}$$

(8)

where η_t represents the level of the economic and public perception rate with the initial value of $\eta_0 = 100$. This parameter is updated in accordance with the action, with more restrictive actions such as lockdowns and vaccination mandates lowering η faster.

Our framework is represented as a flowchart in Fig. 2

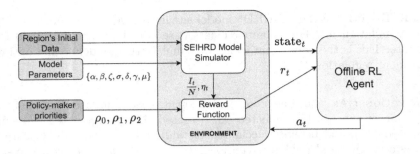

Fig. 2. Mitigation response decision-making process: to initialize the framework, we pass the region's initial values of the population in all compartments of the SEIHRD^v model along with the estimated model parameter values (Sect. 3.2) and policy-maker priorities.

4 Experiments

We run the experiments using an NVIDIA RTX 3090 24GB GPU. For the experiments, we applied our framework to the COVID-19 data collected from New York (NY), USA. We demonstrate that our proposed methodology enables optimization under various sets of priorities. We compare the results with NY, USA data from November 1, 2021 to April 30, 2022.

4.1 Dataset Description

We collected daily observations on cases and their outcomes from New York State Government's recorded COVID-19 data for the period of April 1, 2021 till April 30, 2022.[2] Vaccination data[3] was collected from Centers for Disease Control and Prevention (CDC); used these data to calculate the rate at which the population is getting vaccinated. Hospitalization data[4] was collected from U.S. Department of Health and Human Services. We used these data to estimate the SEIHRD^v model parameters (Sect. 3.2) which we used in our RL framework (Sect. 3.3) to develop a simulation of the epidemic.

4.2 Results

We estimate the model parameters in four week intervals to accurately represent the changes associated with the advances in treatments, public health interventions, and public behavior. The parameter values are represented as a normal distribution in Table 1. The exposure rate $\beta = \mathcal{N}(4.26, 1.07)$

---

[2] https://coronavirus.health.ny.gov/covid-19-data-new-york.

[3] https://covid.cdc.gov/covid-data-tracker.

[4] https://healthdata.gov/Hospital/COVID-19-Reported-Patient-Impact-and-Hospital-Capa/g62h-syeh.

Table 1. Model parameters based on the COVID-19 NY, USA data represented as a normal distribution. The subscripts {s, r, i, h} denote the susceptible, recovered, infected, and hospitalized compartments respectively and the subscripts {uv, fv, b} denote the unvaccinated, fully vaccinated, and booster vaccinated sub-compartments respectively.

Infection rates	Hospitalization rates	Recovery rates	Mortality rates
$\zeta_{s_{uv}} = \mathcal{N}(1.47e^{-2}, 1.63e^{-2})$	$\delta_{uv} = \mathcal{N}(2.30e^{-3}, 1.48e^{-3})$	$\gamma_{i_{uv}} = \mathcal{N}(4.79e^{-2}, 6.83e^{-3})$	$\mu_{i_{uv}} = \mathcal{N}(1.13e^{-3}, 1.11e^{-3})$
$\zeta_{s_{fv}} = \mathcal{N}(3.99e^{-4}, 4.08e^{-4})$	$\delta_{fv} = \mathcal{N}(1.72e^{-3}, 1.39e^{-3})$	$\gamma_{i_{fv}} = \mathcal{N}(5.22e^{-2}, 3.89e^{-3})$	$\mu_{i_{fv}} = \mathcal{N}(5.97e^{-4}, 6.76e^{-4})$
$\zeta_{s_b} = \mathcal{N}(9.63e^{-4}, 1.20e^{-3})$	$\delta_b = \mathcal{N}(1.03e^{-3}, 1.24e^{-3})$	$\gamma_{i_b} = \mathcal{N}(5.28e^{-2}, 7.44e^{-3})$	$\mu_{i_b} = \mathcal{N}(3.65e^{-4}, 3.89e^{-4})$
$\zeta_{r_{uv}} = \mathcal{N}(7.63e^{-3}, 1.67e^{-2})$		$\gamma_{h_{uv}} = \mathcal{N}(3.50e^{-2}, 1.17e^{-2})$	$\mu_{h_{uv}} = \mathcal{N}(4.78e^{-3}, 3.05e^{-3})$
$\zeta_{r_{fv}} = \mathcal{N}(1.82e^{-4}, 2.50e^{-4})$		$\gamma_{h_{fv}} = \mathcal{N}(6.05e^{-2}, 5.04e^{-3})$	$\mu_{h_{fv}} = \mathcal{N}(3.86e^{-3}, 3.49e^{-3})$
$\zeta_{r_b} = \mathcal{N}(1.11e^{-3}, 7.46e^{-4})$		$\gamma_{h_b} = \mathcal{N}(4.67e^{-2}, 1.22e^{-2})$	$\mu_{h_b} = \mathcal{N}(1.01e^{-3}, 3.50e^{-3})$

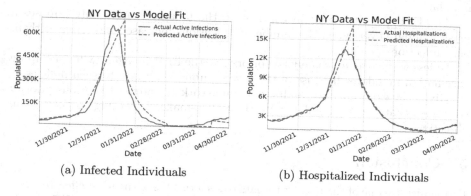

(a) Infected Individuals   (b) Hospitalized Individuals

Fig. 3. SEIHRD^v model fit on COVID-19 data for New York, USA

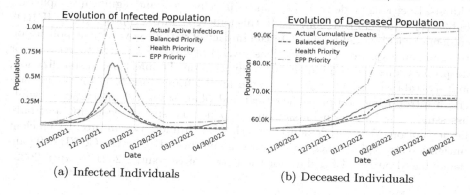

(a) Infected Individuals   (b) Deceased Individuals

Fig. 4. Comparison of population dynamics for agents with different priorities.

We consider the time period from November 1 2021 to April 30 2022 for our experiments. The result of estimating the SEIHRD^v model parameters to fit the NY State data is shown for the Infected and Hospitalized compartments in Fig 3.

Thus, public health authorities can be better prepared as the pandemic evolves based on model forecasts.

Our framework considers policy-maker's priorities to produce an optimal mitigation strategy. The results for three different priorities; health, the economic and public perception rate (EPP), or a balance between the two are shown in Fig 4.

The balanced priority agent enforces a mask mandate initially. When the number of infections starts increasing, it imposes SDMs and mask mandate. When the number of infections goes down significantly it removes the SDMs and finally also removes the mask mandate.

The health priority agent in contrast to the balanced agent imposes a lockdown when the number of infections increases, and as the infections get under control it switches to imposing SDMs. Moreover, it does not remove the mask mandate.

The EPP priority agent in contrast to the balanced agent only imposes a mask mandate even when the number of infections increases and removes them once infections go down.

Unless we give an extremely low priority to the EPP, an agent will not impose vaccination mandates because of the severe public resistance to such policies.

Given the experimental results, our framework can adjust to various priority strategies that can be regulated by the policy-maker according to their main objectives.

5   Conclusion

Pandemics are one of the biggest threats to society. One of the most effective ways to reduce the spread of infection is to reduce the contact rate with infected individuals. Decisions made by policymakers have a direct and significant impact on public behavior and the economy. In this paper, we have proposed the $SEIHRD^v$ epidemiological model to simulate the impact of various government policies on the pandemic spread. The model has several new compartments to account for hospitalizations and the impact of vaccination on the infection, hospitalization, and mortality rates. We have presented an RL framework to assist policymakers in introducing non-pharmaceutical and pharmaceutical interventions while assessing their long-term impact on the pandemic spread, economy, and public perception. We have demonstrated that our framework can produce efficient mitigation strategies under various government priorities for the COVID-19 pandemic based on NY, USA data for the period of November 2021 to April 2022.

References

1. Li, Q., et al.: Early transmission dynamics in Wuhan, China, of novel coronavirus-infected pneumonia. New Engl. J. Med. **382**, 1199–1207 (2020)
2. Kaye, A.D., et al.: Economic impact of Covid-19 pandemic on healthcare facilities and systems: international perspectives. Best Pract. Res. Clin. Anaesthesiol. **35**(3), 293–306 (2021)

3. Chowdhury, P., Paul, S.K., Kaisar, S., Moktadir, M.A.: Covid-19 pandemic related supply chain studies: a systematic review. Transp. Res. Part E Logistics Transp. Rev. **148**, 102271 (2021)
4. Brauer, F.: Compartmental models in epidemiology. In: Mathematical Epidemiology. LNM, vol. 1945, pp. 19–79. Springer, Heidelberg (2008). https://doi.org/10. 1007/978-3-540-78911-6_2
5. Kermack, W.O., McKendrick, A.G.: A contribution to the mathematical theory of epidemics. Proc. Roy. Soc. London. Ser. A Containing Pap. Math. Phys. Charact. **115**(772), 700–721 (1927)
6. Korolev, I.: Identification and estimation of the SEIRD epidemic model for Covid-19. J. Econometrics **220**(1), 63–85 (2021)
7. Smith, M.C., Broniatowski, D.A.: Modeling influenza by modulating flu awareness. In: Xu, K.S., Reitter, D., Lee, D., Osgood, N. (eds.) SBP-BRiMS 2016. LNCS, vol. 9708, pp. 262–271. Springer, Cham (2016). https://doi.org/10.1007/978-3-319-39931-7_25
8. Ranganathan, A.: The levenberg-marquardt algorithm. Tutorial on LM Algorithm **11**(1), 101–110 (2004)
9. Gavin, H.P.: The Levenberg-Marquardt algorithm for nonlinear least squares curve-fitting problems. Department of Civil and Environmental Engineering, Duke University (2019)
10. Zhang, H.F., Wang, L.H., Yin, J.P., Chen, P.H., Zhang, H.F.: Performance of the Levenberg-Marquardt neural network approach in nuclear mass prediction. J. Phys. G Nuclear Part. Phys. **44**(4), 045110 (2017)
11. Aarnink, W., Weishaupt, A., Van Silfhout, A.: Angle-resolved x-ray photoelectron spectroscopy (ARXPS) and a modified Levenberg-Marquardt fit procedure: a new combination for modeling thin layers. Appl. Surf. Sci. **45**(1), 37–48 (1990)
12. Koh, J.M., Cheong, K.H.: Automated electron-optical system optimization through switching levenberg-marquardt algorithms. J. Electron Spectro. Relat. Phenom. **227**, 31–39 (2018)
13. Levine, S., Pastor, P., Krizhevsky, A., Ibarz, J., Quillen, D.: Learning hand-eye coordination for robotic grasping with deep learning and large-scale data collection. Int. J. Robot. Res. **37**(4–5), 421–436 (2018)
14. Levine, S., Finn, C., Darrell, T., Abbeel, P.: End-to-end training of deep visuomotor policies. J. Mach. Learn. Res. **17**(1), 1334–1373 (2016)
15. Vereshchaka, A., Kulkarni, N.: Optimization of mitigation strategies during epidemics using offline reinforcement learning. In: Social, Cultural, and Behavioral Modeling: 14th International Conference, SBP-BRiMS 2021, Virtual Event, 6–9 July 2021, pp. 35–45 (2021)
16. Khadilkar, H., Ganu, T., Seetharam, D.P.: Optimising lockdown policies for epidemic control using reinforcement learning. Trans. Indian Nat. Acad. Eng. **5**(2), 129–132 (2020)
17. Loli Piccolomini, E., Zama, F.: Monitoring Italian Covid-19 spread by a forced SEIRD model. PloS one **15**(8), e0237417 (2020)
18. Fawaz, A., Owayjan, M., Achkar, R.: Development of a robust mathematical model to estimate Covid-19 cases in Lebanon based on seirdv modified model. In: 2021 Sixth International Conference on Advances in Biomedical Engineering (ICABME), pp. 141–146. IEEE (2021)
19. Amona, E., Boone, E., Ghanam, R.: Seirdv model for Qatar covid-19 outbreak: a case study. arXiv preprint arXiv:2204.10961
20. Giordano, G., et al.: Modelling the Covid-19 epidemic and implementation of population-wide interventions in Italy. Nat. Med. **26**(6), 855–860 (2020)

21. Modeling Covid-19 scenarios for the United States. Nat. Med. **27**(1), 94–105 (2021)
22. Borchering, R.K.: Modeling of future Covid-19 cases, hospitalizations, and deaths, by vaccination rates and nonpharmaceutical intervention scenarios-United States, april-september 2021. Morb. Mortal. Wkly Rep. **70**(19), 719 (2021)
23. Scobie, H.M., et al.: Monitoring incidence of Covid-19 cases, hospitalizations, and deaths, by vaccination status-13 us jurisdictions, april 4-july 17, 2021. Morb. Mortal. Wkly Rep. **70**(37), 1284 (2021)
24. Cheng, H.-Y., et al.: Contact tracing assessment of Covid-19 transmission dynamics in Taiwan and risk at different exposure periods before and after symptom onset. JAMA Int. Med. **180**(9), 1156–1163 (2020)
25. Kojima, N., Klausner, J.D.: Protective immunity after recovery from SARS-CoV-2 infection. Lancet Infect. Dis. **22**(1), 12–14 (2022)

Automated Utterance Labeling of Conversations Using Natural Language Processing

Maria Laricheva[1]([✉]) [iD], Chiyu Zhang[1], Yan Liu[2], Guanyu Chen[1], Terence Tracey[1,3], Richard Young[1], and Giuseppe Carenini[1]

[1] The University of British Columbia, Vancouver, BC, Canada
maria.laricheva@ubc.ca
[2] Carleton University, Ottawa, ON, Canada
[3] Arizona State University, Tempe, AZ, USA

Abstract. Conversational data is essential in psychology because it can help researchers understand individuals' cognitive processes, emotions, and behaviors. Utterance labelling is a common strategy for analyzing this type of data. The development of NLP algorithms allows researchers to automate this task. However, psychological conversational data present some challenges to NLP researchers, including multilabel classification, a large number of classes, and limited available data. This study explored how automated labels generated by NLP methods are comparable to human labels in the context of conversations on adulthood transition. We proposed strategies to handle three common challenges raised in psychological studies. Our findings showed that the deep learning method with domain adaptation (RoBERTa-CON) outperformed all other machine learning methods; and the hierarchical labelling system that we proposed was shown to help researchers strategically analyze conversational data. Our Python code and NLP model are available at https://github.com/mlaricheva/automated_labeling.

Keywords: Natural language processing · Conversation analysis · Deep learning · Cognitive and behavioral coding · Emotion classification · RoBERTa

1 Introduction

Analyzing conversational data is essential in psychology because it can help researchers understand individuals' cognitive processes, emotions, etc. One of the conventional methods is to code/label the conversations line by line, also called utterances, by two independent researchers based on a pre-established coding list, which enables further qualitative data analysis. However, the coding is a time-consuming and labor-intensive process that takes approximately 4–6 times of the video recording time [1].

The recent development in natural language processing (NLP) makes it possible to automatically label utterances and significantly reduce the coding time. Some researchers have explored automated labeling for counselling data. For example, Tanana et al. [2] and Lee et al. [3] applied dialogue act classification to therapy transcripts to understand the flow of conversation in therapy sessions. Can et al. [1] conducted automated labeling

R. Thomson et al. (Eds.): SBP-BRiMS 2022, LNCS 13558, pp. 241–251, 2022.
https://doi.org/10.1007/978-3-031-17114-7_23

of counselor's reflections. However, most of these studies do not extensively address the existing challenges of the psychological data.

One challenge is multilabel classification. In psychological conversational data, the behaviours and emotions are often co-occurring, i.e., each utterance may have more than one label. Multilabel classification is not naturally supported by conventional machine learning algorithms, such as Naïve Bayes. **Another common challenge** is a detailed coding system that includes many labels. A large number of classes leads to data imbalance and confounds the classification problem. **The third challenge** is a limited amount of the training data. Due to the privacy concerns and annotation costs, psychological data is hard to access and collect [1, 4], which aggravates the first two challenges.

Several strategies exist to manage mentioned problems. To deal with the multilabel classification (Challenge 1), a task can be decomposed into a series of binary classification tasks using the classifier chain [5]. In the case of a large number of labels (Challenge 2), researchers attempt to aggregate the fine-grained classes into more coarse-grained categories [6–8]. The lack of relevant training data (Challenge 3) may be solved using unsupervised learning algorithms, but in that case, the resulting classes are hard to explain. Another approach to solving the data scarcity is transfer learning from the rich-resource task to a new low-resource task to improve the performance of the latter [9]. A few studies on counseling applications of NLP paid attention to these data problems and none solved them simultaneously.

This study is to investigate how automated labels generated by NLP methods are comparable to human labels in the context of conversations on adulthood transition. We compared several NLP methods, including conventional machine learning and deep learning methods. More specifically, we provided strategies to handle three challenges discussed earlier: (1) demonstrated how to resolve the challenge of one utterance having multiple labels; (2) introduced a hierarchical labeling system to strategically analyze utterances, generate automated labels from general categories to more refined labels; and (3) explored how to pretrain a deep learning model, RoBERTa-CON, on a large data set of counselling conversational data.

2 Data

2.1 Source

We used the data that was collected by Young et al. [10, 11] and that focuses on youth adulthood transition between 2013 and 2016. We utilized a dataset that consisted of 63 text transcripts, each corresponding to the session with a duration of around 10–20 min. The data included conversations between peers (25 transcripts), parents or a parent and an older sibling (29 transcripts), and a parent and a child (9 transcripts). Participants discussed topics that they considered relevant to the theme of the transition to adulthood.

The coding scheme for the original dataset was developed with a perspective of an action theory that conceptualizes the conversation as a joint goal-directed action [12]. After the manual data cleaning, we decided to merge similar labels (e.g., labels *states opinion* and *states perception* were combined into a joint class *express perception or opinion*), and the resulting coding system comprised of 59 unique labels.

2.2 Preprocessing

The final dataset included 7,965 utterances. The data were split into train (90%) and test (10%) sets using stratified sampling to ensure the inclusion of underrepresented labels (such as the label praise with only 12 utterances, which is less than 0.007% of the emotion dataset).

Context is essential for a complete utterance-level dialogue understanding. For our dataset, we extended each utterance with the previous two: to predict the label y_i of the utterance u_i, we used the combination of u_{i-2}, u_{i-1} and u_i utterances. The placeholder was used if there were no utterances preceding.

For conventional machine learning methods, utterances were cleaned by removal of stop-words, punctuation and special symbols and then transformed to numerical vectors, using term-frequency inverse-document-frequency (TF-IDF) technique [13]. For deep learning methods (e.g., RoBERTa), we used the original text without any modification to train the model end-to-end.

2.3 Challenges

Multilabel. A multilabel classification implies that more than one label can be assigned to each utterance. In the original dataset, about 24% of utterances were labeled by two classes, and 12% by three or more. See an example in Fig. 1.

PrtA: (Sigh)
Labels: expresses emotions (worry, etc.)
PrtB: Because the more we talk to people, it's just a, you know, it's real a tough, long grind, right, to get this stuff done.
Labels: elaborates; expresses perception; elicits a response

Fig. 1. An example of a snippet of conversation between a couple

Multiclass. As was mentioned previously, the psychological data has a challenge of large number of labels. To tackle this problem, we introduce the hierarchical labeling system. At the top level, the initial labels constituted two large categories: expressions of emotions and cognitive processes and behaviors. This dichotomy was preserved in our analysis. We refer to this task as **EMO-COG**. The corresponding analysis was conducted on the whole dataset, consisting of 7,965 utterances, with 1,373 utterances corresponding to emotion and 6,592 to non-emotion.

For each of the main categories, we developed an independent higher-level classification consisting of eight classes. For 1,373 emotional utterances, the higher-level classification was based on but not identical to the fundamental emotions from Plutchik's model [14]. We linked 20 original labels to eight classes and referred to this classification as **EMO-8**. For 6,592 utterances corresponding to cognitive processes and behaviors, we developed a coding system by grouping together similar labels. For example, the higher-level category *'clarification'* included the following original labels: *'paraphrase'*, *'ask* *for clarification', 'ask for confirmation', 'clarify', 'confirm', 'elaborate'.* The resulting task included eight cognition labels instead of the original 39 and is referred to as **COG-8**.

Finally, original labels for emotions and cognitive processes and behaviors independently constituted two fine-grained categorization tasks. The fine-grained emotion classification consisted of 20 unique categories and was referred to as **EMO-FULL**. The fine-grained classification for cognitive processes included 39 unique classes and was referred to as **COG-FULL**.

3   Methods

3.1   Conventional Machine Learning Methods

We utilized five popular conventional machine learning methods [13] in the data analysis: (1) Naïve Bayes classifier (**NB**), a probabilistic algorithm, has been widely used for the multiclass text classification; (2) AdaBoost is a boosting ensemble method used to improve the model's performance. We used AdaBoost to enhance the base Naïve Bayes (**AdaBoost+NB**); (3) Random Forest (**RF**) is another ensemble learning method, which can prevent the model from overfitting; (4) Gradient Descent (**GD**) is a popular optimization technique that is used together with linear models. We used support vector machine (**SVM**) as a backbone for the GD; and (5) Logistic regression (**LR**) algorithm applied with L2-norm penalty.

For EMO-COG, we conducted binary classification analysis with all the models described above. For multilabel tasks, we trained each model within a classifier chain framework in order to predict multiple labels for a single utterance.

3.2   Deep Learning Methods

Recently, deep learning models have revolutionized the research in NLP and have been shown superiority to conventional machine learning methods [15]. The deep learning models are data-hungry, i.e., require a large amount of training data. However, our data is limited to train the deep learning model. Hence, we proposed to solve this challenge by using the state-of-the-art pretrained language model.

In our study, we used **RoBERTa** (Robustly Optimized BERT Pretraining Approach [16]) which was trained on a large English dataset, such as Wikipedia and BookCorpus. We utilized the base architecture of RoBERTa that includes 12 Transformer encoder layers, 12 heads each, and 768 hidden units [17]. We used hidden states of "[CLS]" token from the last layer of RoBERTa as a sequence-level representation vector of each input utterance. For EMO-COG, we sent this vector through a non-linear layer with softmax activation function to predict the label and trained the model with cross-entropy loss. For multilabel classifiers, we adopted a similar approach, but we used a sigmoid activation function and trained with binary cross-entropy loss (BCE).

Domain Adaptation. For deep learning models, the performance deteriorates significantly when there is a domain shift [18]. As was mentioned previously, RoBERTa models were pretrained on data that is different from our domain (psychological conversations), therefore, we decided to perform a domain adaptation to improve the model's performance on our tasks. The domain adaptation is a technique that uses a larger dataset of a similar domain, closer to the target, to pre-train the model and learn the relevant characteristics of the target data. In this experiment, we exploited the Alexander Street Press database on Counseling and Psychotherapy Transcripts [19]. This dataset consisted of more than 1,500 conversations between a therapist and a patient. Therefore, we further pretrained RoBERTa on this dataset with masked language modeling objectives [16] which mask 15% of input tokens and task the model to reconstruct the original input sequence. The final model is referred to as **RoBERTa-CON**.

3.3 Hyperparameter

For **conventional machine learning** methods, we used the TF-IDF matrix with a vocabulary size of 3,034. For the AdaBoost+NB, we set the number of estimators as 50, and the learning rate as 0.1. For RF, we used the default hyperparameters of sci-kit learn implementation, which sets the number of estimators as 100 and uses the split criterion of Gini [17]. GD-SVM model was trained with 1,000 epochs and the learning rate was identified by the 'optimal' mode of sci-kit learn. For LR, we used L2-norm penalty and trained it for up to 100 iterations. All conventional models were trained on the training dataset and tested on the test dataset, while RF and GD-SVM were tested three times with different random seeds.

For **deep learning** models, we used 10% of the training data as the development dataset and choose the best hyperparameters based on the development performance (weighted F1). We found the best hyperparameters for RoBERTa and RoBERTa-CON using the grid search. We considered two hyperparameters, i.e., batch size and learning rate. We search the batch size in a set of {*4, 8, 16*}; and the learning rate in a set of {*5e−5, 3e−5, 2e−5, 1e−5, 5e−6, 2e−6*}, with 20 epochs for EMO-COG and 50 epochs for all multilabel tasks. We conducted hyperparameter optimization for two types of tasks, COG-8 and EMO-COG. Due to the high computational costs of the fine-tuning process, the best combination for COG-8 was used for other multilabel tasks, including EMO-8, COG-FULL and EMO-FULL.

Table 1. Best hyperparameters for RoBERTa and RoBERTa-CON used in our experiments

	RoBERTa			RoBERTa-CON		
	Learning rate	Batch size	Best epoch	Learning rate	Batch size	Best epoch
EMO-COG	1e−5	4	8	5e−6	8	3
EMO-8	3e−5	8	12	1e−5	8	19
COG-8	3e−5	8	12	1e−5	8	19
EMO-FULL	3e−5	8	10	1e−5	8	11
COG-FULL	3e−5	8	8	1e−5	8	45

After getting the best hyperparameters, we trained RoBERTa and RoBERTa-CON on the training set for ***three times***. Each time we randomly sampled 10% of the training data as the development set and recorded the development performance of each epoch. We averaged the results of each epoch over three runs and chose the best epoch based on the average development performance (weighted F1 score). For EMO-COG task, we set the maximum number of epochs to 20, and for the other four tasks to 50. Finally, we used the best hyperparameter set to train the models on the whole training set respectively and tested them on the testing set. We summarized the best hyperparameters in Table 1.

3.4 Evaluation Metrics and Baseline

We calculated three metrics: macro F1 score (M-F1), weighted F1 score (W-F1) and accuracy (the latter was replaced by hamming loss for multilabel classification tasks) [13]. M-F1 returns the average of F1 scores across all classes with equal weight. W-F1 computes the average using weights that reflect the proportion of each class in the dataset. M-F1 and W-F1 scores can be calculated using the Eqs. (1) and (2) respectively:

$$Macro\ F1 = \frac{1}{N} \sum_{i=0}^{N} F1_i, \tag{1}$$

$$Weighted\ F1 = \sum_{i=0}^{N} W_i F1_i, \tag{2}$$

where N is the number of classes, and $F1_i$ is the F1 score of the class i, and W_i is the weight, assigned to class i; $W_i = \frac{number\ of\ instances\ of\ class\ i}{training\ set\ size}$. The general formula for F1 is represented by the formula (3):

$$F1 = \frac{TP}{TP + \frac{1}{2}(FP + TP)}, \tag{3}$$

where TP is true positives (correctly labeled as belonging to the class) and FP is the false positives (incorrectly labeled as belonging to the class).

Accuracy (ACC) in machine learning refers to the ratio of correctly predicted items to the total input size, and can be estimated using the following equation:

$$ACC = \frac{number\ of\ correct\ predictions}{total\ number\ of\ predictions}, \tag{4}$$

Since in multilabel classification a prediction can be fully correct, partially correct (some labels were predicted correctly, some were not) or fully incorrect, it is not possible to calculate accuracy using the standard formula. For that reason, we used Hamming loss (HL) instead of accuracy for multilabel classification tasks. HL describes the fraction of incorrectly predicted items and is represented by the formula (5). As this is the loss function, higher scores correspond to less accurate models.

$$HL = \frac{1}{|N||L|} \sum_{1}^{|N|} \sum_{1}^{|L|} xor(y_{ij}, z_{ij}), \tag{5}$$

where y_{ij} is the target, z_{ij} is the prediction, and $xor()$ is the exclusive "or" operator, i.e., $xor(y_{ij}, z_{ij})$ is equal to 0, when target and prediction are equal, and to 1 otherwise.

In the next section, we present the M-F1, W-F1, ACC and HL in the percentage form and use W-F1 as our main metric.

Baseline. To investigate how much models can learn the task, we constructed a simple baseline in which all the utterances were classified as the dominant class (e.g., non-emotion in EMO-COG classification).

4 Results

4.1 EMO-COG Classification

The results of the EMO-COG classification (emotion vs. non-emotion) are provided in the Table 2. Among the conventional machine learning methods, GD-SVM demonstrated the best performance by every metric, achieving the average W-F1 of 88.3. The improvement in M-F1 over the baseline was around 32.61, which demonstrates the model's ability to identify the less represented emotional utterances. Our deep learning model, RoBERTa-CON, achieved the best performance with W-F1 of 98.71.

Table 2. EMO-COG classification results

	W-F1	M-F1	ACC
Conventional machine learning			
Baseline	74.75	45.24	82.61
Naïve Bayes	66.40	53.37	61.93
AdaBoost+Naïve Bayes	72.03	57.74	69.09
Random Forest	84.87 ± 0.41	69.68 ± 0.95	84.25 ± 5.83
GD-SVM	**88.30 ± 0.15**	**77.85 ± 4.53**	**89.43 ± 0.11**
Logistic Regression	87.12	74.93	88.86
Deep learning models			
RoBERTa	90.31 ± 0.47	79.54 ± 2.71	92.92 ± 0.92
RoBERTa-CON	**98.71 ± 0.13**	**98.08 ± 0.21**	**98.38 ± 0.13**

Note. **Bold** font indicates the best performance in each group of methods; underscores indicate the best performance across all the models

4.2 Multilabel Classification

The results of the multilabel classification for the coarse-grained labels (EMO-8 and COG-8) are provided in the Table 3. The results of EMO-FULL and COG-FULL are presented in the Table 4.

Conventional Machine Learning. Similar to the previous task, GD-SVM demonstrated the best performance among conventional models for EMO-8 and COG-8 tasks. While the absolute scores are lower, the improvement over the baseline clearly shows that the models are able to distinguish between classes. W-F1 of GD-SVM are improved over 37.15 points respectively for EMO-8 compared to the baseline; for COG-8 the improvement is slightly smaller with 27.3 points for W-F1. For EMO-FULL, the best W-F1 is still reached by GD-SVM, but NB achieved the best performance on COG-FULL.

Deep Learning. For the most multiclass-multilabel tasks, our RoBERTa-CON again outperformed RoBERTa and all conventional machine learning methods, except for the EMO-FULL task. Our RoBERTa-CON acquired W-F1 of 71.01, 68.31, 45.81 on EMO-8, COG-8, COG-FULL respectively. RoBERTa achieved the best W-F1 of 60.40 on EMO-FULL. Due to a large number of labels and data imbalance, the models however performed poor for minor classes (see error analysis in Sect. 4.3). As the difficulty of tasks increased (from coarse-grained to fine-grained labels), we noticed that the model performance decreased, including the best performed model RoBERTa-CON. There is still a large gap needed to fill for fine-grained classifications of psychological data by using machine learning methods. We will improve this in the future work.

Table 3. EMO-8 and COG-8 classification results

	EMO-8			COG-8		
	W-F1	M-F1	HL	W-F1	M-F1	HL
Conventional machine learning						
Baseline	11.45	5.38	18.55	16.14	6.96	19.51
NB	31.96	23.97	22.06	40.16	23.85	32.78
AdaBoost + NB	31.22	21.34	19.85	35.42	22.32	26.26
RF	40.31 ± 0.61	25.07 ± 0.83	**10.24 ± 0.12**	25.05 ± 0.15	12.50 ± 0.13	17.41 ± 0.02
GD-SVM	**48.60 ± 2.33**	**37.42 ± 4.53**	12.31 ± 0.52	**43.44 ± 1.50**	**24.44 ± 0.35**	17.04 ± 0.34
LR	39.93	24.73	12.83	42.69	24.42	**16.32**
Deep learning models						
RoBERTa	69.08 ± 4.92	60.48 ± 7.78	7.76 ± 0.78	65.45 ± 0.49	49.48 ± 3.88	11.18 ± 0.43
RoBERTa-CON	**71.01 ± 1.84**	**62.21 ± 1.99**	**7.30 ± 0.53**	**68.31 ± 0.39**	**51.76 ± 0.65**	**10.38 ± 0.18**

Table 4. EMO-FULL and COG-FULL classification results

	EMO-FULL			COG-FULL		
	W-F1	M-F1	HL	W-F1	M-F1	HL
Conventional machine learning						
Baseline	8.66	1.91	7.83	4.11	0.70	4.62
NB	16.97	7.87	9.94	**15.09**	**6.80**	15.21

(*continued*)

Table 4. (*continued*)

	EMO-FULL			COG-FULL		
	W-F1	M-F1	HL	W-F1	M-F1	HL
AdaBoost+NB	21.06	9.87	9.33	14.66	6.78	11.03
RF	24.74 ± 0.57	10.46 ± 0.88	**4.69 ± 0.13**	4.56 ± 1.07	2.31 ± 0.55	4.39 ± 0.02
GD-SVM	**40.07 ± 0.85**	**23.93 ± 3.01**	5.76 ± 0.17	9.97 ± 1.06	3.96 ± 0.30	4.34 ± 0.05
LR	24.41	9.42	4.78	7.76	2.82	**4.06**
Deep learning models						
RoBERTa	**60.40 ± 0.18**	**48.01 ± 4.65**	3.97 ± 0.16	44.60 ± 0.77	29.62 ± 2.76	4.13 ± 0.08
RoBERTa-CON	51.92 ± 1.69	27.66 ±3.02	**3.66 ± 0.16**	**45.81 ± 0.13**	**30.26 ± 0.76**	**4.03 ± 0.03**

4.3 Error Analysis

We conducted an error analysis and inspected the best model's (our RoBERTa-CON) performance for each individual class. As was mentioned previously, all models demonstrated poorer prediction accuracy for the non-emotion in the EMO-COG task which can be explained by the data imbalance. Figure 2 visualizes the classification results of RoBERTa-CON model on the EMO-8 and COG-8 tasks. The visualization reveals that the best performance was achieved for labels such as 'joy' and 'anticipation' for EMO-8, and 'agreement' and 'description' for COG-8. Those labels correspond to the dominant classes. The model showed poorer performance for minor classes, such as 'fear' (6% of the EMO-8 dataset) and 'suggestion' (7% of the COG-8 dataset).

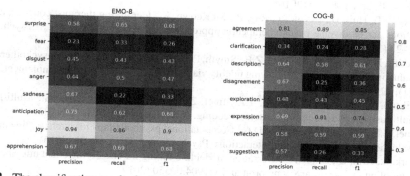

Fig. 2. The classification results for RoBERTa-CON model for EMO-8 (left) and COG-8 (right)

For fine-grained classifications, some less represented labels were not recognized by RoBERTa-CON, e.g., the label 'express fear' for EMO-FULL or 'advise' and 'disapprove' for COG-FULL. It is worth mentioning that for some labels the lack of representation in the training dataset does not affect the model's ability. For example, labels 'pause' and 'unintelligible response' from COG-FULL have the highest precisions among others in the same task.

5   Conclusion and Discussion

In this study, we investigated the utility of conventional machine learning as well as deep learning methods for the automated labeling of utterances in conversations on adulthood transition. To handle three severe data challenges, we developed a hierarchical classification system to tackle our problems from coarse-grained level to fine-grained level. Our results suggested that pretrained deep learning models outperform conventional methods. To further tackle these challenges, we performed a domain adaptation for the original pretrained RoBERTa on large-scale counseling data. Our adapted model, RoBERTa-CON, was almost comparable to the human coder demonstrating W-F1 as high as 98% on EMO-COG task and achieved the best performance on most multiclass-multilabel tasks. Although coarse-grained labels are not equivalent to the fine-grained labels, they can serve as a mid-step to help researchers understand their data.

Some challenges were still persistent. The model performance was substantially decreasing as the number of labels increased. We also noticed that the data imbalance affected the individual performance for minor labels. We plan to improve those limitations in future work by using transfer learning, semi-supervised learning, etc.

References

1. Can, D., Marín, R.A., Georgiou, P.G., Imel, Z.E., Atkins, D.C., Narayanan, S.S.: "It sounds like...": a natural language processing approach to detecting counselor reflections in motivational interviewing. J. Couns. Psychol. **63**(3), 343–350 (2016)
2. Tanana, M., Hallgren, K.A., Imel, Z.E., Atkins, D.C., Srikumar, V.: A comparison of natural language processing methods for automated coding of motivational interviewing. J. Subst. Abuse Treat. **65**, 43–50 (2016)
3. Lee, F.-T., Hull, D., Levine, J., Ray, B., McKeown, K.: Identifying therapist conversational actions across diverse psychotherapeutic approaches. In: Proceedings of the SLPsych, pp, 12–23 (2019)
4. Atkins, D.C., Steyvers, M., Imel, Z.E., Smyth, P.: Scaling up the evaluation of psychotherapy: evaluating motivational interviewing fidelity via statistical text classification. Implement. Sci. **9**(1), 49 (2014)
5. Gibson, J., Atkins, D.C., Creed, T.A., Imel, Z., Georgiou, P., Narayanan, S.: Multi-label multi-task deep learning for behavioral coding. IEEE TAC **13**(1), 508–518 (2022)
6. Imel, Z.E., Steyvers, M., Atkins, D.C.: Computational psychotherapy research: scaling up the evaluation of patient–provider interactions. Psychotherapy **52**(1), 19–30 (2015)
7. Park, S., Kim, D., Oh, A.: Conversation model fine-tuning for classifying client utterances in counseling dialogues. arXiv preprint arXiv:1904.00350 (2019)
8. Valach, L., Young, R. A., Lynam, M.J.: Action Theory: A Primer for Applied Research in the Social Sciences. Greenwood Publishing Group (2002)
9. Acheampong, F.A., Nunoo-Mensah, H., Chen, W.: Transformer models for text-based emotion detection: a review of BERT-based approaches. Artif. Intell. Rev. (2016)
10. Young, R.A., et al.: Transition to adulthood as a peer project. Emerg. Adulthood **3**(3), 166–178 (2015)
11. Young, R.A., Marshall, S.K., Murray, J.: Prospective content in the friendship conversations of young adults. J. Adolesc. **54**(1), 9–17 (2017)
12. Yates, A., Cohan, A., Goharian, N.: Depression and self-harm risk assessment in online forums. arXiv preprint arXiv:1709.01848 (2017)

13. Jurafsky, D.: Speech & Language Processing. Pearson Education India (2000)
14. Plutchik, R.: A general psychoevolutionary theory of emotion. In: Theories of Emotion, pp. 3–33. Academic Press (1980)
15. Collobert, R., Weston, J.: A unified architecture for natural language processing: deep neural networks with multitask learning. In: Proceedings of the ICML 2008, pp. 160–167 (2008)
16. Liu, Y., et al.: RoBERTa: a robustly optimized BERT pretraining approach. arXiv preprint, arXiv:1907.11692 (2019)
17. Scikit-learn. https://hal.inria.fr/hal-00650905. Accessed 10 June 2022
18. Ma, X., Xu, P., Wang, Z., Nallapati, R., Xiang, B.: Domain adaptation with BERT-based domain classification and data selection. In: Proceedings of DeepLo 2019, pp. 76–83 (2019)
19. Alexander Street. https://alexanderstreet.com/. Accessed 15 June 2022

An Exploratory Study on the Author Keyphrases Selection Behaviours in Scientific Articles

Salim Sazzed[✉]

Old Dominion University, Norfolk, VA 23529, USA
ssazz001@odu.edu

Abstract. This study analyzes the keyword selection behavior of authors in scientific articles from multiple perspectives. It first investigates to what extent author-provided keyphrases are retrievable (i.e., abstract coverage) from the abstracts of scientific publications based on phrase-level matching. Afterward, the relations between the abstract coverage with the abstract length and readability scores are investigated. Then, it inspects the performance of domain-independent statistical and co-occurrence-based keyword extraction methods for automatically identifying the author-provided keywords from the abstracts of articles. Finally, it analyzes the agreements between various unsupervised keyphrase extraction methods. It is noticed that author-provided keyphrases are often not present in the abstract. The abstract coverage of around 30% is observed in three different datasets with no perceptible relationships with the abstract length and readability. It is found that unsupervised approaches yield limited accuracy in automatically determining keywords from the abstract (even if they exist in the abstract); They achieve coverage of less than 20%. Besides, the low agreements between various keyword extraction techniques for the automatic keyphrase determination suggest that author keyword selection behavior is not much connected to the statistical attributes (e.g., frequency and co-occurrence of words) or syntactic attributes (i.e., word/sentence length, syllables) of the abstracts.

1 Introduction

Keyphrases enable the mapping of a text document to a set of representative phrases or words. For example, keyphrases constitute a very succinct representation of the documents, such as scientific articles. Keyphrases, if represent a document accurately, can help various downstream tasks such as information retrieval, text summarization, clustering, and classification. Usually, in scientific publications, the authors are instructed to provide a set of keyphrases that they feel represent the corresponding article in the most reasonable ways. The abstract of a scientific article is another short representation of the publication that conveys the outline in some ways. Unlike keyword, which contains only a

R. Thomson et al. (Eds.): SBP-BRiMS 2022, LNCS 13558, pp. 252–260, 2022.
https://doi.org/10.1007/978-3-031-17114-7_24

few words or phrases, the abstract is represented by multiple sentences. Please note that here, we use the terms keyword and keyphrase interchangeably.

In this study, we aim to discover how these two types of synopsis of scientific publications are related based on analyzing around 4000 scientific publications. Note that since this study focuses on comprehending the author keyword selection strategy, all datasets contain only the publications that have keyphrases assigned by the original authors.

In particular, we aim to investigate the following research questions-

- RQ1: Are the author-provided keywords obtainable from the abstracts of the publication? If so, to what extent?
- RQ2: Do the abstract length and readability score have any relation with the abstract coverage (i.e., availability of author-provided keyphrases in the abstract)?
- RQ3: How effective are the unsupervised keyphrase extraction techniques for retrieving the author-assigned keyword from the given abstract?

Here, we analyze three datasets comprised of abstracts and author-provided keyphrases of scientific publications. The first two datasets represent publications from two computer science venues, WWW and KDD, while the third dataset contains a list of biomedical articles. We perform a phrase-level matching to find the proportion of author-suggested keyphrases present in the abstract (i.e., abstract coverage) in all the datasets. We then examine whether the abstract's readability score and length have any impact on the abstract coverage. Finally, we employ various statistical and co-occurrence-based keyphrase extraction techniques in the abstract to find whether they can retrieve author-suggested keywords (when they exist in abstracts). We find that most of the publications have low abstract coverage (i.e., keyphrases do not exist in the abstract). The readability scores and abstract length do not infer any relation with the abstract coverage. Besides, we observe that keywords selected by the statistical co-occurrence-based automatic methods do not resemble high agreement with the author-selected keywords (i.e., low-prediction coverage). In addition, we notice that the agreements on the prediction of various automatic keyphrases extraction methods are very low.

1.1   Contributions

The main contributions of this study can be summarized as-

- We provide various statistics regarding what extent author selected keywords are available in the abstract of scientific articles.
- We reveal that there exists no relationship between the length and readability of the abstract and its coverage on the author-selected keywords.
- We demonstrate that unsupervised keyphrase extraction methods show poor performance for retrieving author-selected keyphrases from the abstracts even when they exist.

– Finally, we show that there exists a low agreement between various unsupervised keyphrase extraction methods for the keyphrase extraction from the short scientific text (i.e., abstract).

2   Related Work

Although keyphrase extraction is a well-studied problem in various domains, including scientific publications, limited analysis has been performed regarding author keyword selection behavior. Lu et al. [5] analyzed author keyword selection strategies and found the presence of keywords in the titles and abstracts around 31% and 52.1%, respectively. The percentage of author-selected keywords in the references was observed at 41.6%. In addition, they noticed prolific authors tend to select fewer keywords from the titles and abstracts; instead, they pick more keywords from references and high-frequency words. The authors also discovered percentages of keywords appearing in titles and abstracts negatively correlate with the citation counts of scientific papers.

Kwon [4] performed a multidisciplinary analysis to understand the ubiquity of author-provided keywords across disciplines. The authors found that 63.7% of the keywords appeared in only one area of the study, which suggests the majority of author keywords for academic papers are not interdisciplinarity but rather topic-specific. The author also noticed that the interdisciplinarity degree of author keywords in art or physical education are lower than in the humanities or social sciences. Gbur Jr and Trumbo [2] provided a set of guidelines for selecting appropriate keywords, such as avoiding repetition of keywords from the title. Mao et al. [6] studied the frequency of the author-assigned keywords in the publications of six different disciplines. The authors found that many of the papers have zero or single keywords.

Wang et al. [10] presented a word embedding-based approach for keyword extraction and generation that yielded comparable performances to the state-of-the-art methods in a dataset. Tripathi et al. [9] performed a study to spotlight the extent of similarity between authors' assigned keywords and Web of Science (WOS) assigned keywords. Hurt et al. [3] examined the differences between author-selected and automatically generated keywords in a particular area of scientific and technical literature. Keywords yielded using both approaches are investigated using inverse frequency and maximum likelihood algorithm. The authors did not notice any statistically significant differences between the two approaches.

3   Dataset

In this study, we utilize three datasets that have author-assigned gold keyphrases. The first two datasets, KDD and WWW, represent publications from the computer science domain. The KDD dataset contains 293 publications, while the WWW dataset has 660 publications. The third dataset, which we refer to as BioMed, is a subset of a biomedical dataset, consisting of 3000 scientific articles.

4   Readability Test

We employ the Flesch Reading Ease (FRE) algorithm to compute the readability scores of the abstracts. FRE provides a readability score between 0 and 100 for a text snippet. A high score indicates the content is easy to read. For example, scores within the range of 90 and 100 can be understood by an average 5th grader, while 8th and 9th-grade students can understand documents with a score between 60 and 70, and college graduates can comprehend documents with a score of 0–30. The FRE score is computed using the following formula-

$$FRE = 206.835 - 1.015 \times \frac{total\ words}{total\ sentences} - 84.6 \times \frac{total\ syllables}{total\ words}$$

5   Unsupervised Keyphrase Extraction Method

We consider four statistical co-occurrence-based unsupervised keyphrase extraction methods that do not require domain-specific labeled data.

5.1   RAKE

Rapid Automatic Keyword Extraction (Rake) [8] is a keyword extraction algorithm that considers the frequency and co-occurrence of the words to determine keywords. It follows the stylistic and semantic characteristics of the text for an adaptive and fine-grained computation of the word co-occurrences to rank candidate keywords

5.2   YAKE

YAKE [1] is a domain-independent unsupervised keyphrase extraction technique. YAKE depends on statistical text features extracted from the textual content to select the most relevant keywords. YAKE considers the characteristics of five types of features that are fused to assign a single value to each keyphrase. A lower score indicates the higher significance of a keyword.

5.3   TextRank

TextRank [7] is a graph-based ranking model that tries to find the most relevant sentences and keywords in the text. To find relevant keywords, the TextRank algorithm constructs a relation network of words by considering the precedence link among words. An edge between two words (vertices) indicates they follow one another; A higher weight is assigned to the edge connecting co-occurring words. Afterward, the Pagerank algorithm is applied to the network to select the top one-third of relevant words. A keywords table is constructed by combining the top relevant words considering their co-occurrence.

5.4   KeyBert

KeyBERT is a transformer-based keyword extraction technique that utilizes BERT-based embeddings and cosine similarity to find relevant keyphrases that are the most similar to the document itself[1]. In KeyBERT, the document-level embeddings (i.e., document-level representation) are first extracted from the BERT. Afterward, word embeddings of word n-grams are retrieved. Finally, the cosine similarity is applied to find the n-grams that are the most similar to the document that best describes the entire document.

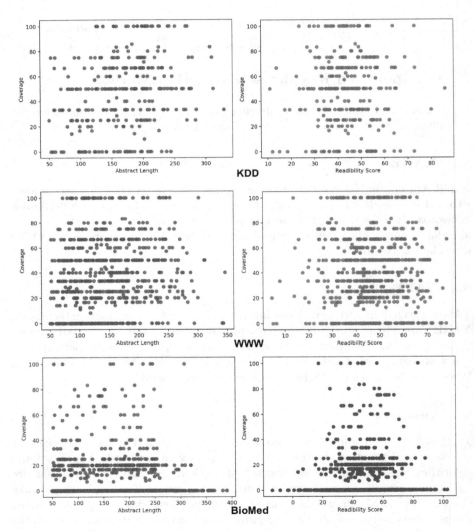

Fig. 1. The relationships of the abstract coverage with the abstract length and readability

---

[1] https://maartengr.github.io/KeyBERT/.

6   Results and Discussion

Abstract Coverage: The term abstract coverage refers to the percentage of author-provided keyphrases available in the abstract based on phrase-level matching. We report the number of publications falls into various ranges of abstract coverage.

Prediction Coverage: The prediction coverage of a keyphrase extraction method with respect to author-provided keyphrases in a corpus is computed in three steps. First, for each abstract, we count how many of the author-provided keyphrases are obtainable. Then for each abstract, we count how many of these obtainable author-keywords exist among the top 10 predicted keyphrases of a method. The prediction coverage of a method is the ratio of the total number of correctly identified keyphrases and the total number of obtainable author-selected keyphrases in a corpus.

Table 1. Statistics of the abstracts coverage and the word-length of non-existent keyphrases

Abstract Coverage Range	KDD #Pub.(%)	WWW #Pub.(%)	BioMed #Pub.(%)
0	36 (12.28%)	106 (16.06%)	2645 (88.16%)
0%–25%	41 (13.99%)	135 (20.45%)	267 (8.90%)
25%–50%	104 (35.49%)	236 (35.75%)	46 (1.53%)
50%–75%	73 (24.91%)	123 (18.63%)	26 (0.086%)
75%–100%	11 (3.75%)	15 (2.27%)	7 (0.023%)
100%	28 (9.55%)	45 (6.81%)	9 (0.03%)
Total	293 (100%)	660 (100%)	3000 (100%)
Unavailable Keyphrases Length	KDD	WWW	BioMed
1	130	516	6725
2	337	922	5504
3	111	270	1835
4	32	167	866
Total	610 (100%)	1835 (100%)	14930 (100%)

Table 2. Prediction coverage of various statistical keyphrase extraction methods (out of obtainable keywords)

Method	KDD	WWW	BioMed
	Out of 553	Out of 1156	Out of 487
YAKE	187 (33.81%)	376 (32.52%)	89 (18.27%)
RAKE	100 (18.08%)	115 (9.94%)	26 (5.33%)
TextRank	82 (14.82%)	264 (22.83%)	79 (16.22%)
KeyBERT	145 (26.22%)	266 (23.01%)	28 (5.74%)

Table 3. Agreements in the predictions of various key phrase extraction methods. The maximum number of matches could be the number of publications × 10, as the top 10 key phrases from each of the methods are considered

Method	KDD (2930)	WWW (6600)	BioMed (30000)
YAKE-RAKE	439 (14.98%)	704 (10.66%)	2868 (9.56%)
YAKE-TextRank	214 (7.30%)	486 (7.83%)	2911 (9.70%)
YAKE-KeyBERT	445 (15.18%)	935 (14.16%)	2747 (9.15%)
RAKE-TextRank	98 (3.34%)	141 (2.13%)	836 (2.78%)
RAKE-KeyBERT	305 (10.40%)	486 (7.36%)	1576 (5.25%)
TextRank-KeyBERT	98 (3.34%)	211 (3.19%)	499 (1.66%)

As shown in Table 1, the abstract coverage values are usually low to fair across publications in various corpora. Among the six groups representing different ranges, we find the 25%–50% group has the most numbers of publications for both the KDD and WWW datasets. In both datasets, we find less than 10% publications have 100% coverage, while 10%–15% publications have 0% coverage. The statistics suggest that while selecting keywords, the authors do not provide much emphasis on the content of the abstract; rather, they select the words/phrases they deem as appropriate.

We also explore whether the abstract length and readability score has any influence on the abstract coverage. Although we anticipated longer abstracts would have higher abstract coverages, we find that this is not true (Fig. 1). A similar outcome we observe regarding the readability; we notice no relation between the readability score and abstract coverage (Fig. 1).

We find unsupervised statistical keyphrase extraction methods exhibit low prediction coverage in all three datasets (Table 2). The YAKE shows the highest prediction coverage among all, over 30% in both KDD and WWW datasets and around 20% in the BioMed dataset. The second best coverage is obtained by transformer-based KeyBERT, which achieves prediction coverage of around

25% in two computer science datasets, although performs poorly for the BioMed dataset. The results indicate that the statistical significances of the words have a low influence (provided the limited content of the abstract) on the author's keyphrases selection strategy.

Besides, we find a lack of consensuses on the predictions of various keyphrase extraction methods (Table 3). Overall, YAKE and KeyBERT yield the highest agreements based on the overlapping terms among the top 10 predicted keyphrases. However, the agreements are still low, between only 10%–15%. The primarily dissimilar results of various methods are observed due to the difference in the statistical algorithms exercised.

7 Summary and Conclusion

This work aims to shed light on how two different kinds of summaries of scientific publications, the abstract and the author's suggested keyphrases, are related. We explore whether the keyphrases obtained through unsupervised methods show high agreements with the author-chosen keywords. The results reveal that automatic keyword selection approaches and author-selected keywords have low agreements in most cases, which suggests that the statistical approaches of keyphrase selection, given the limited content of the abstract, are often unrelated to the author-selected keywords. The future work will investigate larger size datasets and publications from more domains.

References

1. Campos, R., Mangaravite, V., Pasquali, A., Jorge, A., Nunes, C., Jatowt, A.: Yake! keyword extraction from single documents using multiple local features. Inf. Sci. **509**, 257–289 (2020)
2. Gbur, E.E., Jr., Trumbo, B.E.: Key words and phrases-the key to scholarly visibility and efficiency in an information explosion. Am. Stat. **49**(1), 29–33 (1995)
3. Hurt, C.D., et al.: Automatically generated keywords: a comparison to author-generated keywords in the sciences. J. Inf. Organ. Sci. **34**(1), 81–88 (2010)
4. Kwon, S.: Characteristics of interdisciplinary research in author keywords appearing in Korean journals. Malays. J. Libr. Inf. Sci. **23**(2), 77–93 (2018)
5. Lu, W., Liu, Z., Huang, Y., Bu, Y., Li, X., Cheng, Q.: How do authors select keywords? a preliminary study of author keyword selection behavior. J. Inf. **14**(4), 101066 (2020)
6. Mao, J., Lu, K., Zhao, W., Cao, Y.: How many keywords do authors assign to research articles-a multi-disciplinary analysis?. In: iConference 2018 Proceedings (2018)
7. Mihalcea, R., Tarau, P.: Textrank: bringing order into text. In: Proceedings of the 2004 Conference on Empirical Methods in Natural Language Processing, pp. 404–411 (2004)
8. Rose, S., Engel, D., Cramer, N., Cowley, W.: Automatic keyword extraction from individual documents. Text Min. Appl. Theo. **1**, 1–20 (2010)

9. Tripathi, M., Kumar, S., Sonker, S., Babbar, P.: Occurrence of author keywords and keywords plus in social sciences and humanities research: a preliminary study. COLLNET J. Scientometrics Inf. Manag. **12**(2), 215–232 (2018)

10. Wang, R., Liu, W., McDonald, C.: Using word embeddings to enhance keyword identification for scientific publications. In: Sharaf, M.A., Cheema, M.A., Qi, J. (eds.) ADC 2015. LNCS, vol. 9093, pp. 257–268. Springer, Cham (2015). https:// doi.org/10.1007/978-3-319-19548-3_21

Special Panel on Social Good

Computational Models for Social Good: Beyond Bias and Representation

Christopher L. Dancy[1]($\boxtimes$) and Kenneth Joseph[2]

[1] The Pennsylvania State University, University Park, PA 16802, USA
cdancy@psu.edu
[2] The University at Buffalo, Buffalo, NY 14260, USA

Abstract. This panel will bring a timely and overdue discussion to SBP-BRiMS on computational social and behavioral modeling for social good. What's more, we will host a discussion on what it means to critically approach social good in a way that moves beyond discussions of bias and representation. During this panel, panelists will introduce themselves and positions on topics related to social good within computational behavioral and social modeling, and (along with audience members) proceed to discuss sub-topics, queries, and provocations. Chris Dancy will moderate the discussion and ensure an opportunity for interactive experience for all of those in attendance.

Keywords: Computational social good · Behavioral modeling · Social modeling · Systems of oppression · Critical imagination

1 Introduction

The SBP-BRiMS community has long been at the forefront of research at the intersection of computation and the social world. This intersection plays out in a variety of ways with the community being deeply engaged in research that links computational methods with the social sciences. Examples include approaches that combine sociological theory with network science [1, 2], social and/or cognitive psychology with agent-based, computational simulation [3–5], and research linking machine learning with questions in political [6, 7] and health [8] sciences. Efforts within the community have also deeply engaged with core questions and problems in social policy, questions that span myriad computational and social scientific disciplines [9–12].

Recent years have brought yet another dimension to the intersection of computation and the social world that the SBP-BRiMS community, and others like it, have faced with increasing regularity. Broadly known as *computing (or data science) for social good* [13], this domain of research emphasizes the ways in which computation can be used to "do good" in the world. Examples of such research include efforts to use computation to diagnose and/or forecast COVID [14], and to improve traffic flow patterns to ease road congestion [15]. Such research generally takes for granted several notions:

R. Thomson et al. (Eds.): SBP-BRiMS 2022, LNCS 13558, pp. 263–267, 2022.
https://doi.org/10.1007/978-3-031-17114-7_25

a) These tasks can be *solved* with computation.
b) Attempting to solve these tasks provides a net benefit to society.
c) The tasks being addressed will, if *solved*, produce "social good" in self-apparent ways.

The reality, however, is never quite so simple. Scholars in a variety of critical disciplines have emphasized challenges with efforts to perform "Computing for Social Good" (e.g., [16, 17]). With respect to a) above, myriad challenges, from data collection to the inherent difficulty of the task, can create a ceiling for predictive performance on tasks of societal relevance [18]. The result is the expenditure of significant amounts of money on computational tools that were never likely to work, money that could have been spent on low, or even no-tech solutions, that would have produced obvious benefits. With respect to b), there is significant evidence that many problems that have seen attention from computer scientists, including crime prediction [19] and prediction of who need medical care [20], are problems that even if solved will simply serve to reify and further exacerbate existing structural inequalities. What's more, many of these solutions have failed to address the contexts of systems of oppression and understand how such computational systems are likely to interact with institutions that further those systems (for a related discussion see [21]). And with respect to c), similarly, certain problems, such as the development of datasets to evaluate deep fake detection tools [22], have arguably created more problems than they have solved, even if couched in language that such models can ultimately further social good by creating tools that others would have developed anyway.

There are, of course, significant potentials for computation to help improve both our understanding of and ability to live within the social world. The goal of this panel is to engage the SBP-BRiMS community in a debate with experts in the field on how to ensure that efforts to create technology for social good actually do so, and perhaps most importantly, do so for **all**, and not just for those who currently most benefit from existing systems of oppression. The panel will cover at least the following specific questions:

1. What does it really mean for technology to be made for "social good," or "in the public interest"?
2. How might "social good" exclude those from certain communities?
3. How do we best navigate questions about whether or not to build technology *before we actually start to build it?*
4. How do we as an SBP-BRiMS community best advance core issues of social justice, in particular racial inequality?

The format of the panel will be such that it provides time for the panelists listed below to scaffold the discussion with critical perspectives on their experiences, personal and academic, at the intersections of race and technology (Dancy), and technology in the child welfare system (Joseph). It will also provide an array of perspectives, including critical humanist approaches (Castillo), from the intersection of computational modeling, cognitive science, and critical black studies (Dancy), from the computational social sciences (Joseph, and another panelist). After initial, brief statements from the panel participants, attendees will be asked to engage with the panel in a form of critical imagining

[23], where efforts are made to move beyond current boundaries in the field and community to imagine what it would take, currently feasible or not, to truly create technology that is for the social good.

2 Confirmed Participants

Christopher L. Dancy

Chris Dancy is an Associate Professor in Industrial & Manufacturing Engineering and in Computer Science & Engineering at the Pennsylvania State University, University Park. He currently investigates research questions exploring relations between computing systems, cognition, and *the Human*. Dr. Dancy engages with theories and methods from several disciplines, including computational cognitive science, AI, and black studies, to move towards answers to those research questions. His most recent work explores antiblackness in the design, development, and interaction with AI systems. He has served as a Program Committee Chair for SBP-BRiMS since 2018 and has also served as Chair of the Behavior Representation in Modeling and Simulation (BRiMS) Society in the past. Dancy will contribute to the panel through critical reflection and discussion of the ways antiblackness may influence ideas of computing for social good.

Kenneth Joseph

Kenneth Joseph is an Assistant Professor in Computer Science at the University at Buffalo. His research engages with questions at the intersection of sociology, social psychology, social work, and computer science. Recent efforts have focused on understanding how algorithmic biases emerge from structural inequality in social systems, with a specific focus on the American child welfare system. He is a contributing member of the SBP-BRiMS community, including co-organizing the doctoral consortium at the event over the past three years. His contribution to the panel will be a discussion about how qualitative and quantitative methods can be usefully combined to provide critical perspectives on the development of algorithms in high-stakes environments.

3 Invited Participants

David Castillo

David Castillo is a Professor of Romance Languages and Literatures at the University at Buffalo and the Director of the UB Humanities Institute. He also, in 2021, co-founded the Center for Information Integrity at the University at Buffalo, a multidisciplinary effort to study how misinformation spreads online and what might be done to counter that spread. David's expertise is in bringing a critical humanistic perspective, linking contemporary questions about mis- and disinformation on social media to the long trail these questions have wound over time and the ways they are intertwined with the evolution of literature throughout history.

References

1. Uyheng, J., Carley, K.M.: Characterizing bot networks on twitter: an empirical analysis of contentious issues in the Asia-Pacific. In: Thomson, R., Bisgin, H., Dancy, C., Hyder, A. (eds.) SBP-BRiMS 2019. LNCS, vol. 11549, pp. 153–162. Springer, Cham (2019). https://doi.org/10.1007/978-3-030-21741-9_16

2. Clark, M., Frydenlund, E., Padilla, J.J.: Network structures and humanitarian need. In: Thomson, R., Hussain, M.N., Dancy, C., Pyke, A. (eds.) SBP-BRiMS 2021. LNCS, vol. 12720, pp. 214–223. Springer, Cham (2021). https://doi.org/10.1007/978-3-030-80387-2_21

3. Morgan, J.H., Lebiere, C., Moody, J., Orr, M.G.: Trusty ally or faithless snake: modeling the role of human memory and expectations in social exchange. In: Thomson, R., Hussain, M.N., Dancy, C., Pyke, A. (eds.) SBP-BRiMS 2021. LNCS, vol. 12720, pp. 268–278. Springer, Cham (2021). https://doi.org/10.1007/978-3-030-80387-2_26

4. Orr, M.G., Lebiere, C., Stocco, A., Pirolli, P., Pires, B., Kennedy, W.G.: Multi-scale resolution of neural, cognitive and social systems. Comput. Math. Organ. Theory **25**(1), 4–23 (2019). https://doi.org/10.1007/s10588-018-09291-0

5. Atkins, A.A., Brown, M.S., Dancy, C.L.: Examining the effects of race on human-AI cooperation. In: Thomson, R., Hussain, M.N., Dancy, C., Pyke, A. (eds.) SBP-BRiMS 2021. LNCS, vol. 12720, pp. 279–288. Springer, Cham (2021). https://doi.org/10.1007/978-3-030-80387-2_27

6. Shapiro, B., Crooks, A.: Kinetic action and radicalization: a case study of Pakistan. In: Thomson, R., Hussain, M.N., Dancy, C., Pyke, A. (eds.) SBP-BRiMS 2021. LNCS, vol. 12720, pp. 321–330. Springer, Cham (2021). https://doi.org/10.1007/978-3-030-80387-2_31

7. King, C., Bellutta, D., Carley, K.M.: Lying about lying on social media: a case study of the 2019 Canadian elections. In: Thomson, R., Bisgin, H., Dancy, C., Hyder, A., Hussain, M. (eds.) SBP-BRiMS 2020. LNCS, vol. 12268, pp. 75–85. Springer, Cham (2020). https://doi.org/10.1007/978-3-030-61255-9_8

8. Memon, S.A., Tyagi, A., Mortensen, D.R., Carley, K.M.: Characterizing sociolinguistic variation in the competing vaccination communities. In: Thomson, R., Bisgin, H., Dancy, C., Hyder, A., Hussain, M. (eds.) SBP-BRiMS 2020. LNCS, vol. 12268, pp. 118–129. Springer, Cham (2020). https://doi.org/10.1007/978-3-030-61255-9_12

9. Dineen, J., Haque, A.S.M.AU., Bielskas, M.: Formal methods for an iterated volunteer's dilemma. In: Thomson, R., Hussain, M.N., Dancy, C., Pyke, A. (eds.) SBP-BRiMS 2021. LNCS, vol. 12720, pp. 81–90. Springer, Cham (2021). https://doi.org/10.1007/978-3-030-80387-2_8

10. Khaouja, I., Makdoun, I., Mezzour, G.: Using social network analysis to analyze development priorities of moroccan institutions. In: Thomson, R., Hussain, M.N., Dancy, C., Pyke, A. (eds.) SBP-BRiMS 2021. LNCS, vol. 12720, pp. 195–203. Springer, Cham (2021). https://doi.org/10.1007/978-3-030-80387-2_19

11. Lee, K., Braithwaite, J., Atchikpa, M.: Understanding colonial legacy and environmental issues in senegal through language use. In: Thomson, R., Bisgin, H., Dancy, C., Hyder, A., Hussain, M. (eds.) SBP-BRiMS 2020. LNCS, vol. 12268, pp. 23–34. Springer, Cham (2020). https://doi.org/10.1007/978-3-030-61255-9_3

12. Osterritter, L.J., Carley, K.M.: Modeling interventions for insider threat. In: Thomson, R., Bisgin, H., Dancy, C., Hyder, A., Hussain, M. (eds.) SBP-BRiMS 2020. LNCS, vol. 12268, pp. 55–64. Springer, Cham (2020). https://doi.org/10.1007/978-3-030-61255-9_6

13. Ghani, R.: Data science for social good and public policy: examples, opportunities, and challenges. In: The 41st International ACM SIGIR Conference on Research & Development in Information Retrieval, Ann Arbor, MI, USA, p. 3. ACM (2018)

14. Kushwaha, S., et al.: Significant applications of machine learning for COVID-19 pandemic. J. Ind. Integr. Manag. **05**, 453–479 (2020)
15. Yang, F., Vereshchaka, A., Lepri, B., Dong, W.: Optimizing city-scale traffic through modeling observations of vehicle movements. IEEE Trans. Intell. Transp. Syst., 1–12 (2021)
16. Moats, D., Seaver, N.: "You social scientists love mind games": experimenting in the "divide" between data science and critical algorithm studies. Big Data Soc. **6**, 2053951719833404 (2019)
17. Benjamin, R.: Race After Technology: Abolitionist Tools for the New Jim Code. Polity Press, Medford (2019)
18. Salganik, M.J., et al.: Measuring the predictability of life outcomes with a scientific mass collaboration. Proc. Natl. Acad. Sci. **117**, 8398–8403 (2020)
19. Ensign, D., Friedler, S.A., Neville, S., Scheidegger, C., Venkatasubramanian, S.: Runaway feedback loops in predictive policing. In: 1st Conference on Fairness, Accountability and Transparency, pp. 160–171. PMLR (2018)
20. Obermeyer, Z., Powers, B., Vogeli, C., Mullainathan, S.: Dissecting racial bias in an algorithm used to manage the health of populations. Science **366**, 447–453 (2019)
21. Birhane, A., et al.: The forgotten margins of AI ethics. In: 2022 ACM Conference on Fairness, Accountability, and Transparency, pp. 948–958. ACM (2022)
22. Li, Y., Yang, X., Sun, P., Qi, H., Lyu, S.: Celeb-DF: a large-scale challenging dataset for Deep-Fake forensics. In: 2020 IEEE/CVF Conference on Computer Vision and Pattern Recognition (CVPR), pp. 3204–3213 (2020)
23. Cardoso Llach, D., Ozkar, M.: Cultivating the critical imagination: post-disciplinary pedagogy in a computational design laboratory. Digit. Creat. **30**, 257–276 (2019)

Correction to: Chasing the Wrong Cloud: Mapping the 2019 Vaping Epidemic Using Data from Social Media

Parush Gera and Giovanni Luca Ciampaglia

Correction to:
Chapter "Chasing the Wrong Cloud: Mapping the 2019
Vaping Epidemic Using Data from Social Media" in:
R. Thomson et al. (Eds.): *Social, Cultural, and Behavioral*
***Modeling*, LNCS 13558,**
https://doi.org/10.1007/978-3-031-17114-7_1

In an older version of this paper, there was error in figure 2. This has been corrected.

The updated original version of this chapter can be found at
https://doi.org/10.1007/978-3-031-17114-7_1

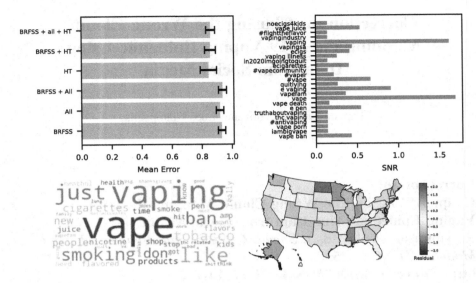

Fig. 2. Top left: Average root mean squared error from 10^3 iterations of 10-fold cross-validation for models trained on different groups of features. Here, 'Tweets (all)' refers to the relative vaping tweets by state, and 'Tweets (by HT)' refers to the relative vaping tweets stratified by the 25 keywords/hashtags from Google Trends (see Table 1). The error bar represent the standard error of the mean. Top right: Signal-to-noise ratio of all the keywords and hashtags used to collect the data (see Table 1). Bottom left: Terms with highest TF-IDF score from vape-related tweets. Only tweets with the keywords vape and vaping and that were posted by a likely human user (bot score ≤ 0.1 were included in the visualization. Word size proportional to TF-IDF score. Bottom right: Map of the residuals of EVALI prediction with the best-performing model.

Author Index

Printed in the United States
by Baker & Taylor Publisher Services

Printed in the United States
by Baker & Taylor Publisher Services